THE PSYCHOLOGY OF SOCCE

Sport psychology, exploring the effects of psychological interventions on important performance-related outcomes, has become ever more popular and prevalent within elite-level soccer clubs in the past decade as teams look to gain psychological as well as physiological advantages over their competitors.

The Psychology of Soccer seeks to present a detailed understanding of the theories underpinning the psychological issues relating to soccer, along with practical insights into effective psychological interventions and strategies.

This book uses contemporary theory and research to elucidate key concepts and applied interventions. It includes world-leading expert commentaries of contemporary theoretical and applied approaches in understanding critical issues in soccer, and provides practical implications and insights into working effectively in soccer-related contexts.

The Psychology of Soccer is an evidence-based resource to guide research and facilitate practice and will be a vital resource for researchers, practitioners, and coaches within the area of sport psychology and related disciplines.

Joseph G. Dixon, PhD, C.Psychol., HCPC, has been working as Club Performance Psychologist with Stoke City Football Club in the English Premier League and Championship Division since 2013. In 2019 he joined Bath Rugby Club in the English Premiership and currently splits his time between both organisations. As a dual-qualified Sport and Occupational Psychologist, Joseph has consulted globally across a variety of sports and commercial organisations.

Jamie B. Barker, PhD, C.Psychol., HCPC, is Senior Lecturer in Sport and Exercise Psychology at Loughborough University, UK, with research interests in applied (sport) psychology, leadership, and stress. Jamie has consulted in business and professional sport, including Sony, the Football Association, the England and Wales Cricket Board, and Great Britain Rowing.

Richard C. Thelwell, PhD, C.Psychol., HCPC, is Professor of Applied Sport Psychology and Head of the School for Sport, Health, and Exercise Sciences at the University of Portsmouth, UK. In addition to his research activities, Richard has extensive applied practitioner experience in professional football and cricket and across a number of sports-governing bodies.

Ian Mitchell, PhD, C.Psychol., HCPC, is currently Head of Performance Psychology at the England Football Association, UK. He previously worked with the Wales men's senior team and Swansea City in the English Premier League. Prior to that he was Senior Lecturer in Sport Psychology at Cardiff Metropolitan University. A former professional and International Schoolboy captain, Ian is UEFA A licensed and has coached national development teams and developed coaches on both UEFA Advanced and Professional licences.

THE PSYCHOLOGY OF SOCCER

*Edited by
Joseph G. Dixon, Jamie B. Barker,
Richard C. Thelwell,
and Ian Mitchell*

NEW YORK AND LONDON

First published 2020
by Routledge
52 Vanderbilt Avenue, New York, NY 10017

and by Routledge
2 Park Square, Milton Park, Abingdon, Oxon, OX14 4RN

Routledge is an imprint of the Taylor & Francis Group, an informa business

© 2020 Taylor & Francis

The right of Joseph G. Dixon, Jamie B. Barker, Richard C. Thelwell, and Ian Mitchell to be identified as the authors of the editorial material, and of the authors for their individual chapters, has been asserted in accordance with sections 77 and 78 of the Copyright, Designs and Patents Act 1988.

All rights reserved. No part of this book may be reprinted or reproduced or utilised in any form or by any electronic, mechanical, or other means, now known or hereafter invented, including photocopying and recording, or in any information storage or retrieval system, without permission in writing from the publishers.

Trademark notice: Product or corporate names may be trademarks or registered trademarks, and are used only for identification and explanation without intent to infringe.

Library of Congress Cataloging-in-Publication Data
Names: Dixon, Joseph (Joseph G.), editor.
Title: Understanding the psychology of soccer / edited by Joseph Dixon, Jamie Barker, Richard Thelwell, and Ian Mitchell.
Description: New York, NY : Routledge, 2020. | Includes bibliographical references and index.
Identifiers: LCCN 2019048490 (print) | LCCN 2019048491 (ebook) | ISBN 9780367350277 (hardback) | ISBN 9780367350284 (paperback) | ISBN 9781003005568 (ebook)
Subjects: LCSH: Soccer—Psychological aspects. | Soccer players—Psychology.
Classification: LCC GV943.9.P7 U64 2020 (print) | LCC GV943.9.P7 (ebook) | DDC 796.334019—dc23
LC record available at https://lccn.loc.gov/2019048490
LC ebook record available at https://lccn.loc.gov/2019048491

ISBN: 978-0-367-35027-7 (hbk)
ISBN: 978-0-367-35028-4 (pbk)
ISBN: 978-1-003-00556-8 (ebk)

Typeset in Bembo
by Apex CoVantage, LLC

Joseph G. Dixon: For Sarah x
Jamie B. Barker: For Mum, Dad, Emma, Lucy, and Molly with love
Richard C. Thelwell: Caroline, Hayden, Isabelle, Elsie, and Flossy - thank you for everything and I love you all x

CONTENTS

List of Figures x
List of Tables xi
List of Contributors xii
Preface xv
Foreward xvi

PART I
Working With Individuals and Teams 1

1 The Transition From Elite Youth to Elite Adult Professional Soccer:
   A Summary of Current Literature and Practical Applications 3
   Robert Morris and Emily Deason

2 The Role of Positive Psychology and Enjoyment in Enhancing Sport
   Commitment and Maximising Strengths in Elite Youth Soccer 19
   Paul J. McCarthy

3 The Psychology of Penalty Kicks: The Influence of Emotions on
   Penalty Taker and Goalkeeper Performance 29
   Philip Furley, Matt Dicks, and Geir Jordet

4 Rational Emotive Behaviour Therapy and Soccer 44
   Andrew G. Wood and Martin J. Turner

5 Developing Effective On- and Off-Field Leadership in Elite Soccer:
   The Social Identity Approach 60
   *Matthew J. Slater, Niklas K. Steffens, Katrien Fransen,
   and S. Alexander Haslam*

6 The Psychology of Soccer Referees   74
   Tom Webb and Denise Hill

PART II
Working Through Others   89

7 Developing Psychological Skills: Emphasising Life Skills for Positive
   Youth Development   91
   Ceri Bowley and Hamish Cox

8 Identifying and Delivering a Team-Based Intervention in Elite Youth
   Soccer: Using Personal-Disclosure Mutual-Sharing to Enhance Team
   Identification, Resilience, and Coping   105
   Andrew L. Evans and Jamie B. Barker

9 The Role of Parents in Developing Elite Soccer Players   121
   Camilla J. Knight and Rachael A. Newport

10 Enhancing Coaching Efficacy in Youth Soccer   133
   Richard Anderson and Chris G. Harwood

PART III
Working in the Environment   153

11 Ecology and Culture in Talent Development—A Four-Step
   Intervention Towards Cultural Leadership in Key Stakeholders in a
   Danish Soccer Academy   155
   Jonas Vestergaard Jensen and Pætur Smith Clementsen

12 Applied Psychology in Academy Soccer Settings:
   A Systems-Led Approach   172
   Cherrie Daley, Chin Wei Ong, and Philippa McGregor

13 A Challenge Culture: Reflections on Implementing a Psychological
   Skills Programme in Elite Youth Soccer   189
   Joseph G. Dixon and Marc V. Jones

14 Understanding the Effects of Organisational Change in
   Professional Soccer   205
   Christopher R. D. Wagstaff and Richard C. Thelwell

15 Understanding the Role of Environment and Culture When
   Delivering Sport Psychology Services in Elite Women's
   International Soccer   220
   Jenn Gandhi and Peter Schneider

16 Assessing the Impact of Psychology Provision in Elite Youth Soccer 234
    Charlotte Chandler, Karl Steptoe, and Martin Eubank

PART IV
Working to Support Injury and Mental Health **247**

17 Effectively Managing Anterior Cruciate Ligament Injury and Return
    to Performance in Elite Women's Soccer 249
    Adam Gledhill, Osman Hassan Ahmed, and Dale Forsdyke

18 Understanding Mental Health and Wellbeing Issues in Elite Soccer
    Players: An Existential Sport Psychology Approach 264
    Alan John Tonge

19 Soccer Referee Mental Health: Developing a Network of Soccer
    Referee Mental Health Champions 278
    Mikel Mellick

20 Stress, Burnout, and Perfectionism in Soccer Players 292
    *Esmie P. Smith, Andrew P. Hill, Sarah H. Mallinson-Howard,
    and Henrik Gustafsson*

Index *317*

FIGURES

4.1	A schematic of the ABC(DE) framework used within the REBT process	45
6.1	Mental fortitude training programme for sustained success	79
7.1	The model for life skill development through coaching	94
8.1	Summary of our PDMS intervention programme	110
8.2	ROPDMS instructions	111
8.3	PDMS contract agreed with athletes for our intervention	111
8.4	COPDMS instructions	113
10.1	Feltz and colleagues' (1999) conceptual model of coaching efficacy	134
10.2	Example of coach-based scenario activity aimed at defining the Cs and identifying behaviours relating to that C as part of building psychosocial coaching efficacy	140
10.3	Guidelines for making PROGRESS with the 5Cs in coaching	142
10.4	Example of u13 coach's training practice with strategies aimed at building communication into the practice	143
10.5	Combined u14 coaches' 5C scoring on the confidence they possessed to use strategies and behaviours to help their players exhibit the 5Cs	147
10.6	Combined u14 player perceptions of their 5C use taken from the players' training diaries	147
11.1	ATDE model. A simplistic description of actors present in the TDE and how they interacted	160
11.2	ESF model. A simplistic description of the most important factors in each category of the talent development environment	161
12.1	Kotter's (2014) eight-step model for leading change	183
20.1	A cognitive behavioural model of Jen's perfectionism	308

TABLES

4.1	Core irrational and rational beliefs accompanied by sport-specific examples	46
4.2	Disputation of Leon's FI irrational belief	54
5.1	A three-month 5R^S programme to develop on- and off-field leadership by creating a shared sense of "us"	67
6.1	Characteristics of performance under pressure	78
6.2	Environment characteristics affecting resilience	80
7.1	Intervention strategies for developing life skills through coaching	99
8.1	Example responses from the social validation questionnaires completed by athletes	115
8.2	Example responses from the social validation questionnaires completed by the head coach	116
11.1	Four-step intervention overview	158
11.2	Schematic representation of the workshop for the characteristic of self-awareness	167
12.1	Kotter's (2014) eight-step model—illustrated against our case study	184
20.1	A summary of research examining burnout in soccer players ($k = 18$)	295

CONTRIBUTORS

Osman Hassan Ahmed, The FA Centre for Disability Football Research, UK, and Bournemouth University, UK

Richard Anderson, Bowling Green State University, UK

Jamie B. Barker, Loughborough University, UK

Ceri Bowley, University of South Wales, UK

Charlotte Chandler, University of Derby, UK

Pætur Smith Clementsen, Faroe Islands Football Association, Faroe Islands, and University of Copenhagen, Denmark

Hamish Cox, Athlos Performance Psychology, UK

Cherrie Daley, Bangor University, UK

Emily Deason, Liverpool John Moores University, UK

Matt Dicks, University of Portsmouth, UK

Joseph G. Dixon, Staffordshire University and Stoke City Football Club, UK

Martin Eubank, Liverpool John Moores University, UK

Andrew L. Evans, The University of Salford, UK

Dale Forsdyke, York City Football Club Foundation Tier 1 Girls' Regional Talent Club, UK, and York St John University, UK

Katrien Fransen, KU Leuven, Belgium

Philip Furley, German Sport University, Germany

Jenn Gandhi, The Football Association, UK

Adam Gledhill, York City Football Club Foundation Tier 1 Girls' Regional Talent Club, UK, and Leeds Beckett University, UK

Henrik Gustafsson, Norwegian School of Sport Sciences, Norway

Chris G. Harwood, Loughborough University, UK

S. Alexander Haslam, University of Queensland, Australia

Andrew P. Hill, York St John University, UK

Denise Hill, Swansea University, UK

Jonas Vestergaard Jensen, University of Copenhagen, Denmark

Marc V. Jones, Manchester Metropolitan University, UK

Geir Jordet, Norwegian School of Sport Sciences, Norway

Camilla J. Knight, Swansea University, UK

Sarah H. Mallinson-Howard, Karlstad University, Sweden

Paul J. McCarthy, Glasgow Caledonian University, UK

Philippa McGregor, Loughborough University, UK

Mikel Mellick, Cardiff Metropolitan University, UK

Robert Morris, Liverpool John Moores University, UK

Rachael A. Newport, Swansea University, UK

Chin Wei Ong, Bangor University, UK

Peter Schneider, Team Sports, USA

Matthew J. Slater, Staffordshire University, UK

Esmie P. Smith, York St John University, UK

Niklas K. Steffens, University of Queensland, Australia

Karl Steptoe, Loughborough University, UK

Richard C. Thelwell, University of Portsmouth, UK

Alan John Tonge, University Campus of Football Business, UK, and Liverpool John Moores University, UK

Martin J. Turner, Manchester Metropolitan University, UK

Christopher R. D. Wagstaff, University of Portsmouth, UK

Tom Webb, University of Portsmouth, UK

Andrew G. Wood, Staffordshire University, UK

PREFACE

Welcome to *The Psychology of Soccer*, a text that brings to practitioners, scholars, coaches, players, and performance directors a comprehensive review of the scientific literature concerning contemporary issues within elite soccer. Our book includes world-leading expert commentaries of contemporary theoretical and applied approaches in understanding critical issues in soccer along with providing practical implications and insights into working effectively. We have arranged the book into the following parts to reflect areas of contemporary research and areas of critical practice in elite soccer: *Working With Individuals and Teams, Working Through Others, Working in the Environment,* and *Working to Support Injury and Mental Health.* We aim to provide the reader with an overview of the broad nature of sport psychology issues in soccer rather than being a definitive text.

As outlined, our intention was to assemble a collection of literature review and evidence-based case studies on key areas that have the potential to influence the provision of psychology within elite soccer. It is hoped that the empirical evidence presented within each chapter, together with the dissemination of this body of research into practical implications for applied practice, offers a comprehensive, essential library for students, graduates, doctoral students, academics, and professionals working in the field of sport psychology. We also hope that the typically standardised format adopted within each chapter enables readers to understand and critique the background literature, clarify and define key terms, and consider the future challenges for research and practice.

Not only do we hope that you enjoy the text and find the content informative, we hope that the contributions are thought-provoking and inspire readers to challenge their current positions and influence future researchers and applied practitioner directions. Finally, we would like to thank the contributors for enabling us to share their fascinating and detailed insights.

Joseph, Jamie, Richard, and Ian, September 2019

FOREWORD

During my professional playing and my early managerial career I have always been interested in the psychology of players and coaches. The ever-increasing demands of professional and international soccer highlight the need for psychological support over and above that of technical, tactical, and the physical nature surrounding the game. At an individual level, players need support around how they think about preparation to optimise their performances and to re-enter after injury. They also need to be aware of how they think about big games, championship run-ins, relegation battles, qualifying periods, and tournaments where the expectation to succeed will be high. The squads that they are part of reflect the importance of group dynamics—how do players interact with other players, how do they respond to competition and when they are competing for places in the line-up, and how do they help starting players if they are non-starters? All of these are essential in the psychology of players and squads. I have always been part of a high-performance culture as a player, coach, and manager. The importance of not just what this is but how to develop it and maintain it at the highest level underpins brilliant performances on the pitch. The importance of how as staff we challenge and support players and each other is an important balance to create a winning mentality. Strong leadership and recognising who we are and what we have to represent when we lead develops a strong sense of identity—something that players and staff will always be able to refer to under pressure situations. Leadership is about the group you lead, so the psychology and understanding of group behaviour cannot be underestimated across all levels of soccer.

I managed Wales during a fantastic period of success that saw us enter the history books; rising to 10th in the world rankings from 117th (the biggest rise in international soccer history). High-performing teams achieve not only through great players but by the support of the environment and the people who work within it. We got that right: the culture, our identity, our game plan, our physicality, and our mentality. All these played a critical part in the success of the national team. Choosing the right people is so important as they have to understand the context and the demands of elite soccer. Aligned to that is the work that they deliver. That work cannot be based upon intuition; it has to be evidence-based and relevant to the nature of elite players who compete at the highest level. The current book will no doubt enhance understanding of some of the key psychological aspects in elite soccer and provide some thought-provoking discussions among readers. Furthermore, and most importantly, applied areas of work are evident throughout each chapter to optimise the performance of those who are lucky enough to work within the great game of soccer.

Chris Coleman, OBE
Ex manager of Fulham, Real Sociedad, Coventry City,
Wales, Sunderland, Hebei China Fortune

PART I
Working With Individuals and Teams

1

THE TRANSITION FROM ELITE YOUTH TO ELITE ADULT PROFESSIONAL SOCCER

A Summary of Current Literature and Practical Applications

Robert Morris and Emily Deason

Brief Introduction

The Young Lions, the English national youth soccer teams, won the Under-17 World Cup, the European Under-19 Championship, and the Under-20 World Cup in 2017, and yet the senior English team hasn't won an international competition since 1966. As these results illustrate, success at the youth level does not always guarantee success at the senior level. Taking this into consideration, recently there has been an increase in research which has focused on understanding development pathways and the psychological aspects of transitions in sport and, more specifically, soccer. This literature (e.g., Morris, Tod, & Oliver, 2015; Morris, Tod, & Eubank, 2016; Wylleman & Lavallee, 2004; Wylleman, Reints, & De Knop, 2013) has identified that elite youth soccer players have to deal with many of the demands that face a typical teenager alongside additional responsibilities and pressures associated with adapting to full-time professional soccer, including pressure from a number of external agencies (e.g., fans, coaches, teammates) to perform at a high level consistently (Morris et al., 2015). Given these additional challenges, it has been highlighted that the transition from elite youth sport to elite senior sport can be difficult, with approximately only 17% of all athletes in youth sport successfully transitioning into elite sport (Vanden Auweele, De Martelaer, Rzewnicki, De Knop, & Wylleman, 2004) and more than 90% of soccer players failing to successfully transition to professional level (Anderson & Miller, 2011). The purpose of the current chapter, therefore, is to highlight to readers the psychological demands of transitioning into an elite adult professional soccer player. In doing so, the chapter will offer practical considerations and challenge practitioners to reflect on the support they currently offer to players entering the world of professional soccer through detailing a case study of supporting an athlete through their move to senior sport. The authors will provide a balanced account of their work with players making the transition, discussing positive examples and those who have not been successful.

Review of Literature

In the preceding ten years, there has been a shift in the focus of career transition literature. Previously, there had been a focus of research on understanding the challenges associated with retirement from sport (e.g., Aquilina, 2013; Park, Lavallee, & Tod, 2013). Through this, and subsequent literature, however, it was identified that other transitions may also be challenging for athletes and warranted investigation so that appropriate support could be put in place to facilitate athlete development. One such transition, the elite youth to elite senior transition, has been of particular focus. This is especially the case because, as highlighted previously, the expected outcomes often result in athletes being released from clubs/organisations or leaving/giving up their respective sport, ultimately failing to make the transition successfully. Even if they are successful in moving to senior sport, it has been identified that this transition can be the most difficult athletes experience due to the multiple developmental demands and simultaneous transitions that characterise this period (Stambulova, Alfermann, Statler, & Côté, 2009; Wylleman et al., 2013). Due to this, it can take between one and four years to become fully established as an elite or professional senior athlete (Finn & McKenna, 2010).

Theories and Models

Across the youth-to-senior transition literature, there have been a number of theories and models outlined which have aimed to describe and explain when and how transitions occur and the process that athletes will go through as they experience this progression.

Descriptive Models

Models (e.g., Bloom, 1985; Côté, 1999) have identified that there are several stages within the life of a sports performer, including development, elite performer, and retirement phases, and that there are transitions which occur between these phases in the athletic level. Wylleman and colleagues (2004, 2013), while agreeing that there are several stages within the life of a sports performer, also posited the interaction of athletic transitions with non-athletic transitions, suggesting that areas outside athletes' sporting career may influence their development. Specifically, initially it was suggested that athletes will experience transitions in four domains: athletic, psychological, psychosocial, and academic/vocational. Later developments of the theory also added a financial domain (Wylleman et al., 2013).

The transition from youth-to-senior sport is incorporated within the transition from development to mastery athletic level, but its exact position in the athletic career will depend on the sporting context and the individual athlete. As the holistic athletic career model (Wylleman et al., 2013) illustrates, this athletic transition is likely to occur in conjunction with multiple non-athletic transitions across the four other life domains, such as the transition from puberty/adolescence to (young) adulthood; the corresponding change in support network (in particular, the lesser influence of parents or guardians); and the transition from secondary education to a professional or semi-professional sport contract, higher education, or a vocation. The challenge of coping with concurrent athletic and non-athletic transitions can increase the level of stress experienced by athletes and the likelihood of any one of the transitions becoming a crisis or failed transition (Stambulova, 2000). Therefore, if attempts to aid adaption are to be successful, it is important to take a holistic perspective and situate the athletic transition in the context of concurring (athletic or non-athletic) transitions.

In addition to increased stress occurring when transitions happen concurrently, it has been posited that the changes athletes encounter during a transition process can result in the development of (new) identities. Specifically, this development of identity may be disrupted or curtailed by transition periods, meaning that athletes become unsure of who they are and what they represent (Morris et al., 2016). The psychological transition from (late) adolescence to (early) adulthood is a period for exploration and personal identity development; however, as illustrated by the holistic athletic career transition model, this psychological transition is likely to occur at a similar period to the transition from junior to senior sport (Wylleman et al., 2013). The impact of an individual's athletic involvement on their identity development and the degree to which they define their identity through their athletic pursuits (i.e., their athletic identity) has the potential to become problematic. In particular, the premature over-identification with one's athletic role (i.e., identity foreclosure) has been shown by research to have a negative impact on the athlete's exploration of other career, education, and lifestyle options (Brewer, Van Raalte, & Linder, 1993; Brewer, Van Raalte, & Petitpas, 2000; Murphy, Petitpas, & Brewer, 1996). To expand, an exclusive focus on sport during this period can lead to the development of an exclusive or foreclosed athletic identity (Murphy et al., 1996). A multidimensional identity, on the other hand, developed through the exploration of various interests, provides a more rounded identity for the individual to rely upon in adverse situations (e.g., difficulty in transitions; Erikson, 1994; Lang & Lee, 2005). This ensures that when athletes' identities are threatened (i.e., injury threatens retirement from sport), they can rely on the other dimensions of their identity (i.e., their other interests, hobbies, or roles). Therefore, although a strong athletic identity is recognised as beneficial for commitment to sport and sporting performance, a diverse understanding of the self through multiple interests, hobbies, and roles is considered advantageous for navigating athletic and non-athletic transitions.

Explanation Models

When exploring the concept of transition, initial theories drew upon wider psychological literature (such as thanatology and social gerontology) to explain transitions and, in particular, athletic retirement. These theories viewed athletic retirement as either a version of "social death" or as retirement from a vocational career, indicating that this event was one characterised by loss and grieving (Stambulova et al., 2009). However, the understanding of retirement from sport as a form of "death" was criticised in the literature because the theories proposed were unable to explain the nuances of the sport experience and the influence of sport-specific factors (e.g., retirement due to injury, the view of athletic retirement as a new opportunity rather than the negative experience that "social death" suggests, or the need for adaption to a second non-athletic career). Given this criticism, there was a need for other theories which may help to explain the process of transition in sport.

The model for analysing human adaptation to transition (Schlossberg, 1981) was considered advantageous in explaining the complexities of retirement from sport because it embraces individual differences within a transition. This theory defines transition as "an event or non-event which results in a change in assumptions about oneself and the world and thus requires a corresponding change in one's behavior and relationships" (Schlossberg, 1981, p. 5). It is postulated by Schlossberg's theory that individuals' adaption to transitions is determined by their perception of the change (e.g., whether it was expected or not expected and the timing of the event/non-event), the characteristics of the individual (e.g., their psychological resources and coping strategies), and the characteristics of the pre-transition and post-transition environments (e.g., the social support available). Although this model instigated widespread research in transition by sport psychology, the description of a transition as an event/non-event was considered too simplistic for sporting contexts (Stambulova, 2003). To expand, athletic retirement studies showed that it takes an athlete, on average, a year to adapt to their post-athletic career (Sinclair & Orlick, 1993; Alfermann, 2000). Consequently, transition in sport is understood as a process of change that athletes are required to cope with (Taylor & Ogilvie, 1994; Stambulova, 2003), rather than a singular event which may take place over a short period of time, as this model suggests.

Given these limitations, Stambulova (2003) published a sport-specific model of transition, designed to explain the process of a single transition that could be applied across sport careers (e.g., youth-to-senior and retirement from sport). This work was also among the first to start to try and explain the process of transition across sport, rather than solely athletic retirement. Stambulova (2003) suggested that a transition is the athletes' ability to deal with specific demands which pose a conflict between "what the athlete is" and "what he or she wants or ought to be" in their sport career. Each transition can be viewed as a process which has a number of demands, barriers, coping resources, outcomes, and long-term consequences. The model predicted that demands, resources, barriers, and coping mechanisms interact throughout each sport career transition and the outcomes and long-term consequences of transition are dependent upon athletes having sufficient and appropriate coping resources to manage any demands and barriers they may encounter throughout the process.

Empirical Research

Empirical research in the area has highlighted that the youth-to-senior transition is characterised by a series of challenges that permeate across both athletic and non-athletic domains. Specifically, the youth-to-senior transition can challenge athletes physically and mentally (Bruner, Munroe-Chandler, & Spink, 2008; Pummell, Harwood, & Lavallee, 2008) and may result in anxiety and uncertainty around aspects such as level of performance and social interaction with senior players (Lorenzo, Borrás, Sánchez, Jiménez, & Sampedro, 2009). Additionally, the amount and appropriateness of social support can also help or hinder the transition to senior sport. Specifically, where appropriate support, which is emotional in nature and facilitative to athlete development, is provided, athletes are less likely to feel anxious and nervous about unrealistic expectations from key stakeholders and experience a positive transition (Bruner et al., 2008; Jones, Mahoney, & Gucciardi, 2014). Contrastingly, where support is more focused on performance outcomes and pressure is put on athletes to succeed, they are likely to experience enhanced difficulties (Pummell, 2008; Pummell & Lavallee, 2019).

Specific soccer-based research has also highlighted that the transition from elite youth to elite senior soccer is made difficult by a number of pertinent challenges. From an individual perspective, it has been highlighted that the transition is characterised by a large increase in the standard of play, more physical and technical demands, and a greater psychological demand (e.g., when recovering from mistakes; Finn & Mckenna, 2010; Morris et al., 2016; Relvas, 2010). Research within soccer has identified both individual (e.g., athletic identity and athlete competencies; Brown & Potrac, 2009; Gledhill & Harwood, 2015; Larsen, Alfermann, & Christensen, 2012) and environmental factors (e.g., support available and environment culture; Gledhill & Harwood, 2015; Mitchell et al., 2014) which facilitate this transition. Additionally, from a cultural/environmental perspective, there are a number of complications. Particularly, it has been highlighted that soccer players moving to senior sport experience challenges fitting in with standards of first-team environment (e.g., handling social dynamics in the first-team group) and communicating with first-team staff (Røynesdal, Toering, & Gustafsson, 2018). Additionally, physical, philosophical, and/or cultural distance can exist between the youth and the professional environments. This distance can lead to a lack of trust and/or belief by the first-team coach(es) in youth development, meaning players can suffer from a lack of first-team opportunities which help them to establish themselves effectively in senior sport (Relvas, 2010).

To help overcome these barriers some key attributes have been identified, including good sporting skills (i.e., an equal balance of physical, technical, tactical, and psychosocial skills; Relvas, 2010), goal-directed attributes (e.g., passion, professional attitude), intelligence (e.g. sport intelligence, emotional competence; Mills, Butt, Maynard, & Harwood, 2012), survival strength, practice behaviour, and social competence (Røynesdal, 2015). Social support, from family, friends, coaches, and teammates, can also provide emotional, technical, and tangible support to players throughout the transition which can help them overcome some of the challenges they may experience but cannot manage on their own (e.g., technical deficiencies; Morris et al., 2016).

Practical Implications—Case Study

Background and Context

Brian (pseudonym) was a player I (First author) had spent time working with previously in a sport psychology role as he was contracted to play for one of the teams which I was employed by. At the time, I was spending one day a week in the environment, an elite academy within England, supporting youth players with their psychosocial development and helping them develop the skills that they would require to be successful in senior sport. Previous to the situation below occurring, Brian had not been particularly forthcoming towards sport psychology support, and beyond sessions which he was required to attend as outlined by the club, he had not engaged in many individual sessions with me. A central midfielder, Brian was a player who had been very successful in the youth development teams, often playing in teams that were for athletes older than he was and competing in international games at various age group levels (e.g., Under-15, Under-16, Under-17 age groups). In addition, he was often the focal point of teams he played in and was well respected by the players he played with at all levels, becoming captain of his youth team in the last year of his youth career. He believed that he was able to manage many of the psychological challenges he came across in his sport without specific support from me. However, this changed a number of months into my work at the club. Brian was approaching the time where he was due to be informed about whether or not he would be moving up to senior sport when he contacted me to ask for additional support in relation to some fears and anxieties he was experiencing regarding this process and the subsequent outcomes which would occur.

Presenting Issue(s)

When Brian approached me, we agreed that we would meet on a one-to-one basis during the coming days to explore his fears and anxieties around the transition. I felt meeting on a one-to-one basis would give him the opportunity to be open about his fears and anxieties and allow us to explore together methods and approaches to overcome these. Given that Brian had also identified that many of his fears were around soccer and his future within the game, we also agreed that meeting within the club would be inadvisable, and we agreed that we would meet at his house.

A couple of days later, as we started to talk, it immediately became clear that many of Brian's fears were permeated by a strong athletic identity. Brian referred to being "unsure of what he would do" if he was released, not being "any good" at anything else, and as soccer "being his life." These descriptions of the value he placed on soccer led me to start to explore the notion of identity foreclosure with Brian. Previous literature (e.g., Park et al., 2013) has identified that athletes who may suffer from identity foreclosure (i.e., commitment to an identity to the detriment of others) could also experience the negative consequences of this which may include mental health problems (Morris et al., 2016) if this identity, for whatever reason, is removed. In the case of Brian, he was identifying that he would have nothing that would fill the void of soccer if he were to be released, which highlighted that he may be vulnerable to negative consequences as a result of having an exclusive athletic identity.

In addition to considering soccer as his life, Brian also had concerns around his ability to be successful in senior sport. Although appreciating the excitement and joy he would get were he to be offered a professional senior contract, Brian had already been informed by the club that if he was to be offered a contract, it would only be for one year in the initial instance, with the option of extending for a second year thereafter were the first year was successful. Brian had perceived this as a reflection of him not being "as successful as the other guys" and "that they [the club/coaches] were doubting his ability" to be a senior player. He perceived that the club, and more specifically his current coaches and the senior team coaches, did not believe in his technical or physical ability to perform within senior sport. This was also highlighted by an uncertainty and lack of clarity around (a) how good he believed the other players to be and (b) the challenges he might face as he moved up to senior sport. Research (e.g., Morris et al., 2015) has identified that technical and physical competence is a concern for soccer players moving up to senior sport and that athletes do not want to be seen as someone incapable of being successful at the senior level. With Brian, it was evident that this was also something that he was concerned about, and this was having an impact on his confidence and concentration during training and matches.

A final fear that Brian had was that he did not want to let those around him down as he moved to senior sport. For ten years, Brian's parents had travelled throughout the country, taking him to and from tournaments, supporting him during his first game through to his international debut, and ensuring he was well nourished and looked after at home prior to him moving out when he got his youth development contract. Brian feared letting his parents down—he repeated continually that he wanted to be able to "pay them back" for what they were able to do for him in his younger days by performing well in senior sport—something he was not sure he was capable of doing. Brian also feared letting his coaches, manager, and senior peers down in this regard—he did not want to move up to senior sport to then be seen as a failure when performing under heightened levels of pressure and where mistakes are more criticised. He wanted to gain the respect of these senior peers and members of the management team. It has been highlighted that performing under new levels of pressure and making mistakes in this senior environment can be detrimental to performance and add additional mental strain (e.g., Finn & McKenna, 2010), especially when players lose confidence in their own ability to be successful, and Brian was showing signs of this "fear" of failure. What Brian was experiencing, while not uncommon, was something he indicated he was unsure of how to cope with.

Intervention/Work Conducted

To support Brian (and other players in a similar position), it was decided in conjunction with coaches and academy staff that we would work together on an intervention, which was focused on giving players an understanding of the transition they are about to experience, an understanding of the factors which may be important to them making this transition, and also appropriate support at an individual level to highlight any additional challenges they may be facing. To do this, three main approaches were used, namely short-, medium-, and long-term goal-setting on the transition, workshops to players and related parents/guardians on the transition and factors which may impact successful outcomes, and humanistic counselling designed to offer individual athletes the opportunity to discuss apprehensions and fears they may be having in relation to the transition (or more general areas of their sport and life).

Goal-Setting

It is argued that the reason goal-setting is effective is that it facilitates four key areas of performance, namely the technique (a) directs attention of the athlete, (b) mobilises them to maintain and enhance effort, (c) enhances persistence to achieve, and (d) helps develop new learning strategies (Locke, Shaw, Saari, & Latham, 1981). Because of these outcomes, goal-setting has been a technique that has been used successfully as a way to support and facilitate the development of athletic performance (see Burton & Weiss, 2008; Weinberg, 2013). This technique has also been outlined as part of previously suggested broader interventions as a way to facilitate athlete transitions (see Stambulova, 2010, 2011). Given that many of Brian's fears permeated from not being confident with his ability to be successful in senior sport and his lack of planning for life after sport (were he not to be successful), using goal-setting as a way to reframe his thinking was a technique we agreed may be effective. In addition to what was highlighted previously, conversations with him had highlighted that he did not have clear goals that he was working towards other than "he wanted to play in the Premier League." When discussing this with Brian, I asked him to identify any shorter-term goals which were facilitating this end goal and, consequently, his self-belief in his ability to achieve his end goal. In particular, we aimed to identify goals which facilitated or directed his attention to specific skills or roles, motivated him to continue to improve, and enhanced his drive to achieve—all of which would be crucial were he to be successful in moving to senior sport and thereafter. From this conversation, it was apparent that he had not considered many of these aspects and how to maintain his motivation and was merely working to an end goal of English Premier League success.

In addition to using goal-setting for performance and confidence purposes, I also discussed with Brian the value of using goal-setting to think more broadly about the transition, whether to senior sport or out of sport, and what he would like to achieve in his sport, life, and other domains he has an interest in. The purpose of this was to ensure that the strong athletic identity he had was facilitative rather than debilitative to his development. Brian had indicated that his sole focus for a number of years had been on sport. Now he was coming to what he considered "crunch time", he was starting to be fearful of what he was going to do next in life, regardless of being successful or unsuccessful moving up to senior sport.

Once Brian and I had agreed that there was value in the technique of goal-setting for his situation, the next stage was to identify specific goals for him. Goals should be specific, measurable, attainable, realistic, and within a set time frame and could (and should) include a range of outcome goals, performance goals, and process goals (Weinberg & Gould, 2015). With Brian, as highlighted previously, he had outcome goals for his sport, but beyond this he did not have clearly aligned goals for any other aspects of performance. In relation specifically to his transition, he did not have any goals which were outcome-, performance-, or process-based. Given this, Brian and I worked together to identify appropriate goals which covered a range of outcome, performance, and process elements and were especially related to aspects he could control independent of others. Specific goals included achieving over 80% in pass and tackling success rate in every game he played between now and the end of the season; work on his pass and tackling technique three times a week for 30 minutes post his normal training session; between now and the end of the season start to explore other opportunities which he could perhaps do were he to be unsuccessful in becoming a senior player, including joining the army, teacher training, and coaching; and being happy with what he has achieved post-transition.

Workshops

Workshops have been identified previously as an effective way to educate athletes and key stakeholders on a number of different areas of sport psychology and athlete development, including the role of sport psychology in helping develop key psychological skills (e.g., Clement & Shannon, 2009), and the influence that parents can have on children's youth sport experiences (e.g., Vincent & Christensen, 2015).

Given that a lot of Brian's worries appeared to be stemming from a lack of knowledge about the transition, specifically what challenges he might face as he moved up to senior sport or the challenges he might face if he were to be released, educating him on the process and the ways he might be able to overcome such worries may have alleviated some of the challenges he was experiencing. In addition, Brian was also fearful of letting people, more specifically his parents, down. Given this, to support Brian and the other players coming towards the end of their youth career, it was decided that workshops which were designed to educate parents/guardians on the process and their role in transition might be effective in ensuring they were supporting their sons and helping facilitate rather than debilitate their progress.

In total, there were three workshops with the players and one with the parents on the transition and the potential challenges that may be faced. Specific workshop content for the players, which was drawn from previous research in this area, including Morris et al. (2015, 2016), consisted of what transitions are and the process they will go through, the potential challenges that may be faced by athletes as they prepare for and then move to senior sport, and what challenges they may face if they are unsuccessful in being given a senior team contract and are released from the club. Specific parent/guardian workshop content, which was also drawn from previous literature in the area, included what transitions are, the process their children will go through, their role in transition, and what they can do to facilitate the process.

Humanistic Counselling

Humanistic psychology has become more prevalent within sport psychology in recent times due to its focus on positive virtues and exploring the positive aspects of humankind such as love, individuality, creativity, hope, and actualisation. Rogers (1951) pioneered this type of client-centred therapy, with the focus of the interaction between client and practitioner on helping the client achieve self-actualisation (fulfilment/happiness with life). This is achieved through empathic understanding and rephrasing of what the client says in order to clarify and help them objectify their thinking and their understanding of their situation (Rogers, 1951).

As identified earlier, Brian had fears which were permeated by a strong athletic identity and a focus on sporting success—something that Brian was unable to control to a large extent. In addition, he continually referenced that he did not want to let his family, coaches, or peers down; thus, he was attributing his own success to thoughts and feelings of external parties, aspects he could not control. These aspects, as a collective, meant that self-actualisation or fulfilment were elements that became a focus of many of our conversations due to the distinct possibility of him being released from sport.

With Brian, I had a number of conversations which covered a variety of topics, including his personal life, what he wanted to achieve in his life, and his working life. In other words, Brian and I discussed what aspects of his life made or could make him happy, achieve and understand love, individuality, creativity, hope, and actualisation, the main underpinning features of humanism. Maintaining conversations about the need to focus on athletic performances, which were still vital to the work being carried out, was important, but our one-to-one conversations in this time period focused on broadening Brian's thinking and understanding of what would allow him to achieve fulfilment. Through these conversations, Brian identified that he wanted to be in a position in a few years where he was married with children, was able to support his parents, was perceived as being a good person, and was happy with his achievements in life. Brian also identified that, although he wanted to play soccer for a living, it was not essential for him to achieve this. Indeed, he mentioned that he knows a number of players who were very successful in soccer but not happy with their lives, something Brian "did not want to be."

Outcome Analysis

Brian was successful in being awarded a one-year contract with the first team and was delighted with this, perceiving that it was the culmination of the effort he had put in for a number of years to be successful. However, as identified earlier, the main focus of the work Brian and I carried out together was around three areas: his strong athletic identity, his doubt over his ability to be successful both short term and long term as an athlete, and his fear of letting those around him down—areas which were not necessarily directly performance related, especially in the instances of athletic identity and fear of letting others down. Therefore, in the following I will identify changes in the way Brian was perceiving each element before discussing his and his coaches' reflections on the process, which may offer insight into the value of maintaining a holistic perspective on athlete development to performance.

Overall Outcomes

Prior to intervention, Brian identified that were he not be successful in getting a senior team contract, then he would be unsure of what he could or should do to fill the void of soccer. Post-intervention, it was clear that, while Brian still had a drive to be successful in sport, he had a broader perspective on what success and happiness meant. He identified that he may be able to achieve success as an athlete at another organisation or even external to sport with additional opportunities that may be available to him, such as coaching. Ultimately, for Brian, rather than just focusing on getting a first-team contract, he was more focused on enjoying what he was doing and achieving self-actualisation.

In addition, Brian also had a more positive perception of his ability to perform well both within sport and externally. As discussed previously, specific goals Brian set included achieving over 80% in pass and tackling success rate in every game he played between now and the end of the season; work on his pass and tackling technique three times a week for 30 minutes post his normal training session; between now and the end of the season start to explore other opportunities which he could perhaps do were he to be unsuccessful in becoming a senior player, including joining the army, teacher training, and coaching; and being happy with what he has achieved post-transition. When reflecting back upon these goals, Brian identified that he had become more confident in his ability to be successful because he had achieved what he had set out to do. He also identified that because he was not reliant upon others to achieve these goals, he had a greater understanding of his own capacity to learn how to manage his private and sporting lives. This achievement of goals had also helped Brian to achieve greater self-actualisation, where he was more content in his own ability to be happy and achieve individuality. Additionally, Brian took part in a range of workshops which meant that, were he to be successful in getting a senior team contract, he had a greater understanding of what he could expect and be required to do post-transition. Brian reflected that such knowledge was crucial for him as he now had a greater understanding of what could happen, both within his sport and external to his sport, and the way these outcomes could influence his self-actualisation.

Finally, Brian feared letting those around him down, especially his parents, by not achieving ultimate success of getting a first-team contract. A workshop with players' parents prior to the contract decision was designed to ensure that parents were more informed about their role in transition and how they can help (or hinder) their child's development. Brian reflected on this workshop by identifying that his parents were now more supportive in their approach, especially as they had a greater understanding of their role in transition and the support they can provide. Brian also identified that, although there was still expectation placed upon him from his parents, this was more aligned to aspects that could facilitate performance, not the performance itself—for example, hard work. Ultimately, this led to Brian reflecting that, even if he was not successful in his sport in the future, his parents would be proud of him because he was and had put appropriate effort into his training and matches.

Client Reflections

After Brian had been awarded his senior team contract, I asked him to reflect back upon the work we had done together and whether or not he believed it influenced how he was perceiving the transition and the eventual outcome he got. He offered the following reflection:

> There is no doubt working with you has made a difference to the way I perceive what I am doing and how I am feeling about playing in the senior team. Before working with you I was really unsure about a number of things, including the challenges I was about to face, the way my parents would react if I was released, and what I would do if I were not successful. I know I have the contract now, but I think my broader understanding of me and making sure I am happy has given me a different perspective on it—ultimately I now know that even if I do get released in a year, I will still be ok. I have relaxed a lot as a result, meaning I am doing OK in training and the games I have played so far in the first team.

From this reflection from Brian, I perceived that the main benefit of the work we carried out together was that it gave him a broader perspective on both his sport and his life, which meant he was able to relax knowing he was and would be successful regardless of the outcome of his contract decision. This led to him enjoying his sport, something which was facilitative to his performances in the lead up to his contract decision.

Coach Reflections

To further understand the outcomes that happened as a consequence of the work between Brian and me, I also asked the coach to reflect upon Brian and the way he had performed and presented himself in recent months. The coach offered the following reflection:

> We offered Brian a contract because, in a time that is often difficult for players, he has been able to remain focused and relaxed, performing well, and generally showing he can handle the challenges he is about to face. Six months ago, we weren't sure on him, but I think he has now got a bit more about him—he isn't as bothered by making a mistake and isn't fearful of the reaction, he just gets on with it and goes again.

Although not specifically asked to reflect upon the intervention but about Brian and the way he had developed, the coach's reflections (in addition to Brian's) do help to show the potential benefits of interventions, such as the above, from a performance perspective. By being more aware of his own thoughts and feelings, Brian was able to demonstrate competence in a relaxed manner, leading to contract success.

Case-Study Reflections

Overall, I was pleased with the intervention which was carried out with Brian and the outcomes which he achieved, which he perceived were in part to do with this work. There was evidence that Brian was now closer to understanding self-actualisation, and this had resulted in him being more relaxed in himself. That said, some reflections on the strengths and limitations of the use of goal-setting, workshops, and humanistic counselling as part of a career transition strategy may help to inform future applied practice.

First, practitioners should be aware of when to intervene and make an informed decision about the length of time the intervention may take to implement. With Brian, when he first came to see me, there were a couple of months remaining before the decision was being made about whether or not he was to be awarded a contract. This meant that we had to work on both short-term and longer-term issues in tandem, to ensure that he was able to achieve short-term results and longer-term outcomes. Ordinarily, when working with athletes who are preparing for transition, the majority of my time would be working with athletes from a humanistic counselling perspective, helping them to understand and achieve fulfilment regardless of decisions made which they have no control over (i.e., contract decisions). With Brian, given there were some immediate issues needing to be managed, including his parents' expectations and his fear of failure, I worked from a more eclectic approach to ensure the intervention covered the challenges he was presenting with. This reflection also highlights the value of both early intervention and intervention that focuses on the individual needs of athletes.

Additionally, the case reinforced my beliefs around ensuring practitioners are trained in a variety of approaches and use the best approach which is to the benefit of the client. In the case of Brian, it would have been easy for me to decide to take one approach out of goal-setting, workshops, and humanistic counselling, rather than combining these methods. By mixing approaches, I was able to target the same presenting issues from a variety of angles, ensuring that Brian was educated and was then able to make appropriate decisions about the said concerns. Reflecting upon the work, using one of these approaches in isolation may have been perfectly viable and may have achieved desired outcomes. However, I also believe that such an approach may have elongated the time it took for Brian to achieve understanding of the issues at play and make informed decisions about next steps. By broadening my approach, I gave Brian the opportunity to achieve both short term and long term, through short-term goals and longer-term self-actualisation conversations.

Summary and Conclusions

In summary, this chapter has provided an overview of factors impacting the elite youth to elite senior transition in soccer. We have provided an overview of this by providing a summary of main literature in the research area before providing a practical example of the case of Brian, a soccer player who was on the verge of being informed whether or not he was going to be awarded a senior team contract and was experiencing heightened anxiety as a consequence. This case highlights the value of taking an eclectic approach when supporting athletes experiencing transitions, while also aiming to highlight to the readers the complexity of transitions and various factors which may influence the smoothness of such. Practitioners and researchers in the field should consider these elements when researching or working with athletes in transition to ensure that the support provided to athletes in future is appropriate and helps to facilitate transition where possible.

Key Messages and Further Reading

From this chapter you should now have a greater understanding that:

- In order to support athletes effectively we need to be able to identity and understand factors that influence the quality of soccer players' transition from elite youth to elite adult professional soccer.
- The elite youth to elite adult professional athletic transition is considered to be a normative transition, which can be predicted and prepared for in advance.
- The elite youth to elite adult professional athletic transition is likely to occur simultaneously with transitions in other life domains, for example psychological development from adolescence to (early) adulthood and financial transitions to financial independence.
- Being able to interpret signs that athletes are experiencing negative transitions and the factors influencing the transition from elite youth to elite adult professional soccer is important to ensure that appropriate and individualised support is provided.
- To support athletes effectively through transition, the focus of intervention can be on sport performance but can also take an eclectic approach which ensures athletes have a greater understanding of managing transitional challenges and how they may be impacting performance.

If you wish to find out more about transitions in soccer, and particularly the elite youth to elite senior transition, please refer to the following works:

Morris, R., Tod, D., & Oliver, E. (2015). An analysis of organizational structure and transition outcomes in the youth-to-senior professional soccer transition. *Journal of Applied Sport Psychology*, 27, 216–234. doi:10.1080/10413200.2014.980015

Morris, R., Tod, D., & Eubank, M. (2016). From youth team to first team: An investigation into the transition experiences of young professional athletes in football. *International Journal of Sport and Exercise Psychology*, 1, 1–17. doi:10.1080/1612197X.2016.1152992

Stambulova, N. B. (2010). Counseling athletes in career transitions: The five-step career planning strategy. *Journal of Sport Psychology in Action*, 1(2), 95–105. doi:10.1080/21520704.2011.598223. This article outlines an intervention usable with athletes through the junior-to-senior transition.

Stambulova, N. B., & Ryba, T. V. (2013). *Athletes' careers across cultures*. East Sussex: Routledge. This book outlines and discusses a number of aspects of careers in sport in relation to different cultures across the world, including transitions in sport.

Wylleman, P., Alfermann, D., & Lavallee, D. (2004). Career transitions in sport: European perspectives. *Psychology of Sport and Exercise, 5,* 7–20. This article provides a summary of some of the main career transition in sport literature.

References

Alfermann, D. (2000). Causes and consequences of sport career termination. In D. Lavallee & P. Wylleman (Eds.), *Career transitions in sport: International perspectives* (pp. 45–58). Morgantown, WV: Fitness Information Technology.

Anderson, G., & Miller, R. M. (2011). *The academy system in English professional football: Business value or following the herd*. Liverpool: University of Liverpool Management School No. 43.

Aquilina, D. (2013). A study of the relationship between elite athletes' educational development and sporting performance. *International Journal of the History of Sport, 30*(4), 374–392. https://doi.org/10.1080/09523367.2013.765723

Bloom, B. S. (1985). *Developing talent in young people*. New York, NY: Ballantine Books.

Brewer, B. W., Van Raalte, J. L., & Linder, D. E. (1993). Athletic identity: Hercules' muscles or Achilles' heel? *International Journal of Sport Psychology, 24*(2), 237–254.

Brewer, B. W., Van Raalte, J. L., & Petitpas, A. J. (2000). Self-identity issues in sport career transitions. In D. Lavallee & P. Wylleman (Eds.), *Career transitions in sport: International perspectives* (pp. 29–43). Morgantown, WV: Fitness Information Technology. doi:10.1037/0090–5550.45.1.20

Brown, G., & Potrac, P. (2009). You've not made the grade, son: De-selection and identity disruption in elite level youth football. *Soccer & Society, 10*(2), 143–159. doi:10.1080/14660970802601613

Bruner, M. W., Munroe-Chandler, K. J., & Spink, K. S. (2008). Entry into elite sport: A preliminary investigation into the transition experiences of rookie athletes. *Journal of Applied Sport Psychology, 20*(2), 236–252. https://doi.org/10.1080/10413200701867745

Burton, D., & Weiss, C. (2008). The fundamental goal concept: The path to process and performance success. In T. S. Horn & T. S. Horn (Eds.), *Advances in sport psychology* (3rd ed., pp. 339–375, 470–474). Champaign, IL: Human Kinetics.

Clement, D., & Shannon, V. (2009). The impact of a workshop on athletic training students' sport psychology behaviors. *The Sport Psychologist, 23*(4), 504–522. https://doi.org/10.1123/tsp.23.4.504

Côté, J. (1999). The influence of the family in the development of talent in sport. *The Sport Psychologist, 13,* 395–417. https://doi.org/10.1123/tsp.13.4.395

Erikson, E. H. (1994). *Identity and the life cycle*. New York, NY: W. W. Norton & Company.

Finn, J., & McKenna, J. (2010). Coping with academy-to-first-team transitions in elite English male team sports: The coaches' perspective. *International Journal of Sports Science & Coaching, 5*(2), 257–279. https://doi.org/10.1260/1747-9541.5.2.257

Gledhill, A., & Harwood, C. (2015). A holistic perspective on career development in UK female soccer players: A negative case analysis. *Psychology of Sport and Exercise, 21,* 65–77. https://doi.org/10.1016/j.psychsport.2015.04.003

Jones, R., Mahoney, J., & Gucciardi, D. (2014). On the transition into elite rugby league. *Sport, Exercise, and Performance Psychology, 3*(1), 28–45. https://doi.org/10.1016/S0140-6736(13)61957-1

Lang, J. C., & Lee, C. H. (2005). Identity accumulation, others' acceptance, job-search self-efficacy and stress. *Journal of Organizational Behavior, 26*(3), 293–312. doi:10.1002/job.309

Larsen, C., Alfermann, D., & Christensen, M. (2012). Psychosocial skills in a youth soccer academy: A holistic ecological perspective. *Sport Science Review, 21*(3–4), 51–74. doi:10.2478/v10237-012-0010-x

Locke, E. A., Shaw, K. N., Saari, L. M., & Latham, G. P. (1981). Goal setting and task performance: 1969–1980. *Psychological Bulletin, 90*(1), 125–152. https://doi.org/10.1037/0033-2909.90.1.125

Lorenzo, A., Borrás, P. J., Sánchez, J. M., Jiménez, S., & Sampedro, J. (2009). Career transition from junior to senior in basketball players. *Cuadernos de Psicología del Deporte, 9,* 38.

Mills, A., Butt, J., Maynard, I., & Harwood, C. G. (2012). Identifying factors perceived to influence the development of elite youth football academy players. *Journal of Sports Sciences, 30*(15), 1593–1604. https://doi.org/10.1080/02640414.2012.710753

Mitchell, T. O., Nesti, M., Richardson, D., Midgley, A. W., Eubank, M., & Littlewood, M. (2014). Exploring athletic identity in elite-level English youth football: A cross-sectional approach. *Journal of Sports Sciences, 32*(13), 1294–1299. https://doi.org/10.1080/02640414.2014.898855

Murphy, G. M., Petitpas, A. J., & Brewer, B. W. (1996). Identity foreclosure, athletic identity, and career maturity in intercollegiate athletes. *The Sport Psychologist, 10*, 239–246.

Park, S., Lavallee, D., & Tod, D. A. (2013). Athletes' career transition out of sport: A systematic review. *International Review of Sport and Exercise Psychology, 6*(1), 22–53. https://doi.org/10.1080/1750984X.2012.687053

Pummell, B. (2008). *Junior to senior transition: Understanding and facilitating the process*. Loughborough: Loughborough University.

Pummell, B., Harwood, C. G., & Lavallee, D. (2008). Jumping to the next level: A qualitative examination of within-career transition in adolescent event riders. *Psychology of Sport and Exercise, 9*(4), 427–447. https://doi.org/10.1016/J.PSYCHSPORT.2007.07.004

Pummell, E. K., & Lavallee, D. (2019). Preparing UK tennis academy players for the junior-to-senior transition: Development, implementation, and evaluation of an intervention program. *Psychology of Sport and Exercise, 40*, 156–164. https://doi.org/10.1016/j.psychsport.2018.07.007

Relvas, H. (2010). *A qualitative exploration of the transition from youth to professional football across Europe: A critique of structures, support mechanisms and practitioner roles*. Liverpool: Liverpool John Moores University.

Rogers, C. (1951). *Client-centered therapy: Its current practice, implications and theory*. London: Constable.

Røynesdal, Ø. (2015). *The transition from academy to professional football*. Norway: Norwegian School of Sport Sciences.

Røynesdal, Ø., Toering, T., & Gustafsson, H. (2018). Understanding players' transition from youth to senior professional football environments: A coach perspective. *International Journal of Sports Science and Coaching, 13*(1), 26–37. https://doi.org/10.1177/1747954117746497

Schlossberg, N. K. (1981). A model for analyzing human adaptation to transition: The *Counseling Psychologist, 9*(2), 2–18. https://doi.org/10.1177/001100008100900202

Sinclair, D. A., & Orlick, T. (1993). Positive terminations from high-performance sport. *The Sport Psychologist, 7*, 138–150. https://doi.org/10.1123/tsp.7.2.138

Stambulova, N. B. (2000). Athlete's crises: A developmental perspective. *International Journal of Sport Psychology, 31*(4), 584–601.

Stambulova, N. B. (2003). Symptoms of a crisis-transition: A grounded theory study. In N. Hassmén (Ed.), *Årsbok: Svensk idrottspsykologisk förening SIPF* (pp. 97–109). Örebro: Svensk idrottspsykologisk förening. Retrieved from http://urn.kb.se/resolve?urn=urn:nbn:se:hh:diva-5911

Stambulova, N. B. (2011). The mobilization model of counseling athletes in crisis-transitions: An educational intervention tool. *Journal of Sport Psychology in Action, 2*(3), 156–170. https://doi.org/10.1080/21520704.2011.598223

Stambulova, N. B., Alfermann, D., Statler, T., & Côté, J. (2009). ISSP Position stand: Career development and transitions of athletes. *International Journal of Sport and Exercise Psychology, 7*(4), 395–412. https://doi.org/10.1080/1612197X.2009.9671916

Taylor, J., & Ogilvie, B. C. (1994). A conceptual model of adaptation to retirement among athletes. *Journal of Applied Sport Psychology, 6*(1), 1–20. https://doi.org/10.1080/10413209408406462

Vanden Auweele, Y., De Martelaer, K., Rzewnicki, R., De Knop, P., & Wylleman, P. (2004). Parents and coaches: A help or harm? Affective outcomes for children in sport. In Y. Vanden Auweele (Ed.), *Ethics in youth sport* (pp. 174–194). Leuven, Belgium: Lannoocampus.

Vincent, A. P., & Christensen, D. A. (2015). Conversations with parents: A collaborative sport psychology program for parents in youth sport. *Journal of Sport Psychology in Action, 6*(2), 73–85. https://doi.org/10.1080/21520704.2015.1054535

Weinberg, R. S. (2013). Goal setting in sport and exercise: Research and practical applications. *Revista Da Educacao Fisica, 24*(2), 171–179. https://doi.org/10.4025/reveducfis.v24.2.17524

Weinberg, R. S., & Gould, D. (2015). *Foundations of sport and exercise psychology*. Champaign, IL: Human Kinetics.

Wylleman, P., & Lavallee, D. (2004). A developmental perspective on transitions faced by athletes. In M. Weiss (Ed.), *Developmental sport and exercise psychology: A lifespan perspective* (pp. 503–524). Morgantown, WV: Fitness Information Technology.

Wylleman, P., Reints, A., & De Knop, P. (2013). A developmental and holistic perspective on athletic career development. In P. Sotiriadou & V. De Bosscher (Eds.), *Managing high performance sport* (pp. 191–214). London: Routledge.

2

THE ROLE OF POSITIVE PSYCHOLOGY AND ENJOYMENT IN ENHANCING SPORT COMMITMENT AND MAXIMISING STRENGTHS IN ELITE YOUTH SOCCER

Paul J. McCarthy

Brief Introduction and Review of Literature

The positive psychology movement studies "the conditions and processes that contribute to the flourishing or optimal functioning of people, groups and institutions" (Gable & Haidt, 2005, p. 104). In soccer, most people aim to flourish within the game by harnessing strengths and enjoying what they do (McCarthy & Jones, 2007). This dual purpose encourages most young soccer players to begin, develop, and thrive within the soccer environment to youth elite and adult elite levels. In this chapter, I shall explore the role of positive psychology and enjoyment in enhancing sport commitment and maximising strengths in elite youth soccer. I begin with an understanding of the foundations of positive psychology and positive psychological interventions (PPIs) before illustrating how an elite youth soccer player chose to help himself using PPIs.

The neologism—positive psychology—arrived in the late 1990s with a short history but a long past. In the previous 100 years, a deficit-based approach to psychological upkeep seemed reasonable because fixing what is wrong seems prudent; however, leaning on human strengths and possibilities harnesses the boundless potential of the person. Martin Seligman and his colleagues laid the foundations for a positive psychology movement to complement deficit-based approaches (Seligman, 2002; Seligman & Csikszentmihalyi, 2000), and since this watershed, scientific research and applied practice blossomed. In sport and exercise contexts, especially soccer, we can readily see the match between the positive psychology movement and optimal functioning in its broadest sense: psychological wellbeing and performance. Because positive psychology represents the science of positive aspects of human life, including happiness, optimism, and flourishing, it is easy to recognise common denominators with soccer. For instance, young soccer players pursuing a career in professional soccer require a mix of attributes and characteristics such as resilience, hope, positivity, and optimism (Carr, 2011). Crucially, we can develop these characteristics through simple but efficacious and effective PPIs. PPIs include gratitude visits, finding three good things in one's life, random acts of kindness, active-constructive responding, identifying signature strengths, savouring, best possible self, and positive reminiscence. These interventions are evidence-based and promote optimal functioning of people, groups, and institutions (Carr, 2011). What is most encouraging for applied sport psychologists is that these evidence-based PPIs often occur organically within soccer environs because of the nature and goals of teams at the heart of their social and cultural history. For instance, positive coaching alliances, working with local communities, and charity work are the cornerstones of most, if not all, professional soccer clubs.

Researchers examining PPIs have demonstrated the efficacy of such interventions to increase happiness and reduce depressive symptoms (Parks & Schueller, 2014). Efficacy refers to the difference an intervention can make. This efficacy is captured principally within laboratory settings, but for an intervention to be effective, we need to know how these interventions work in the real world. In other words, what actual difference does this intervention make under ordinary circumstances to bring about a desired effect? And although PPIs work for some individuals, they do not work for all. When we consider the efficacy of psychological support, we need to acknowledge that some people simply get better over time—something Eysenck referred as "spontaneous remission" (Eysenck, 1957). Notwithstanding this possibility, the argument within the literature strongly suggests that people get better because of the support provided by a psychologist (Cooper, 2008). The accumulated research evidence illustrates the effectiveness of PPIs to harness enjoyment, signature strengths, and commitment to activities within our lives. Soccer players and coaches can work alone or together to benefit from PPIs; however, even more can be gained through relational depth with a sport psychologist in a healthy working alliance. I work from a person-centred perspective in private practice. A person-centred approach resonates strongly with the positive psychology movement and the basic assumptions I hold: a positive view of humanity; humans are optimistic and growth-oriented; clients are responsible and in charge; the psychologist believes in the inner resources of the client and creates the right ingredients for growth; a client's self-healing is activated when they become empowered; clients bring about change. This way of being as a sport psychologist means that many of the assumptions of positive psychology are inherent in my work. The following case study illustrates the centrality of positive psychology, enjoyment, and flourishing in my work.

Practical Applications—Case Study

Background and Context

The following case study involves professional support offered to a professional youth soccer player through referral from a head coach. My professional working relationship with the soccer club offered soccer players the opportunity to meet privately with me without notifying the club directly. Also, if the coaches felt a player might benefit from psychological support, they would discuss this idea with the player and then involve me if the player agreed. I shared my contact details with all the players and staff at the soccer club. My private offices are located in the city centre, with private parking and a secure entrance. Clients attend by appointment, and the receptionist receives the clients if I am in session.

As a practising psychologist, I hold various assumptions about the work that I do and those with whom I work. I feel that the way in which I work reflects my values and assumptions about people and how I as a sport psychologist can support personal change. My therapeutic line of inquiry, frameworks, and interventions reflects these values and assumptions. Some of these assumptions include the following: People deserve respect, understanding, and acceptance because they are human. People are experts on themselves. People are capable of change. People have a powerful desire to maximise their potential. People work purposefully towards values and goals they own. By recognising these basic assumptions, I can openly discuss and debate them. I can challenge them and modify them through my reading, research, experience, and supervision. If I hold these assumptions as footholds, I can assess my actions against them. For example, if I repeatedly advise a client to follow my guidance, one could argue that I believe this client is incapable of choosing for himself and needs my support for direction.

Presenting Issue(s)

The manager at a local professional soccer club referred Adam to me because of "a lack of form on the pitch." The manager, Ally (a pseudonym), explained that Adam was

> as good as I've seen at his age. He'll have a fantastic career but I'm concerned the move to the first team might have been too much for him—it's a big step you know for a 17 year old because I can remember the same thing for myself. Anyway, he'll be in touch and you'll know what's best for him.

Adam called to my office on his way home from training. We had a brief conversation. During this conversation, I asked Adam what he knew about sport psychology and how a sport psychologist works with soccer players. I also asked him which changes he felt he needed to make, how he planned to make those changes, and how such changes might unfold in the weeks and months ahead. I normally engage clients in this way because it allows me to gauge whether we can work together and critically the client's view of the psychotherapeutic process (Cooper, 2008). Following our conversation, I decided that psychological contact was available and possible. We arranged a meeting time for the following evening.

Adam: I thought about what you said yesterday, you know, about you learn to see things from one perspective and may not consider other's perspectives.
Me: You've been thinking about how you see what's been happening to you.
Adam: It's like I'm worried about what other people think of me but I guess I'm not seeing it from their perspective—I'm still seeing things from my perspective. I thought that when I was thinking about what others thought of me, then I was thinking about the way they see things, you know from their point of view.
Me: And it will seem like you're . . . concerned only with how things seem to you?
Adam: Yes, I suppose it does. The thing is, I thought I was humble but maybe I'm not?
Me: And that's important to you—to be humble. . . .
Adam: Yeah, I'm a team player, no ego here
Me: You were really annoyed when you said that.
Adam: No—you're wrong. I'm not an angry person at all. Anger only causes problems.
Me: Getting angry . . . might be a weak thing to do?

Adam: Yes

Pause

Adam: That's the one thing I can't be—ever.

Adam is clever and insightful; he seems keen to speak about things that are not going well for him. And he has done so since he began playing soccer. At this point, I am aware of the ways in which the client might lead the content of our work. Content refers to what the client brings to the interaction—thoughts, feelings, behaviours, and experiences. In this instance, I am trying to understand what the client is saying to me verbally and non-verbally. But we also need to understand the process. The process refers to the dynamics of the relationship. How am I and my client working together? What is happening between us?

Person-centred theory is phenomenological, which means it is a philosophical approach to understanding based on the experience and perceptions of the person. In short, we are interested in the subjective experience of the client. Based on this underpinning, we focus entirely on understanding the world of the client. Person-centred therapy is non-directive, and being non-directive means taking a non-expert stance as the psychologist. When a client enters person-centred therapy, it is because he or she is in a state of incongruence. The psychologist's role is to reduce the level of incongruence between the ideal self and actual self and help the client to become a more fully functioning person. Congruence, or genuineness, is one of the most important attributes in person-centred therapy. The psychologist presents himself or herself authentically so that the client experiences the psychologist as he or she really is. Rogers (1980) suggested that the psychologist or counsellor accepts the therapeutic conditions as a set of principles for living rather than as a set of professional practices.

From my perspective as the sport psychologist, I am focused on presenting the attitudes and values of person-centred therapy because the client becomes an "active self-healer" in the process of psychological support. The client uses what the psychologist has to offer but uses it in his or her own way. The client is active in the therapeutic process, not a passive recipient of the psychologist's suggestions, advice, or therapeutic conditions. In short, the client is running the client's change programme by the client's rules. These principles echo those of the broad positive psychology movement where clients mobilise their strengths and values.

The Intervention/Work Conducted

During our first session, I explained to Adam how I work and what person-centred therapy means practically. His initial perception about the therapeutic process was that the psychologist will "tell me how to get better." When I explained that he was running his change programme by his rules, I got the sense through his expressions (gestures and words) that this circumstance was alien to him.

Adam: "So what you're saying is that I set out the rules and no one tells me what to do or how to do it? That's so strange to me. I'm told what to do and how to do everything by my coaches, the manager, S&C, physio—you name it! And in here, I do what I want with your support—is that right?"

Me: Um hmm

Adam: So . . . I'm in charge (smiling)?

Me: You sound excited by that notion?

Adam: Yeah. It's like . . . when I'm at home in my house, I have to brush my teeth and get my clothes on or whatever but as soon as I get to the training ground it's like 'Stand here, run there, get this, sit there' as if I don't know what to do or I'm too stupid to figure things out for myself

Me: You are being pulled from pillar to post without a say in it, is that right?

Adam: Right, right! 100 percent man! The only place I can relax is when I go home because I'm second guessing myself all the time at training and even more so at games.

Me: I sense your concern and exhaustion . . . second guessing yourself all the time.

Adam: Yeah! I'm all over the place and I know that's not right—it can't be. It's not how I play my best soccer.

Our first session helped Adam to see himself as psychologically independent, and it offered him an insight about how to maintain his psychological integrity. My focus was on empowering Adam by listening deeply to his experience of his world. The psychologist–client relationship is a relationship of change, and the catalyst for that change comes from all parties involved. The psychologist influences but does not interfere with the client's work regardless of opinions and preferences.

Adam was keen to understand more about human potential. He felt he had "shut down" so much of himself to fit into the team. He explained this "shut down" as accepting only the best and dismissing the rest. In his view, his "ideal self" "played above and beyond himself, made no mistakes and impressed the manager and fans in every game." His "real self" was quite different. His "real self" made mistakes as a matter of routine, had little to offer the manager and fans, and felt that the only way to contribute to the team was by making as few mistakes as possible.

Person-centred therapy aims to help the client to achieve independence. In other words, the client controls his world from the inside out and gains a sense of empowerment realising this internal locus of control. An external locus of control (i.e., being governed from the outside) pervaded Adam's life in soccer. He submitted to the coach and manager's directions and established dependence, rather than independence, with most of the support staff also. Through our second session, Adam began to recognise the appropriate balance of listening and learning while retaining an internal locus of control. I explained to Adam about the analogy of "keeping his hands on the reins." In this way, "you are still travelling to where you wish to go; you're acknowledging the terrain around you but your hands are on the reins."

Adam felt that he had "lost his voice" and was not sure if he would recognise it. He added that he 'wasn't sure what his own thoughts were anymore because he rarely gave them "airtime." In person-centred therapy, the client chooses how the change process works for the client. In Adam's view, he felt he would benefit from writing down his opinions and providing justification from a professional soccer player's stance. He began "to find his voice" by writing down his analysis of a game before reading the newspaper or watching highlights on television. Adam used to enjoy planning his day but over the past six months fell into a routine of "getting up, driving to training, driving home and not much else." He resolved to get his diary out again and asked for suggestions about planning one's day and gaining a sense of achievement from the day.

I met with Adam weekly for eight weeks. By his own volition, Adam scored himself on a one-to-ten scale, with one representing "not at all good" and ten representing "top of the world" before attending our sessions. When he attended on the first day, he had scored himself a 2 out of ten. In his second session, he scored himself a 4 out of ten, and it gradually increased to 9 out of ten by our final session. He revealed in his final session what he had been doing because he felt that the only way he would know if he was feeling better was to make a note that no one else would influence directly.

Adam's final session was most intriguing. Adam's manner and expression conveyed a confidence that he recognised but was intrigued by the reaction of his manager towards him.

Adam: It's almost as if he sees me differently. He trusts me. You know that's everything for a soccer player. I used to be shy and withdrawn around him but the weird thing now is that he seems to be shy and withdrawn around me! I've been scoring goals, making lots of assists, working hard for the team and of course I'm getting recognised, you know what I mean. My agent has been getting lots of calls but I'm happy where I am. But there's one part I need to better understand: Did I help myself or did you help me?

Me: Um hmm . . . pause

Adam: Good question! I've been trying to answer it over the last few weeks. I knew at the beginning that I needed some help and that's why I turned up. But I was so uneasy. But your way of doing things really got me going and I know that I decided what to do and when and everything. But I think I get it now. I do, I get it now. I get it now (laughing). That last thing you said. You didn't ask me a question, did you?

Me: No I didn't.

Adam: But you left space for me to answer it, didn't you? And I answered it. You see that's it—it's the space to answer it. And you don't judge me, do you? I don't get that anywhere else in soccer that kind of trust and respect. You think, no, you believe I can help myself . . . I guess you believe in me . . . yeah that's quite a good feeling to get from someone.

Outcome Analysis

Outcome studies that assess how clients feel at the end of therapy have reported large differences between pre- and post-therapy with a medium to large "treatment" against "control" effect size for client-centred/non-directive therapy (Elliott, Greenberg, & Lietaer, 2004). Within person-centred therapy, the focus is on the process of growth and facilitating that growth which is inherent in the organism rather than fixing something that is broken. To facilitate this growth, we focus on the therapeutic conditions. Rogers' (1961, p. 130) six therapeutic conditions coalesce around one idea: the client experiences himself as being fully received. Received, in this instance, means that the feelings, expressions, and whatever he is being in this moment is received by the psychologist.

But not all psychological support has the desired outcome for the client. On this occasion, Adam did report confidently on his experience. In his view, he felt much better and was performing on the pitch better than he expected when our work finished. I remained in the background while Adam decided how he could and would help himself. Adam chose to use two PPIs: writing down three good things in his life each day and identifying and exercising signature strengths. He engaged in the PPIs while we work together. He responded well to this psycho-therapeutic support; however, it may not suit all clients. It would be folly to discount all the other factors that might have influenced Adam's progress towards becoming a more fully functioning person. For example, the first-team coach and manager, being aware of Adam's difficulties and concerned about his recovery, explained that they were keen to boost his confidence in training and games by listening to him before they gave feedback to him. The first-team coach and manager were eager to know how to interact with Adam and the other players in a more facilitative fashion and lessen the usual sermonising they did. We discussed the issue, and they decided to "listen first, speak second." This approach seemed to diminish stifled conversations and especially the players speaking in defence of their actions.

The psychologist doing the work forms part of the change equation through their relationship with the client and the expectations of the client seeking support. Although debate abounds about the comparative efficacy of different therapies, there appears little difference in how efficacious different psychological therapies are (Luborsky et al., 2002). If there is little difference among therapies, then the non-specific factors (e.g., quality of relationship) truly matter. According to the estimates known as the Lambert Pie, 85% variance in therapeutic outcomes can be accounted for by client factors (40%), relationship factors (30%), and expectancy or hope (15%), with 15% relating to specific techniques or models. If we accept these estimates, then developing a strong therapeutic alliance, challenging cognitive appraisals, and appropriate self-disclosure (Cooper, 2008) is what matters in the therapeutic process.

Case-Study Reflections

I typically work from a non-directive (i.e., person-centred therapy) or directive approach (i.e., cognitive behavioural therapy) when I work with clients. My experience to date suggests a pluralistic approach (i.e., a set of principles and meta-strategies which can be adopted by psychologists from various backgrounds) meets most clients' needs most often (Cooper & McLeod, 2011). But to serve the client best, it is critical that we meet the client's needs. In this instance, and many others in professional sport, I feel that athletes need and value the opportunity to help themselves in their own way—central principles within positive psychology. Adam expressed that his life "was in someone else's hands" whether it was his agent, the club manager, support staff, and so forth. Adam embraced the opportunity to help himself though many of my previous experiences in soccer highlighted a dependency on others for guidance and a concomitant dissatisfaction with being "told what to do all the time."

Stories about clients are often the unit of analysis (i.e., what we study) in sport and exercise psychology programmes. Researchers have shown that students in medicine and nursing acquire skills for practice by memorising what was wrong with particular patients and what happened to them in "illness scripts" (Greenhalgh, 2010). We can learn meaningfully from anecdotes and acknowledge the drawbacks of decision-making by anecdote. The challenge for applied sport psychologists is to be evidence based (i.e., using research evidence to systematically inform one's decisions) and narrative based (i.e., distilling the richness of the corralled anecdotes and focusing on the client's unique story).

What the present case study demonstrates is that the psychologist working with the client has some answers but not all the answers. The client is central to the client's success in applied practice; therefore, we need to cope with change, guided by our philosophical stance, and recognise that what we have read in the past guides what we need to read and learn in new situations. Scientific uncertainty exists in applied sport psychology. As skilled as we become as practitioners, we cannot answer all questions that arise in therapeutic practice. We can read widely on a particular topic, but the most valuable skill will be to distil practically from the close-written text we have read. Knowledge alone will not suffice—we need wisdom. This wisdom is gained through evidence-based practice, reading widely within the field and beyond, sharing best practice with others, learning from others, and remembering that sound applied practice is a mixture of science (i.e., why it fits together) and art (i.e., how it fits together).

Summary and Conclusions

There is no text that is self-interpreting. What is taken by the applied sport psychologist from what is written in books and journals depends on various personal, professional, and contextual factors. The applied sport psychologist, therefore, depends on judgement and preference in professional practice. In this chapter, I suggested that PPIs within a person-centred approach to sport psychology delivery holds several advantages in a soccer context and sport more broadly. Working from a person-centred perspective means psychological support can be simple (though not easy), warm, and optimistic. The warmth, genuineness, and understanding of the psychologist can improve the condition of the client because the client holds within vast resources of self-understanding to change one's attitudes and behaviours, and this climate of change is facilitated by the psychologist. The client knows his world best and so is an expert on himself. Understanding how the client is thinking and feeling now is critically important in the process, and the client chooses how to help himself.

Sport psychology, like many other fields, has an exceptionally high noise-to-signal ratio (lots of modest research and incalculable unsubstantiated speculation on the topic). We realise that evidence-based practice (e.g., PPIs) is growing, but such evidence or "facts" are neither final nor incontrovertible. Rather, we value precision and accuracy alongside logical argument and detailed analysis. Our questioning, challenging, and replication of other researchers' work will bring generalisable findings for everyone's benefit.

Key Messages and Further Reading

One's self-concept—beliefs one has about oneself—incorporates valuing what I am and what I do. If a soccer player perceives himself to be strong, he might behave with confidence (e.g., a signature strength) and consider those actions as the actions of a confident person. The challenge might emerge mostly when the way we see ourselves differs from how others see us. A soccer player might be skilful on the ball yet consider himself incompetent. He judges and evaluates the image he holds of himself as incompetent, thus derailing his self-esteem. In person-centred therapy we refer to the client as a client—not a patient—because the psychologist and client are equal. This equality means the client is responsible for improving his or her life circumstances, not the psychologist. The psychologist provides the conditions to allow the client to consciously and rationally understand what is wrong and what could be done to put it right. The relationship, therefore, is vital. To build this relationship, the psychologist listens, understands, accepts, and shares with the client. Clients learn to understand their view of the world and themselves. By reducing incongruence between the ideal and actual self, a person can become a more fully functioning person with increased feelings of self-worth. A person-centred way of practising, therefore, prizes the client, the client's resources and abilities to help himself or herself. In short, the personal relationship the clients develop with themselves sets them free to flourish within and outside sport.

Key Readings

Carr, A. (2011). *Positive psychology: The science of happiness and human strengths* (2nd ed.). London: Routledge.

Mearns, D., & Cooper, M. (2017). *Working at relational depth in counselling and psychotherapy* (2nd ed.). London: Sage Publications.

Mearns, D., Thorne, B., & McLeod, J. (2013). *Person-centred counselling in action* (4th ed.). London: Sage Publications.

Rogers, C. R. (1961). *On becoming a person: A therapist's view of psychotherapy*. London: Constable.

Seligman, M. E. (2011). *Flourish: A new understanding of happiness and well-being- and how to achieve them*. London: Nicholas Brealey Publishing.

References

Cooper, M. (2008). *Essential research findings in counselling and psychotherapy: The facts are friendly*. London: SAGE Publications.

Cooper, M., & McLeod, J. (2011). *Pluralistic counselling and psychotherapy*. London: SAGE Publications.

Elliott, R., Greenberg, L. S., & Lietaer, G. (2004). Research on experiential therapies. In M. J. Lambert (Ed.), *Bergin and Garfield's handbook of psychotherapy and behavior change* (5th ed.). Chicago, IL: John Wiley & Sons.

Eysenck, H. J. (1957). The effects of psychotherapy: An evaluation. *Journal of Consulting Psychology, 16*(5), 319–324.

Gable, S. L., & Haidt, J. (2005). What (and why) is positive psychology? *Review of General Psychology, 9*, 103–110.

Greenhalgh, P. (2010). *How to read a paper: The basics of evidence-based medicine* (4th ed.). Chichester: Wiley-Blackwell.

Luborsky, L., Rosenthal, R., Diguer, L., Andrusyna, T. P., Berman, J. S., Levitt, J. T. . . . Krause, E. D. (2002). 'The Dodo bird verdict is alive and well-mostly'. *Clinical Psychology: Science and Practice, 9*(1), 2–12.

McCarthy, P. J., & Jones, M. V. (2007). A qualitative study of sport enjoyment in the sampling years. *The Sport Psychologist, 21*, 400–416.

Parks, A. C., & Schueller, S. M. (2014). *The Wiley-Blackwell handbook of positive psychological interventions.* Oxford: Wiley-Blackwell.
Rogers, C. R. (1961). *On becoming a person.* Boston, MA: Houghton Mifflin.
Rogers, C. R. (1980). *A way of being.* Boston, MA: Houghton Mifflin.
Seligman, M. E. P. (2002). *Authentic happiness.* New York, NY: Free Press.
Seligman, M. E. P., & Csikszentmihalyi, M. (Eds.). (2000). Positive psychology: An introduction. *American Psychologist, 55,* 5–14.

3
THE PSYCHOLOGY OF PENALTY KICKS

The Influence of Emotions on Penalty Taker and Goalkeeper Performance

Philip Furley, Matt Dicks, and Geir Jordet

Introduction and Review of Literature

The intense emotional nature of many sports contributes to explaining why millions of spectators watch such major events in front of the television or in fan arenas. Think, for example, of the quarter-final match during the 2018 Soccer World Cup between England and Colombia that was decided in a penalty shootout. Given England's history of unsuccessful performance in major penalty shootouts during World Cups, it was not surprising to see the nervous anticipation of players and fans in their bodily and facial expressions after the match had ended and they knew that the game would be decided by penalty kicks. This feeling of an entire English nation is nicely captured in the following quote:

> However, after 120 minutes of intense soccer raised all our blood pressure to dangerous levels, a familiar sinking feeling crept up on England fans like a delegation of Dementors.
> *(www.bbc.com/sport/football/44705768; retrieved on the 29.08.18)*

The shootout started well for England as both Harry Kane and Marcus Rashford scored with perfectly executed penalties. However, everything seemed to go "back to normal" when the Colombian goalkeeper David Ospina made the first save in the shootout, stopping Jordan Henderson's kick, leading to buoyant expressions of joy among Colombian players. These feelings were quickly changed, however, after Colombia's fourth penalty hit the crossbar and England scored. The emotions of the English players and fans then unloaded when England's goalkeeper, Jordan Pickford, saved Carlos Bacca's penalty in spectacular fashion and England's Eric Dier scored the winning penalty.

While a penalty shootout during a World Cup in soccer serves to illustrate the experience and expression of emotions that most people can relate to, science has struggled in dealing with the study of such emotions. Prominent emotion researcher Alan Fridlund stated, "The only thing certain in the emotion field is that no one agrees on how to define emotion" (Beck, 2015, p. 1). Further, the scientific study of emotions is complicated by the fact that some sport performance emotions are difficult to induce under laboratory conditions. The complication of inducing emotions is exemplified by the fact that identical methods have been found to be both successful (Wilson, Wood, & Vine, 2009) and unsuccessful (Noel & van der Kamp, 2012) in eliciting an emotional response.

Further to such experimental complications are the challenges in measuring emotions; in sport, this has led to the development of an array of different questionnaires (e.g., Hanin, 2000; Jokela & Hanin, 1999; Martens, Vealey, Burton, Bump, & Smith, 1990; Smith, Smoll, Cumming, & Grossbard, 2006), observational (Jordet, 2009a, 2009b), and physiological (Laborde, Mosley, & Thayer, 2017; van Paridon, Timmis, Nevison, & Bristow, 2017) measures. Despite such development, a fair appraisal is that there is currently no consensus on how best to study and measure emotions. The controversy in the research literature on emotions led Paul Ekman—another pioneering scientist on emotions—to publish a recent article with the title "What scientists who study emotion agree about" (Ekman, 2016), in which he interviewed the leading experts on emotion research. Although, this paper revealed some consensus in psychology on emotional theory (e.g., on the emotions of anger, fear, sadness, and disgust), evidence-based guidelines for sports practitioners are still hard to derive from research. This is further complicated by the observation from Richard Lazarus (2000) on research in sport:

> In the past, two almost separate research literatures have grown up, one centered on stress and coping, the other on emotion. [. . .] This is illogical and counterproductive. Stress is important in its own right, but emotion encompasses all of the important phenomena of stress. I believe the emotions provide a far richer understanding of the adaptational struggles of human and infrahuman animals.
>
> *(p. 231)*

Unfortunately, most research findings in sports have narrowly focused on the emotions of anxiety or stress and have led to potential theoretical misunderstandings on the role of emotions in influencing peoples' behaviour (Lazarus, 2000). Thus, the present chapter seeks to provide an up-to-date synthesis of emotional theorising and use this as background to integrate a selection of research findings in the context of soccer penalties. Subsequently, practical guidelines for goalkeepers, players, and coaches are extracted to inform evidence-based practice when preparing and performing soccer penalties.

Emotion Theory

It has recently been suggested that an evolutionary approach to emotions might help to address the lack of consensus in this field of study in the psychological literature (Al-Shawaf, Conroy-Beam, Asao, & Buss, 2016)—in particular in applied settings—as this perspective allows one to think about emotions from a broader perspective (Furley, 2018). Charles Darwin (1871, 1872) inspired this big-picture approach to emotions that has proven to be highly fruitful to integrate piecemeal research findings into a bigger picture of life on earth. Darwin's general perspective regarded emotions as bodily adaptations (e.g., specialised brain networks) that transform sensory information into adaptive behaviour. This approach has been successfully applied to increase understanding of emotions in everyday life (Ekman, 2007, 2016; Al Shawaf et al., 2016). Evolutionary-inspired theories regard emotions to be specialised neuronal networks that evolved to prepare the organism for different categories of recurring situations/stimulus patterns in the environment and the body. More specifically, Ekman (2007) described emotions as a complex pattern of physiological and psychological changes that are adapted to meaningful situations. These changes include physiological arousal, feelings, cognitive processes, expressions, behavioural tendencies, and overt behaviour that prepare humans and other animals to respond adaptively to recurring problems and opportunities in their environment (e.g., threat or disgust).

Following Ekman (2007), an emotion is assumed to be a very brief episode and is typically experienced as happening to us, instead of chosen by us. Longer-lasting emotional experiences are not conceptualised as emotions but as moods. An important component of emotions are cognitive appraisal processes (e.g., Lazarus, 2000; see Moors, Ellsworth, Scherer, & Frijda, 2013, for a recent review), in which people automatically scan the environment for things that are of importance to them, even though they are not typically aware of this appraisal process. People only become aware of an emotion when this automatic appraisal process is complete. After people become aware that they are in the grip of an emotional experience, they can, if desired, reappraise the situation and potentially change the nature and intensity of the emotional experience. According to Ekman (1992), there are certain universal emotional themes (basic emotions; e.g., fear, anger, disgust, joy, sadness) that reflect our evolutionary history, in addition to many culturally learned variations that reflect our individual experiences. However, other emotion researchers have argued against distinct categories of emotions and advocate a dimensional approach that typically involves the dimensions of pleasant–unpleasant and low–high intensity (Gendron, Crivelli, & Feldman Barrett, 2018; Russell, Weiss, & Mendelsohn, 1989; see Cowen & Keltner, 2017, for a recent integration of these competing theories).

Emotions are accompanied by changes in physiological processes—mainly via the autonomic nervous system (e.g., Levenson, 2014, for a recent review)—and non-verbal signals that inform others in the social group of how an individual is feeling (Darwin, 1872; Ekman, 1992) and/or likely to behave in the immediate future (Fridlund, 1994; Crivelli & Fidlund, 2018). Emotions in general are assumed to serve two main functions: (i) to prepare the organism to respond adaptively to recurring stimuli and (ii) to communicate important social information (Darwin, 1872; see Shariff & Tracy, 2011, for a review). In the next section, we focus on research findings that show how individual physiological changes associated with emotions have the potential to affect behaviour and performance via arousal and attentional processes in the penalty situation. Further, the assumed social or expressive function of emotions is of relevance in the penalty situation given the interactive nature of penalty kicks or shootouts.

Selected Research on Emotions in Penalties

Individual Effects of Emotions in the Penalty Situation

Given the overwhelming amount of information that humans have to integrate to behave adaptively, it has been proposed that cognitive processes have evolved to guide goal-directed behaviour to orient and attend to subsets of information. In this respect, research on penalties in soccer has adopted the attentional control theory (ACT, Eysenck, Derakshan, Santos, & Calvo, 2007) as a theoretical background in explaining performance in high-pressure situations (e.g., Wilson et al., 2009; Wood & Wilson, 2010). The main tenet of ACT is that human behaviour is controlled by two attentional systems: a top-down system that is guided by activated contents in working memory (goals, expectations, knowledge) and a bottom-up system that is guided by salient stimuli in the environment. An assumption of ACT is that performance pressure can lead to the emotion of anxiety and this causes an imbalance between these two systems in favour of the bottom-up system, facilitating the detection and adaptation of behaviour towards threatening stimuli in the environment (Eysenck et al., 2007). That is, with increasing anxiety, attention to threatening stimuli increases in order to allow rapid behaviours to escape any potential negative consequences for one's wellbeing. Wilson et al. (2009) found evidence for this in the penalty context by demonstrating that anxious participants were more likely to focus on the goalkeeper in a penalty kick than less anxious players. The goalkeeper was deemed to be a "threatening" stimulus given that this opponent ultimately stood between success and failure in the penalty kick, a suggestion that is supported by the observation that the mere presence of a goalkeeper leads to a decrease in penalty kick accuracy (Navarro, van der Kamp, Ranvaud, & Savelsbergh, 2013). Of further relevance, the increase in attention to the goalkeeper has been shown to lead to performance decrements in both laboratory (Wilson et al., 2009) and competitive penalty kick situations (Furley, Noel, & Memmert, 2017). Subsequently, it has been demonstrated that if a goalkeeper attempts to distract a penalty taker by waving their arms, for instance, this has the potential to further orient the penalty taker's attention towards them and thereby impair performance (Wood & Wilson, 2010).

A related series of findings have shown that pressure-induced anxiety can lead to paradoxical or ironic effects (Wegner, 1994) in penalty situations (Bakker, Oudejans, Binsch, & van der Kamp, 2006). Bakker and colleagues (2006) demonstrated that the instruction "not to shoot near the goalkeeper" during a penalty kick had the ironic effect that penalty takers shot closer to the goalkeeper. The authors argued that anxiety can lead to the worrying thought of not wanting to place the ball close to the goalkeeper, which has the ironic effect that attention is drawn towards the goalkeeper, which in turn leads to shots being placed closer to the goalkeeper (cf. Wilson et al., 2009). Moreover, performance decrements in pressurised performance contexts have been attributed to paralysis by analysis (e.g., Baumeister, 1984; Gray, 2004). Baumeister (1984) suggested that pressure-induced anxiety raises self-consciousness and worry about performing correctly. Studies have shown that self-conscious thoughts induce an attentional shift to monitoring the step-by-step execution of movement in an attempt to stabilise performance (Gray, 2004). Paradoxically, instead of stabilising performance by directing attention to skill execution, studies (e.g., Gray, 2004) have demonstrated that the explicit monitoring of well-learned skills disrupts skill execution, because step-by-step movement control is too slow to deal with the real-time control of otherwise well-learnt, proceduralised skills (e.g., when a professional player executes a penalty kick).

As considered earlier in the chapter, laboratory-based manipulations that aim to affect emotions are not without their complications (e.g., Noel & van der Kamp, 2012). Thus, an alternative and highly fruitful line of inquiry has been to develop video analysis methods that enable researchers to systematically observe players while they participate in major penalty shootouts, under different pressure conditions. Collectively, results highlight a clear tendency that players score fewer goals under high-pressure conditions (e.g., Jordet, 2009a, 2009b; Jordet & Hartman, 2008; Jordet, Hartman, & Jelle Vuijk, 2012). Moreover, players respond with more avoidance-oriented behaviours (primarily speeding up their preparation times and, in some instances, diverting their gaze away from the goal) when they are under extra high-pressure conditions such as performing shots where a miss instantly would produce a loss (Jordet & Hartman, 2008); having high individual status and thus more pressure to deliver (Jordet, 2009a); playing for countries with high team status (Jordet, 2009b); or playing for countries with a preceding history of penalty shootout losses (Jordet et al., 2012). Generally, there is also a tendency that quicker, self-imposed preparation times come with lower performance; but, with externally imposed waiting times, the tendency is the opposite, longer waiting times are associated with lower performance (Jordet, Hartman, & Sigmundstad, 2009). However, with all these results, it is important to keep in mind that they at most indicate a probability that something might happen, as no causality has been established. This means, for example, that one should be careful to recommend players to just take longer preparation times, without also helping them buffer against or cope with some of those debilitative emotional processes through which pressure exerts a negative effect on performance. We will elaborate on this implication for applied practice in the case-study section.

Together, the literature shows how performance pressure, which can lead to the emotion of fear or anxiety in the penalty context, can negatively impact on the control processes that underpin skilled behaviour. It is theorised that the emotions of fear or anxiety originally served to prepare an adaptive response that helped early humans to avoid potential harm can actually have detrimental effects in the soccer penalty situation. Before giving practical guidelines on how penalty takers can avoid these negative effects of anxiety, we further review studies that have focused on social effects of certain emotions on penalty interactions.

Social Effects of Emotions in the Penalty Situation

As considered in the observational studies of Jordet and colleagues (e.g., 2009a; Jordet et al., 2012), waiting for stressful events has been shown to potentially lead to feelings of discomfort and dread, which can lead to behaviour intended to get out of the situation as quickly as possible. Jordet and Hartman (2008) found evidence that this also seems to be observable in penalty shootouts. Penalty takers reduced the time they took preparing the penalty kick when the pressure was extraordinarily high. Moreover, penalty takers displayed hastening behaviour for negative valence shots, where a miss would lead to the team losing compared to positive valence shots, where a goal would lead to the team winning. In addition, negative valence shots resulted in a greater likelihood that penalty takers would turn their back towards the goalkeeper after placing the ball on the penalty spot before subsequently walking back to the spot prior to commencing their run-up. Jordet and Hartmann reported that such avoidance behaviour was correlated with negative penalty-taking performance. Furley and colleagues (Furley, Stendtke, Dicks, & Memmert, 2012) examined the communicative function of such hastening and hiding behaviour in penalty kicks. The study found that penalty takers showing hastening and hiding behaviours were perceived more negatively by both soccer goalkeepers and outfield players. Observers considered the penalty takers to possess less positive attributes, to have less accuracy in their penalties, and to be less likely to perform well in penalty situations. A further behavioural experiment provided initial evidence that goalkeepers who were confronted with hastening and hiding behaviours of the penalty taker during this preparation initiated their first movement attempting to save the penalty slightly later. This later movement may have been caused by the fact that the goalkeepers formed a negative impression of the penalty taker and anticipated a not very accurate kick. By waiting a little longer, goalkeepers could increase their chances of saving an inaccurate kick as the spatiotemporal demands would be less challenging, while, in contrast, a goalkeeper would have to move earlier if the kick was anticipated as likely to be highly accurate (Navia, Dicks, van der Kamp, & Ruiz, 2017).

These findings exemplify how the actions of a goalkeeper are based on the non-verbal information available from the penalty taker's behaviour. Indeed, an extensive body of research now exists that has examined which non-verbal information (cues) from a penalty taker is likely to be most useful to a goalkeeper. This literature indicates that penalty takers' use of deception ensures that early cues (e.g., approach angle) are incongruent with kick direction (Lopes, Jacobs, Travieso, & Araújo, 2014). However, if goalkeepers attend to later movement information such as the orientation of the non-kicking foot, this increases the likelihood of goalkeeper success (Dicks, Button, & Davids, 2010). Promising evidence indicates that training can be designed so that goalkeepers learn to attend to these later, more reliable cues (Dicks, Pocock, Thelwell, & van der Kamp, 2017). The application of such evidence has the potential to benefit goalkeepers who, when compared to penalty takers, are often said to have no pressure in shootouts because the likelihood of success is stacked heavily in the favour of the penalty taker. Despite such suggestion, Bar-Eli, Azar, Ritov, Keidar-Levin, and Schein (2007) have argued that due to the presence of pressure and social evaluation, goalkeepers do not adopt an optimal behaviour when facing penalties. They also argued that the optimal strategy for goalkeepers is to stay in the centre of the goal. Goalkeepers, however, almost always dive, a behaviour that was interpreted as evidence that a goal conceded following inaction (staying in the centre) elicits more negative emotions and evaluation from others than following action (diving).

These findings exemplify how all players involved in penalty shootouts are likely to encounter some emotional affects that are likely to impact (negatively) on performance. Importantly, as considered in the social information displayed by penalty takers to goalkeepers, certain emotional expressions have the potential to influence social interactions in the penalty kick situation. That is, when soccer players feel a certain emotion, this tends to be expressed and observers recognise this and are subsequently influenced by such emotional expression (Furley, Dicks, & Memmert, 2012; Furley & Schweizer, 2018). Of importance to this line of argumentation, several theorists have proposed that emotional expressions can be both deliberately and unintentionally used to influence others (van Kleef, Van Doorn, Heerdink, & Koning, 2011, p. 154): "Emotion is not just a feeling. Emotion is for influence." Increasing evidence suggests that emotions do not only affect those who experience and express them but also those who perceive them (Furley & Schweizer, 2014; Hareli & Rafaeli, 2008; Van Kleef, 2009). Moll, Jordet, and Pepping (2010) demonstrated that 80% of soccer players who celebrated a successful penalty by showing the positive emotion of pride (in comparison to those who did not show pride after a successful penalty) during penalty shootouts in the European and World Championships between 1972 and 2008 ended up winning the shootout. Similarly, a trend was evident indicating that players who showed non-verbal signs that are typical of the negative emotion of shame (i.e., gazing down) were less likely to win the shootout.

To explain interpersonal effects of emotions, the *emotions as social information model* (EASI model; van Kleef, 2009) was proposed and transferred to the penalty kick situation (Furley, Moll, & Memmert, 2015). The EASI model suggests two specific processes via which emotional expressions influence observers: inferential processes and/or affective processes. Inferential processes describe how an observer of emotional expressions is able to infer certain information about the internal states (e.g., feelings and attitudes) of other people. Observers use this information to better understand the situation, and it helps to inform an adaptive response (e.g., to initiate a later movement response as a goalkeeper when perceiving anxious non-verbal behaviour). In addition, observed emotional expressions can elicit affective reactions within the observer. One type of affective reaction occurs via the process of emotional contagion whereby individuals catch the expresser's emotions through their facial expressions, bodily movements and postures, or vocalisations (Hatfield, Cacioppo, & Rapson, 1993). Importantly, the nature of the social interaction (i.e., whether it is cooperative or competitive) will influence if an observer of an emotional expression will be "infected" with the same emotion via emotional contagion or will have different emotional, cognitive, and behavioural reactions via inferential processes.

After having established that emotions can have performance-relevant effects on penalty shootouts and emotional expressions can influence opponents and teammates, the next section of the chapter provides practical guidelines to soccer coaches and players when preparing for penalty shootouts. While much has been written on emotion regulation (Gross, 1998, 2014), also with the specialised aim of stabilising performance in sports (e.g., Friesen et al., 2013; Lane, Beedie, Jones, Uphill, & Devonport, 2012), the next section does not intend to give an exhaustive review of tools and techniques used in this field but instead to give broad behavioural recommendations that follow from the reviewed research. In this endeavour, we choose a case-study scenario to exemplify a strategic approach to the preparation of penalty shootouts. According to an influential process model of emotion regulation (Gross, 1998, 2014), emotions can be regulated at five points in the emotion generative process: (a) selection of the situation, (b) modification of the situation, (c) deployment of attention, (d) change of cognitions, and (e) modulation of behaviour. The chosen case study focuses on the behavioural aspect of emotion regulation and exemplifies behaviours that actors (players, staff, coaches) can employ across the five points of the emotion regulation model to help stabilise performance in penalty shootouts.

Practical Applications—Case Study

The following case descriptions are inspired by and built upon several applications and experiences of communicating with teams as they prepare for single games or entire tournaments that may lead to a penalty shootout.

Background and Context

Preparing for penalties presents a challenging circumstance for soccer coaches and teams, for a few reasons. Prior to a tournament, teams will never be able to establish with certainty that they will end up with a shootout. First, this presupposes the team will advance to the knockout stage where kicks from the penalty spot are a way to decide tied games and, second, that a knockout stage game will be tied after full-time and extra-time. Players and coaches can sometimes resist the mere idea of preparing penalties, as this necessarily implies that the team would not be able to win the game after full-time, which can be deemed by some as an overly pessimistic attitude.

Presenting Issue(s)

How can a team increase their chances of winning a penalty shootout? Further to this over-arching aim, coaches typically ask questions such as follows: (a) Which players should be picked to take a kick? (b) What type of kick is the best penalty? (c) Should penalties be practised? The studies considered in this chapter indicate that pressure can lead to anxiety and, in turn, can have a momentous impact on the outcome of a penalty shootout (e.g., Jordet & Hartman, 2008; Jordet, Hartman, Visscher, & Lemmink, 2007; Jordet & Elferink-Gemser, 2012). Thus, a penalty shootout, perhaps more than any other aspect of soccer, can be considered a psychological game. This necessitates a psychological approach to preparation, where a fundamental aim is to identify, get acceptance for, and prepare a strategy that helps the coach, the supporting staff, the team, and each individual player to effectively deal with pressure and the emotions accompanying it. Thus, the questions typically asked by coaches are better reframed accordingly: (a) What should coaches and support staff do prior to and during a penalty shootout to help players better deal with the pressure/emotions of the shootout (which also includes addressing *how* should you pick players to take a shot)? (b) What should players *focus on* during a shootout? (c) *How* should penalties be *prepared and trained*? Interventions could be structured around these questions.

Intervention

Ideally, an intervention should be comprehensive, and this includes promoting a full and adaptive mindset and culture around pressure, emotions, penalties, and performance, as well as identifying concrete solutions to optimise management, communication, and individual coping/focus around these shots. Because of the wide-ranging nature of such an approach, it needs to start early and well ahead of the actual tournament or game. A recent real-world example of such comprehensive preparation is the England national team leading up to and during the 2018 World Cup. England had not won a major penalty shootout since 1996 (across five attempts), and English players exhibit more avoidance-oriented coping strategies in shootouts than any other players representing leading European soccer nations (Jordet, 2009b). In 2018, the England team was reported to prepare very differently for a penalty shootout (see media accounts, e.g., Lyttleton, 2018; Davis, 2018). England started preparing a long time before the actual tournament; they took a psychologically mature stance towards what constitutes success at penalties (it's not about luck but skill under pressure); there was an overarching aim ("Owning the shootout"); multiple meetings on this topic were conducted between players and staff; players trained frequently and repeatedly; they adopted a penalty shooting routine where they were encouraged to take more time than English players have done in the past; and the newly appointed psychologist had sessions and did psychometric testing with the players (Lyttleton, 2018; Davis, 2018) to identify players who would likely perform well under pressure. Fortunately for England, they won their first major tournament, senior penalty shootout in 22 years against Colombia.

Prior to a penalty shootout, you want to build competence and confidence in the team, the staff and each individual player's ability to perform under this type of pressure and keep debilitative emotions in check. In our experience, knowledge about what actually takes place in penalty shootouts can be very powerful, and one simple way to start to build competence and confidence is to educate everyone in and around the team about known success factors in these events. These factors (such as the ones referred to earlier in this chapter) can be communicated with some very simple key data, which are best presented with videos from actual penalty shootouts. Now, let us address some of the practical questions that come up when assisting teams with penalty shootouts:

How should the coaches identify and select which players to take a shot, and in what order? Often, coaches ask the players, who wants to take a shot? (For descriptions of ways this can be played out, see Jordet & Elferink-Gemser, 2012.) A problem with this approach is that you, as a coach, do not know the exact reasons why a player will volunteer to take a shot. It could be because that player feels confident or that they should take responsibility. When a player puts up their hand in the spur of the moment, this in itself may add even more pressure on that player's shoulders—as this player not only just accepted responsibility but also asked to have the responsibility. A better approach is for the coach to make the decision and tell which players he or she wants to take a shot. But leading up to this decision, as much information as possible should be gathered—about each player's penalty kick skills, players' abilities under pressure, and also whether a player genuinely wants to take a shot or not.

Another popular question is that of whether penalty kicks should be trained or not. Logically, training penalty kicks is likely to make a player better at taking penalty kicks. It is also likely to increase players' confidence in these situations. Importantly, even though it will be hard or even impossible to practice these kicks under exactly the same emotional conditions as in a game, players should practice as realistically as possible. Specifically, there is a big difference between penalty training and penalty shootout training. Penalty shootout training means taking only one kick in a training session; performing the kick under conditions of intense fatigue, after a long and hard game-based training session; walking from the centre-circle to the penalty spot; being alone with the goalkeeper, not with all your teammates standing around the penalty area; and performing under competitive conditions, not while teammates are laughing and joking around you. Some of these conditions may indirectly add some pressure, but pressure can also be induced by having spectators and by creating different types of internal competitions.

Ultimately, each player needs to acquire and rehearse their own individual way to deal with these events. What do they focus on at different points in time? From the moment the referee has blown the whistle after extra time to the moment their foot contacts the ball on the penalty spot (for a detailed review, see Jordet & Elferink-Gemser, 2012). A complete psychological approach to helping each player prepare for penalties should take players through the event, step by step, to make sure each player knows what to focus on, what to do, and how to deal with complications, distractions, or anxieties—should any of these occur. A detailed account of this is beyond the scope of this chapter, but one aspect that briefly can be addressed is, what do you do in that moment that the referee signals (with a whistle and sometimes a hand movement) that you can start moving towards the ball and shoot. Back to the 2018 England–Colombia penalty shootout, much was said in English media about English players historically having been among the fastest penalty takers in the world and that Gareth Southgate's team this time was educated about this and then encouraged to take more time (e.g., Lyttleton, 2018; Davis, 2018). The English players indeed took longer time than they have before. However, taking time is not a guarantee that you will score more goals. We have worked with players who have felt that the recommendation to take time can actually add pressure, rather than taking it away, because it does not feel natural to wait to approach the ball when all you want to do is to get the situation over and done with as soon as possible. A better translation of this research finding into practice (the finding that taking short time is associated with fewer goals; Jordet et al., 2009) is to help players find a strategy that will make them feel more in control of the situation right before and during the kick, so they're not just behaving in what sometimes seems to be a panic-driven frenzy. One way to establish this type of control can be to be in charge of the time and to use this time to take 1–2 deep breaths. We see many top players take these types of deep breaths right after the referee has given his signal, with some noteworthy examples being Cristiano Ronaldo, Neymar, and Harry Kane. However, it is imperative that the breath is diaphragmatic, thus deep and full—not just a short breath located high up in the chest. Ideally, you also want players to systematically practice this type of breathing far in advance (Vickery, 2007). An important part of this advice for a penalty shootout is that it also gives the players something to focus on at a stressful moment, which in itself will anchor a player's focus onto something different than their tension and anxiety.

How about the goalkeeper? The goalkeeper is obviously a foundational participant in all parts of the shootout, yet psychologically players in these roles are perhaps less obvious intervention targets than the penalty takers because the pressure to deliver is assumed to be more on the penalty taker than the goalkeeper. That said, a goalkeeper's task should stretch beyond that of being a shot stopper. They can effectively do a lot to distract and make the pressure even more palpable for the opponent penalty takers (Wood & Wilson, 2010), and they can effectively do a lot to support their teammates. Regarding the former, we considered above how the time interval where the shooter is waiting for the referee to get ready is negatively correlated with performance (from Jordet et al., 2009). This time interval can be heavily influenced by the goalkeeper's actions—if the goalkeeper takes his or her time to get ready, the referee will also take more time to blow the whistle and the player will therefore have to wait longer. About supporting your teammates, the England team against Colombia showed an interesting way to do this, where their goalkeeper Jordan Pickford held the ball after every single shot he faced from the Colombian players and then personally handed it over to his teammate as they made the walk from the half-way line to the penalty spot. In this handover process, Pickford would have been able to say some supportive words as well, making one of the final steps of the preparation for the English penalty takers a potentially more familiar and positive one than it typically is.

Finally, during the shootout, it is not just about what you do as a shooter or goalkeeper when you are involved with the ball, it is also about what you do as a team and staff to support the others. We considered earlier how teams in penalty shootouts sometimes either do not communicate or communicate in a potentially non-helpful manner (Jordet & Elferink-Gemser, 2012). In the phase right after extra-time, coaches need to already have a plan in place and then communicate this plan with clarity, focus, and confidence. For example, England in the 2018 World Cup were very mindful in this phase about who would speak to whom, to preserve their focus for the messages that needed to be heard and to minimise the amount of extraneous noise affecting the players. Interestingly, when observing this particular penalty shootout, at one specific moment in time, one can see the Colombian goalkeeper being spoken to by five members of staff or teammates at the same time. Although positively intended, there is no way that the goalkeeper can effectively process all this information within such a limited time, and it is likely to distract him, rather than help. On the England team, the atmosphere around the goalkeeper was much more composed and seemingly more focused as he was approached by one staff member at a time. Furthermore, when in the centre-circle, one of our studies shows that this is the time where the pressure may be most intensely felt, as anxiety statements from this phase are plentiful (Jordet & Elferink-Gemser, 2012). We have experience with having very specific plans for how players can support each other at this stage. When a teammate scores, teammates' should take time to celebrate the shot (an indirect implication of the findings by Moll et al., 2010). When a teammate misses, the team can make sure they actively get that teammate back into the group again as soon as possible. Our experience with presenting these messages is that players and teams respond positively to them.

Outcome Analysis

Even though penalty shootouts obviously are crucial for the outcome of the game, one always needs to evaluate performance, not just the outcome of these events. With penalties, a player who simply closes his eyes and fires in the direction of the goal may still score, even if the ball placement was horrible, if indeed the goalkeeper happened to guess the other corner, as is possible due to inherent action biases likely to inform goalkeeper actions (Bar-Eli et al., 2007). Similarly, a player may execute a great penalty kick, with the ball headed for the bottom corner of the goal, but the goalkeeper's performance may be even better and the kick is saved. A thorough analysis of performance should include not only the outcome (goal/miss) of a shot but an analysis of the precise speed and placement of the ball, goalkeeper movement times (i.e., did he or she anticipate too early or late; Dicks, Davids, & Button, 2010), as well as the quality with which a player manoeuvres different types of goalkeeper-distracting behaviours.

Case-Study Reflections

In conclusion, teams should prepare a penalty shootout as a psychological game, and this requires comprehensive and detailed planning that focuses on not just the tactical and technical aspects of a penalty shot but different types of strategic decisions, communication, support strategies, and pre-shot routines. The next generation of penalty shootout preparation will almost certainly address all these issues, and perhaps somewhat ironically, the nation that has had more trauma than any others over the last 30 years in penalty shootouts, England, has led the way with their highly deliberate and holistic approach to their 2018 World Cup, culminating with their penalty shootout win against Colombia.

Summary and Conclusion

This chapter used the 2018 England–Colombia penalty shootout as an opening example to introduce contemporary theorising on the impact that emotions can have on behaviour and performance. Subsequently, a broad range of research findings from diverse methodological backgrounds on the effects of emotions in the soccer penalty situation (Jordet, 2009a) were described to set up practical recommendations for preparing penalty shootouts situated within the behavioural aspect of emotion regulation models (Gross, 1998, 2014). While there is still much to be learned about emotions in general (e.g., Beck, 2015; Ekman, 2016), and especially concerning their impact and regulation in high-pressure situations as soccer penalty shootouts, the present chapter was aimed at providing a timely review of relevant literature to inform evidence-based practice when preparing for penalties and inspiring new research in advancing emotional theory in performance situations.

Key Messages and Further Reading

- Emotions have an impact on soccer penalty kicks.
- Penalty shootouts are not a lottery, and training interventions can help to keep emotions in check.
- Emotion regulation strategies can target specific behaviours to help all actors (penalty takers, coaches, goalkeepers, and staff) in a penalty shootout scenario to be in control of the situation and perform well under pressure.

Recommended Reading on Emotion Theory

Al-Shawaf, L., Conroy-Beam, D., Asao, K., & Buss, D. M. (2016). Human emotions: An evolutionary psychological perspective. *Emotion Review*, *8*, 173–186. doi:10.1177/175407391456551

Ekman, P. (2007). *Emotions revealed: Recognizing faces and feelings to improve communication and emotional life*. New York, NY: St. Martin's Griffin.

Ekman, P. (2016). What scientists who study emotion agree about. *Perspectives on Psychological Science*, *11*, 31–34. doi:10.1177/1745691615596992

Hanin, Y. (2000). *Emotions in sport*. Champaign, IL: Human Kinetics.

Recommended Reading on Emotion Regulation (in Penalties)

Gross, J. J. (2014). *Handbook of emotion regulation*. New York, NY: Guilford Press.

Jordet, G., & Elferink-Gemser, M. T. (2012). Stress, coping, and emotions on the world stage: The experience of participating in a major soccer tournament penalty shootout. *Journal of Applied Sport Psychology*, *24*, 73–91.

Jordet, G., Hartman, E., & Sigmundstad, E. (2009). Temporal links to performing under pressure in international soccer penalty shootouts. *Psychology of Sport and Exercise*, *10*, 621–627.

References

Al-Shawaf, L., Conroy-Beam, D., Asao, K., & Buss, D. M. (2016). Human emotions: An evolutionary psychological perspective. *Emotion Review*, *8*, 173–186. doi:10.1177/175407391456551

Bakker, F. C., Oudejans, R. R. D., Binsch, O., & van der Kamp, J. (2006). Penalty shooting and gaze behavior: Unwanted effects of the wish not to miss. *International Journal of Sport Psychology*, *37*, 265–280.

Bar-Eli, M., Azar, O. H., Ritov, I., Keidar-Levin, Y., & Schein, G. (2007). Action bias among elite soccer goalkeepers: The case of penalty kicks. *Journal of Economic Psychology*, *28*(5), 606–621.

Baumeister, R. F. (1984). Choking under pressure: Self consciousness and paradoxical effects of incentives on skilful performance. *Journal of Personality and Social Psychology*, *46*, 610–620.

Beck, J. (February 24, 2015). Hard feelings: Science's struggle to define emotions. *The Atlantic*. Retrieved from www.theatlantic.com

Cowen, A. S., & Keltner, D. (2017). Self-report captures 27 distinct categories of emotion bridged by continuous gradients. *Proceedings of the National Academy of Sciences*, *114*(38), E7900-E7909. doi:10.1073/pnas.1702247114

Crivelli, C., & Fridlund, A. J. (2018). Facial displays are tools for social influence. *Trends in Cognitive Sciences*. doi:10.1016/j.tics.2018.02.006

Darwin, C. (1871). *The descent of man*. New York, NY: D. Appleton and Company.

Darwin, C. (1872). *The expression of emotions in man and animals*. London: Murray.

Davis, B. (2018). How England conquered their penalty shootout hoodo – From review of past failures to new routines. Retrieved from www.telegraph.co.uk/world-cup/2018/07/04/england-conquered-penalty-shootout-hoodo-review-past-failures/

Dicks, M., Davids, K., & Button, C. (2010). Individual differences in the visual control of intercepting a penalty kick in association football. *Human Movement Science, 29*(3), 401–411.

Dicks, M., Pocock, C., Thelwell, R., & van der Kamp, J. (2017). A novel on-field training intervention improves novice goalkeeper penalty kick performance. *The Sport Psychologist, 31*(2), 129–133.

Ekman, P. (1992). An argument for basic emotions. *Cognition and Emotion, 6*, 169–200. doi:10.1080/02699939208411068

Ekman, P. (2007). *Emotions revealed: Recognizing faces and feelings to improve communication and emotional life.* New York, NY: St. Martin's Griffin.

Ekman, P. (2016). What scientists who study emotion agree about. *Perspectives on Psychological Science, 11*, 31–34. doi:10.1177/1745691615596992

Eysenck, M. W., Derakshan, N., Santos, R., & Calvo, M. G. (2007). Anxiety and cognitive performance: Attentional control theory. *Emotion, 7*, 336–353. doi:10.1037/1528-3542.7.2.336

Fridlund, A. J. (1994). *Human facial expression: An evolutionary view.* San Diego, CA: Academic.

Friesen, A. P., Lane, A. M., Devonport, T. J., Sellars, C. N., Stanley, D. N., & Beedie, C. J. (2013). Emotion in sport: Considering interpersonal regulation strategies. *International Review of Sport and Exercise Psychology, 6*, 139–154.

Furley, P. (2019). What modern sports competitions can tell us about human nature. *Perspectives on Psychological Science, 14*, 138–155. https://doi.org/10.1177/1745691618794912

Furley, P., Dicks, M., & Memmert, D. (2012). Nonverbal behavior in soccer: The influence of dominant and submissive body language on the impression formation and expectancy of success of soccer players. *Journal of Sport and Exercise Psychology, 34*, 61–82. doi:10.1123/jsep.34.1.61

Furley, P., Dicks, M., Stendtke, F., & Memmert, D. (2012). Get it out the way: The wait's killing me: Hastening and hiding during soccer penalty kicks. *Psychology of Sport and Exercise, 13*, 454–465.

Furley, P., Moll, T., & Memmert, D. (2015). Put your hands up in the air? The interpersonal effects of pride and shame expressions on opponents and teammates. *Frontiers in Psychology, 6*, 1361. doi:10.3389/fpsyg.2015.01361

Furley, P., Noel, B., & Memmert, D. (2017). Attention towards the goalkeeper and distraction during penalty shootouts in association football: A retrospective analysis of penalty shootouts from 1984–2012. *Journal of Sports Sciences, 35*, 873–879. doi:10.1080/02640414.2016.1195912

Furley, P., & Schweizer, G. (2014). I'm pretty sure that we will win! The influence of score-related nonverbal behavioral changes on the confidence in winning a basketball game. *Journal of Sport and Exercise Psychology, 35*, 316–320. doi:10.1123/jsep.2013-0199

Furley, P., & Schweizer, G. (2020). Body language in sport. In G. Tenenbaum & R. C. Eklund (Eds.), *Handbook of sport psychology* (4th ed., pp. 1201–1219). Hoboken, NJ: Wiley.

Gendron, M., Crivelli, C., & Feldman Barrett, L. (2018). Universality reconsidered: Diversity in making meaning of facial expressions. *Current Directions in Psychological Science, 20*, 286–290.

Gray, R. (2004). Attending to the execution of complex sensorimotor skill: Expertise differences, choking and slumps. *Journal of Experimental Psychology: Applied, 10*, 42–54. doi:10.1037/1076-898X.10.1.42

Gross, J. J. (1998). The emerging field of emotion regulation: An integrative review. *Review of General Psychology, 2*, 271–299.

Gross, J. J. (2014). *Handbook of emotion regulation.* New York, NY: Guilford Press.

Hanin, Y. (2000). *Emotions in sport.* Champaign, IL: Human Kinetics.

Hareli, S., & Rafaeli, A. (2008). Emotion cycles: On the social influence of emotion. *Research in Organizational Behavior, 28*, 35–59. doi:10.1016/j.riob.2008.04.007

Hatfield, E., Cacioppo, J. T., & Rapson, R. L. (1993). Emotional contagion. *Current Directions in Psychological Science, 2*, 96–99. doi:10.1111/1467-8721.ep10770953

Jokela, M., & Hanin, Y. (1999). Does the individual zones of optimal functioning model discriminate between successful and less successful athletes? A meta-analysis. *Journal of Sports Sciences, 17*, 873–887. doi:10.1080/026404199365434

Jordet, G. (2009a). When superstars flop: Public status and choking under pressure in international soccer penalty shootouts. *Journal of Applied Sport Psychology, 21*, 125–130.

Jordet, G. (2009b). Why do English players fail in soccer penalty shootouts? A study of team status, self-regulation, and choking under pressure. *Journal of Sports Sciences, 27*, 97–106.

Jordet, G., & Elferink-Gemser, M. T. (2012). Stress, coping, and emotions on the world stage: The experience of participating in a major soccer tournament penalty shootout. *Journal of Applied Sport Psychology*, 24, 73–91.

Jordet, G., & Hartman, E. (2008). Avoidance motivation and choking under pressure in soccer penalty shootouts. *Journal of Sport and Exercise Psychology*, 30, 450–457.

Jordet, G., Hartman, E., & Jelle Vuijk, P. (2012). Team history and choking under pressure in major soccer penalty shootouts. *British Journal of Psychology*, 103, 268–283.

Jordet, G., Hartman, E., & Sigmundstad, E. (2009). Temporal links to performing under pressure in international soccer penalty shootouts. *Psychology of Sport and Exercise*, 10, 621–627.

Jordet, G., Hartman, E., Visscher, C., & Lemmink, K. A. (2007). Kicks from the penalty mark in soccer: The roles of stress, skill, and fatigue for kick outcomes. *Journal of Sports Sciences*, 25, 121–129.

Laborde, S., Mosley, E., & Thayer, J. F. (2017). Heart rate variability and cardiac vagal tone in psychophysiological research-recommendations for experiment planning, data analysis, and data reporting. *Frontiers in Psychology*, 8, 213. doi:10.3389/fpsyg.2017.00213

Lane, A. M., Beedie, C. J., Jones, M. V., Uphill, M., & Devonport, T. J. (2012). The BASES expert statement on emotion regulation in sport. *Journal of Sports Sciences*, 30, 1189–1195.

Lazarus, R. S. (2000). How emotions influence performance in competitive sports. *The Sport Psychologist*, 14, 229–252.

Levenson, R. W. (2014). The autonomic nervous system and emotion. *Emotion Review*, 6, 100–112.

Lopes, J. E., Jacobs, D. M., Travieso, D., & Araújo, D. (2014). Predicting the lateral direction of deceptive and non-deceptive penalty kicks in football from the kinematics of the kicker. *Human Movement Science*, 36, 199–216. doi:10.1016/j.humov.2014.04.004

Lyttleton, B. (2018). How Gareth Southgate overcame England's World Cup penalty hoodoo. Retrieved from www.theguardian.com/football/2018/jul/05/england-gareth-southgate-penalties-overcome-hoodoo

Martens, R., Vealey, R. S., Burton, D., Bump, L., & Smith, D. E. (1990). Development and validation of the competitive sports anxiety inventory-2. In R. Martens, R. S. Vealey & D. Burton (Eds.), *Competitive anxiety in sport* (pp. 127–173). Champaign, IL: Human Kinetics.

Moll, T., Jordet, G., & Pepping, G.-J. (2010). Emotional contagion in soccer penalty shootouts: Celebration of individual success is associated with ultimate team success. *Journal of Sports Sciences*, 28, 983–992. doi:10.1080/02640414.2010.484068

Moors, A., Ellsworth, P. C., Scherer, K. R., & Frijda, N. H. (2013). Appraisal theories of emotion: State of the art and future development. *Emotion Review*, 5, 119–124.

Navarro, M., van der Kamp, J., Ranvaud, R., & Savelsbergh, G. J. P. (2013). The mere presence of a goalkeeper affects the accuracy of penalty kicks. *Journal of Sports Sciences*, 31(9), 921–929.

Navia, J. A., Dicks, M., van der Kamp, J., & Ruiz, L. M. (2017). Gaze control during interceptive actions with different spatiotemporal demands. *Journal of Experimental Psychology: Human Perception and Performance*, 43, 783–793.

Noel, B., & van der Kamp, J. (2012). Gaze behaviour during the soccer penalty kick: An investigation of the effects of strategy and anxiety. *International Journal of Sport Psychology*, 41, 1–20.

Russell, J. A., Weiss, A., & Mendelsohn, G. A. (1989). Affect grid: A single-item scale of pleasure and arousal. *Journal of Personality and Social Psychology*, 57, 493–502.

Shariff, A. F., & Tracy, J. L. (2011). What are emotion expressions for? *Current Directions in Psychological Science*, 20, 395–399. doi:10.1177/0963721411424739

Smith, R. E., Smoll, F. L., Cumming, S. P., & Grossbard, J. R. (2006). Measurement of multidimensional sport performance anxiety in children and adults: The sport anxiety scale-2. *Journal of Sport and Exercise Psychology*, 28, 479–501.

Van Kleef, G. (2009). How emotions regulate social life: The emotions as social information (EASI) model. *Current Directions in Psychological Science*, 18, 184–188. doi:10.1111/j.1467-8721.2009.01633.x

Van Kleef, G. A., Van Doorn, E. A., Heerdink, M. W., & Koning, L. F. (2011). Emotion is for influence. *European Review of Social Psychology*, 22, 114–163. doi:10.1080/10463283.2011.627192

van Paridon, K. N., Timmis, M. A., Nevison, C. M., & Bristow, M. (2017). The anticipatory stress response to sport competition: A systematic review with meta-analysis of cortisol reactivity. *BMJ Open Sport & Exercise Medicine*, 3, e000261, doi:10.1136/bmjsem-2017-000261

Vickery, R. (2007). *The effect of breathing pattern retraining on performance in competitive cyclists*. Master's thesis. Auckland University of Technology.

Wegner, D. M. (1994). Ironic processes of mental control. *Psychological Review, 101*, 34–52.

Wilson, M. R., Wood, G., & Vine, S. J. (2009). Anxiety, attentional control, and performance impairment in penalty kicks. *Journal of Sport and Exercise Psychology, 31*(6), 761–775.

Wood, G., & Wilson, M. R. (2010). A moving goalkeeper distracts penalty takers and impairs shooting accuracy. *Journal of Sports Sciences, 28*, 937–946. doi:10.1080/02640414.2010.495995

4
RATIONAL EMOTIVE BEHAVIOUR THERAPY AND SOCCER

Andrew G. Wood and Martin J. Turner

Introduction and Review of Literature

This following quote by Bill Shankly (ex-manager of Liverpool FC) exemplifies an extreme and dogmatic irrational belief about success and failure: "Some people think football is a matter of life and death. I assure you, it's much more serious than that." Often misinterpreted, the quote was in fact given during a TV chat show where he explained the strain that his managerial career had placed on his family life, admitting his misplacement of his priorities and the adverse effects it had placed upon his personal life. Both his tough upbringing and time within the Royal Air Force meant he knew all too well the triviality of sport, stating:

> Pressure is working down the pit. Pressure is having no work at all ... pressure is not the European Cup or the Championship or the Cup Final. That's the reward.

As such, we understand that those operating in elite sport and especially professional soccer can become absorbed into a world obsessed with winning and losing, resulting in a dogmatic and irrational shift from "wanting to" towards "having to" win (Botterill, 2005), which may come at a cost to their performances (Wood, Barker, & Turner, 2017; Turner, Kirkham, & Wood, 2018) and, more significantly, psychological wellbeing (Turner, Carrington, & Miller, 2018).

In the present chapter we introduce and describe the integration of rational emotive behavior therapy (REBT; Ellis, 1957) in elite soccer. Based upon our applied experiences we map the real-world and pragmatic integration of four core rational beliefs using separate case-examples. Each case combines real-life and hypothetical elements to protect client confidentiality and anonymity, while providing insights into the formulation and practical application for the readership. Each case differs in context, which determined the modality (i.e., formal/informal), targeted core belief, intervention aims, and the intended recipient/s, ultimately highlighting the flexible and dynamic nature by which REBT can be used by practitioners to meet the contextual and client needs.

Originally associated with the treatment of psychological disorders in clinical settings, REBT is a cognitive behavioural approach that over the past five years has received marked attention within sport psychology as an effective intervention to help athletes overcome adversity (e.g., Turner & Bennett, 2018). REBT is based on the premise that adversity (i.e., failure, rejection, or setbacks) is inevitable and when encountered those with irrational beliefs will experience *unhealthy* negative emotions (UNEs; e.g., anxiety, depression, unhealthy rage) and maladaptive behaviours (e.g., avoidance, disproportionate behaviours) that hinder goal achievement (Vîsla, Flückiger, Grosse Holtforth, & David, 2016; David, Szentagotai, Eva, & Macavei, 2005). Instead, those who hold rational beliefs will experience *healthy* negative emotions (HNEs; e.g., concern, sadness, healthy anger) and adaptive behaviours (problem-focused, proportionate behaviours) that help goal achievement (Dryden & Branch, 2008).

In practice, REBT is centred on the ABC(DE) framework (Ellis & Dryden, 1997; see Figure 4.1), where practitioners help the client to comprehend that it is one's beliefs about the adversity (A) and not the situation that determines how adaptive the consequences (C; adaptive/maladaptive) are for goal achievement. Though for some a difficult and surprising realisation, the notion that irrespective of the situation (A) they themselves can dictate how they respond offers a liberating and significant realisation for many athletes we have worked with. Using three main strategies (i.e., empirical, logical, and pragmatic) practitioners will dispute (D) and replace the athlete's irrational beliefs with effective and rational alternatives (E) (see Table 4.1). The framework helps clients comprehend that their thoughts, feelings, and subsequent actions are interrelated and changes in one lead to changes in the other/s (David, Miclea, & Opre, 2004). As such, REBT is not exclusively focused on changing thoughts (e.g., core beliefs/attitudes) but also draws upon a range of emotional (e.g., rational emotive imagery; Lipsky, Kassinove, & Miller, 1980) and behavioural methods (e.g., in vivo desensitisation, risk-taking, shame attacking; Ellis, 2003). A common misconception of REBT is that a rational view promotes indifference to adversity. On the contrary, researchers have proposed that rational beliefs may be associated with greater self-determined motivation (Turner, 2016; Turner & Davis, 2018). A rational view ensures players experience a minor blip, rather than a large dip in either psychological wellbeing or functioning, in response to adversity.

Humans are inherently rational and irrational, even more so when important goals are compromised or their core values/beliefs are challenged. From an evolutionary perspective, the extreme and exaggerated response associated with irrational beliefs would have served adaptive functions for our ancestors (David, Lynne, & Ellis, 2010). For example, the physical violence associated with unhealthy anger/rage (i.e., UNE) would be helpful in one's attempts at nullifying

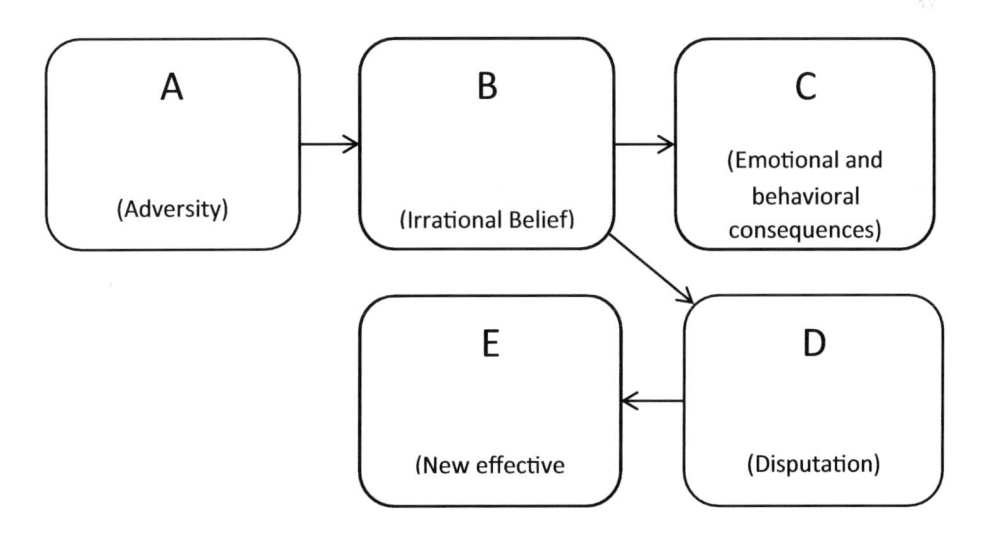

FIGURE 4.1 A schematic of the ABC(DE) framework used within the REBT process (Turner & Barker, 2014)

TABLE 4.1 Core irrational and rational beliefs accompanied by sport-specific examples

Core Irrational Beliefs	Core Rational Beliefs
Demandingness "I want to, and therefore I must be successful"	**Preference** "I want to, but that does not mean I must, be successful"
Awfulising "It would be absolutely terrible if I did not win"	**Anti-awfulising** "It would be bad, but it certainly wouldn't be terrible if I did not win"
Self/Life/Other-Depreciation "Losing makes me a complete failure"	**Unconditional Self/Life/Other-Acceptance** "If I lost it does not make me a complete failure, only that I have failed this time"
Frustration Intolerance "I could not tolerate losing today"	**Frustration Tolerance** "Although uncomfortable, I could tolerate losing, and it is worth it to do so"

a member of an attacking tribe, yet the same reactions after an unfavourable refereeing decision would result in, at the very least, the player being cautioned through to prosecution, depending on the severity. Similarly, feeling extremely anxious (i.e., UNE) would allow our ancestors to have remained vigilant for extended periods of time, yet the prevalence of incessant thoughts at night before an important game would hinder sleep rather than help a player perform. In sum, human irrationality beliefs are probably a vestige of our pre-civilised past.

Though recent research indicates no differences in the prevalence of irrational beliefs across athletic standard (Turner et al., 2018), there are social and cultural factors that will exert an influence on a player's irrationality. You only have to observe a manager's response to mistreatment/unfairness to appreciate that disproportionate actions in soccer could be considered normal and even favourable, often described as a "showing commitment and passion." This is problematic because, such actions are contagious and may become the norm—to the extent players may feign a disturbed response (e.g., pretending to be angry; Dryden, 2007) to conform to normative behaviour while warding off the costs of appearing "not to care."

"*There were terrible mistakes*" (Redmond, 2018, p. 2) is a quote taken from a news article that describes the two errors ex-Liverpool FC goalkeeper Loris Karius made during a champions league final. The quote presents a common example of irrational language (i.e., awfulising) often portrayed within the media to grab the attention of fans and/or readers via the use of sensationalism, and this is certainly not a new phenomenon. Further, the introduction of social media and subsequent competition between news sources has proliferated the extent and type of sensationalism (Kilgo, Harlow, García-Perdomo, & Salaverría, 2018). This has ramifications for players in the spotlight who are faced with perpetual intense media scrutiny. Any failings are intentionally sensationalised by the media or fans to evoke unpleasant emotions and dramatise ordinary people and often entrenched in irrationality. For example, suggestions players/teams are complete failures for underperforming (i.e., other-downing), as well as dogmatic requests for success (i.e., "this is a must win game") are commonplace. Of course, winning and playing well are important for a player, yet the prospect of future scrutiny and the belief it would be "awful" if they lost may render a player too anxious to perform or too depressed to return from injury. With no sign that the media scrutiny will soften, REBT offers an effective means by which a player and coach are able to mitigate against the adversities they encounter by challenging irrational beliefs and reinforcing a rational view of success and failure.

Considering all of the inherent challenges associated with elite soccer, there is a promising and critical mass of literature that has examined the use of REBT with athletes to enhance performance (e.g., Elko & Ostrow, 1991; Wood et al., 2017), reduce anxiety (e.g., Turner & Barker, 2013; Wood, Barker, Turner, & Thompson, 2018; Turner, Ewen, & Barker, 2018), increase autonomous motivation (Turner & Davis, 2018), and increase resilience (Deen, Turner, & Wong,

2017). Nevertheless, based upon our own experiences sport psychology practice is dynamic, unpredictable, and often time-constrained contrasting with the linearity and control characteristic of applied research. Thus, in the following section we portray the flexible, pragmatic, and mostly opportunistic integration of rational principles that best reflects the real-world application of REBT within elite soccer that has its origins within clinical settings.

Practical Application

Case Study 1

"I would prefer others and life to be fair to me, but this doesn't have to be the case"

Preference for Fairness

Background and Context

The present case arose after I (first author) observed a minor altercation between two players during a training session. The player, named Tom (pseudonym), had physically lashed out at another player after what he deemed to be a dangerous tackle. Tom's response was considered out of character and an occurrence I considered worthy of exploration. I had acted as the sport psychologist for Tom for two years and was well placed to broach this topic with him. Knowing the busy schedule ahead, I used the walk back from the training pitch to the changing rooms to start the conversation with Tom to gauge his initial reflections of what had happened.

Presenting Issue(s)

During this initial conversation it was apparent that Tom was remorseful yet unsurprised by his outbreak. He noted feeling extremely frustrated and angry in the build-up which had been internalised. Tom cited very little issues with the player involved, instead attributing his outbreak to a series of questionable refereeing decisions that had gone against him. During what was a five-minute "walk and talk" I felt assured that he was open and ready to follow this up. I suggested that we meet later for a coffee, which he accepted. Based upon the magnitude of his aggressive outburst and his reference to poor refereeing decisions, I anticipated he was harbouring a dogmatic and immoveable demand for fairness (i.e., I must be treated fairly, others and/life must be fair to me).

The Intervention

The aim of session 1 was to help Tom understand that, first, it was his beliefs, rather than the situation, that determined the functionality of his response; second, that rather than the negative emotion/response (valence) itself, it was the functionality of his response that would help him overcome adversity; third, to help Tom conceptualise a functional and adaptive response if this situation were to arise again.

Finally, and most importantly, I wanted to ascertain the critical adversity (A) that he found most challenging, which would provide clues about his core irrational belief via a technique known as "inference chaining" (Neenan & Dryden, 1996). Inference chaining involves taking the clients swiftly from the superficial to the core of their emotional disturbance. In Tom's case, the initial adversity was highlighted as a bad tackle, I then asked "why this was so bad?", in which he noted that the tackle should have been given as a foul. I then queried why this was so bad? We repeated this (why is this so bad?) line of questioning until we came to the most poignant and core irrational belief. Tom was consumed in how unjust the situation was during training and demanded that the referee had to be fair towards him. Together we agreed Tom would reflect on what we had covered and become aware of moments he felt angry (C) or was faced with unfairness (A).

Session 2 was conducted over the phone and where we aimed to establish, dispute, and replace his old irrational belief with a rational alternative. After reviewing our first session Tom mentioned that he had observed, in other teams, how unhelpful it was to become embroiled in refereeing decisions that were outside of their control. He pointed to the association between individuals/teams who battled with the referees and poor performances. I then began to dispute Tom's irrational belief that "referees had to treat him fairly, and that life must be fair" with three key questions. (1) How true was it that he had to be treated fairly? (2) How logical was it that because he wanted referees to treat him fairly, that he had to be? (3) How helpful was this belief for his respective goal? Once Tom largely concurred with the disputation process, we then worked to create the rational equivalents. Tom was asked to record his irrational and rational self-statements to use as a trigger and reappraise the situation the next time he felt aggrieved across any aspects of his life.

After reflecting on the last session, in session 3 we continued to dispute and reinforce his newly held rational view of fairness. Tom noted that he was now aware and was able to "catch his own thoughts" when feeling aggrieved/treated unfairly. It was important to ensure that Tom was not becoming indifferent to unfairness, instead experiencing a negative healthy emotion (e.g., frustration) rather than the unhealthy equivalent (e.g., rage), a credible notion welcomed by Tom. As a behavioural task I asked Tom to continue placing himself in competitive or refereed game scenario sessions to reinforce his new and rational belief that just because he wanted life/others to be fair, it did not mean that it/they had to be.

Outcome Analysis

After three sessions an informal assessment of the intervention was completed. First, Tom's self-reported sensitivity to his core irrational beliefs and new rational alternatives indicated that he had both engaged with and accurately conceptualised the ABC(DE) model. During training games, I observed Tom's ability to better transition between passages of play after a poor refereeing decision interjection. Thus, this indicated Tom was displaying a functional and adaptive behavioural response that was more focused on his and the team's plan instead of becoming caught-up in controversial refereeing decisions. In an ideal world I would have used the irrational Performance Beliefs Inventory (iPBI; Turner & Allen, 2018) to ascertain Tom's endorsement of irrational beliefs prior to and after the intervention delivery; however, time constraints did not permit.

Case-Study Reflections

From all four examples the present case offers an intervention that is most closely aligned with the formal and typical application of REBT, consisting of three x 30 minute one-to-one sessions. Short enough to be considered a brief contact intervention (Giges & Petitpas, 2000) the brief application of REBT appeared to offer an effective intervention to assuage the player's frustration and anger over life's unfairness within elite soccer. It would be prudent to note that Tom was a very self-aware, engaged, and proactive player who would have accelerated his progress through the ABC(DE) model.

Case Study 2

"It would be bad, but certainly not the end of the world if lost today"

Finding perspective—Anti-awfulising

Background and Context

The present case-example arose after a team meeting with players and staff after what was deemed an extremely disappointing exit from a major championship. As a new appointment to the team I (first author) was eager to garner player and staff input, from which emerged the desire to want to play soccer without feeling as if it were "do or die." Players noted that the prospect of failure rendered the team too anxious and thus unable to stick to the game plan. Instead, the players became desperate in their decision-making, inefficient in their physical effort, whereby the harder they tried the more it hindered their performance. In addition, all of the team were still very sensitive about the game and carried much of the baggage of the past six months after the tournament had finished.

Presenting Issue(s)

From the meeting, it became evident that the team were collectively awfulising failure in soccer. To explain, those who awfulise perceive a past/present/future event to be disproportionately worse than what the situation warrants. Awfulising can also be characterised by words such as "terrible," "awful," and "the end of the world," indicating that there is nothing conceivably worse that could happen (i.e., 100% bad, Froggatt, 2005). Of course, losing a game is bad, but rationally speaking it is certainly not terrible; there is much worse that a human could and has experienced in their life. Within the sometimes-insular world of elite soccer both players and staff have a propensity to awfulise and lose perspective, as a result perceiving the consequences of an adversity to be worse than they are in reality. Based upon the above I decided to run a single anti-awfulising workshop with the entire team, using a commonly known activity named the "badness scale" (Turner, Slater, & Barker, 2014).

The Intervention/Work Conducted

The badness scale provided an effective and engaging way to challenge and dispute awfulising beliefs while providing a simple tool members of the team could take away individually to further reinforce the core rational belief of anti-awfulising beliefs. To begin, the team were arranged into small groups made up of both staff and players. I then asked them to place and rate a series of adversities unrelated to sport onto a scale from 0 to 100% (100% = awful and 0% = not bad at all). For example, "as a % how bad would it be to: lose your wallet? Have a cold? Forget your passport at the airport?"

I then asked them to place a series of soccer-related adversities (e.g., losing in a final, de-selection) on the badness scale. Expectedly, the soccer-related adversities were placed much higher (70–100% badness) on the badness scale compared to the everyday alternatives (5–50% badness). At this juncture, I asked if they were all happy with their existing ratings, and then I asked them to place a series of what we consider major adversities (e.g., losing a loved one, an earthquake) on the badness scale. It was at this point the team started to realise their propensity to awfulise what could be considered relatively trivial compared to major adversities. How could missing a penalty be 100% bad if losing their partner was 100% bad. As in this case, typically we find those who complete the badness scale will then reduce all soccer-related adversities by about 50%. Finally, I emphasised the point that nothing can be 100% bad, as there is always something that could be worse however bad they perceived it to be. I asked the team to keep the badness scale with them or at home whenever they started to feel overwhelmed by a situation.

Outcome Analysis

From a single 60-minute workshop, anecdotal accounts suggested the badness scale was successfully comprehended and received positively. Although superficially players would verbalise that there was more to life than soccer, it took to completion of an activity for them to truly appreciate that they held core awfulising beliefs about achievement and failure in soccer. There was not pre- and post-assessment of this session; instead, the theme of anti-awfulising and the notion of placing unnecessary pressure upon themselves during important games continued to be a central theme that myself, players, and the coaching team alluded to. In particular, I observed the coach starting to use anti-awfulising techniques (i.e., "it doesn't matter you are allowed to make mistakes, move on") with players' mistakes during training and as part of team meetings in attempts to reduce their fear of failure and to foster an environment that encouraged players to make the right decision rather than the easiest.

Case-Study Reflection

On reflection, this workshop was not sufficient to dispute and replace the core beliefs of every member of the team within the allotted 60 minutes, and research largely supports this (Turner et al., 2014). However, it offered a starting point for players and staff to ponder and reflect on their propensity to awfulise when faced with particular adversities. Subsequently, following the session the theme of anti-awfulising was informally integrated into the sport psychology support, which then became both a familiar and normative term for all in the team. Indeed, little is currently known about the mechanisms by which sport psychologists can foster a rational culture within a team or organisation; nonetheless, far-reaching and broad workshops such as this seem to offer the first initial steps.

Case Study 3

> "It is tough, but I can tolerate being disrespected and it is worth it to do so. Yes the coach has treated me badly, but he is not a wholly bad person"

Frustration Tolerance and Unconditional Other Acceptance

Background and Context

I (second author) had noticed that Leon (pseudonym) was not as enthusiastic in training as he normally is and seemed distant from the rest of the team in the cool down. This change in behaviour was, I felt, worth exploring casually with Leon, so I walked with him back to the changing rooms to give me an opportunity for a brief chat. I asked how training went, to which he replied "ok I suppose," triggering me to dig a little deeper and convey my observations to Leon concerning his uncharacteristic lack of enthusiasm. "I just feel down," he said. We scheduled an appointment for later that afternoon. I wanted to give Leon a chance to offload whatever was bothering him and really had no idea what the resultant conversation would cover.

Presenting Issue(s)

I already had a general sense for Leon's affective state, so started there in our meeting. I wanted to understand more about the "down" that he was experiencing and so undertook a C (consequences) analysis to gain information on the emotional, behavioural, and cognitive aspects of what he was experiencing. He was having trouble sleeping, felt constantly frustrated, and kept asking "what's the point?"

when it came to his engagement with the sport. The maladaptive influence this was having on this wellbeing was clear, and I arrived at the decision that he was experiencing a UNE about something. I wanted to know what had triggered this state, and it became clear that a situation had arisen recently with his club coach. After training one evening, the coach told him he was dropped for the next game, and when Leon asked why, the coach "it's none of your business" and maintained that he didn't need to explain his decision. Leon felt that this was disrespectful, and he had been ruminating on it ever since. Now, in the present, he was still feeling angry about the situation and couldn't shake this feeling. I decided to conduct inference chaining to help us to understand what his critical A might be. The chain resembled the below:

Leon: The coach disrespected me
SP: Yes it would seem that way. Why is this causing your anger?
Leon: Well, it's just not right is it?
SP: No I agree. But why would that cause your anger and affect your sleep?
Leon: Because I train hard and am playing well.
SP: Yes you are. So why would the coach's disrespect of you affect you in this way?
Leon: People shouldn't just disrespect me like that.
SP: That sounds like a tough rule to live by.
Leon: Not really. People shouldn't be disrespectful at all.
SP: But what if they do disrespect you?
Leon: I just can't stand it. I can't abide by that sort of behavior at all.
SP: OK. Its intolerable to you?
Leon: Yeah! And it shows what a bad person the coach is. The way he handled it. Appalling.

This short exchange reveals various potential avenues for further exploration. The notion of being disrespected in general, not just by the coach, comes through here. So too do a range of potential irrational beliefs. Leon's language reflects demandingness ("People shouldn't be disrespectful at all"), frustration intolerance (FI) ("I just can't stand it. I can't abide by that sort of behaviour at all"), and other-depreciation ("it shows what a bad person the coach is"). Of course, working with athletes is rarely simple and usually a range of As, Bs, and Cs will emerge during exchanges. I posited a number of ideas to Leon in line with the ABC framework of REBT. First, I suggested that his rigid rule that "People shouldn't be disrespectful at all" leaves him open to feeling angry when people do inevitably disrespect him. Second, I proposed to him that his belief that "I just can't stand it. I can't abide by that sort of behaviour at all" and that the coach is "bad person" might serve to deepen his frustration. Leon agreed, and I was able to educate him in the ABC framework, placing an emphasis on how disrespect (A) may trigger his deeply held beliefs (B; demandingness, FI, and depreciation), which then causes his unhealthy anger and associated sleep issues (C).

The Intervention/Work Conducted

Leon connected with the ABC framework quickly, and to organise our work, I asked him which belief he would like to work on first. Choice in REBT is important, because when I am not around, or our work is finished, Leon has to work by himself to apply REBT to occurring adversities. Leon felt that his FI belief was particularly pervasive and even thinking about this belief in the room with me caused him to tense up and feel annoyed. I wanted to make sure we were both clear on what he meant by "I can't stand," so I checked with him "When you say, 'I can't stand it', does this mean you would do anything to avoid it, or do you just dislike it?" (Harrington, 2011). It's important that we are on the same page here; just because an athlete says "I can't stand it" doesn't mean they truly and deeply believe it. At this point, we ran out of time, but we both knew there was unfinished business that could wait. Therefore, we schedule a morning meeting for the following day. I furnished him with some homework. He was to complete the iPBI and the ABC self-assessment worksheet between now and the morning session. I asked him to complete the ABC sheet in line with what we had discussed, which would allow me to check his understanding in the morning and allow him to physically capture what we had covered to aid recollection.

In the morning, Leon seemed a little less down. He was smiling, seemed more energetic, and reported that he had slept well. This could be due to the period of time that had now passed from the event, but could be in part due to the session we had the day before. I have noticed that by helping the athlete to frame their issues using the ABC framework, alongside helping them to understand the routes of their emotions, they develop a sense of direction quickly. With this direction, the athlete can become more hopeful that their emotions can be assuaged. In REBT, I consider the introduction of the ABC framework to be a significant intervention, even though I am yet to help the client restructure their irrational beliefs. However, the disputation phase of REBT is where meaningful change can take place. With Leon I was happy to undertake disputation with him in this session as he had shown a good understanding of the ABC framework as related to his situation and was able and willing to work on his beliefs. To confirm this with Leon, I asked him if the direction we are heading is "ok" frequently. The process of REBT can be very collaborative, which is in contrast to the misconception that REBT is only didactic. REBT can be very directive, but we can offer direction without being authoritative and rigid.

Disputation

I wrote the FI irrational beliefs in large letters on my notepad so that Leon could see it, making it the focus of our conversation. I then introduced the evidence, logic, and pragmatic arguments that we would use to challenge this belief. My first task with Leon before disputation was to construct a rational alternative belief for his FI. I find that the conversation about what kind of belief the athlete could use instead of the irrational beliefs is useful as it tells me where the client is at in terms of their ability to think rationally and engages the client in the intellectual process of generating thoughts that are helpful and healthy. Leon and I collaborated on this for a while, until I was broadly (but not fully) happy with the rational alternative belief we had developed. As it stood, Leon's new belief was "I actually can stand being disrespected." After disputation, I knew we would return to the new rational beliefs to refine and strengthen it. To aid clarity, I have included the main aspects of the disputation Leon and I went through in Table 4.2.

TABLE 4.2 Disputation of Leon's FI irrational belief

Irrational FI belief
I just can't stand it. I can't abide by that sort of behaviour at all.

Evidence
Where is it written that you can't stand it? Is your belief consistent with reality? What do the data tell us? Is this how the world works?

Logic
Does it make sense that you can't stand being disrespected? Have you been disrespected in the past? Did you survive? If so, how can it be the case that you are unable to stand disrespect then?

Pragmatics
Is believing that being disrespected is intolerable helpful for your goal attainment or wellbeing? Is holding this belief helping you get to where you want to go? Under what circumstances could you tolerate this disrespect? If I told you your life depended on it, could you tolerate it? If so, why can't you tolerate for your mental wellbeing?

Some debate ensued concerning his ability to selectively tolerate things he didn't like versus things he thought it was worth tolerating. For example, he would not be able to stand disrespect from the coach but could stand disrespect from his father because it is worth tolerating this behaviour in order to maintain the relationship. Therefore, whether or not Leon chooses to tolerate disrespect is a choice he can make, rather than a rigid rule that is applicable across his life. Leon's rigid belief does not reflect the reality that he actually can, and does often, make choices about what he can stand.

Next, we returned to Leon's new rational belief "I actually can stand being disrespected" with a view to strengthening the belief in terms of its validity from an evidence, logic, and pragmatic perspective. It is important to recognise that the situation is tough, that the disrespect can be tolerated, and that it is worth tolerating in order to maintain wellbeing and performance. Evidently, Leon's intolerance of the situation is hindering his engagement and drive to fight for a place in the team. Therefore, together we developed the rational beliefs that "It is tough, but I can tolerate being disrespected and it is worth it to do so." This belief is subjected to the same disputation process as the irrational beliefs went through, to ensure a scientific approach to the cognitive restructuring process.

Once the new rational belief had been settled on, it was important to move onto reinforcing this belief and helping Leon to incorporate this belief into his philosophy of life. This took place in the following session. To do this, I used the athlete rational resilience credo (ARRC), a tool I developed in 2015 (Turner, 2016), which builds on the work of Windy Dryden (2007). The ARRC comprises five sections, one dealing with each of the four core irrational/rational beliefs and one dealing with irrational beliefs concerning the credo itself. Section three relates to FI and reads:

> Not having my desires met is very tough and difficult to tolerate. But I know I can tolerate this, because not getting what I want will not kill me or cause so much pain that I disintegrate. Even if my strongest desires are not met it is not

unbearable. It is very hard not to be successful, not to perform consistently, not be secure in my team, and not to keep developing my skills, but I know that I can stand this. I also realize that I can tolerate being treated unfairly and with disrespect, not being accepted and valued by coaches and teammates, and not being given opportunities. Although I may feel frustrated and upset and my goal attainment may be hindered, I know that I have the capacity to tolerate failure, setbacks, and poor treatment. Importantly, I accept that facing tough situations that do not meet my desires is OK as this provides me with valuable opportunities to grow as an athlete and as a person. Ultimately, tolerating bad situations is worthwhile because of the strength it gives me to face future adversity.

The main purpose of the credo is to provide a set of beliefs by which Leon can live, but sections of the ARRC were used separately as self-talk to provide in the moment rationality when As arise. Also, Leon read and reflected on the ARRC as a daily task, and to aid this, Leon audio-recorded the credo onto his smartphone so he could listen to it throughout the day. The ARRC helped Leon to internalise a rational philosophy that he could draw upon across multiple adversities, and as he started to use the credo more over time, he began to think critically about what is written within it, instigating conversations about how the credo applied to him and his specific issues.

Back to Depreciation

Based on Leon's preference, FI was addressed first in our work, but his irrational other-depreciation belief of "it [being disrespectful to me] shows what a bad person the coach is" was yet to be worked with. Rather than reiterate the process I have detailed above, it would perhaps be more fruitful to share an activity I use often with athletes who harbour depreciation beliefs. It's called the "Big I little i technique" (Lazarus, 1977). That is, of course, in practice I would complete a full assessment of Leon's ABCs in relation to his other-depreciation, and would for sure employ collaborative disputation to the belief, and work on developing new rational alternative beliefs with him. But I would also often complete practical activities with clients to aid disputation in a more creative way. With Leon, the Big I little i technique worked well because he was able to generate his own content and come to his own realisation as to the irrationality of his global negative evaluation of people who he perceived to have disrespected him.

The Big I little i technique involved drawing a big letter I that fills a side of paper. Then, I asked Leon to tell me all of the *good* things the coach has done since Leon has known him. For each answer, I draw a small letter i within the big letter I and label it with the "good" thing. After we exhausted this set of "good" things, I asked him to now tell me all of the *bad* things the coach has done since Leon has known him. Again, for each answer I draw a small letter i within the big letter I and label it with the "good" thing. Once this is complete, we now have a big letter I with loads of small letter i's inside it, each associated with a "good" or "bad" coach behaviour.

Then we reflect on the task, and how it might relate to the coach being a "bad person." The key takeaway here is that while the coach and indeed all human beings are capable of good and bad, it is not possible, and more to the point is irrational, to rate any human being as completely good or completely bad.

Once the depreciation belief was disputed, Leon and I then moved onto developing a new rational belief that could be supported on evidential, logical, and pragmatic grounds. We arrived at "*The coach has treated me badly, but is not a wholly bad person*," which recognises that the coach did disrespect Leon (we assume this to be true), but that this action does not mean that the coach is *all* bad. Again, once we arrived at this belief, reinforcement using the ARRC was undertaken, and we worked together to strengthen his new rational beliefs over the final two sessions.

Outcome Analysis

Leon and I had six one-to-one sessions together, and in between sessions, Leon was in touch with me numerous times to update me on his progress and to ask about the ABC(DE) process. This additional support is important, especially because I set Leon some homework assignments between sessions, and supporting him in these was paramount to their successful undertaking. The work could be considered brief, but we saw shifts in his irrational beliefs on the iPBI from above the norm (Turner & Allen, 2018) to below the norm. A reassessment of C revealed more functional behaviours in relation to the coach's disrespectful behaviour. Leon was still frustrated when the coach spoke to him disparagingly, but now Leon has made a commitment to fight for his place in the team and not *disturb himself* about the situation. Leon was now making choices about his emotions and behaviours, rather than letting his emotions and behaviours be driven by the coach's actions.

Case-Study Reflection

The work with Leon quickly snowballed from the first interaction we had. In that first chat, it was enough for me to understand that there was something bothering Leon, but it is typical for me to arrange a separate session to really try to understand what is going on. At the second session, I really had no idea what was going to be discussed and whether REBT would be applicable or not. My choice to employ REBT is driven by my analysis of the client and does not always focus on the disputation of irrational beliefs. Leon could well have been harbouring *rational beliefs* but still be experiencing difficult emotions, which could be addressed using a variety of CBT-derived techniques. Once it occurred to me that Leon was holding irrational beliefs and that these beliefs were in some way leading to UNEs, I adopted the REBT approach. One of the important aspects of REBT that distinguishes it from other CBTs is the focus on irrational beliefs as the chief cause of UNEs. Note that I do not challenge the evidence that Leon has been disrespected (A). In other forms of CBT it is more common to question the inference of perception at A, but in REBT we usually accept A to be true and focus on the rationality of the underlying beliefs triggered by A. In

> this way, we hope to achieve a more elegant solution (DiGiuseppe & Bernard, 2006) that aids the client across many As, not just the A at the centre of the present issues they are experiencing. Finally, the multiple irrational beliefs at play in this case are typical across the athletes I have worked with. That is, there is often more than one irrational belief that is triggered by an adverse situation (A), and therefore I would try to work through the beliefs in an order dictated by the client. It is important to do a thorough job in dealing with each irrational belief, to reduce relapse and to more fully teach the model to the client with a view to helping them to use REBT independently in the future.

Summary and Conclusions

Drawing upon our applied experience, we took REBT out of the consultancy room into the world of elite soccer using three distinct cases that targeted prevalent core irrational beliefs. In the first case, we outlined the application of a brief contact REBT intervention (3 x 30 minutes) to foster a flexible preference in a player who was demanding that others should treat them fairly and that life had to be fair. In case two, we described the rationale and delivery of an REBT workshop focused on disputing the core irrational belief of awfulising with a group who had a tendency to respond excessively to adversity (i.e., losing a game). Finally, in case three we chart the application of REBT with a player who harboured high frustration intolerance and other-downing in response to being disrespected by the coach. Both researchers and practitioners alike should be mindful that irrational beliefs are considered a remnant of our ancestry, and in today's society this propensity to demand core desires is not always met and is strongly linked to psychological ill-health. More specifically, in response to an adversity the endorsement of extreme and illogical beliefs will lead to unhelpful decisions and/or actions that prevent goal achievement, certainly unhelpful considering the plethora of barriers that those who work in elite soccer will inevitably encounter during their rocky road to success. Combining irrational tendencies with the domain of elite soccer may unwittingly cultivate irrationality and a setting that propagates mental ill-health within some and fosters an unhealthy relationship with the game for others. Our experience of applying REBT reveals those who abandon and replace their irrational view with rational alternatives will rekindle their intrinsic love for the game, which had become a pursuit they "had to do" rather than "wanted to do." Researchers and practitioners should look to proactively endorse and integrate rationality as a cultural pillar to support the sustained functioning of all those who operate in elite soccer (i.e., players, coaches, and support staff), with little cost to their psychological or physical wellbeing.

Key Messages and Further Reading

1. Though REBT was originally conceived to as a psychotherapy, the ABC(DE) presents a logical and yet flexible framework practitioners can draw upon to foster rationality within the dynamic and ever-changing context of elite soccer.
2. Whatever the client perceives the adversity (A) to be, REBT practitioners will initially consider the (A) to be true (e.g., coach does not like me) and instead tackle core beliefs (B). Markedly, it is when clients accept and endorse rational beliefs about the adversity (A) does perception (e.g., "coach does not like me") often change implicitly.

3. The ABC(DE) framework of REBT is anything but superficial, rather targeting deeply held beliefs. Successful shifts to flexible and logical rational beliefs and the associated psychological benefits are typically meaningful and maintained over time and transcend contexts.
4. Though originally a clinical therapy, the ABC(DE) framework is a fruitful approach that sport psychologists can employ re- and/or proactively to bolster psychological health and performance. Nonetheless, it should not be/we do not endorse practitioners to apply REBT with clients who present with clinical symptoms without the necessary training, requisite knowledge, and the associated professional accreditation.

Further Reading

1. Turner, M. J., & Bennett, R. (2018). *Rational emotive behavior therapy in sport and exercise*. London: Routledge.
2. Wood, A. G., Barker, J. B., & Turner, M. J. (2017). A case study with an elite archer: Developing performance using rational emotive behavior therapy (REBT). *The Sport Psychologist, 31*, 78–88.
3. Turner, M. J. (2016). Rational Emotive Behavior Therapy (REBT), irrational and rational beliefs, and the mental health of athletes. *Frontiers in Psychology, 7*, 1423.
4. Turner, M. J., & Barker, J. B. (2014). Using rational emotive behavior therapy with athletes. *The Sport Psychologist, 28*(1), 75–90.
5. Dryden, W., & Branch, R. (2008). *Fundamentals of rational emotive behavior therapy: A training handbook*. Chichester: John Wiley & Sons.

References

Botterill, C. (2005). Competitive drive: Embracing positive rivalries. In S. Murphy (Ed.), *The sport psych handbook* (pp. 37–48). Champaign, IL: Human Kinetics.
David, D., Lynn, S. J., & Ellis, A. (Eds.). (2010). *Rational and irrational beliefs: Research, theory, and clinical practice* (pp. 339–348). Oxford: Oxford University Press.
David, D., Miclea, M., & Opre, A. (2004). The information processing approach to the human mind: Basic and beyond. *Journal of Clinical Psychology, 60*(4), 353–369.
David, D., Szentagotai, A., Eva, K., & Macavei, B. (2005). A synopsis of Rational-Emotive Behavior Therapy (REBT): Fundamental and applied research. *Journal of Rational-Emotive and Cognitive- Behavior Therapy, 23*, 175–221.
Deen, S., Turner, M. J., & Wong, R. S. (2017). The effects of REBT, and the use of credos, on irrational beliefs and resilience qualities in athletes. *The Sport Psychologist, 31*, 249–263. doi:10.1123/tsp.2016-0057
Digiuseppe, R., & Bernard, M. E. (2006). REBT assessment and treatment with children. In A. Ellis & M. E. Bernard (Eds.), *Rational emotive behavioral approaches to childhood disorders*. Boston, MA: Springer Publishing Company.
Dryden, W. (2007). Resilience and rationality. *Journal of Rational-Emotive & Cognitive-Behavior Therapy, 25*(3), 213–226.
Dryden, W., & Branch, R. (2008). *Fundamentals of rational emotive behavior therapy: A training handbook*. Chichester: John Wiley & Sons.
Elko, K. P., & Ostrow, A. C. (1991). Effects of a rational-emotive education program on heightened anxiety levels of female collegiate gymnasts. *The Sport Psychologist, 5*, 235–255. doi:10.1123/tsp.5.3.235
Ellis, A. (1957). Outcome of employing three techniques of psychotherapy. *Journal of Clinical Psychology, 13*, 344–350.
Ellis, A. (2003). Similarities and differences between Rational Emotive Behavior Therapy and Cognitive Therapy. *Journal of Cognitive Psychotherapy, 17*(3), 225–240. doi: 10.1891/jcop.17.3.225.52535
Ellis, A., & Dryden, W. (1997). *The practice of rational emotive behavior therapy*. New York, NY: Springer Publishing Company. Retrieved from www.telegraph.co.uk/men/thinking-man/10489571/Seriously-sport-is-not-a-matter-of-life-and-death.html

Froggatt, W. (2005). A brief introduction to rational emotive behavior therapy. Retrieved from www.rational.org.nz/prof-docs/Intro-REBT.pdf

Giges, B., & Petitpas, A. (2000). Brief contact interventions in sport psychology. *The Sport Psychologist, 14*, 176–187. doi:10.1123/tsp.14.2.176

Harrington, N. (2011). Frustration intolerance: Therapy issues and strategies. *Journal of Rational-Emotive & Cognitive-Behavior Therapy, 29*(1), 4–16.

Kilgo, D. K., Harlow, S., García-Perdomo, V., & Salaverría, R. (2018). A new sensation? An international exploration of sensationalism and social media recommendations in online news publications. *Journalism, 19*, 1497–1516.

Lazarus, A. A. (1977). Towards an egoless state of being. In A. Ellis & R. Grieger (Eds.), *Handbook of rational-emotive therapy*. New York, NY: Springer Publishing Company.

Lipsky, M., Kassinove, H., & Miller, N. (1980). Effects of rational-emotive therapy, rational role reversal and rational-emotive imagery on the emotional adjustment of community mental health center patients. *Journal of Consulting and Clinical Psychology, 48*, 366–374.

Neenan, M., & Dryden, W. (1996). The intricacies of inference chaining. *Journal of Rational-Emotive & Cognitive-Behavior Therapy, 14*, 231–243.

Turner, M. J. (2016). Proposing a rational resilience credo for use with athletes. *Journal of Sport Psychology in Action, 7*, 170–181.

Turner, M. J., & Allen, M. (2018). Confirmatory factor analysis of the irrational Performance Beliefs Inventory (iPBI) in a sample of amateur and semi-professional athletes. *Psychology of Sport and Exercise, 35*, 126–130. doi:10.1016/j.psychsport.2017.11.017

Turner, M. J., & Barker, J. B. (2013). Examining the efficacy of Rational-Emotive Behavior Therapy (REBT) on irrational beliefs and anxiety in elite youth cricketers. *Journal of Applied Sport Psychology, 25*, 131–147. doi:10.1080/10413200.2011.574311

Turner, M. J., & Bennett, R. (2018). *Rational emotive behavior therapy in sport and exercise*. London: Routledge.

Turner, M. J., Carrington, S., & Miller, A. (2018). Psychological distress across sport participation groups: The mediating effects of secondary irrational beliefs on the relationship between primary irrational beliefs and symptoms of anxiety, anger, and depression. *Journal of Clinical Sport Psychology*, 1–38.

Turner, M. J., & Davis, H. S. (2018). Exploring the effects of rational emotive behavior therapy on the irrational beliefs and self-determined motivation of triathletes. *Journal of Applied Sport Psychology*, 1–20.

Turner, M. J., Ewen, D., & Barker, J. B. (2018). An idiographic single-case study examining the use of Rational-Emotive Behavior Therapy (REBT) with three amateur golfers to alleviate social anxiety. *Journal of Applied Sport Psychology*, 1–19.

Turner, M. J., Kirkham, L., & Wood, A. G. (2018). Teeing up for success: The effects of rational and irrational self-talk on the putting performance of amateur golfers. *Psychology of Sport and Exercise, 38*, 148–153.

Turner, M. J., Slater, M. J., & Barker, J. B. (2014). Not the end of the world: The effects of rational emotive behavior therapy on the irrational beliefs of elite academy athletes. *Journal of Applied Sport Psychology, 26*, 144–156. doi:10.1080/10413200.2013.812159

Vîsla, A., Flückiger, C., Grosse Holtforth, M., & David, D. (2016). Irrational beliefs and psychological distress: A meta-analysis. *Psychotherapy and Psychosomatics, 85*, 8–15. http://dx.doi.org/10.1159/000441231

Wood, A. G., Barker, J. B., & Turner, M. J. (2017). Developing performance using Rational-Emotive Behavior Therapy (REBT): A case study with an elite archer. *The Sport Psychologist, 31*, 78–87.

Wood, A. G., Barker, J. B., Turner, M. J., & Thomson, P. (2018). Exploring the effects of a single rational emotive behavior therapy workshop in elite blind soccer players. *The Sport Psychologist, 32*, 321–334.

5

DEVELOPING EFFECTIVE ON- AND OFF-FIELD LEADERSHIP IN ELITE SOCCER

The Social Identity Approach

Matthew J. Slater, Niklas K. Steffens, Katrien Fransen, and S. Alexander Haslam

Brief Introduction and Literature Review

Paul Pogba addressed his teammates in the dressing room ahead of the World Cup Final versus Croatia on the 15th of July 2018 with the following words:

> Boys, I don't want to talk too much. We all know where we are. We all know what we want. We all know how far we have come. We know it in our hearts, in our eyes, I can see it boys, we are concentrated. We cannot forget. Maybe I am repeating myself. We are 90 minutes away from possibly making history, 90 minutes. One match. One match. I don't know how many matches we have played in our careers but this is one match that changes everything, that changes all of history. There are two teams, there is one trophy. For them, it's the same, they want it. We know we lost a final [Euro 2016]. We know it. We feel it here [points to heart]. It's still in our heads. Today we are not going to let another team take what is ours. Tonight, I want us to be in the memory of all the French people who are watching us, their kids, their grandkids, even their great grandkids. I want us to go on the pitch, as warriors, as leaders.

As this address clearly communicates, at its core, leadership is a collective endeavour, a group process. It is not about the individual leader but about the team; it's not about me, it's about us. The social identity approach endeavours to capture and explain these collective underpinnings of leadership (Haslam, Reicher, & Platow, 2011). It argues that to understand (and develop) leadership we need to recognise that leaders and followers are part of a particular social group (e.g., a nation, a political party, a soccer team). Accordingly, in his speech, Pogba looked to motivate and inspire his teammates by focusing not on himself or teammates *as individuals* but on what they *shared*—history, ambition, and opportunity. In this chapter, we show how leadership is inextricably bound up with group processes of this form and how successful and enduring leadership involves developing, managing, and advancing a sense of shared identity within a given group or team. We then use a case study from the field of elite soccer to show how the social identity approach can be applied to develop on- and off-field leadership. We start, though, by introducing the social identity approach and reviewing the evidence that speaks to the benefits of cultivating a shared special sense of "us."

The Benefits of Cultivating a Shared Sense of "Us" in Sports Contexts

The social identity approach (comprised of *social identity theory*, Tajfel & Turner, 1979; and *self-categorisation theory*, Turner, Hogg, Oakes, Reicher, & Wetherell, 1987) is based on the premise that individuals can understand themselves not only as individuals (in terms of a personal identity as "I" or "me") but also, and often more significantly, as members of a social group (in terms of a social identity as "we" or "us"). In soccer, for example, a player can think, feel, and behave as an individual vis-à-vis other individuals (e.g., seeking personal gain, perhaps by moving to another club with a better reputation), but also as a group member (e.g., acting in the group's interests, perhaps by helping out a teammate who is going through a difficult time). Although the social identity approach does not have a long history of being applied to the study of sport and exercise, in recent years researchers have made significant strides by generating a large body of evidence which speaks to the role of social identity processes in shaping key outcomes in this area (e.g., Fransen, Boen, Stouten, Cotterill, & Vande Broek, 2016; Rees, Haslam, Coffee, & Lavallee, 2015; Slater, Coffee, Barker, & Evans, 2014; Stevens et al., 2017).

Social identity is important in sporting (and other) contexts because when athletes define themselves in terms of a given social identity (e.g., as a member of a given team), then this identity informs their values, norms, goals, and behaviour (Turner, 1991). In other words, rather than acting with reference to "me" they act with reference to "us"—and look to behave in ways that align with, and promote, the group's perspective. At the same time, social identity creates a sense of togetherness and common purpose that encourages those who share it (e.g., players, coaches, and sport science/medicine staff) to coordinate their actions, not least by cooperating, communicating, and supporting one another in pursuit of their common goals (Haslam, 2004).

The consequences of a shared social identity should all have a bearing on behaviours that under peak performance. Confirming this, at an individual level, research indicates that the more strongly athletes identify with their team, the more likely they are (a) to have a positive sense of self-worth (Martin, Balderson, Hawkins, Wilson, & Bruner, 2018), (b) to engage in goal-setting that contributes to their own development (Bruner et al., 2017), and (c) to show commitment and effort and go the extra mile for their team (i.e., by engaging in social labouring; De Cuyper, Boen, Van Beirendonck, Vanbeselaere, & Fransen, 2016). At a group level, too, social identification with a team has been shown to be associated with (a) greater collective efficacy (Fransen et al., 2014), (b) higher task and social cohesion (Fransen, Decroos, Vande Broek, & Boen, 2016), and also (c) better performance (e.g., Fransen, Steffens et al., 2016; Slater, Haslam, & Steffens, 2018).

The claim that shared identification is implicated in sporting performance has also received support from a study by Slater and colleagues (2018) of soccer teams playing in the 2016 UEFA European Championships. This assessed the level of collective passion shown by teams during their rendition of their country's national anthem and examined the capacity for this to predict the team's subsequent performance in the tournament. Here it was reasoned that teams whose members identified more strongly with their team would be likely to show greater collective passion and that this would feed into team functioning and performance. Supporting this prediction, results indicated that the teams that showed greater collective passion conceded fewer goals (but did not score more goals) and were more likely to win the subsequent match in the knockout, but not the group, phase of the tournament. Thus, at the highest level of competition, social identity dynamics appear to influence team performance, and it appears that this is particularly true when the stakes are high (e.g., in the knockout phase of a competition).

Leaders as Cultivators of a Shared Sense of "Us"

Having highlighted the benefits of a shared social identity for team performance, it is important to know how this can best be cultivated. At this point, then, leadership becomes our focus. The social identity approach to leadership argues that the effectiveness of leaders hinges on their capacity to cultivate a shared sense of "we" and "us" in their teams—in others words, their capacity to demonstrate identity leadership (Haslam et al., 2011). To provide effective identity leadership, leaders need to engage with four principles (Haslam et al., 2011; Steffens et al., 2014): they need to be seen as (1) prototypical for the in-group; (2) in-group champions; (3) identity entrepreneurs; and (4) identity embedders. First, acting as *in-group prototypes* involves leaders representing the unique qualities of the group and what it means to be a group member. Second, acting as *in-group champions* involves individuals promoting the core interests of the group and acting to the best of the group's interests. Third, acting as *entrepreneurs of identity* involves individuals bringing the group together by creating a shared and distinct sense of "we" and "us" in the group. Fourth, acting as *embedders of identity* involves individuals developing structures/strategies and organising activities that allow the group to live out our values in reality and achieve our vision.

It's reasoned that leading in-line with social identity principles optimises team effectiveness, and this notion has been confirmed by substantial evidence across methodologies and contexts. For example, evidence has supported the positive effect of leadership that aligns with the social identity approach on outcomes such as perceived trust (Giessner & van Knippenberg, 2008), influence (Subašić, Reynolds, Turner, Veenstra, & Haslam, 2011), and followers' job performance (Zhu, He, Trevino, Chao, & Wang, 2015). Leadership that creates a shared identity has also been found to predict the development of a special relationship between leader and follower (Steffens, Haslam, & Reicher, 2014), and this personal bond has been found to implicate followers' psychophysiological responses to stress (Slater, Turner, Evans, & Jones, 2018). Further, the measurement of the extent to which an individual leads in-line with social identity principles (established by assessment with the Identity Leadership Inventory: ILI; Steffens et al., 2014) has recently been validated across 20 countries (van Dick et al., 2018), demonstrating the cross-cultural applicability of the approach.

These endeavours bring to light leaders as cultivators of a shared sense of team identity. Yet, as with the social identity approach more generally, only in recent years have sport and exercise researchers made strides with evidence demonstrating how such leadership shapes key outcomes (see Rees et al., 2015; Slater et al., 2014; Stevens et al., 2017, for reviews). In a study surrounding the London 2012 Olympic Games, successful performance directors were observed to mobilise their athletes by communicating a positive, distinctive, and enduring sense of team identity in their media communication (Slater, Barker, Coffee, & Jones, 2015). In another investigation of leaders seeking to mobilise the efforts of their followers, Slater and colleagues (2018) found that when athletes perceive there to be a strong (versus weak) connection to their coach, they reported greater levels of intentional effort and were willing to spend 18.7% more time dedicated to a task asked of them by the coach (Slater et al., 2018). In other words, if soccer coaches ask their team to spend time on a task away from training (e.g., watch and analyse additional video of upcoming opponents), having a strong (compared to weak) connection with the athletes will result in the team investing more time on the task.

In exercise contexts (as well as sport), follower perceptions of social identity leadership (e.g., the instructor leading a team or an exercise class) has been found to positively relate to group identification, which in turn is associated with greater attendance at training/classes (Stevens et al., 2018). Crucially too, in the same study, mediation analyses suggested that there was a positive indirect effect of identity leadership on group members' attendance through group identification. Thus, it seems that it is through the creation of a shared sense of "us" that the leading in-line with the four principles can positively contribute to exercise and sport attendance. In other words, if soccer coaches wish to maximise attendance, leading in-line with social identity principles will achieve this through the creation of a shared team identity. In sum, there is growing evidence that engaging in identity leadership behaviours is crucial for sport and exercise leaders (e.g., soccer coaches) to mobilise their athletes' effort levels and boost attendance at training (through the creation of a shared social identity).

The growing application of the social identity approach to leadership in sport and exercise has been coupled with developments in the field of athlete leadership. Returning to the speech by Paul Pogba to his teammates, Pogba was one of the athletes on the team (he was neither the coach nor the formal captain) who demonstrated leadership in a way that sought to inspire his fellow athletes. Recent evidence has indeed corroborated that not only the coach but also athletes within the team have the unique capacity to manage—that is create, embody, advance, and embed—a collective sense of "us" within their teams. For example, experimental work in basketball and soccer settings evidenced that high-quality athlete leaders are able to create a shared team identity among their team members, which in turn nurtures team members' confidence in their team's abilities and improves their performance (Fransen et al., 2015; Fransen, Steffens et al., 2016).

An additional study has demonstrated that the four principles of identity leadership may have different consequences for athletes in sport. In a sample of 421 athletes (who completed the ILI in reference to their team captain) across a range of team sports (31% soccer), Steffens et al. (2014: Study 4) found that (a) being prototypical was a particularly powerful predictor of the captain's influence, (b) championing the group was a particularly powerful predictor of athletes' confidence in the team, (c) being an entrepreneur of identity was also a particularly powerful predictor of the captain's influence, as well as of athletes' team identification and task cohesion, and (d) embedding the identity was a particularly powerful predictor of athletes' team confidence and task cohesion. Accordingly, certain aspects of identity leadership behaviours may carry more weight when coaches or leaders within the team aspire to have influence or create a united, confident, and cohesive team.

Programmes to Develop a Shared Sense of "Us"

How can leaders cultivate a shared sense of "us"? The social identity approach to leadership proposes a shared sense of "us" can be crafted via the 3Rs: *Reflect*, *Represent*, and *Realise* (Haslam et al., 2011). First, *Reflecting* involves leaders listening and observing to understand the identities that are important to the athletes and staff within the sport team/club. Second, *Representing* involves leader's role modelling the unique qualities of the sport team/club and acting in the team's/club's interests. Finally, *Realising* involves leaders embedding in reality the sport team's/club's identity in terms of its values and aspirations/vision. Leadership development programmes can apply and embed these Rs by engaging leaders and their team members in a range of activities.

In the first application of the 3Rs in sport (and in soccer), Slater and Barker (2019) investigated the influence of embedding the 3Rs with an international-level disability sport team across two years. To implement the 3Rs, the authors created a Senior Leadership Team (SLT) that comprised members of staff and four athletes. Within each phase, the SLT completed a series of activities. For example, during the Reflecting phase, two identity mapping exercises were completed. The first, in line with Cruwys et al. (2016), involved members documenting all the groups that they felt that they belonged to. The second identity mapping activity captured what values members associated with the team and what it meant to them to be part of the group. Then, one of the activities within the Representing phase involved reviewing and discussing these suggested values to create a set of shared values. Finally, one of the activities in the Realising phase involved environmental changes to bring these values to life (e.g., posters of the shared values were placed in changing rooms). Across these SLT activities, the athletes involved were tasked with completing the same activities with the remaining squad, bringing information outcomes back to the next SLT session. Findings indicated that, compared to before the programme, following the 3Rs athletes' strength of team identification and perceptions of staff as identity leaders increased. Accordingly, Slater and Barker (2019) concluded that the 3R model holds promise for researchers and practitioners whose purpose it is to develop leadership and create a shared sense of "us" in sport.

Leaders, too, who participate in a similar leadership development programme designed for organisational leaders (the 5R programme) report similar self-reflective benefits. In soccer, this could relate to members of staff (e.g., coaches, sport science/medicine) or the SLT in accordance with Slater and Barker's (2019) approach. Haslam and colleagues (2017) ran a leadership development programme that extended the 3Rs by including a *Readying* (at the start) and *Reporting* (at the end) phase with managers of Allied Health teams in Australia. Compared to baseline data, following the 5R programme leaders reported that they were better able to engage in identity leadership behaviours, they had greater team goal clarity, and small positive effects were seen in their strength of team identification. Thus, the 5R programme is also perceived to be a useful framework by leaders themselves, and in soccer this could mean coaches, support staff, and captains are better placed to have influence.

Broadening our perspective on leadership, the 5R programme has been extended to a holistic approach that not only focuses on the coach as an identity leader but strengthens the identity leadership skills of athlete leaders. To realise this aim, Fransen et al. (2020) brought together insights from organisational and sport psychology to design a *5R Shared Leadership Programme ($5R^S$)*, which (a) encourages a structure of shared leadership (through *Shared Leadership Mapping*) and (b) further develops the leadership potential of athlete leaders (through the *5R Programme*). More specifically, an initial analysis of the leadership structure within the team (through social network analysis) inspires the appointment of athlete leaders in different leadership roles (ranging from task and motivational leadership roles on the field to the roles of social and external leader off the field; for a more elaborate discussion on this Shared Leadership Mapping procedure, we refer to Fransen et al., 2015). Afterwards, the appointed athlete leaders receive the lead role in guiding their teammates through the five phases; together with their team they reflect on their joint core values and norms (Reflecting phase); they come up with new task, motivational, social, and external goals (Representing phase) and devise strategies to attain each of these goals (Realising phase). In the final Reporting phase, they evaluate the team's progress and, by doing so, provide new input to start this 5R cycle again. By teaching athlete leaders in soccer teams how to create, embody, advance, and embed a collective sense of "us" in their team, the participation in the programme allows leaders not only to be perceived as better leaders themselves but also to gain an important lever through which they can attain other outcomes, such as increased team confidence and cohesion, and improved performance.

Practical Applications—A Hypothetical Case Study of the Social Identity Approach to Leadership

Background and Context

The hypothetical professional soccer team in question has experienced significant and repeated change over the previous few seasons. The first-team squad included 25 professionally contracted athletes from multiple nations. Following a poor season of results, the previous head coach left his position at the end of the last season, and the case study begins with the new head coach in place at the start of the pre-season. Together with the new head coach, numerous new members of staff came into the club, while some members of backroom staff remained from the previous structure.

Presenting Issue(s)

The primary areas for improvement related to a lack of leadership and players' lack of identification with the team. First, in terms of leadership, as the head coach and a number of backroom staff were new to the club, there was a lack of connection between staff and players. Regarding the players, there was a formal captain, but he was not seen as effective by the team. Second, in terms of the team's identity, while previously players have "agreed to disagree," there remained cliques in the team, the team did not come together effectively in performance terms, nor did they enjoy spending time together off the field.

With near-constant change in elite soccer, it can be difficult to establish shared values and behaviours that all team members buy-in to. This can be compounded by arrivals of new staff who bring their own philosophy and style of play that they wish to implement. This happens frequently and is exactly what Claudio Ranieri did when he started at Leicester City (Haslam & Reicher, 2016). He told his players about the tactics that they were going to employ for the forthcoming season. At this point, however, Ranieri did something different to the norm. He paused. He listened:

> When I spoke with the players, I realised that they were afraid of [my] tactics. They did not look convinced, and neither was I. I have great admiration for those who build new tactical systems, but I always thought the most important thing a good coach must do is to build the team around the characteristics of his players. So I told the players that I trusted them and would speak very little of tactics.
> *(Percy, 2016)*

So rather than imposing his personal will over the players, Ranieri seemingly understood that he was there to serve the players to discover and live out their collective will (Haslam & Reicher, 2016). Going back to our point regarding the difficultly of establishing shared values and behaviours in the context of serial change, this can cascade into the team not being clear on "who we are," "what we are about," and "where we want to go." The team lacks an identity. Therein lies an opportunity for growth and improvement.

The 5R^S Intervention

Following discussions with the coach it was clear that there was a need to develop the team's leadership and create a cohesive unit that was orientated by a clear collective identity. To achieve this vision, an intervention was proposed based on the 5R^S (Fransen et al., 2020) which incorporated five phases: Readying, Reflecting, Representing, Realising, and Reporting (see also Haslam et al., 2017; Slater & Barker, 2019). Given that the head coach was new to the club and that team building is often the focus of the pre-season, we planned a three-month programme to begin at the start of the pre-season (see Table 5.1 for an overview).

Following Slater and Barker (2019), the first objective of the intervention was to establish a Senior Leadership Team. An SLT is not a mainstay in elite soccer, but more recently there are anecdotal examples (e.g., England national team, Brentford, who at the time of writing plays in the English Championship, one league below the Premier League, and in hockey—the men's Australian hockey team) of teams establishing SLTs that include athletes. In our intervention, the SLT provided the cornerstone through which on- and off-field leadership and the creation of a shared sense of "us" flourished. The head coach liked the idea of the SLT but was also cautious about maintaining appropriate "distance" from athletes. As a result, we agreed that the SLT would comprise the head coach, the assistant coach, and the captain (as formal leaders) and that we would introduce four additional players onto the SLT. The four players would fit the four athlete leadership roles. On-field: the task leader (who focuses on technical and tactical guidance to optimise performance) and the motivational leader (who galvanises the team to perform to their best). Off-field: the social leader (who fosters team morale and a positive atmosphere) and the external leader (who represents the team in dealing with external groups, e.g., media).

In accordance with Fransen et al. (2015), we adopted a bottom-up approach that identified the players who were perceived by their teammates to be the most effective leaders in the four roles of athlete leadership. To achieve this end, we created a roster of all 25 players in the squad and had all athletes rate each other on a scale of 0 (*very poor leadership*) to 10 (*very good leadership*) for each of the four athlete leadership roles separately. As a result, we had data on how the 24 members of the squad perceived each other player's leadership in each of the four roles. With these data, we completed the social network analysis (SNA) to identify the best leaders in each of the four roles (i.e., the players who received on average the highest leadership scores). We then shared the results with the team and proposed to appoint the four most highly scoring athletes as leaders. The players were happy and motivated to take on the responsibility, and thus we had the final SLT structure in place ($n = 7$): the head coach, the assistant coach, the captain, and the four athlete leaders.

TABLE 5.1 A three-month 5R^s programme to develop on- and off-field leadership by creating a shared sense of "us"

Month	July	July 2	Aug	Aug 2	Sept	Sept 2
Session title	Athlete leadership mapping	Readying—Introduction	Reflecting—Walking a mile in your team's shoes	Representing—Championing the group	Realising—Achieving our ambitions	Reporting
Activities	Rate teammates on four athlete leadership roles	Overview SLT established	Identity mapping (understand who we are/values) What's your vision?	Review and agree on shared values Develop aligned behaviours Athlete leadership goals	Identify possible barriers and an action plan Agree vision Environmental changes	Launch event Monitoring and review progress
SLT athlete activities	N/A	N/A	Complete identity mapping and vision activity with team	Discuss shared values and behaviours with team	Discuss barriers/action plan and vision with team	Monitoring and review progress with team
Measures	Pre: Team identification ILI-SF x 2		Mid: Team identification ILI-SF x 2			Post: Team identification ILI-SF x 2

Note. SLT = Senior Leadership Team; ILI-SF = Identity Leadership Inventory-Short-form (Steffens et al., 2014).

Readying

In the first phase we introduced the programme and its aim to the team and announced the four athlete leaders by discussing the results of the SNA. This session was delivered to all the athletes and staff. It was outlined that the SLT would start to meet and that the members would complete a series of activities during each of the sessions, which, following each session, would be completed with the remaining squad by the athlete leaders. This is in line with the approach taken previously (Slater & Barker, 2019) and serves to assure all players feel empowered and part of the programme—where the athletes' voice drives "what we do" and "who we become."

Reflecting

The SLT met for the first time in the reflecting stage to complete two activities: *identity mapping* and *what's our vision?* In the *identity mapping* task, SLT members were asked to "Draw a map of your [team name] identity (player or staff). Consider the values and goals associated with your identity, and what it means to you to be part of this team." Members listed values such as being creative, unity, honour/integrity, resilience, and excellence. In the *what's our vision* task, SLT members considered the team's vision. After both activities, each SLT member talked through their ideas, beginning to build an understanding of shared values and the team's vision. The completed handouts were collected, and the session was closed by providing the four athlete leaders with the materials needed to complete the same tasks with the remaining squad. At this point, the captain said that they wished to be involved, and, thus, the five athletes on the SLT facilitated a group session with the remaining 20 players. Once completed, these handouts were added to the SLT information ahead of the representing (focusing on values) and realising (focusing on vision) phases.

Representing

Ahead of the Representing SLT session, the values that the SLT and the squad had identified were anonymously collated. The Representing SLT session involved three activities: *our shared values, our shared behaviours*, and *athlete leadership goals*. In the *our shared values* task, the SLT discussed the values identified and agreed on four values. The intent was that these four values represented the core (i.e., most important/unique) aspects of "who we are" while also connecting with each team member without the list becoming too long (3–5 core values are often optimal).

In the *our shared behaviours* task, the SLT members generated a series of behaviours under each value. Initially, a range of behaviours were listed, and through discussions, the three most important/closely aligned behaviours per value were agreed. These behaviours reflected observable actions in the context of each value. For example, providing encouragement to teammates was a behaviour connected to the value of unity. While it was the expectation that all staff and players role modelled (i.e., Represented) the shared values and behaviours, the athlete leaders were given the responsibility to champion these values/behaviours in action (e.g., around the club, in the changing rooms). In the *athlete leadership goals* task the athlete leaders facilitated discussions that generated goals for each athlete leadership role—task, motivational, social, and external.

Following the SLT session, the captain and athlete leaders facilitated a group session with the playing squad to discuss the shared values, behaviours, and goals. No amendments were made to the values or goals, while small changes were made to the behaviours and ideas that were fed into the next SLT session (e.g., the players leading a post-match debrief on the values/behaviours following the coaches debrief).

Realising

The Realising session started with the captain and players reflecting on the session that they had facilitated with the squad. The remainder of the session involved two activities: *barriers/solution action plan* and *our vision*. In the *barriers/solution action plan* task, the SLT discussed potential barriers that would interfere with the team "living out" their shared values before developing solutions to overcome the identified barriers in an action plan. Examples of ideas contained in the action plan included the performance analyst creating video/motivational montages showing the team embodying the shared values/behaviours. Another suggestion was to create infographics and send these to all staff and players and to make environmental improvements (e.g., in the changing rooms, in the corridors at the club) so that the values/behaviours and accompanying quotes/pictures are visible day-to-day. In the *our vision* task, the SLT were provided with all vision statements generated in the Reflecting phase and worked together to generate a single vision for the team. The SLT session closed with the athlete leader autonomously stating that they would facilitate another group player session to seek feedback on the barriers/solution action plan and vision. At this point, the head coach proposed the idea that as everything is beginning to take shape (e.g., values, behaviours, vision) we should have a launch event where all elements are brought together.

Reporting

Following the head coach's suggestion, all players and staff met for a launch event to share the progress made on our values, behaviours, and vision. This was led by the SLT and provided a holistic picture of how the activities undertaken in the 5R^S programme had helped to cultivate a shared sense of "us." The SLT also met to discuss progress on the 5R^S programme (e.g., "Are we demonstrating our core values and behaviours?"). The session closed with a discussion on how to continue. It was agreed that the SLT would continue to meet, as they had done over the previous three months.

Outcome Analysis

The primary areas for improvement related to a lack of leadership and players' lack of identification with the team. These two variables were assessed by validated social identity-related questionnaires. To assess the influence of the 5Rs on leadership, first, all 25 athletes completed the short-form of the ILI (ILI-SF: Steffens et al., 2014) in reference to the head coach. This scale includes four items (e.g., "This leader is a model member of the team), which generate a mean score for identity leadership. Second, 24 of the athletes (all but the captain) completed the scale in reference to the captain's leadership. To assess the influence of the 5R programme on team identification, all staff and players completed Doosje, Ellemers, and Spears' (1995) four-item measure of team identification (e.g., "I feel strong ties with members of the team").

We assessed these outcomes before the intervention (week 1), at the mid-point (week 6), and at the end of the intervention (week 12). At the start of the pre-season we found levels of team identification and perceived leadership to be moderate. We found gradual increases in the three variables from pre- to mid-intervention and then mid- to post-intervention. Improvements in performance were also observed. Further, informal discussions and observations of staff/player behaviour provided valuable signs of the influence of the $5R^S$ intervention. For example, coaches used more collective language, the head coach referred to values/behaviours/vision in his team-talks, and the players began to "go the extra mile" by, for example, staying on after training to support an injured athlete in rehabilitation.

Case-Study Reflections

In the preceding hypothetical case study we have drawn on our experiences of applying social identity interventions to develop leadership and team identification. There are a number of strengths that we can reflect on, including the theoretically driven, empirically based, and inclusive approach adopted in the $5R^S$ programme. Therefore, the $5R^S$ programme is more likely to (a) bring about meaningful change as team members are intrinsically invested in the process and empowered to contribute to a shared sense of "us," and (b) endure, that is, bring about significant and lasting benefit. In contrast, there are areas that could have occurred differently depending on the time available and the creation of the SLT.

First, the $5R^S$ programme takes time to deliver and it evolves (e.g., Representing builds on Reflecting), meaning that sufficient time to schedule SLT sessions and for SLT athletes to work with the squad is a challenge. This challenge can be intensified in the often short-term world of elite soccer where the results-focused narrative dominates. As an illustration, we presented a three-month $5R^S$ programme in the context where the average tenure of managers across the four top divisions in England and Wales is 1.16 years (League Managers Association, 2017). Being clear and transparent on the time and investment required prior to the intervention is crucial. Moreover, we completed the rating of team members' leadership in the context of the four roles early on in pre-season. Arguably, more time for leadership dynamics to unfold would be welcomed before doing this.

There are various ways in which the SLT can be created. The most fruitful way of going about this is likely to depend on the context. Some head coaches will want to be involved and may request that other members of staff will be too (e.g., an assistant coach). Other coaches may wish for the SLT to involve players only, particularly given staff members' already tight schedules. Aligned with the collective and inclusive social identity approach, our view is that coach involvement is important and should be encouraged where possible. In terms of the make-up of the SLT, here we followed Fransen et al. (2020) and asked the playing squad to select the best-quality leaders across the four roles. Another approach that has not been documented in the literature but has been reported anecdotally (e.g., by England in the build-up to and at the World Cup, 2018) is to use a rotation system. This involves changing the four SLT athletes on a regular basis so that the squad are part of the SLT at some stage and therefore have an opportunity to develop their leadership skills and to make meaningful contributions to the team.

Summary and Conclusions

In this chapter we have demonstrated the theoretical underpinnings and empirical evidence that point to leadership as an action that cultivates a shared sense of "us." Further than this, we outlined and presented evidence detailing the positive influence of the 3R, 5R, and 5R^S programmes wherein the overall vision is to foster team identity and leadership. Finally, we outline a hypothetical case study to show how a social identity programme can harness the power of on- and off-field leadership.

Key Messages and Further Reading

1. When athletes define themselves in terms of a given social identity (e.g., as a member of a soccer team), rather than acting with reference to "me," they act with reference to "us"—and look to behave in ways that align with, and promote, the team's perspective.
2. Leadership is inextricably bound up with group processes, and successful leadership involves developing, managing, and advancing a sense of shared identity within a given team.
3. There are multiple and profound individual-, group-, and organisational-level benefits of cultivating a shared sense of "us" in elite soccer.
4. The 3R and 5R^s programmes are inclusive, empowering, and evidence-based approaches to leadership development.
5. Cultivating a shared sense of "us" through the 5R^s—Readying, Reflecting, Representing, Realising, and Reporting—will optimise on- and off-field leadership.

We have highlighted the five most pertinent further reading resources below:

Haslam, S. A., Reicher, S. D., & Platow, M. J. (2011). *The new psychology of leadership: Identity, influence and power*. Hove: Psychology Press.
Haslam, S.A., Steffens, N. K., Peters, K., Boyce, R.A., Mallet, C., & Fransen, K. (2017). A social identity approach to leadership development: The 5R program. *Journal of Personnel Psychology, 16*, 113–124. doi:10.1027/1866-5888/a000176
Rees, T., Haslam, S. A., Coffee, P., & Lavallee, D. (2015). A social identity approach to sport psychology: Principles, practice, and prospects. *Sports Medicine, 45*(8), 1083–1096. doi:10.1007/s40279-015-0345-4
Slater, M. J., & Barker, J. B. (2019). Doing social identity leadership: Exploring the efficacy of an identity leadership intervention on perceived leadership and mobilization in elite

disability soccer. *Journal of Applied Sport Psychology, 31*, 65–86. doi:10.1080/10413200.2017.1410255

Steffens, N. K., Haslam, S. A., Reicher, S. D., Platow, M. J., Fransen, K., Yang, J. . . . Boen, F. (2014). Leadership as social identity management: Introducing the Identity Leadership Inventory (ILI) to assess and validate a four-dimensional model. *Leadership Quarterly, 25*, 1004–1025.

References

Bruner, M. W., Balish, S., Forrest, C., Brown, S., Webber, K., Gray, E. . . . Shields, C. A. (2017). Ties that bond: Youth sport as a vehicle for social identity and positive youth development. *Research Quarterly for Exercise and Sport, 88*, 209–214. Retrieved from http://dx.doi.org/10.1080/02701367.2017.1296100

Cruwys, T., Steffens, N. K., Haslam, S. A., Haslam, C., Jetten, J., & Dingle, G. (2016). Social Identity Mapping: A procedure for visual representation and assessment of subjective multiple group memberships. *British Journal of Social Psychology, 55*(4), 613–642. doi:10.1111/bjso.12155

De Cuyper, B., Boen, F., Van Beirendonck, C., Vanbeselaere, N., & Fransen, K. (2016). When do elite cyclists go the extra mile? Team identification mediates the relationship between perceived leadership qualities of the captain and social laboring. *International Journal of Sport Psychology, 47*(4), 355–372. doi:10.7352/IJSP2016.47

Doosje, B., Ellemers, N., & Spears, R. (1995). Perceived intragroup variability as a function of group status and identification. *Journal of Experimental Social Psychology, 31*, 410–436.

Fransen, K., Coffee, P., Vanbeselaere, N., Slater, M., De Cuyper, B., & Boen, F. (2014). The impact of athlete leaders on team members' team outcome confidence: A test of mediation by team identification and collective efficacy. *The Sport Psychologist, 28*(4), 347–360. doi:10.1123/tsp.2013-0141

Fransen, K., Decroos, S., Vande Broek, G., & Boen, F. (2016). Leading from the top or leading from within? A comparison between coaches' and athletes' leadership as predictors of team identification, team confidence, and team cohesion. *International Journal of Sports Science & Coaching, 11*(6), 757–771. doi:10.1177/1747954116676102

Fransen, K., Haslam, S. A., Steffens, N., Mallett, C., Peters, K., & Boen, F. (2020). *All for us and us for all: Introducing the 5R Shared Leadership Program*.

Fransen, K., Steffens, N. K., Haslam, S. A., Vanbeselaere, N., Vande Broek, G., & Boen, F. (2016). We will be champions: Leaders' confidence in 'us' inspires team members' team confidence and performance. *Scandinavian Journal of Medicine and Science in Sports, 26*(12), 1455–1469. doi:10.1111/sms.12603

Fransen, K., Van Puyenbroeck, S., Loughead, T. M., Vanbeselaere, N., De Cuyper, B., Vande Broek, G., & Boen, F. (2015). Who takes the lead? Social network analysis as pioneering tool to investigate shared leadership within sports teams. *Social Networks, 43*, 28–38. doi:10.1016/j.socnet.2015.04.003

Giessner, S. R., & van Knippenberg, D. (2008). License to fail: Goal definition, leader group prototypicality, and perceptions of leadership effectiveness after leader failure. *Organizational Behaviour and Human Decision Processes, 105*, 14–35.

Haslam, S. A. (2004). *Psychology in organizations: The social identity approach* (2nd ed.). Thousand Oaks, CA: Sage Publications.

Haslam, S. A., & Reicher, S. D. (2016). Leicester's lesson in leadership. *The Psychologist, 29*(6), 446–449.

Haslam, S. A., Steffens, N. K., Peters, K., Boyce, R. A., Mallet, C., & Fransen, K. (2017). A social identity approach to leadership development: The 5R program. *Journal of Personnel Psychology, 16, 113–124*. doi:10.1027/1866-5888/a000176

League Managers Association. (2017). End of season manager statistics: Research and report. Retrieved August 26, 2018, from www.leaguemanagers.com/documents/55/LMA_End_of_Season_Report_and_Statistics_2016-17.pdf

Martin, L. J., Balderson, D., Hawkins, M., Wilson, K., & Bruner, M. W. (2018). The influence of social identity on self-worth, commitment, and effort in school-based youth sport. *Journal of Sports Sciences, 36*(3), 326–332. http://dx.doi.org/10.1080/02640414.2017.1306091

Percy, J. (2016). Claudio Ranieri reveals the secrets behind Leicester City's Premier League success. Retrieved August 24, 2018, from www.telegraph.co.uk/sport/football/teams/leicester-city/12146839/Claudio-Ranieri-reveals-the-secrets-behind-Leicester-Citys-Premier-League-success.html

Rees, T., Haslam, S. A., Coffee, P., & Lavallee, D. (2015). A social identity approach to sport psychology: Principles, practice, and prospects. *Sports Medicine*, *45*(8), 1083–1096. doi:10.1007/s40279-015-0345-4

Slater, M. J., & Barker, J. B. (2019). Doing social identity leadership: Exploring the efficacy of an identity leadership intervention on perceived leadership and mobilization in elite disability soccer. *Journal of Applied Sport Psychology*, *31*, 65–86. doi:10.1080/10413200.2017.1410255

Slater, M. J., Barker, J. B., Coffee, P., & Jones, M. V. (2015). Leading for gold: Social identity leadership processes at the London 2012 Olympic Games. *Qualitative Research in Sport, Exercise and Health*, *7*(2), 192–209. doi:10.1080/2159676X.2014.936030

Slater, M. J., Coffee, P., Barker, J. B., & Evans, A. L. (2014). Promoting shared meanings in group memberships: A social identity approach to leadership in sport. *Reflective Practice: International and Multidisciplinary Perspectives*, *15*(5), 672–685.

Slater, M. J., Haslam, S. A., & Steffens, N. (2018). Singing it for us: Team passion during national anthems is associated with subsequent success. *European Journal of Sport Science*, *18*, 541–549. doi:10.1080/17461391.2018.1431311

Slater, M. J., Turner, M. J., Evans, A. L., & Jones, M. V. (2018). Capturing hearts and minds: The influence of leader relational identification on followers' mobilization and cardiovascular reactivity. *The Leadership Quarterly*, *29*, 379–388. doi:10.1016/j.leaqua.2017.08.003

Steffens, N. K., Haslam, S. A., & Reicher, S. D. (2014). Up close and personal: Evidence that shared social identity is a basis for the 'special' relationship that binds followers to leaders. *The Leadership Quarterly*, *25*, 296–313.

Steffens, N. K., Haslam, S. A., Reicher, S. D., Platow, M. J., Fransen, K., Yang, J. . . . Boen, F. (2014). Leadership as social identity management: Introducing the Identity Leadership Inventory (ILI) to assess and validate a four-dimensional model. *Leadership Quarterly*, *25*, 1004–1025.

Stevens, M., Rees, T., Coffee, P., Haslam, S. A., Steffens, N. K., & Polman, R. (2018). Leaders promote sport and exercise participation by fostering social identity. *Scandinavian Journal of Medicine and Science in Sports*. Advance online publication. doi:10.1111/sms.13217

Stevens, M., Rees, T., Coffee, P., Steffens, N. K., Haslam, S. A., & Polman, R. (2017). A social identity approach to understanding and promoting physical activity. *Sports Medicine*, *47*, 1911–1918.

Subašić, E., Reynolds, K. J., Turner, J. C., Veenstra, K. E., & Haslam, S. A. (2011). Leadership, power and the use of surveillance: Implications of shared social identity for leaders' capacity to influence. *Leadership Quarterly*, *22*, 170–181.

Tajfel, H., & Turner, J. C. (1979). An integrative theory of intergroup conflict. In S. Worchel & W. G. Austin (Eds.), *The psychology of intergroup relations* (pp. 33–47). Monterey, CA: Brooks-Cole.

Turner, J. C. (1991). *Social influence*. Milton Keynes: Open University Press.

Turner, J. C., Hogg, M. A., Oakes, P. J., Reicher, S., & Wetherell, M. S. (1987). *Rediscovering the social group: A self-categorisation theory*. Oxford: Basil Blackwell.

van Dick, R., Lemoine, J. E., Steffens, N. K., Kerschreiter, R., Akfirat, S. A., Avanzi, L. . . . Haslam, S. A. (2018). Identity leadership going global: Validation of the Identity Leadership Inventory (ILI) across 20 countries. *Journal of Occupational and Organizational Psychology*. doi:10.1111/joop.12223

Zhu, W., He, H., Trevino, L. K., Chao, M. M., & Wang, W. (2015). Ethical leadership and follower voice and performance: The role of follower identifications and entity morality beliefs. *The Leadership Quarterly*, *22*, 702–718. http://dx.doi.org/10.1016/j.leaqua.2015.01.004

6
THE PSYCHOLOGY OF SOCCER REFEREES

Tom Webb and Denise Hill

Introduction and Review of Literature

The current climate of soccer across Europe is one of intense pressure given the increased financial benefits attributed to success (Webb, 2017). The pursuit of immediate success has created a "short-termist" culture in professional soccer and is particularly evident in the most prominent European leagues (Premier League, England; La Liga, Spain; Serie A, Italy; Bundesliga, Germany; and Ligue 1, France). Such a short-term approach in the modern game has led to a significant turnover of players and coaches/managers at soccer clubs and placed significant pressure on players and coaches/managers (Larner, Wagstaff, Thelwell, & Corbett, 2017; Wagstaff, Gilmore, & Thelwell, 2015, 2016). The situation is exacerbated by the interest shown by the national and international media in professional soccer (Webb, 2016, 2018a, 2018b). Domestic leagues receive considerable media attention, as does the Champions League and Europa League in Europe, with almost every match either receiving live coverage or covered as part of a highlight programme. For example, the Champions League final is estimated to receive between 112 and 200 million viewers during live match broadcasts in countries across the world (Ashby, 2014).

It is within this setting that the modern referee must operate. Referees are not immune to the scrutiny placed on the game. In fact, referee decisions are debated at length, utilising a number of camera angles to discuss the accuracy of a decision. Referees are also assessed at each of the matches they officiate, often by more than one assessor; making them some of the most accountable individuals in soccer (Webb, 2017). Indeed, their decisions are subjected to continued scrutiny and focus, by players, spectators, managers, and the media during the game and then within the post-match interviews and press conference. Moreover, much of this scrutiny is negative and critical, rather than constructive (Cleland, O'Gorman, & Webb, 2018; Webb, Cleland, & O'Gorman, 2017; Webb, Dicks, Thelwell, van der Kamp, & Rix-Lievre, 2019). This focus on the referee can often be used as a means of deflecting from a poor performance or result. Alongside this sustained scrutiny, the elite referees are exposed to a number of stressors, which hold the potential to impact them and their performance. These stressors include the remote geographical management of the group of elite referees (meaning that isolation can be a concern for the individual referee on a day-to-day basis); the demands of training; travel requirements; performance evaluation; technological innovations; supporter, player, and coach behaviour; and their fundamental job security (Webb, Wagstaff, Rayner, & Thelwell, 2016).

This case study is an amalgamation of our experiences working with referees and match officials across a number of sports, specifically soccer. These experiences, observations, and outcomes are focused particularly upon the changing environment in which modern soccer referees operate and how, through the management of the stressors/demands placed upon them, referees can strive to improve performance under pressure, while attempting to maintain their wellbeing. The underpinning evidence is informed by our research and consultancy activities within a number of countries and sports. It is supported specifically by data collection involving interviews with 64 elite referees, ex-elite referees, referee managers, referee assessors, and referee coaches across England, Spain, Italy, France, and Portugal (operating at UEFA and FIFA level). Referee organisations exist in every soccer-playing country in Europe, and some organisations operate across countries, working with referees from different countries. Both of these organisations predominantly manage, train, and develop the elite referees who operate in the top professional league in a given country and in continent-wide-based competitions. Therefore, we present a hypothetical case-study approach that could be accepted and adopted in any country in world football, which is based on extensive research-informed practice that has been implemented previously.

Practical Applications—Case Study

We were contacted to work with the soccer referees of a European-based organisation, to achieve two key aims. The first was to examine in detail and address (where possible) the poor retention rate of their elite-level referees. Thus, an increasing number of the elite referees were leaving the sport, citing low levels of job satisfaction (including concerns regarding personal safety), lowered wellbeing, and poor mental health as the cause.

The second aim of the work was to support the referees to cope effectively with the demands of their role, so they were better placed to maintain their wellbeing/mental health throughout the season and perform more effectively under pressure during matches. Specifically, the organisation had noted that the elite referee group were performing less consistently under pressure towards the end of the season—with some (not all) failing to make the "big calls" (i.e., choking under the pressure), despite the opportunity to use video assistant referees (VAR).

In terms of the initial approach adopted, we established a detailed understanding of the factors affecting the elite referees within the organisation via an online quantitative survey (completed by the referees) and follow-up interviews (with the referees and key members of the organisation). The survey was designed to identify (i) the main demands/stressors experienced by the referees (on and off the pitch) during the season; (ii) their adopted coping strategies to those demands; (iii) the perceived effectiveness of their coping strategies; (iv) their key sources of support; (v) their level of wellbeing and mental health indicators; and, finally, (vi) their level of mental health literacy (MHL).

The 1:1 interviews were completed with a number of the elite referees ($n = 12$) from various stages of the career, in order to gauge differing perspectives (i.e., those new into the elite officiating, through to those who were close to retirement). The interviews focused specifically on exploring the impact that the range of stressors had on their pressurised performance and wellbeing/mental health, alongside further consideration of their effective and ineffective coping mechanisms. Furthermore, key stakeholders (8) within the organisation (leadership/assessors/selectors) were also interviewed (individually) to discuss their perspective on the demands placed on elite referees and the role they, and more broadly, their organisation, played in the development and support of the refereeing group.

The organisation also provided data regarding the reasons their elite referees had left the role in the previous five years (i.e., low levels of job satisfaction, lowered wellbeing, and poor mental health—due to player/crowd abuse, sustained scrutiny, job insecurity, and a lack of work–life balance). Moreover, we completed a critical review of the extant literature pertaining to effective management of pressure and determinants of wellbeing among officials/referees across sport and countries. Together, these data, information, and evidence base afforded enough information to devise a proposed intervention.

Of note, throughout the intervention we become increasingly mindful of the recent and emerging technological advancements enabling the introduction of goal-line technology and the implementation of VAR (Webb, 2016, 2018a). While these innovations have broadly been welcomed within soccer, and by referees, it has meant additional training for referees, changes to performance, and adaptations to routines, all of which has led to additional demands placed on referees relating to the environment in which they operate. For example, the use of goal-line technology is not standardised; different providers are utilised for different competitions; and some competitions (until recently) did not use goal-line technology at all, preferring to introduce additional goal-line assistant referees. These issues produce challenging circumstances for referees themselves and referee managers, which is difficult to prepare for, and requires dynamic leadership and training mechanisms to best support the referees.

We were also required to reflect on the pertinent emergent theme, of abuse to which referees are being exposed. This evidently impacted the performance and wellbeing of the referees and presents issues for those in managerial and training positions. Predominantly, this abuse is perpetrated by players, coaches, and supporters, and the abuse at the elite level tends to be verbal in nature, rather than physical—with aggression, threats, and abuse from players and crowd, the most recognised and examined stressor/demand (Friman, Nyberg, & Norlander, 2004; Webb & Thelwell, 2015; Webb, Rayner, & Thelwell, 2018).

Therefore, the available empirical evidence, alongside primary data from the case study clearly identified that the "demands" of the role were impacting directly on the health and performance of the referees. Accordingly, an integrated training and intervention was designed to increase recruitment and retention of match officials, through supporting the mental health and pressurised performance of the officials (Belkacem & Salih, 2018; Kellett & Warner, 2011; Warner, Tingle, & Kellett, 2013).

The Intervention/Work Conducted

The intervention was multi-modal and addressed personal resilience, alongside enhancing organisational resilience, while also encouraging broader cultural changes. Therefore, while the initial premise was to work directly with the individual referees (i.e., micro-level), it became evident that in order to achieve our aim, it was also necessary to explore and address organisational (i.e., meso-level) and the broader contextually driven factors (i.e., macro-level), which detrimentally affected the referees' performance and wellbeing. In short, in order to focus on the individual, it became apparent that the meso and macro external factors required attention, as they had the potential to impact positively and negatively on the performance and wellbeing of the elite referee.

In terms of the micro-level, we first provided group and individual psychological skills training to the elite referees, which aimed to enhance their capacity to cope (more) effectively with the stressors/demands they faced on and off the pitch. This work was designed to improve their performance (i.e., decision-making) under pressure throughout the season, including the times when called upon to make the highly critical/pressurised "big call."

Thus, we encouraged the referees to appraise positively the demands/stressors they encountered on and off the pitch, by introducing them to a number of problem- and emotion-focused coping strategies that have been demonstrated to be effective among soccer referees (e.g., Mathers & Brodie, 2011; Neil, Bayston, Hanton, & Wilson, 2013). This included imagery, positive self-statements, relaxation, a pre-match routine, simulated practice, and cognitive restructuring (of the stressor and emotions). We also utilised research from other sports (e.g., rugby union) to help the elite referees appreciate that certain proactive, problem, and emotion-focused coping strategies can be used to manage effectively specific stressors and encourage positive appraisal (see Table 6.1).

Thereafter, and building on the development of coping strategies, the individual referees and key individuals within the organisation were introduced to resilience training. *Robust* psychological resilience is the ability of individuals to withstand pressure, so they are able to maintain functioning, wellbeing, and performance when under pressure (Bonanno, 2004; Carver, 1998; Fletcher & Sarkar, 2013); while *rebound* resilience enables the individual to return to normal functioning after minor/temporary disruptions to their wellbeing and performance when under pressure. Accordingly, by delivering psychological resilience training, we aimed to enhance the referees' robust and reactive resilience. This was achieved through the application of the mental fortitude training programme for sustained success (Fletcher & Sarkar, 2016; see Figure 6.1), whereby the referees were supported to develop the necessary personal qualities of resilience. That is, (i) gaining an awareness of oneself/others, and the environment (i.e., self-awareness and social awareness); (ii) directing thoughts and mental images (through the use of self-talk, imagery, mental rehearsal, and visualisation); (iii) directing attention appropriately (i.e., through attentional control); (iv) learning to regulate arousal levels (through relaxation, activation, and arousal control); (v) setting effective goals (i.e., goal-setting); and, finally, (vi) planning for expected and unexpected events.

Thereafter, to ensure that the referees' resilience was developed fully, and they established an "optimal" challenge mindset, it was necessary to consider the manner in which they could be exposed to (and work within) a facilitative environment. This

TABLE 6.1 Characteristics of performance under pressure

Stressor/Demand	Effective Coping Response	Details
Unfamiliarity	Proactive-coping Informational social support	Prepare for unexpected/best-case/worse-case scenarios before the game, through imagery and accessing expert advice from significant others
Performance Errors	Acceptance Ownership Reflective practice	Own (rather than deny) the error and use reflective practice (with a significant other) to constructively consider and address the reasons for the mistake. Use (mindfulness) acceptance during/after the game (re: the error).
Interpersonal Conflict	Proactive coping Emotion-focused coping	Manage abuse/threatening behaviour through preparation (imagine worst-case scenario and rehearse effective personal response) and individualised emotion-focused coping strategy (e.g., relaxation, centring, distancing). Note specifically the importance of emotional contagion (the player/crowd responding to (i.e., "catching") the referee's emotions) in a hostile context.
Important Game/moment	Proactive-coping Emotion-focused Task/process-focused	Manage important games by preparing best/worse case in advance (see aforementioned) and use individually tailored behavioural coping strategies to modify emotional state (see aforementioned). Utilise process goals to remain focused on task-relevant performance information under high levels of pressure
Scrutiny	Task/process-focused	Adopt process goals to remain focused on task, when under high levels of pressure

Source: (Adapted from Hill, Matthews, & Senior, 2016)

included, specifically, a challenging but supportive culture within the organisation and (ideally) across the broader refereeing/soccer community.

To engender an organisational culture that supports the wellbeing and mental health of the referees, we delivered an educational programme devised to increase the mental health literacy (MHL) of the referees and the key stakeholders within the organisation. MHL training aims to improve the recipients' understanding of mental health, increase their awareness of poor wellbeing/mental health (in oneself and others), and enhance confidence in supporting others with mental health concerns. It

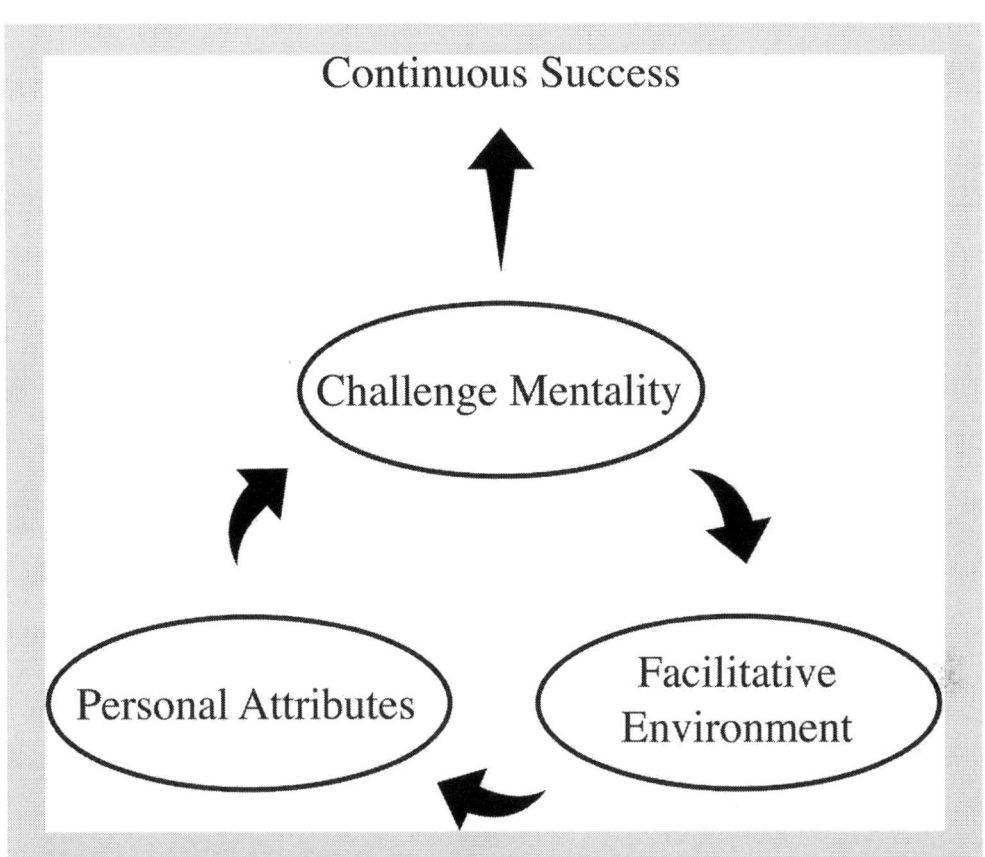

FIGURE 6.1 Mental fortitude training programme for sustained success
Source: (Adapted from Fletcher & Sarkar, 2016).

can also promote help-seeking behaviours for those experiencing poor mental health and reduce stigma associated with mental ill-health (e.g., Morgan, Ross, & Reavely, 2018). Accordingly, it was assumed that this approach could elicit an organisational climate that would improve the wellbeing and mental health of the referees and the organisation's leadership group (see Gorczynski et al., 2019; Jorm, 2012).

Then, in terms of the organisational culture that the referees operate within, we discussed with the key stakeholders of the leadership group how to create a facilitative environment for the referees, while limiting the factors relating to an unrelenting, stagnant, and comfortable environment (see Table 6.2). Together, it was intended that the development of personal qualities, within this facilitative environment, would support the referees to develop robust and reactive resilience, performance success, and wellbeing.

When considering the broader culture of professional soccer that affected the referees (performance and wellbeing), the particular issues presented were mainly relating to player behaviour altering between competitions, with referees amending their preparation and performance due to the perceived pressures of changing player behaviour dependent on the competition in which they were officiating (Webb &

TABLE 6.2 Environment characteristics affecting resilience

Stagnant Environment	Unrelenting Environment	Comfortable Environment	Facilitative Environment
Unseen leaders and managers	Unhealthy competition	Over-caring, parent like culture	Supportive challenge towards a goal
People are not stimulated	Leader exposes / ridicules under performers	People are "nice"	People thrive in a challenging but supportive environment
People are just going through the motions	Blame culture if high standards not met	Too cosy	Individuals have input into and take ownership of goals
Culture of mediocrity	Avoidance mentality	People working in their comfort zones	Individuals seek out challenges to develop
Little going on	Little care for well-being	People are bored	Individuals crave constructive feedback
Good performance by accident more than by design	People feel isolated	Ambiguity and uncertainty	Good relationships between performers and leaders / coaches
people don't know what to do or don't care	Potential conflict	Stifling for individuals wanting to be stretched	Psychologically safe environment that encourages sensible risk-taking
	Performance is not sustainable	Difficult conversations avoided	healthy competition
	Stress / potential burnout	Lack of personal / professional development	Everyone supporting one another
	"Sink or swim"	Lack of celebration of achievement	Learn from mistakes / failures
		Underperformance not addresses	Success recognised and celebrated
		"A happy performer will be a great performer"	"We're in this together"

Source: (Adapted from Fletcher & Sarkar, 2016).

Thelwell, 2015). Referee and player behaviour can be considered and classified by country and culture, particularly regarding attitudes that are principally organised around specific cultural dimensions such as the measurement of work goals, values, needs, and attitudes (Ronen & Shenkar, 1985), all of which can be applied to referees and their training, development, and performance. As such, we focused on these dimensions, recognising that differences in the management of stressors, performance under pressure, players, and the demands of their job are dependent on the country or region from which the referee originates.

The countries tend to be grouped in certain clusters, such as "Latin Europe"—which can demonstrate explicit characteristics such as high variance in masculinity, high uncertainty-avoidance, and a high-power distance, among the wider population and players and referees on the field of play. In contrast, countries grouped in the "Anglo" cluster, including the United States, Canada, New Zealand, the United Kingdom, Ireland, and South Africa, exhibit low to medium scores on the power distance index (a measure of the interpersonal power or influence between those in power/control and a subordinate perceived as the less powerful of the two in a given situation; Hofstede, 1980), a low to medium score on the uncertainty-avoidance index, and high scores on the individualism and masculinity indices. These dimensions and characteristics were taken into account in the design and delivery of content to the referees; given the differences in the cultural dimensions between referees from different countries and leagues, we needed to understand how this might manifest itself in training and decision-making differences (Webb & Thelwell, 2015).

We also took into account how aspects such as national culture ingrained through collective cultural norms, and cultural differences between nations, can impact upon referee performance—with referee decision-making conditioned in part by national cultural factors and influenced by life experiences, the family, and later educational experiences in schools and organisations which differ across national boundaries (Hofstede, 1980, 1983).

Overall, the cultural influence outlined previously can be considered in two significant ways.

1. The country in which referees operate;
2. The competition in which referees operate.

In terms of the intervention, this meant we were required to understand the potential impact and effect both aspects could have on training and performance, both in terms of the individual referee (micro-level) and the culture of the wider organisation (meso-level).

Therefore, we delivered training both individually to referees and to the referees as a group, to enable them to deal effectively with players from around the world with different cultures, both societally and in terms of the style and type of soccer played in specific countries. To elaborate, we know that players behave variably, depending on the competition in which they are competing (Webb, 2017; Webb & Thelwell, 2015), and we also know that referees alter their behaviour and performance accordingly (Webb & Thelwell, 2015). Hence, we incorporated cultural knowledge into training packages, and an understanding of attitudinal dimensions through cultural classification, in order to potentially impact positively on referee behaviour on the field of play (Ronen & Shenkar, 1985). We supported the referees to understand how behaviour might vary dependent on the cultural classification of players and what type of behavioural traits might be displayed or expected.

As a result, our work with the referees revealed differences in culture and the acceptance of cultural difference by national refereeing organisations. Indeed, and critically, because of the behavioural/attitudinal differences we uncovered that affected referee performance, standardisation, and uniformity of officiating would improve if cultural training was included in the referee training packages offered for European Championships.

Outcome Analysis

Our principal aims for this intervention were to examine and address the poor retention rate of elite-level referees in a European refereeing organisation. Issues concerning an increasing number of the elite referees leaving the sport, with low levels of job satisfaction, lowered wellbeing, and poor mental health, were noted as the causes of discontinuation. Therefore, the second aim was to support the referees to cope effectively with the demands of their role, so that they were better placed to maintain their wellbeing/mental health throughout the season and perform more effectively under pressure during matches.

In terms of the micro-level work, it was evident that the individually tailored psychological skills intervention and resilience training enhanced the referees' performances under pressure and robust/reactive resilience. This was noted through self-report questionnaires completed at five points through the season, which included (i) the Test of Performance Strategies 2 (Hardy, Roberts, Thomas, & Murphy, 2010), which identified the increased use of psychological skills by the referees during pressurised performance, and (ii) the Connor-Davidson Resilience Scale (CD-RISC, Gonzalez, Moore, Newton, & Galli, 2016), which demonstrated the improved levels of personal resilience. Moreover, qualitative data gathered from interviews with a sample of the referees also indicated that those who had engaged with the psychological training "felt" more confident and focused during their matches and reported that, in particular, they experienced higher levels of perceived control (over self and their performance). The latter point is of importance, as perceived control is recognised as being a critical component of optimal performance under pressure (see Otten, 2009; Hill, Hanton, Matthews, & Fleming, 2010). Such findings were also supported by objective performance data, whereby those referees who had engaged fully with the intervention did receive higher scores for their performance (from assessors) for their games, where decision-making became more consistent, and the "big calls" were more accurate.

However, it is important to note that not all referees engaged with the psychological skills/resilience training, as there were a number of individuals who were reticent towards sport psychology. It remains the case, therefore, that in certain sporting domains, there is either a misunderstanding or even a mistrust of sport psychology that needs to be addressed before psychological interventions are delivered. Nevertheless, with the improved performance of those referees who did take part in the intervention, it can be anticipated that engagement with future psychological training programmes will improve.

Through our observations, and interviews with the referees, it also became apparent that the leadership group within the organisation had implemented strategies/processes to engender a facilitative environment for the referees to work within. In turn, this may have played a role in the referees' enhanced personal resilience. Specifically, the referees and leadership group created in partnership a "team" culture (i.e., team ethos, supportive ethos, and team goals), while the referees also developed/took ownership of individual goals. Finally, attempts were also made to identify, focus on, and celebrate success far more (Fletcher & Sarkar, 2016). However, this work was tempered by the organisations' continued desire to offer "short-term" contracts to the referees, whereby poor performance or absence from the game (from injury/illness) led to removal from the elite refereeing group. Such job insecurity encouraged an unhealthy competitive context, which is associated with an unrelenting environment. Furthermore, the continued intense level of scrutiny (from assessors and media) and the sustained hostility (from players, managers, crowd, and the media) experienced by the referees did reinforce an "avoidance-mentality," associated with the need to avoid mistakes. Accordingly, the broader, macro-level environment in which the referees operated within remained unrelenting. As such, it is the case that while the referees' resilience (for the most part) was enhanced, further improvement is likely to be limited by their unrelenting working environment.

In regard to mental health, it was found that the mental health literacy training (i.e., Mental Health First Aid) received by the referees and key stakeholders within the organisation impacted positively their awareness of mental ill-health and enhanced their confidence to signpost others with poor mental health to relevant supporting/professional agencies (as ascertained through the Mental Health Literacy Scale; O'Connor & Casey, 2015). However, it was also identified (through the General Help-Seeking Questionnaire; Wilson, Deane, Ciarrochi, & Rickwood, 2005) that the referees remained reluctant to engage with help-seeking behaviours, if they (hypothetically) suffered from poor mental health. As indicated through the interviews, this appears to relate to the stigma associated with mental health and the referees being concerned that they will be judged as "weak" and unable to carry out their refereeing duties, if that admitted to suffering from poor mental health. With help-seeking behaviours, critical to the prevention of poor wellbeing/the development of mental ill-health, this was a concerning finding and may have influenced the level of wellbeing remaining relatively low across the refereeing group through the season (as measured by the Warwick–Edinburgh mental wellbeing scale, Tennant et al., 2007).

While it is too early to recognise whether this work will influence retention, the indications are that if further improvements to the referees' personal resilience and the facilitative environment of the organisation can be achieved, then the factors affecting retention (job satisfaction, wellbeing/mental health) can be influenced positively. However, the main challenge remains within the wider context of the soccer community (i.e., players, media, fans, and audiences), whereby a multi-organisational approach is needed to address the critical scrutiny and hostile attitudes of "significant others" towards referees. As part of this process, there is a need to examine why the current programmes of work designed to protect the referee from such hostility has been ineffectual (e.g., the Respect Programme, England).

Case-Study Reflections

The interventions and work conducted as part of the case study have resulted in mixed conclusions. For the organisations that are involved in the governance of elite referees, the findings and outcomes on a micro (individual) level were generally beneficial. The organisations also have a greater understanding of their requirement to develop a supportive and facilitative environment, in order to enable referees to train, develop, and operate as effectively (and resiliently) as possible. However, there are factors which are beyond the control of the organisation but which can impact negatively upon the individual referee. There are aspects operating at the meso- and macro-level. For example, it is impossible for referee organisations to control the media or changes to the way the game is played or governed, although they have to react to these changes. That is the most challenging aspect of this case study. How can organisations ensure that referees perform as effectively as possible, given the meso- and macro-related factors which are involved?

Our work centred around the modification of variables which can be controlled and preparing the referee to manage the demand placed on them by their role and the referee organisations. Improvements were made in the development of psychological specific skills by individual referees. These skills assisted the referees in coping effectively with the stressors which are involved in their day-to-day activities both on and off the pitch, resulting in improved performance during the season. The next challenge is for this improvement to be continuous and extended over a prolonged period, despite the aforementioned extraneous and uncontrollable meso/macro factors impacting upon individual referees. Nevertheless, as the delivery of the psychological resilience training improved referees' reactive resilience, it is anticipated they will be better prepared for the unexpected stressors and unrelenting environment in which they work

All of these pressures resulted in a requirement for referees to understand and embrace MHL. This was also true of the refereeing organisation, because in order for MHL to be effective, it must be widely supported and integrated through the provision of training and educational provision (something which we introduced in our case study). While the work around MHL improved referee awareness of mental health issues, as well as of the relevant stakeholders within the organisation, the positive impact will be short-lived, without the organisation addressing the stigma that evidently existed with regard to mental ill-health.

The cultural training was integrated in order to improve referee understanding of the impact that culture can have on their training and performance, as well as the behaviour of players, and was an important aspect of our intervention. The referee organisation was required to understand how culture can influence behaviour and performance, as well as decision-making in referees, leading to an acceptance of these cultural norms and differences and an integration of these concepts into the training and support provided for the referees. This training and educational content improved referee training and performance, as cultural norms and the impact of the particular domestic league in which the referees officiated were taken into account and accepted. This novel approach improved standards, and referees began to understand the influence of culture on their actions and behaviour on the pitch when dealing with players and teams from various countries. The comprehension that players will expect certain behaviour and decision-making of referees, based on historic and socially developed cultural norms formed and held over time (also dependent on the competition in which they are playing), was an aspect of the intervention which took time to develop. The longer-term impact of this work will be evident in the evolution of training material provided to referees, and it is anticipated that the development of cultural understanding by both the individual referees and the referee organisation itself, combined with the underpinning training, will further improve performance.

Summary and Conclusions

Our experiences during this case study have led to a greater understanding of the influence of external factors, which are beyond the control of individual referees, key stakeholders, and national referee associations. These factors include the role and coverage of the media, the organisation of the national leagues and European and international competition, supporter/coach/player abuse towards the referee, and the influence of cultural differences both at individual behavioural level and within competitions. External factors have a significant bearing on the wellbeing and performance of the referees, and yet these factors are difficult to influence. Nevertheless, there are internal factors within refereeing organisations which can be positively affected, such as organisational culture, career development, assessment pressures, and the performance of individual referees

The issue of pressure elevates the importance of a facilitative environment (created by support networks, mentors, referee coaches, other referees, and management), which is linked to improved performance and wellbeing. An unrelenting environment, with ineffective management of the stressors experienced by referees, means it is difficult to perform effectively, maintain wellbeing, and sustain job satisfaction. The introduction of goal-line technology, VARs, rule interpretations/changing player behaviour in different competitions and as a reaction to the introduction of different innovations, all have an effect on the individual referee. In light of these matters, the management and leadership of elite referees has never been so important. If managed effectively, the associated impact on individual referee performance can see sustained improvement.

Key Messages and Further Reading

We recommend that in order to develop this work further, organisations from different countries are involved and undertake similar processes to those outlined in this case study. This will enable a greater understanding of the different national and international challenges which referee organisations face, as well as provide increased understanding of some of the cultural aspects outlined in this chapter. As the countries involved in this delivery grow, so the understanding of the cultural implications in each of the countries develops.

The wellbeing and mental health of referees in soccer has never been such an essential area of investigation. We need to work with referees and referee organisations further, to support referees to develop the capabilities and tools needed to manage the demands placed on them—while maintaining wellbeing and mental health. However, to progress, there may be a need to understand and challenge the stigma associated with mental ill-health within this context,

We also have to ensure that referee organisations provide infrastructures, procedures, and frameworks within which individual referees operate, which promote facilitative and supportive environments—while avoiding factors that contribute to an unrelenting environment. This, in turn, will provide referees with the setting to train and perform to an improved level, through the development of robust and reactive resilience.

Referees, for their part must be assisted in developing resilience, given the modern game in which they operate, and our intervention has sought to provide this. Our intervention has provided the tools to improve performance, but, as we have outlined, the current operational environment for referees is one with numerous external pressures and uncontrollable factors. We have sought to mitigate and control these factors, although what has become clear during the course of this case study is that the macro factors are beyond the control of individual referees and even key stakeholders involved in the management of referees at national and international levels in some cases.

Five Most Pertinent References

> Belkacem, C., & Salih, K. (2018). The relationship between the sources of psychological stress and the level of self-esteem among football referees. *European Journal of Physical Education and Sport Science*, *3*(12), 575–593. doi:10.5281/zenodo.1145469
>
> Fletcher, D., & Sarkar, M. (2016). Mental fortitude training: An evidence-based approach to developing psychological resilience for sustained success. *Journal of Sport Psychology in Action*, *7*(3), 135–157. doi:10.1080/21520704.2016.1255496
>
> Hill, D. M., Matthews, N., & Senior, R. (2016). The psychological characteristics of performance under pressure in professional rugby union referees. *The Sport Psychologist*, *30*(4), 376–387.
>
> Webb, T. (2017). *Elite soccer referees: Officiating in the Premier League, La Liga and Serie A*. London: Routledge.
>
> Webb, T., Wagstaff, C., Rayner, M., & Thelwell, R. (2016). Leading elite association football referees: Challenges in the cross-cultural organization of a geographically dispersed group. *Managing Sport and Leisure*, *21*(3), 105–123. doi:10.1080/23750472.2016.1209978

References

Ashby, K. (2014). Worldwide reach of the Lisbon final. *UEFA website*. Retrieved March 5, 2019, from https://fr.uefa.com/uefachampionsleague/news/newsid=2111684.html

Bonanno, G. A. (2004). Loss, trauma, and human resilience: Have we underestimated the human capacity to thrive after extremely aversive events? *American Psychologist, 59*, 20–28. doi:10.1037/0003-066X.59.1.20

Carver, C. S. (1998). Resilience and thriving: Issues, models, and linkages. *Journal of Social Issues, 54*(2), 245–266. doi:10.1111/j.1540-4560.1998.tb01217.x

Cleland, J., O'Gorman, J., & Webb, T. (2018). Respect? An investigation into the experience of referees in association football. *International Review for the Sociology of Sport, 53*(8), 960–974. doi:10.1177/1012690216687979

Fletcher, D., & Sarkar, M. (2013). Psychological resilience: A review and critique of definitions, concepts and theory. *European Psychologist, 18*(1), 12–23. doi:10.1027/1016-9040/a000124

Friman, M., Nyberg, C., & Norlander, T. (2004). Threats and aggression directed at soccer referees: An empirical phenomenological psychological study. *The Qualitative Report, 9*(4), 652–672.

Gonzalez, S. P., Moore, E. W. G., Newton, M., & Galli, N. A. (2016). Validity and reliability of the Connor-Davidson Resilience Scale (CD-RISC) in competitive sport. *Psychology of Sport and Exercise, 23*, 31–39. doi:10.1016/j.psychsport.2015.10.005

Gorczynski, P., Gibson, K., Thelwell, R., Papathomas, A., Harwood, C., & Kinnafick, F. (2019). The BASES expert statement on mental health literacy in elite sport. *The Sport and Exercise Scientist, 59*, 6–7.

Hardy, L., Roberts, R., Thomas, P. R., & Murphy, S. M. (2010). Test of performance strategies (TOPS): Instrument refinement using confirmatory factor analysis. *Psychology of Sport and Exercise, 11*(1) 27–35. doi:10.1016/j.psychsport.2009.04.007

Hill, D. M., Hanton, S., Matthews, N., & Fleming, S. (2010). Choking in sport: A review. *International Review of Sport and Exercise Psychology, 3*(1), 24–39. doi:10.1080/17509840903301199

Hofstede, G. (1980). *Culture's consequences: International differences in work related values*. London: Sage Publications.

Hofstede, G. (1983). The cultural relativity of organizational practices and theories. *Journal of International Business Studies, 14*(2), 75–89.

Jorm, A. F. (2012). Mental health literacy: Empowering the community to take action for better mental health. *American Psychologist, 67*(3), 231–243. doi:10.1037/a0025957

Kellett, P., & Warner, S. (2011). Creating communities that lead to retention: The social worlds and communities of umpires. *European Sport Management Quarterly, 11*(5), 471–494. doi:10.1080/16184742.2011.624109

Larner, R. J., Wagstaff, C. R. D., Thelwell, R. C., & Corbett, J. (2017). A multistudy examination of organizational stressors, emotional labor, burnout, and turnover in sport organizations. *Scandinavian Journal of Medicine & Science in Sports, 27*(12), 2103–2115. doi:10.1111/sms.12833

Mathers, J. F., & Brodie, K. (2011). Elite refereeing in professional soccer: A case study of mental skills support. *Journal of Sport Psychology in Action, 2*(3), 171–182. doi:10.1080/21520704.2011.609018

Morgan, A. J., Ross, A., & Reavley, N. J. (2018). Systematic review and meta-analysis of mental health first aid training: Effects on knowledge, stigma, and helping behaviour. *PLoS ONE, 1*(35), e0197102. doi:10.1371/journal.pone.0197102

Neil, R., Bayston, P., Hanton, S., & Wilson, K. (2013). The influence of stress and emotions on association football referees' decision-making. *Sport & Exercise Psychology Review, 9*(2), 22–41.

O'Connor, M., & Casey, L. (2015). The Mental Health Literacy Scale (MHLS): A new scale-based measure of mental health literacy. *Psychiatry Research, 229*(1–2), 511–516. doi:10.1016/j.psychres.2015.05.064

Otten, M. (2009). Choking vs. clutch performance: A study of sport performance under pressure. *Journal of Sport & Exercise Psychology, 31*(5), 583–601. doi:10.1123/jsep.31.5.583

Ronen, S., & Shenkar, O. (1985). Clustering countries on attitudinal dimensions: A review and synthesis. *Academy of Management Review, 10*(3), 435–454.

Tennant, R., Hiller, L., Fishwick, R., Platt, S., Joseph, S., Weich, S. . . . Stewart-Brown, S. (2007). The Warwick-Edinburgh mental well-being scale (WEMWBS): Development and UK validation. *Health and Quality of Life Outcomes, 5*(1), 63.

Wagstaff, C. R. D., Gilmore, S., & Thelwell, R. C. (2015). Sport medicine and sport science practitioners' experiences of organizational change. *Scandinavian Journal of Medicine & Science in Sports, 25*(5), 685–698. doi:10.1111/sms.12340

Wagstaff, C. R. D., Gilmore, S., & Thelwell, R. C. (2016). When the show must go on: Investigating repeated organizational change in elite sport. *Journal of Change Management, 16*(1), 38–54. doi:10.1080/14697017.2015.1062793

Warner, S., Tingle, J. K., & Kellett, P. (2013). Officiating attrition: The experience of former referees via a sport development lens. *Journal of Sport Management, 27*(4), 316–328. doi:10.1123/jsm.27.4.316

Webb, T. (2016). "Knight of the Whistle": W. P. Harper and the impact of the media on an Association Football referee. *The International Journal of the History of Sport, 33*(3), 306–324. doi:10.1080/09523367.2016.1151004

Webb, T. (2017). *Elite soccer referees*. London: Routledge.

Webb, T. (2018a). Managing match officials: The influence of business and the impact of finance in the Premier League era. In S. Chadwick, D. Parnell, P. Widdop & C. Anagnostopoulos (Eds.), *Routledge Handbook of Football Business and Management* (Chapter 29). London: Routledge.

Webb, T. (2018b). Referees and the media: A difficult relationship but an unavoidable necessity. *Soccer & Society, 19*(2), 205–221. doi:10.1080/14660970.2015.1133414.

Webb, T., Cleland, J., & O'Gorman, J. (2017). The distribution of power through a media campaign: The respect programme, referees and violence in association football. *Journal of Global Sport Management, 2*(3), 162–181. doi:10.1080/24704067.2017.1350591

Webb, T., Dicks, M., Thelwell, R., van der Kamp, J., & Rix-Lievre, G. (2019). An analysis of soccer referee experiences in France and the Netherlands: Abuse, conflict, and level of support. *Sport Management Review*. Retrieved from https://doi.org/10.1016/j.smr.2019.03.003

Webb, T., Rayner, M., & Thelwell, R. (2018). An explorative case study of referee abuse in English rugby league. *Journal of Applied Sport Management, 10*(2). doi:10.18666/JASM-2017-V10-12-8834

Webb, T., & Thelwell, R. (2015). He's taken a dive: Cultural comparisons of elite referee responses to reduced player behaviour in association football. *Sport, Business and Management: An International Journal, 5*(3), 242–258. http://dx.doi.org/10.1108/SBM-04-2014-0019

Wilson, C. J., Deane, F. P., Ciarrochi, J., & Rickwood, D. (2005). Measuring help-seeking intentions: Properties of General Help-Seeking Questionnaire. *Canadian Journal of Counselling, 39*(1), 15–28.

PART II
Working Through Others

7
DEVELOPING PSYCHOLOGICAL SKILLS

Emphasising Life Skills for Positive Youth Development

Ceri Bowley and Hamish Cox

Introduction and Review of Literature

Current Leicester City (and former Swansea City, Liverpool, and Celtic) manager, Brendan Rogers, has a coaching philosophy that stretches further than improving soccer skills: "I started coaching for one reason. To make a difference for people, not just as footballers, but as human beings." Sport offers an opportunity for young people to experience the elations of success and the disappointments of failure. Irrespective of the outcome, both experiences present potential teaching moments for sports coaches and learning opportunities for participants. Subsequently, sport has been regarded as an ideal vehicle for *positive youth development* (PYD) and an environment in which young people can learn the life skills and psychological attributes required for success in both sport and life (Bowley, Cropley, Neil, Hanton, & Mitchell, 2018; Gould & Carson, 2008; Santos et al., 2017). Life skills development has received increasing interest in the literature over recent years as it is becoming more widely accepted that sport plays a fundamental role in a child's overall development, perhaps above and beyond their sole progression as an athlete in their chosen sport (e.g., Jones & Lavallee, 2009a; Pierce, Kendellen, Camiré, & Gould, 2016; Vella, Oades, & Crowe, 2011). In line with this research interest, many authors have attempted to define the term to aid the integration of life skills into practice, as well as improve understanding and measurement of their development (e.g., Hodge & Danish, 1999; Jones & Lavallee, 2009a). One definition, seemingly accepted in the sport domain, suggests that life skills are "[t]hose skills that enable individuals to succeed in the different environments in which they live, such as school, home and in their neighbourhoods" (Danish, Forneris, Hodge, & Heke, 2004, p. 40). Such skills are thought to include cognitive (e.g., decision-making), emotional (e.g., coping with stress), physical (e.g., physical literacy), intellectual (e.g., problem solving), and social (e.g., communication) attributes (cf. Jones & Lavalle, 2009a; Neely & Holt, 2014). Further, the skill learned in one context (e.g., sport) must be transferrable to another before it can be considered a life skill. For example, if an individual develops *problem-solving* skills in soccer, then it must transfer and be used in other domains (e.g., solving problems in the classroom) that are not similar to the sporting environment (Allen, Rhind, & Koshy, 2015).

The development of young people's life skills when participating in soccer can be influenced by many stakeholders (e.g., parents, teachers, peers), with sports coaches potentially playing the most substantial role (Bowley et al., 2018; Camiré, Trudel, & Forneris, 2012). Consequently, this chapter aims to (a) discuss the role of the soccer coach as a person of significant importance in the development of psychological life skills, focusing on the nature of such skills and the theoretical implications of their development, and (b) offer an evidence-based practical framework for how soccer coaches can integrate life skills development within their coaching practice.

The Role of the Soccer Coach in Developing Life Skills

In recent years, the psychological and social development of young people has become an important focus for coach education programmes largely due to the holistic development of athletes being targeted globally by national governing bodies (NGBs) of sport. This is amplified in football by the emergence of the *four-corner* model, which focuses on the technical, physical, psychological, and social development of players. Further, the role of the coach in developing life skills through their practice has been widely explored. For example, McCallister, Blinde, and Weiss (2000) found the coach to be the most significant individual in teaching the life skills of fair play, respect for others, cooperation, decision-making, and leadership, because coaches are in a position of influence. Indeed, Bowley et al. (2018) supported such a notion as the coaches, parents, and teachers in their research expressed how the relationship between a coach and athlete is different from the relationships that the young person has with others (e.g., teachers) due to the context of sport. Consequently, coaches are in an efficacious position to positively influence the young person, who sees the coach as an authority figure without the level of coercive power (e.g., the ability to deliver punishment) of teachers or parents.

The importance of the coach–athlete relationship for the development of life skills has also been discussed in relation to initial learning of skills within a sporting context. For example, in a study with award-winning coaches Gould, Collins, Lauer, and Chung (2005) found support for the value of a continual process of learning that allowed life skills to be developed as opposed to adopting isolated strategies or techniques (e.g., integrating life skill development as a fundamental part of practice rather than simply an "add-on" to practice). Further, Gould et al.'s (2005) participants reported that, along with a philosophical base and trust, a strong coach–athlete relationship was fundamental in guiding a continual process of delivery. The adult–child relationship has also been deemed as vital in helping young people develop resilience (Cox, Neil, Oliver, & Hanton, 2016; Henley, Schweizer, de Gara, & Vetter, 2007), as well as teamwork, fair play, ethics, and the social skills that support these values (Boyden & Mann, 2005). As a result, it is clear that coaches must have skills beyond those required for solely teaching sport and game activities. Coaches should also be able to facilitate the understanding of emotions and interpersonal communication between children and help children develop effective coping skills (Henley et al., 2007). Indeed, the protective enabling forms of relationships that players develop with the coach assist in the development of a variety of internal problem-solving skills, coping, and adaptation strategies that enhance a person's functioning processes (Connor & Davidson, 2003).

While soccer can be used as a vehicle for developing life skills, participation in any sport does not guarantee personal growth. To develop life skills and enhance the psychological and social development of young people, therefore, coaches and leaders in youth sport must shape and facilitate the environment in which young people participate and perform while explicitly considering their learning as a priority (Camiré, Forneris, Trudel, & Bernard, 2011). This involves purposeful teaching of skills, as life skills are *taught* and not *caught* through participation alone (Danish, Forneris, Hodge, & Heke, 2004). In addition, simply giving players ownership or naïvely applying athlete-centred principles (which seem to be considered as the gold standard approach in youth development) is not enough to aid the development of life skills and the understanding of how they might be transferred outside of the sport. In consideration of

Vygotsky's (1978) theory that young people are more likely to learn and develop quicker with the support of a *more capable other* who is able to facilitate growth within the individuals' *zone of proximal development*, the role of the coach should, therefore, never be underestimated. Certainly, the "just let them play" approach has to be challenged with careful consideration afforded to the principles of effective pedagogy.

Coaches should always aim to *enhance their players' understanding of what they are doing and why they are doing it* as this will help the athlete make sense of what they are learning, thus enhancing their understanding of the relevance and consequently increasing the likelihood of transferring learning from training to competition and/or from soccer to other life domains. Coaches must also make explicit the relevance of the skill(s) in focus to other aspects of life away from soccer to assist players in transferring what they have learnt. Without this transfer, it is unlikely that coaches actually enhance players' personal development (Pierce et al., 2016). For example, if we develop a young person's ability to work as part of a team in soccer without improving their understanding of the utility of teamwork skills in other aspects of life, all we are doing is developing *sport skills*. Youth soccer coaches have a duty of care for the young people under their guidance to ensure that each participant develops as a person first and foremost to maximise their potential not only in sport but also in wider life domains, including home, school, society, and later when entering employment.

In summary, soccer (and or sport) participation does not automatically result in participants' psychological and/or social growth, which has pertinent practical implications for soccer coaches. First, life skills are *taught* rather than *caught*, meaning that coaches must adopt a purposeful and integrated approach where the participant and the coach work together to enhance the learning experience. Second, the coach–athlete relationship lies at the heart of life skill development given the nature of the skills and interaction required to help participants understand how skills are transferred from one context to another. As a result, coaches must place emphasis on developing a relationship with their athletes that is built on trust and mutual respect. Finally, coaches need to develop a philosophy that embraces the concept of supporting *the person* in order to develop the athlete.

Practical Applications—Case Study

Background and Context

The importance of understanding context has been discussed in the coaching and life skills literature alike where recognising the needs of the learner is of particular significance for coaches (e.g., Gould & Carson, 2008). For example, within a soccer club, a coach delivering a session on communicating when defending could be presented with a squad of 18 players with differing levels of ability, experience of defending, roles when defending (e.g., a centre back versus a winger), and motivation for the session (likely to be linked to the perception of importance based upon role). As a result, the coach must tailor their approach for each individual to ensure that the challenge set and subsequent expectations are appropriate. Thus, to help with structuring context-specific coaching practice, an evidence-based model for coaching life skills is presented in Figure 7.1 and discussed in the intervention section.

94 Ceri Bowley and Hamish Cox

```
┌─────────────────┐     ┌─────────────────┐     ┌─────────────────┐     ┌─────────────────┐
│   Philosophy    │     │      Plan       │     │   Environment   │     │ Coaching Practice│
│                 │     │                 │     │   Development   │     │                 │
│ Develop people  │     │   Curriculum    │     │  Constructivism │     │   3-step process│
│   & athletes    │ ⇨   │                 │ ⇨   │                 │ ⇨   │                 │
│ Understand      │     │ Individual      │     │  Orchestration  │     │ Intervention    │
│ athlete & parent│     │ sessions        │     │                 │     │ Strategies      │
│ expectations    │     │                 │     │ Structure:      │     │ Questions &     │
│ Know your club/ │     │                 │     │ Performance Time│     │ Challenges      │
│ organisation    │     │                 │     │                 │     │ Facilitate      │
│ ethos & your    │     │                 │     │                 │     │ Transfer        │
│ values          │     │                 │     │                 │     │                 │
└─────────────────┘     └─────────────────┘     └─────────────────┘     └─────────────────┘

              ⇦───────────────── Reflective Practice ─────────────────⇨
```

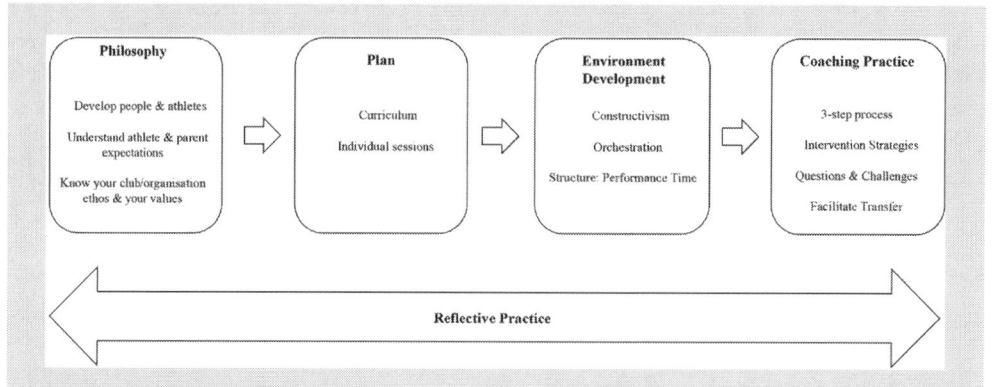

FIGURE 7.1 The model for life skill development through coaching

This case study presents the approach taken by the first author to developing the life skills (commitment, reflection, confidence, coping with challenges, leadership, discipline, teamwork, communication) of young players in a professional football club academy. Specifically, working with the Youth Development Phase (12–16 years) a holistic approach was taken whereby the life skill was fully integrated within the technical and tactical practice of the coach. The model for coaching life skills (Figure 7.1) was utilised as a framework for (a) educating the academy coaches and (b) shaping coaching practice.

Presenting Issue(s)

The case study set out to address two issues specifically:

1. The myth that sport (soccer) itself develops life skills;
2. That coaches felt unprepared for developing players psycho-socially (Bowley et al., 2018).

The Intervention

This section will be structured in line with the model presented in Figure 7.1 which contains five key elements: *philosophy, plan, environment development. coaching practice*, and *reflective practice* that was used to (1) educate coaches and (2) support coaches with developing the life skills of their players. Each element will be discussed in turn, with consideration towards the practical applications to utilise the model in practice.

Philosophy

Given the need for an appropriate set of values that drive coach behaviour towards valuing the holistic development of a person, a coach's philosophy is said to be of great importance for developing young people's life skills (Camiré et al., 2012). Indeed, various studies have shown that a well-articulated coaching philosophy is a crucial element in a coach's repertoire (e.g., Bowley et al., 2018; Gould & Carson, 2008). To elaborate, a well-conceived coaching philosophy provides the foundation upon which coaches and players can learn in a consistent and coherent manner without becoming too situation specific or too reactive (Cassidy, Jones, & Potrac, 2009). Indeed, a coaching philosophy "will remove uncertainty about training rules, styles of play, discipline, codes of conduct, competitive outlook, short- and long-term objectives, and many other facets of coaching" (Martens, 2004, p. 5). Further, Collins, Gould, Lauer, and Chung (2009) found that model high school football coaches have well-established coaching philosophies that recognise the importance of coaching life skills. In doing so, coaches hold the "person" at the heart of their practice through developing an athlete-centred philosophy, the importance of which is clear given the number of youth involved in organised sport today (McGladrey, Murray, & Hannon, 2010). A workshop was delivered to the coaches to explore their individual coaching philosophies and align them to that of the club. Coaches were asked to:

1. Determine their values and beliefs through asking questions such as: Why do I coach? What is important to me in sport? What do I expect of my athletes? What is my role? Reflecting on past experiences, as a coach and/or player served to help to answer these.
2. Understand your players and parents' expectations. Why do they come to your sessions? What do they hope to achieve? How do they see your role as a coach? Coaches were encouraged to speak to their players and parents on an individual basis to verify their own thoughts and gain a credible understanding of how each player is motivated. This served as an opportunity to develop a relationship with the player and their parents.
3. There needs to be congruence between what we say, what we value, and what we actually do. Therefore, if we say we want to develop our players foremost as people, our actions must reflect this. A lack of congruence between values and behaviours can have a detrimental impact on the effectiveness of practice and the relationship a coach has with athletes. Thus, a philosophy needs to contain a series of *value statements* that are linked with *observable behaviours* that outline how these values are manifested. Coaches were challenged to develop their own value statements and highlight observable behaviours that best represent them. These statements and behaviours were developed with the club philosophy in mind, and sharing and discussing their value statements and observable behaviours served to align each coach with the academy philosophy.

Plan

It is important to know where you want your athletes to finish and what you want them to learn in order to provide focus to coaching delivery (Reece & Walker, 2007). Indeed, being clear about the *learning outcomes* of a session gives the practice a purpose and focus that will facilitate learning of life skills beyond more implicit and activity-focused approaches (e.g., "by the end of the session the players will know/be able to . . ." is better than "in this session we will do this activity/topic"; Husbands & Pearce, 2012). To facilitate the development of appropriate learning outcomes that support life skill development, it is important to consider the expectations of the players and their parents, the coach's own values, and what life skills need to be taught. Taking into consideration the expectations of the players is important as Knight and Trowler (2001) argued that if students are given a real stake in their own learning they will learn more effectively and will be more motivated and enthusiastic.

Once the learning outcomes have been determined it is important that coaches plan their players' learning through the development of a *curriculum*. When designing the curriculum, the following were considered:

1. Which life skills are most important for the players to develop? The academy philosophy and demands of professional academy football were central to this.
2. How to shape the curriculum. Consideration was given to (a) which life skills needed developing first to provide the foundations for developing others (e.g., communication was regarded as an underpinning life skill for many others) and (b) the life skills that may become most important at a specific time of the season (e.g., coping with challenges at a time when the level of opposition may exceed the norm, thus providing additional learning stress).

Within the *curriculum* coaches were tasked with designing individual sessions to explicitly develop an individual life skill over a four-week period to offer multiple opportunities for players to practice the life skill in a soccer situation to enhance understanding which in turn would offer a greater chance of successful transfer away from soccer and into other life domains (e.g., at home, school). Coaches followed two clear guidelines:

1. Think about which coaching practices activate the life skill to ensure an integrated approach (e.g., attacking phases in soccer require players to overcome problems as a team rather than to act independently and so a focus on developing problem-solving as the life skill).
2. Think about *coaching*, *teaching*, and *learning*. Good teaching and learning stem from a range of complex interactions between the students, teacher, setting, and learning activities (Maher, 2004). Emphasis should be placed on motivating athletes through posing challenges and questions, along with deciding which intervention strategies would be most applicable for creating and maximising learning opportunities. Through this approach a flexible framework for a session based upon a maximum of three attacking/defending (e.g., play through, play around, play over/press to win the ball, press to force backwards, always show outside) principles that remained consistent was created that allowed the coach to react to the players' engagement and comprehension and adjust the session as required (cf. Jones & Wallace, 2006). This offered a level of consistency which allowed the players to focus on the key learning for the session rather than their attention being drawn towards an ever-changing way of playing.

Environment Development

The development of an appropriate environment is an important factor in life skill development as coaches are highly involved in creating motivational climates that influence the way athletes evaluate themselves (Keegan, Harwood, Spray, & Lavallee, 2014) as well as environments that are conducive to learning and PYD (Chak, 2001). Given some of the philosophical underpinnings of athlete-centred approaches, as well as recent research findings (e.g., Bowley et al., 2018), an environment built upon *constructivist* approaches to learning was adopted.

The term *constructivism* covers a diverse range of theories about human learning commonly seen as falling into the two areas of cognitive/psychological and sociocultural constructivism (Davis & Sumara, 2003; Fosnot, 2005). From a cognitive constructivism perspective, learning is seen as a process through which the individual draws on past experience and knowledge to actively construct ways of knowing (Cobb, 1996). For example, through learning life skills in training players were encouraged to draw upon their experience in order to effectively apply the learned life skill in another environment (e.g., at school).

Sociocultural constructivism views learning as being culturally and socially situated and thus typically focuses on learning as part of a broader activity system and participation in culturally organised practices (Light & Wallian, 2008). For example, life skills can be developed through interaction with teammates or the coach (Vygotsky, 1978). The *Model for Life Skill Development Through Coaching* advocates a theoretically pragmatic approach whereby the interplay between the two approaches is considered (Cobb, 1996). Consequently, opportunities for interaction and discussion with (coach–player) and between (player–player) were created to help players understand:

1. What life skill they are learning;
2. Why the life skill is important in soccer;
3. Where else the life skill is important;
4. How to plan the transfer away from soccer.

Making the learning explicit served to enhance the players' ability to transfer the life skill away from the sport. In using a constructivist approach the role of the coach can be viewed as an *orchestrator* of coaching practice and learning. The concept of orchestration was derived from Wallace and Pocklington's (2002) theory about the management of educational change. When applied to coaching, Jones and Wallace (2006) defined orchestration as a

> [c]oordinated activity within set parameters expressed by coaches to instigate, plan, organise, monitor, and respond to evolving circumstances in order to bring about improvement in the individual and collective performance of those being coached.
>
> *(p. 61).*

Orchestration implies *steering* as opposed to *controlling*, a dynamic interactive process involving much *behind-the-scenes string pulling* towards desired objectives; constant analysis, evaluation, and scrutiny to keep things going; maintaining detailed oversight of minutiae of each coaching situation (Jones & Wallace, 2006). The coach's work is then viewed as being much more outside of the limelight, as unobtrusively arranging, guiding, and generally scaffolding the resultant athletes' public performance (Jones, Bailey, & Thompson, 2013).

Coaching Practice

The process for developing life skills was *message-reinforce-transfer* (Bodey, Schaumleffel, Zakrajsek, & Joseph, 2009). Through the application of this approach coaches communicated the life skill *message* to the athletes at the beginning of the session before engaging in discussion about the importance of the life skill, first, to soccer and, then, importantly, in other areas of life. For example, a soccer coach teaching problem-solving skills may outline the message "For players to develop their problem-solving skills in the session" and have it written on a whiteboard board to serve as a visual reminder. They would then discuss what problem-solving means to the players and ask the players to share what good problem-solving looked like in soccer or to name a player who displays good problem-solving skills. Then, players were asked to share ideas of what good problem-solving might look like at school or at home. During the *reinforce* phase coaches use intervention strategies to reinforce the key life skill message. Through a synthesis of the extant literature (e.g., Bowley et al., 2018; Camiré et al., 2012) seven intervention strategies were used for reinforcing messages to facilitate successful development of life skills (see Table 7.1). Finally, during the *transfer* phase coaches encouraged players to reflect on their learning from within the session on their own and then with peers, before asking them to identify a different context in which they will attempt to apply the life skill learnt. For example, following the soccer theme from the aforementioned example, at the end of the session the coach would ask players to think about (individually) or discuss in small groups when in the session they displayed good problem-solving and not only why this was important for the session but also why it may be important in their next competition. Then, players were asked to consider how they will attempt to demonstrate good problem-solving ability in a different environment over the next week and to communicate this individually to the coach before leaving the session.

Message-reinforce-transfer is an effective process for structuring coaching practice, particularly in light of life skill development, because in its application coaches provide opportunities for athletes to build up knowledge, rather than the coach being the dispenser of knowledge (Patton, Parker, & Pratt, 2013). In applying this process, the role of the coach is to find ways to encourage athletes to explore their world, discover knowledge, set and solve problems, and to reflect and think critically (Brooks & Brooks, 1993). This approach, therefore, encourages athletes to take ownership and make sense of their own learning through interaction with their surroundings and in doing so develop a stronger awareness of self which can help facilitate the transfer of life skills (Fosnot, 2005).

TABLE 7.1 Intervention strategies for developing life skills through coaching

	Intervention Strategy	Description
1	Reinforcing the message based on observation of successful application	The coach identifies correct use of life skill and asks the athlete to explain/demonstrate what they did to their teammates/peers.
2	Reinforcing the message with individual athletes	The coach questions an athlete on the action(s) they have just performed and how they could improve the performance of the action further
3	Reinforcing the message through group work	Athletes are separated into groups (of two or more athletes) to discuss their performance in the practice so far and identify ways to improve their performance further
4	Reinforcing the message with the whole group of athletes	A combination of the above strategies can be used
5	Reinforcing the message with video footage	Video demonstrating successful performance of the message can be a powerful tool for painting a clear picture for athletes. Video of them performing the message can be a useful motivator too
6	Use of challenges	The coach plans a series of challenges that can be presented to/set for the athletes. These challenges should encompass specific individual athlete, small group, unit, and whole group (as applicable) challenges to tailor the approach to suit the development needs of the individual
7	Use of cue words	When performing athletes have lots to concentrate on and messages can easily be forgotten. The coach may use single words (cue words) of meaning rather than a full sentence to help athlete's concentrate on the message

Reflective Practice

The growing interest in reflective practice has been consistent in its acknowledgement towards the importance of the process for coaches to learn about the landscape of the context in which they are working and about their own coaching practice (e.g., Cropley, Miles, & Nichols, 2015). The value of reflective practice here is no different. It is a process that underpins the *Model for Life Skill Development Through Coaching* and enables all four elements to be linked and integrated. This ensures a cohesive approach to life skill development that considers *people* (e.g., the coach, the athlete, the parent), *practices* (e.g., reinforcement of message through group challenge), and the *environment* (e.g., facilitating a place for growth). Without such cohesion it is unlikely that life skill development will be effective or efficient given the difficulties associated with athletes being able to successfully transfer the skills outside of sport (cf. Neely & Holt, 2014). Consequently, reflective practice offers coaches an approach to explore their *knowledge-in-action* (e.g., the sum of a coach's social norms, values, prejudices, experiences, empirical knowledge, aesthetical knowledge, personal knowledge, and ethical knowledge) in a way that brings into question how well their values align with their actions. This can be a challenging process as it is likely to bring about the questioning of cultural norms and accepted practices. However, if coaches are committed to personal and professional development and want to strive to support the holistic development of the individuals for whom they are responsible, then such questioning is required (Peel, Cropley, Hanton, & Fleming, 2013).

A range of approaches were adopted to facilitate both coaches' and players' reflective practice (e.g., reflective conversations, written diaries/reports, mind maps, audio/visual methods; cf. Cropley et al., 2015). In any case the following approaches were taken:

1. Reflective practice is more powerful when structured. It is not likely that coaches will naturally ask the critical level of questions required to thoroughly explore their actions, values, emotions, and cognitions. As a result, using a model to guide your reflective practices will encourage a deeper and more meaningful approach.
2. Reflective practice can be more powerful when *shared*. Certainly, our reflection is bound in what we know (and hindered by what we do not know). Reflecting with another person (or people) can help us to develop additional knowledge and insight that reflecting alone may not.
3. Reflective practice has to be about the positives as much, if not more, than the negatives. Reflecting on our strengths can help us to create more opportunities to use them, and it is our strengths that often lead to successful practice. Being clear about what works for us and why it works will facilitate ongoing *good* practice that will only be of benefit to the learning of life skills.

Outcome Analysis

In line with previous life skills research (e.g., Bowley et al., 2018) we determined the effectiveness of our intervention through social validation interviews with coaches, observations of training and matches, a focus group with players, and reflective diary inputs by coaches and players. Social validation is considered integral to intervention-based research because it informs researchers and practitioners about the delivery and effect of psychological interventions (Barker, McCarthy, Jones, & Moran, 2011). Social validation interviews focused on determining (1) the coaches' experiences of integrating life skills in practice and (2) any noticeable change in players' ability to transfer life skills from training to competition (and vice versa) and from the pitch to off the pitch. Observations enhanced understanding of the context and afforded us the opportunity to explore beyond the selective perceptions of the coach through drawing on personal knowledge and experience. Specifically, observations conducted over a six-month period focused on determining (1) the life skill coached; (2) the intervention strategies used; and (3) whether or not all elements of the three-step process were utilised. Reflective diaries were completed by players to offer a deeper understanding of (1) the experiences of the players and (2) the learning that had occurred as a result of the life skills being integrated within sessions.

The evaluation of the intervention revealed that coaches (a) felt better able to deliver sessions with a psycho-social focus, (b) had developed an understanding of what "good" might look like when observing the application of different life skills, (c) were able to effectively integrate life skill development within their coaching practice, and (d) expressed a feeling of adding value to each individual's development beyond that as a player; and that players (a) could recall how their coaches had emphasised the development of key life skills in their delivery and (b) were able to articulate examples of how they had transferred the life skills beyond soccer.

Case-Study Reflections

As outlined in our outcome analysis, our life skills intervention using the *Model for Life Skills Development through Coaching* elicited some change in coaching delivery over a six-month period that also resulted in the successful development of some life skills among soccer academy players.

In the early stages of the intervention, the initial discussions with coaches and observations of coaching practice highlighted an uncertainty around the development of psychological skills. With coaches showing vulnerability, the importance of building rapport and creating psychological safety struck home. I set about demonstrating the "how" and "why" through being very aware of the importance of speaking the same language as the coaches (and players). Finding the means to deliver the key psychological messages in a way that made sense was the priority. The club's existing game model in and out of possession and the overall philosophy was deemed the most effective and quickest way of doing this, with the life skills required to effectively implement these brought to life through video examples of "what good looks like" to (a) provide clarity and consistency and (b) enhance coach engagement in the process. Progress in the early stages was slow as coaches got to grips with the new approach; however, structured planning and reflection were paramount to the coaches' development throughout the intervention, and it was clear that over time the psychological development of their players became a more prominent focus in their practice. As the coaches became more confident and began to understand the approach to developing life skills better, they began to embrace other ways to engage in reflective practice, including collaborative reflections with other coaches while they were also more forthcoming in seeking my support. These approaches were particularly beneficial, and it was clear that the access to other opinions, knowledge, and ways of thinking, and thus new ways of understanding and learning from experience, accelerated the journey of coaches towards competent and confident delivery of an integrated approach to life skill development.

Throughout the academy there is now a greater awareness of the impact of coaching practice on the players as performers and people, and the scope of the psychologist's role is evolving as a result of the noticeable impact of the intervention on coaches and players alike, which has led to an increased receptiveness and buy-in.

Summary and Conclusions

Coaches are responsible for the holistic development of the people with whom they are working. This includes athletes' technical, tactical, physical, and psychosocial attributes. In addition, it is becoming more widely accepted that coaches should consider their athletes as *people first*, requiring them to adapt their philosophies to encourage more athlete-centred principles that include a focus on life skill development. Indeed, facilitating life skill development in young people can help to improve their functioning in both sport and life as well as enhance the contribution that these people can make to society. Life skill development has to be formally integrated into coaching practice as it is the athlete's interaction with the coach, sport, and other athletes that encourages them to be learned (it is unlikely that life skills will be efficiently and effectively learned through participation in sport alone). To do this, we have presented the *Model for Life Skill Development Through Coaching*, which encourages coaches to (a) develop an appropriate philosophy; (b) plan an integrated curriculum; (c) develop an environment built on principles of constructivist learning; (d) utilise a range of intervention strategies to deliver and reinforce the life skill message and encourage transfer; and (e) engage in reflective practice to facilitate ongoing learning and development.

Key Messages and Further Reading

1. Soccer is a vehicle for developing life skills.
2. The coach plays a significant role in developing players' life skills—life skills are "taught not caught."
3. A collaborative approach to developing life skills is needed between the coach and other significant influencers of young people (e.g., parents, teachers, peers).
4. The *Model for Life Skill Development Through Coaching* should be used as a framework for developing players' life skills.
5. Reflection enhances a coach's ability to purposefully coach life skills and a player's ability to transfer life skills.

To gain a more detailed understanding of life skill development the following reading is recommended:

> Bowley, C., Cropley, B., Neil, R., Hanton, S., & Mitchell, I. (2018). A life skills development programme for youth football: Programme development and preliminary evaluation. *Sport & Exercise Psychology Review, 14*(1), 3–22.
> Cox, H., Neil, R., Oliver, J., & Hanton, S. (2016). PasSport4life: A trainee sport psychologist's perspective on developing a resilience-based life skills program. *Journal of Sport Psychology in Action, 7*(3), 182–192.
> Gould, D., & Carson, S. (2008). Life skills development through sport: Current status and future directions. *International Review of Sport and Exercise Psychology, 1*, 58–78.
> Pierce, S., Kendellen, K., Camiré, M., & Gould, D. (2016). Strategies for coaching for life skills transfer. *Journal of Sport Psychology in Action*. doi:10.1080/21520704.2016.1263982

References

Allen, G., Rhind, D., & Koshy, V. (2015). Enablers and barriers for male students transferring life skills from the sports hall into the classroom. *Qualitative Research in Sport, Exercise and Health, 7*, 53–67.
Barker, J. B., McCarthy, P. J., Jones, M. V., & Moran, A. (2011). *Single-case research methods in sport and exercise psychology*. London: Routledge.

Bodey, K. J., Schaumleffel, N. A., Zakrajsek, R., & Joseph, S. (2009). A strategy for coaches to develop life skills in youth sports. *The Journal of Youth Sports, 4,* 16–20.

Bowley, C., Cropley, B., Neil, R., Hanton, S., & Mitchell, I. (2018). A life skills development programme for youth football: Programme development and preliminary evaluation. *Sport & Exercise Psychology Review, 14*(1), 3–22.

Boyden, J., & Mann, G. (2005). Children's risk, resilience, and coping in extreme situations. In M. Ungar (Ed.), *Handbook for working with children and youth: Pathways to resilience across cultures and contexts* (pp. 3–25). Thousand Oaks, CA: Sage Publications.

Brooks, J. G., & Brooks, M. G. (1993). *In search of understanding: The case for constructivist classrooms.* Alexandria, VA: Association for Supervision and Curriculum Development.

Camiré, M., Forneris, T., Trudel, P., & Bernard, D. (2011). Strategies for helping coaches facilitate positive youth development through sport. *Journal of Sport Psychology in Action, 2*(2), 92–99.

Camiré, M., Trudel, P., & Forneris, T. (2012). Coaching and transferring life skills: Philosophies and strategies used by model high school coaches. *The Sport Psychologist, 26,* 243–260.

Cassidy, T., Jones, R. L., & Potrac, P. (2009). *Understanding sports coaching: The social, cultural and pedagogical foundations of coaching practice* (2nd ed.). New York, NY: Routledge.

Chak, A. (2001). Adult sensitivity to children's learning in the zone of proximal development. *Journal for the Theory of Social Behavior, 31,* 383–396.

Cobb, P. (1996). Where is the mind? A coordination of sociocultural and cognitive constructivist perspectives. In C. T. Fosnot (Ed.), *Constructivism: Theory, perspectives, and practice* (pp. 34–52). New York, NY: Plenum.

Collins, K., Gould, D., Lauer, L., & Chung, Y. (2009). Coaching life skills through football: Philosophical beliefs of outstanding high school football coaches. *International Journal of Coaching Science, 3,* 29–54.

Connor, K. M., & Davidson, J. (2003). Development of a new resilience scale: The Connor-Davidson resilience scale (CD-RISC). *Depression and Anxiety, 18,* 76–82.

Cox, H., Neil, R., Oliver, J., & Hanton, S. (2016). PasSport4life: A trainee sport psychologist's perspective on developing a resilience-based life skills program. *Journal of Sport Psychology in Action, 7*(3), 182–192.

Cropley, B., Miles, A., & Nichols, N. (2015). Learning to learn: The coach as a reflective practitioner. In J. Wallace & J. Lambert (Eds.), *Becoming a sports coach* (pp. 11–26). London: Routledge.

Danish, S., Forneris, T., Hodge, K., & Heke, I. (2004). Enhancing youth development through sport. *World Leisure Journal, 46,* 38–49.

Davis, B., & Sumara, D. (2003). Why aren't they getting this? Working through the regressive myths of constructivist pedagogy. *Teaching Education, 14*(2), 123–140.

Fosnot, C. T. (2005). *Constructivism: Theory, perspectives, and practice.* New York, NY: Teachers College Press.

Gould, D., & Carson, S. (2008). Life skills development through sport: Current status and future directions. *International Review of Sport and Exercise Psychology, 1,* 58–78.

Gould, D., Collins, K., Lauer, L., & Chung, Y. (2005). Coaching life skills: A working model. *Sport and Exercise Psychology Review, 2,* 4–12.

Henley, R., Schweizer, I. C., de Gara, F., & Vetter, S. (2007). How psychosocial sport and play programs help youth manage adversity: A review of what we know and what we should research. *International Journal of Psychosocial Rehabilitation, 12,* 51–58.

Hodge, K., & Danish, S. (1999). Promoting life skills for adolescent males through sport. In A. M. Horne & M. S. Kiselica (Eds.), *Handbook of counselling boys and adolescent males: A practitioner's guide* (pp. 55–71). Thousand Oaks, CA: Sage Publications.

Husbands, C., & Pearce, J. (2012). *What makes great pedagogy? Nine claims from research.* National College for School Leadership, Nottingham, England. Retrieved from https://assets.publishing.service.gov.uk/government/uploads/system/uploads/attachment_data/file/329746/what-makes-great-pedagogy-nine-claims-from-research.pdf

Jones, M., & Lavallee, D. (2009a). Exploring the life skills needs of British adolescent athletes. *Psychology of Sport and Exercise, 10,* 159–167.

Jones, R. L., Bailey, J., & Thompson, I. (2013). Ambiguity, noticing, and orchestration: Further thoughts on managing the complex coaching context. In P. Potrac, W. Gilbert & J. Denison (Eds.), *The Routledge handbook of sports coaching* (pp. 271–283). London: Routledge.

Jones, R. L., & Wallace, M. (2006). The coach as orchestrator: More realistically managing the complex coaching context. In R. L. Jones (Ed.), *The sports coach as educator: Re-conceptualizing sports coaching* (pp. 51–64). London: Routledge.

Keegan, R. J., Harwood, C. G., Spray, C. M., & Lavallee, D. (2014). A qualitative investigation of the motivational climate in elite sport. *Psychology of Sport and Exercise, 15*, 97–107.

Knight, P. T., & Trowler, P. R. (2001). *Departmental leadership in higher education*. Buckingham: Open University Press.

Light, R., & Wallian, N. (2008). A constructivist-informed approach to teaching swimming. *Quest, 60*, 387–404.

Maher, A. (2004). Learning outcomes in higher education: Implications for curriculum design and student learning. *Journal of Hospitality, Leisure, Sport and Tourism Education, 3*, 46–54.

Martens, R. (2004). *Successful coaching* (3rd ed.). Champaign, IL: Human Kinetics.

McCallister, S. G., Blinde, E. M., & Weiss, W. M. (2000). Teaching values and implementing philosophies: Dilemmas of the coach. *Physical Educator, 57*, 35–45.

McGladrey, B., Murray, M., & Hannon, J. (2010). Developing and practicing an athlete-centered coaching philosophy. *Youth-first: Journal of Youth Sports, 5*, 4–8.

Neely, K., & Holt, N. (2014). Parents' perspectives on the benefits of sport participation for young children. *The Sport Psychologist, 28*, 255–268.

Patton, K., Parker, M., & Pratt, E. (2013). Meaningful learning in professional development: Teaching without telling. *Journal of Teaching in Physical Education, 32*, 441–459.

Peel, J., Cropley, B., Hanton, S., & Fleming, S. (2013). Learning through reflection: Values, conflicts, and role interactions of a youth sport coach. *Reflective Practice, 14*, 729–742.

Pierce, S., Kendellen, K., Camiré, M., & Gould, D. (2016). Strategies for coaching for life skills transfer. *Journal of Sport Psychology in Action*. doi:10.1080/21520704.2016.1263982

Reece, I., & Walker, S. (2007). *Teaching, training & learning: A practical guide*. Houghton le Spring: Business Education Publishers.

Santos, F., Camiré, M., Macdonald, D. J., Campos, H., Conceição, M., & Silva, P. (2017). Youth sport coaches' perspective on youth development and its worth in mainstream coach education courses. *International Sport Coaching Journal, 4*, 38–46.

Vella, S., Oades, L., & Crowe, T. (2011). The role of the coach in facilitating positive youth development: Moving from theory to practice. *Journal of Applied Sport Psychology, 23*, 33–48.

Vygotsky, L. S. (1978). *Mind in society*. Cambridge, MA: Harvard University Press.

Wallace, M., & Pocklington, K. (2002). *Managing complex educational change: Large-scale reorganization of schools*. London: Routledge.

8
IDENTIFYING AND DELIVERING A TEAM-BASED INTERVENTION IN ELITE YOUTH SOCCER

Using Personal-Disclosure Mutual-Sharing to Enhance Team Identification, Resilience, and Coping

Andrew L. Evans and Jamie B. Barker

Brief Introduction and Review of Literature

Reports of athletes participating in activities underpinned by personal-disclosure mutual-sharing (PDMS) are widespread. For example, the Buffalo Bills American Football team has regularly concluded team meetings with one athlete preparing and delivering personal stories to teammates detailing their upbringing, motivations, influences, and elements of their life that they value most (see Kahler, 2017). In soccer, Wayne Rooney (former Manchester United and England soccer international) has explained how meetings between England players during training camps involved them discussing how to improve as a team following the 2014 World Cup tournament in Brazil (see BBC Sport, 2014). More recently, Theo Walcott (former Arsenal soccer player) has described how a meeting between Arsenal players was organised to enable them to express their feelings to one another regarding a period of poor team form (see BBC Sport, 2016). Within anecdotal reports, athletes have attributed a range of benefits to participating in such activities, including improved team dynamics (see Kahler, 2017), increased team cohesion (see BBC Sport, 2014), and elevated team performance (see BBC Sport, 2016). Based on anecdotal evidence, applied sport psychology researchers have systematically explored the potential effects and athlete perceptions of participating in PDMS activities. In this chapter, we aim to further raise the profile of PDMS as a valuable psychological intervention for athletes of all levels with a focus on a youth soccer context. Specifically, we (a) briefly introduce PDMS, (b) review extant PDMS research, (c) detail a hypothetical case study, and (d) conclude with key messages, future research directions, and suggested key further reading.

PDMS is a communication-based intervention originating from counselling settings introduced into applied sport psychology literature by Crace and Hardy (1997) and Yukleson (1997) as an approach to team building. The PDMS intervention process begins with a needs analysis where practitioners gather information (e.g., through questionnaires) from key individuals (e.g., coaches) to inform the nature of their PDMS intervention (e.g., Barker, Evans, Coffee, Slater, and McCarthy, 2014). After planning their PDMS intervention, practitioners may deliver an introductory sport psychology education session (e.g., Evans, Slater, Turner, & Barker, 2013). Accordingly, practitioners introduce the notion of PDMS to athletes who are given time to prepare previously unknown information and/or personal stories that are later mutually shared with group or team members during a PDMS activity/session (see Dunn & Holt, 2004). PDMS activities conclude with a reflective component and debrief where the PDMS process and information communicated during the PDMS activity are discussed by practitioners and athletes (see Evans et al., 2013). Like counselling procedures, athletes communicate information and/or personal stories during PDMS activities focused on a situation, issue(s), and/or aspiration(s) with the aim of gaining resolution through interpersonal interaction (Olarte, 2003). The role of a practitioner during PDMS activities is diverse and includes organising the PDMS intervention, facilitating disclosures, supporting athletes with disclosures, and leading reflections and debriefs.

Intuitively, the application of PDMS in soccer could benefit team and athlete functioning. For teams to function effectively, athletes require an understanding of themselves and others (e.g., roles and values; Crace & Hardy, 1997). PDMS activities therefore enable athletes to mutually share thoughts, feelings, and experiences pertaining to a topic or theme such as transitioning from youth to senior soccer (Yukleson, 1997) which generates shared perceptions and meanings among group or team members (see Evans et al., 2013). Developing shared perceptions and meanings through PDMS activities provides a basis for collectively shared psychological constructs (e.g., team cohesion) and understandings to emerge (Windsor, Barker, & McCarthy, 2011). For athletes to function effectively, they would benefit from increased self-awareness and a range of individual-level psychological factors such as resilience, coping, and self-efficacy, which could all be enhanced through PDMS activities. For example, theories of stress appraisal (e.g., Cognitive Appraisal Theory, Lazarus, 1999) would suggest that increasing athlete awareness of demand and resource appraisals through PDMS activities could develop an athlete's coping potential for an upcoming event such as making a first-team soccer debut (Evans et al., 2019). To this end, PDMS could manipulate a host of group-/team-level and individual-level psychological outcomes pertinent in sport.

PDMS activities are theorised to instigate positive changes in group/team and individual-level psychological variables through mechanisms underpinning person-centred counselling approaches (see Rogers, 1951). During person-centred counselling (see Rogers, 1951), a practitioner develops empathy with their client as they are provided with a greater understanding of their client's thoughts, feelings, and experiences. Throughout counselling, a client and practitioner work together to address a client's needs which is considered therapeutic for the client (Dryden, 2006). According to Dryden (2006), activities founded on PDMS also encourage empathetic understanding among group or team members because individuals (athletes) are provided with a greater understanding of one another by receiving information and listening to personal stories. Additionally, Evans et al. (2013) suggested that PDMS can be a challenging experience for athletes because athletes can have underdeveloped public-speaking skills which could be attributable to the environment they operate in. For instance, Evans et al. (2019) revealed that soccer academy athletes are seldom provided with opportunities in their academy life to open-up to their teammates in a safe and therapeutic environment where teammates are fully attentive and respectful of one another. Evans et al. (2013) therefore proposed that athletes support one another through a challenging PDMS experience which perhaps underpins changes in psychological variables (e.g., social identification). Emerging research conducted with sports students has provided initial support for this hypothesis in that perceptions of emotional, esteemed, and informational support availability significantly increased from pre-PDMS to post-PDMS intervention phases (Evans, Slater, & Turner, in press).

Presently, four forms of PDMS are documented in applied sport psychology literature. First, Dunn and Holt (2004) delivered a relationship-oriented PDMS (ROPDMS) activity to 27 male intercollegiate ice hockey athletes at a national university tournament. ROPDMS activities involve athletes preparing and sharing personal stories to teammates or group members based on an event in their personal or sporting life that defines their character, motives, and desires (see Dunn & Holt, 2004). Several benefits to participating in ROPDMS were reported by athletes in

Dunn and Holt's (2004) study, including increased understanding of the self and others, heightened confidence and trust in teammates, and improved feelings of closeness. Such benefits were later confirmed by Holt and Dunn (2006) and Windsor et al. (2011) in male intercollegiate ice hockey and professional soccer samples respectively. However, in Windsor et al., ROPDMS failed to elicit any immediate performance gains in a competitive soccer match while cohesion and communication did not significantly change from pre-ROPDMS to post-ROPDMS. Windsor and colleagues suggested that the effect of ROPDMS on performance may have been confounded by a host of variables, such as the strength of the opposition. Meanwhile, the effect of ROPDMS on cohesion and communication could have been attributable to the nature of psychometrics used. Subsequent research examined the effects of ROPDMS on a wider set of psychological variables. For example, Evans et al. (2013) found that ROPDMS significantly increased the value 14 male soccer academy athletes placed on friendships within their team. Goal difference and goal discrepancy exhibited sustained improvement following ROPDMS while qualitative data revealed ROPDMS improved social identities among athletes. Barker et al. (2014) later confirmed that ROPDMS elicits increases in social identities and the value athletes place on friendships within a team of 15 elite male academy cricketers. Ten days after completing ROPDMS, cricketers also completed a mastery-oriented PDMS (MOPDMS) activity. MOPDMS activities involve athletes preparing and sharing information and/or personal stories pertaining to best sporting performance. Data from Barker et al. (2014) indicated that collective efficacy and the value athletes placed on results within their team remained unchanged following ROPDMS but significantly increased following MOPDMS. Additionally, the significant increases in social identities and the value athletes placed on friendships within their team that occurred following ROPDMS were maintained following MOPDMS.

The third form of PDMS that has recently emerged in literature is rational emotive PDMS (REPDMS). REPDMS activities involve athletes sharing experiences of applying rational emotive behaviour therapy (REBT) principles in life (see Turner & Barker, 2014). Athletes outline their irrational and rational beliefs about a life event before explaining how they applied cognitive restructuring (Turner & Davis, 2018). Preliminary research explored the effects of REPDMS on irrational and rational beliefs in 20 male adolescent athletes from sports including soccer and tennis (Vertopoulos & Turner, 2017). Athletes in condition 1 completed four REBT education workshops while athletes in condition 2 completed the same four REBT education workshops before an REPDMS activity. Further reductions in irrational beliefs and improvements in rational beliefs were reported following REPDMS which were beyond changes in irrational and rational beliefs reported by athletes who received REBT education only. Accordingly, Turner and Davis (2018) examined the effects of REPDMS versus ROPDMS (containing no REBT elements) following five REBT education workshops on the irrational beliefs and self-determined motivation of 23 triathletes. Both REPDMS and ROPDMS activities led to further increases in self-determined motivation, but neither REPDMS nor ROPDMS was effective at further reducing irrational beliefs. The authors explained that perhaps athletes experienced further distress when realising irrational beliefs were still present when recounting events during PDMS activities. Furthermore, the emotional intensity of PDMS activities may have been questionable due to the timing of their delivery (see Turner & Davis, 2018).

The final form of PDMS to also recently emerge in literature is coping-oriented PDMS (COPDMS), which was developed by Evans et al. (2019) for 18 male youth soccer academy athletes approaching a time where they would be awarded a professional contract or released from their soccer academy. During their COPDMS activity, athletes communicated demand and resource appraisals pertaining to transitional events based on theoretical postulations that the balance between demand and resource appraisals determines emotional, physiological, and performance outcomes (see the Theory of Challenge and Threat States in Athletes; Jones, Meijen, McCarthy, & Sheffield, 2009). Athlete insights into COPDMS outcomes indicated that COPDMS encouraged an approach focus for potential upcoming transitions, enhanced understanding of the self and others, increased self-confidence, and benefitted cognitive appraisal around being released or gaining a professional contract. It is important to note that not all athletes provided insights into COPDMS outcomes, meaning the effects of COPDMS are not yet fully established.

Ultimately, research suggests that PDMS activities can manipulate psychological variables aligned to the form of PDMS administered. For example, ROPDMS instructions used to guide personal stories (see Dunn & Holt, 2004) focus on facilitating group integration, relationships, and belongingness which would be anticipated to manipulate aligned group dynamic variables such as social identification and the value athletes place on friendships within groups or teams (see Barker et al., 2014). Alternatively, MOPDMS instructions require athletes to discuss past performance accomplishments while athletes receive verbal persuasion information and vicariously experience sporting success by listening to information and personal stories communicated by others (Barker et al.). Previous success, verbal persuasion, and vicarious experiences are sources of efficacy beliefs in athletes (see Bandura, 1997). That said, it is noteworthy that certain PDMS outcomes may be a product of undergoing the PDMS experience rather than participating in a particular form of PDMS. For example, enhanced understanding of the self and others has been found following both ROPDMS (Dunn & Holt, 2004; Holt & Dunn, 2006) and COPDMS activities (Evans et al., 2019). In sum, extant PDMS literature provides practitioners working in soccer with four forms of PDMS activities that could benefit athletes and/or teams depending on their needs. ROPDMS activities would appear beneficial for teams seeking to develop group-/team-level outcomes such as social identification while MOPDMS activities would appear beneficial for teams aiming to improve efficacy-related outcomes (e.g., collective efficacy). Although there is mixed evidence regarding the benefits of REPDMS for irrational beliefs, REPDMS (like ROPDMS) would seem beneficial for promoting self-determined motivation. Finally, athlete insights suggest that COPDMS may be beneficial for developing coping-related outcomes (e.g., an approach focus).

Practical Applications—Hypothetical Case Study

In this section, we provide background and contextual information about a hypothetical scenario of being approached by a head coach to provide psychological support to a soccer team. Accordingly, we present how we (as practitioners) addressed psychological issues raised during needs analyses through a PDMS intervention. We then explain how we evaluated the effectiveness and efficacy of our PDMS intervention and provide a synopsis of anticipated intervention outcomes. Finally, we present key reflections relating to our hypothetical use of PDMS.

Background and Context

The head coach of an English Premier League soccer academy club contacted us during the off-season to provide psychological support to an Under-18s team. The team comprised a squad of 18 athletes with all main positions in a soccer team represented (goalkeeper, defender, midfielder, and attacker). Initial discussions with the head coach revealed the team had recently recruited many talented athletes from across the world but had collectively underperformed in the previous two seasons. Moreover, when athletes had been confronted with challenging situations, they had often fallen short of their expectations and struggled to cope with performance demands. During further conversations, the head coach provided insight into the dynamics of the club, the performance environment, and the performance expectations of the club. The head coach informed us that we had eight weeks to work with the team during pre-season but would have no access to athletes outside or beyond our intervention due to competing athlete commitments. Due to demands on staff time at the club, the head coach also explained that we only had access to themselves as the head coach and their athletes.

Presenting Issue(s)

Before commencing our work, a needs analysis for the team was undertaken to outline key psychological areas for development. We determined the requirements for our work through a reflective meeting lasting around 90-minutes which we facilitated with the head coach and team captain (Pain & Harwood, 2009). During our reflective meeting, we explored the key psychological challenges the team were experiencing. To facilitate reflections, we raised awareness to the group by showing video-clips from the previous season of the team performing in highly pressurised situations and discussed the psychological factors impacting the team. Following the meeting, we reflected on what we heard and tried to make sense of the salient issues. During our practitioner reflections, we aimed to challenge our preconceptions and suggestions while being mindful of the need to be pragmatic in our postulations. Based on our group meeting and our practitioner reflections, a series of action points were generated to guide our work: (a) facilitate team identification among athletes, (b) allow team members to understand themselves and each other, (c) develop resilience, and (d) help athletes to cope with the demands of being a soccer academy athlete.

The Intervention/Work to Be Conducted

One method of addressing action points emanating from the needs analysis was to develop a dual-phased PDMS intervention programme incorporating ROPDMS and COPDMS activities (see Figure 8.1 for an overview). ROPDMS was used to facilitate team identification (see Evans et al., 2013), while COPDMS was used to develop coping (see Evans et al., 2019). By undergoing the PDMS experience, we anticipated that athletes would gain enhanced understanding of themselves and others (see Dunn & Holt, 2004; Holt & Dunn, 2006) and develop resilience. Previously, only Barker et al. (2014) have implemented a dual-phase PDMS intervention. Athletes in Barker et al.'s research explained that the second PDMS activity (MOPDMS) was effective but did not instigate the same intense benefits as the first PDMS activity (ROPDMS). Such

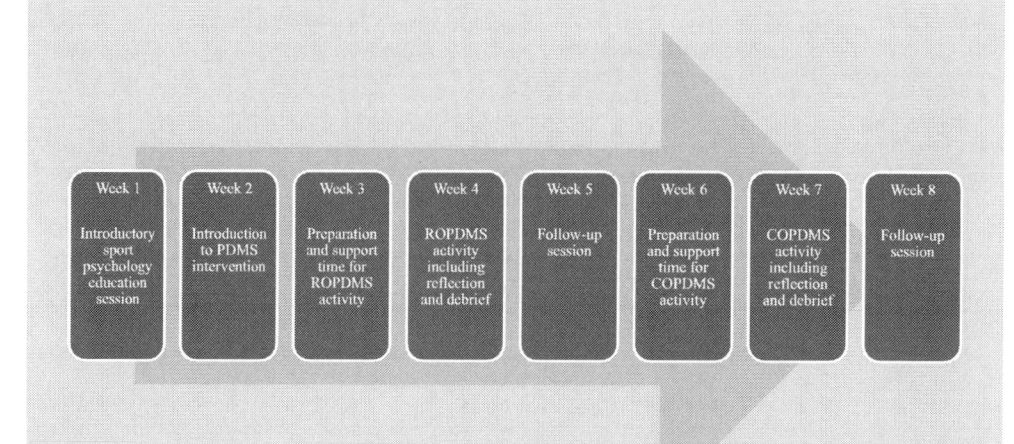

Week 1	Week 2	Week 3	Week 4	Week 5	Week 6	Week 7	Week 8
Introductory sport psychology education session	Introduction to PDMS intervention	Preparation and support time for ROPDMS activity	ROPDMS activity including reflection and debrief	Follow-up session	Preparation and support time for COPDMS activity	COPDMS activity including reflection and debrief	Follow-up session

FIGURE 8.1 Summary of our PDMS intervention programme

data suggest that athletes perhaps became somewhat desensitised to PDMS having undergone a previous and recent PDMS experience. We therefore separated our PDMS activities by a longer time frame while drastically altering the form of PDMS to ensure that our athletes could experience the same intense outcomes relevant to both forms of PDMS. Before implementing our intervention, we determined the suitability of using PDMS with our athletes (see Evans et al., 2019). Indeed, we could have opted to build team identification (for example) through an alternate activity such as identity mapping (see Haslam, Eggins, & Reynolds, 2003). During a follow-up meeting with the head coach and team captain, we therefore established our athletes' experiences of public speaking. Checking for potential public speaking anxiety was important because athletes can feel apprehensive about PDMS (see Barker et al.) while public speaking anxiety is common in youth populations (Furmack et al., 1999). The head coach explained that athletes completed weekly sessions aimed at personal development which involved athletes speaking in front of others. The team captain also explained that athletes had typically responded well to public speaking activities with little signs of resistance or distress. Based on such comments, we concluded that PDMS was suitable to base our intervention programme upon for our athlete case.

Our intervention programme was conducted over the full eight weeks of pre-season. Completing ROPDMS seemed appropriate during pre-season because a soccer team's structure typically changes due to athletes exiting and entering the team. Completing COPDMS also appeared suitable during pre-season because the team could develop resilience and coping prior to the season ahead. Our intervention programme comprised six structured sessions and two sessions used to support athletes which took place in the academy's education room, as this location was used frequently by our athletes for sports science support. We included the head coach in all structured sessions as he supported our work and presence at the club, which professional practice literature suggests would help us secure buy-in from team members

(Mellalieu, 2017). Involving the head coach also meant they could promote task engagement (see Evans et al., 2013) and provide insightful data to help evaluate our intervention programme.

In line with PDMS research, our intervention began with a 45-minute introductory sport psychology education session where we aimed to establish our presence, build some rapport with athletes, and discuss the role and importance of psychology in soccer (e.g., Evans et al., 2013). The following week, we delivered a 45-minute session to introduce PDMS to athletes, inform athletes about the nature of each PDMS activity, distribute ROPDMS instructions (see Figure 8.2), and agree on a PDMS contract (see Figure 8.3). PDMS contracts are important to establish because

Instruction 1: Describe a personal story/situation that will help your teammates understand you more.

Instruction 2: Tell the group why you play soccer and what you think you bring to the team.

Instruction 3: Detail a personal story that you would want everyone to know about you that would make them want you in the trench beside them before going over the top and into battle. Your story can be related to any event that took place in your personal or sporting life and should illustrate something that defines your character, motives, and desires.

FIGURE 8.2 ROPDMS instructions taken from Evans et al. (2013)

1. Respect and uphold confidentiality by not discussing information and/or personal stories with those individuals not included within PDMS activities.
2. Delivering information and/or personal stories is not a test and you will not be given preferential treatment or discriminated against at the academy based on what you decide or do not decide to share.
3. Answer all parts of the instructions to provide a detailed account of your thoughts, feelings, and experiences.
4. Be open and honest with your disclosures. There are no right or wrong answers and all that is required is that you detail information aligned to instructions administered.
5. Be professional at all times by respecting, listening, and attending to others when speaking.

FIGURE 8.3 PDMS contract agreed with athletes for our intervention

they highlight and promote key ethical and procedural elements that contribute to the potential success of PDMS interventions (Evans et al., 2019). Athletes were informed that the quality rather than the length of information and/or personal stories mutually shared during PDMS activities was of utmost importance to maximise empathetic understanding (Evans et al., 2013). Nevertheless, we were mindful that athletes may appreciate guidance on speaking time so we advised that our athletes spoke for between two and five minutes (see Barker et al., 2014; Vertopoulos & Turner, 2017). Athletes were then given one week to prepare information and/or personal stories aligned to ROPDMS instructions. Since athletes can feel apprehensive prior to PDMS activities (see Barker et al.), we followed Evans et al's. (2019) suggestion that each athlete should be provided with support ahead of their ROPDMS activity. For the ROPDMS activity, chairs were arranged in a semi-circle to promote openness (Dunn & Holt, 2004). As per PDMS guidelines (see Dunn & Holt, 2004; Windsor et al., 2011), athletes then took it in turns to stand at the front of the room and share information and/or personal stories. For the final part of the ROPDMS activity, we led a reflection on the main information mutually shared by athletes to draw together the key themes and messages emanating from athlete disclosures. Overall, the ROPDMS activity lasted around 75 minutes.

In week 5, we delivered a 45-minute follow-up session to the ROPDMS activity to provide athletes with further opportunity for reflection, to distribute COPDMS instructions (see Figure 8.4), and to reinforce our PDMS contract. Information communicated about the COPDMS procedure was consistent with information we provided ahead of our earlier ROPDMS activity. Likewise, athletes were again given one week to prepare for their COPDMS activity (and receive support), which was delivered in the same way as our earlier ROPDMS activity. The final follow-up session (circa 45 minutes) delivered as part of our intervention programme enabled athletes to further reflect on the COPDMS activity but also provided an opportunity for discussion around how athletes would use key messages emanating from the PDMS intervention programme for the season ahead.

Outcome Analysis

In keeping with PDMS research (e.g., Barker et al., 2014; Windsor et al., 2011), we determined the effectiveness of our intervention programme in a systematic manner. Yet working in a fluid environment can make it difficult to consistently and objectively determine change and effectiveness (Barker, McCarthy, Jones, & Moran, 2011). To evaluate the effectiveness of our programme, we tracked potential change in team identification, resilience, and coping throughout our PDMS intervention by using relevant quantitative measures. To measure team identification, we used a single-item measure ("To what extent do you feel you identify strongly with your team"; see Postmes, Haslam, & Jans, 2013) which was anchored on a seven-point Likert scale ranging from 1 (*not at all*) to 7 (*completely*). To measure resilience, we used the 25-item Five-by-Five Resilience Scale (5x5RS; Desimone, Harms, Vanhove, & Herian, 2017), which included five subscales (adaptability,

Instruction 1: As an academy soccer athlete you will encounter difficult scenarios or moments within your soccer career. Provide a brief account of some of the main difficult scenarios or moments you have encountered so far as a soccer athlete. What were the demands or challenges associated with these difficult scenarios or moments? How did you think, feel, and behave before, during, and after the scenarios or moments you have identified?

Instruction 2: Describe a difficult scenario or moment you have previously encountered within your soccer career that you did not deal with effectively. Explain the demands or challenges associated with this scenario or moment. Describe any factors (e.g., thoughts, feelings, or behaviors) that you feel contributed to you not dealing effectively with this scenario or moment.

Instruction 3: Describe a difficult scenario or moment you have previously encountered within your soccer career that you did deal with effectively. Explain the demands or challenges associated with this scenario or moment. Describe any factors (e.g., thoughts, feelings, or behaviors) that you feel contributed to you dealing effectively with this scenario or moment.

Instruction 4: What difficult scenarios or moments do you think you will encounter during the upcoming season? What have you learnt from those previously difficult scenarios or events you have discussed that could help you deal effectively with future difficult encounters?

FIGURE 8.4 COPDMS instructions adapted from Evans et al. (2019)

emotion regulation, optimism, self-efficacy, and social support), with each subscale including five items (e.g., self-efficacy: "I excel in what I do"). Items within the 5x5RS were anchored on a five-point Likert scale ranging from 1 (*very inaccurate*) to 5 (*very accurate*). Finally, to measure coping, we used the 18-item Coping Function Questionnaire for Adolescents in Sport (CFQ; Kowalski & Crocker, 2001), which included three subscales assessing problem-focused (six items: e.g., "I tried to find a way to change the situation"), emotion-focused (seven items: e.g., "I worked through my emotions in order to feel better"), and avoidance-focused (five items: e.g., "I tried to get away from the situation to reduce the stress") coping functions. Our instruction stem encouraged athletes to respond to items in relation to a recent stressful moment that had occurred in training or competition. Items within the CFQ were anchored on a five-point Likert scale ranging from 1 (*not at all*) to 5 (*very much*). As we evaluated our work through a quantitative lens, we drew on some key principles associated with single-case research methods (Barker et al., 2011). For example, we collected quantitative data at the beginning of our introductory sport psychology education session (baseline), immediately following the ROPDMS reflective component (post-ROPDMS), immediately following the COPDMS reflective component (post-COPDMS), and four weeks after the final follow-up session (maintenance).

Based on our rationales for using PDMS and previous PDMS research (e.g., Barker et al., 2014), we found that team identification significantly improved from baseline to post-ROPDMS (a medium to large effect), significantly improved from post-ROPDMS to post-COPDMS (a small effect), and then rescinded to baseline values from post-COPDMS to maintenance. Alternatively, we found that resilience significantly improved from baseline to post-ROPDMS (a medium to large effect), significantly improved from post-ROPDMS to post-COPDMS (a small effect), but then rescinded to baseline values from post-COPDMS to maintenance. Finally, we found that problem-focused and emotion-focused coping use remained unchanged from baseline to post-ROPDMS but significantly increased from post-ROPDMS to post-COPDMS (a medium to large effect) before rescinding to baseline from post-COPDMS to maintenance. Meanwhile, avoidance-coping use remained unchanged from baseline to post-ROPDMS but significantly reduced from post-ROPDMS to post-COPDMS (a medium to large effect) before rescinding to baseline from post-COPDMS to maintenance.

To further explore the efficacy of our work, we collected social validation data typical in PDMS research (e.g., Evans et al., 2013) using principles outlined in literature (see Page & Thelwell, 2013). Social validation is integral to intervention-based research because it informs researchers and practitioners about the delivery and effect of psychological interventions (Barker et al., 2011). We distributed a social validation questionnaire to athletes that was completed immediately after each PDMS activity to explore balanced athlete perceptions and feelings about the PDMS activities and procedures. The athlete social validation questionnaire included five open-ended questions: (1) How did you find preparing and delivering personal information and stories? (2) How did the PDMS activity make you feel before, during, and after the PDMS activity? (3) How do you think the PDMS activity has impacted and will impact you and your team? (4) How has the PDMS activity affected the way you view yourself and your teammates? (5) What have you learnt about yourself and your teammates as a product of doing the PDMS activity? We also distributed a social validation questionnaire to the head coach that was completed at the maintenance phase to explore their perceptions and feelings about the intervention activities and procedures. Including coach evaluations provided more detailed data regarding the efficacy of our work and helped us to determine whether the head coach who approached us for our service was satisfied with our intervention programme. The coach social validation questionnaire included five open-ended questions: (1) How did you find being involved in PDMS activities? (2) How do you think the PDMS activity has impacted and will impact your team? (3) How do you think the PDMS activity has benefitted you as a head coach? (4) How satisfied where you with the delivery of the PDMS intervention? (5) How successful do you feel the PDMS intervention was at tackling the issues you approached us to address? Example responses from athlete and coach social validation questions are presented in Tables 8.1 and 8.2.

TABLE 8.1 Example responses from the social validation questionnaires completed by athletes

Question	Responses
1	• It was difficult initially to know what to include within personal stories (post-ROPDMS). • It was difficult to know what to include within personal stories because the instructions had changed (post-COPDMS). • Increased confidence and feelings of being respected when delivering information because athletes listened and the environment was supportive (post-ROPDMS and post-COPDMS).
2	• Initially apprehension about whether athletes would take one another seriously (post-ROPDMS). • Feelings pleased with reactions from teammates when information and/or personal stories were being shared (post-ROPDMS and post-COPDMS). • Feeling relieved but proud after completing the session (post-ROPDMS and post-COPDMS). • Feeling calmer ahead of the PDMS session because it was known how athletes were likely to react (post-COPDMS).
3	• Increased belongingness to the team (post-ROPDMS and post-COPDMS). • Increased resilience when undergoing recent and future difficult experiences (post-ROPDMS and post-COPDMS). • Increased frequency of facing-up and confronting recent and future stressful situations (post-COPDMS).
4	• Increased understanding of the self and teammates because of the information and/or personal stories shared (post-ROPDMS and post-COPDMS).
5	• Learning about being similar and not that different to teammates (post-ROPDMS). • Learning that avoiding situations is generally ineffective and facing-up to overcoming problems and dealing with emotional consequences associated with stressful events is more effective (post-COPDMS).

Case-Study Reflections

As explained within our outcome analysis, our PDMS activities elicited short-term change in psychological variables. Indeed, Evans et al. (2013) found that certain psychological variables that significantly improved immediately following a ROP-DMS session returned to baseline values at follow-up and maintenance phases. Perhaps additional psychological interventions or further PDMS-related activities would need to be implemented following our PDMS intervention for the benefits of our PDMS sessions to be maintained over time. Within our hypothetical context, the head coach explained that we only had eight weeks to intervene with athletes. In such contexts, it would be advisable for practitioners to consider negotiating more time with athletes so additional interventions can be delivered to promote more long-lasting psychological change. Time restrictions associated with our hypothetical context also influenced our proposed methods for evaluating our intervention. Being granted limited access to athletes beyond our planned intervention meant that conducting semi-structured interviews or focus groups to evaluate our work was not viable. Finally, it would have been useful for us to have determined whether

TABLE 8.2 Example responses from the social validation questionnaires completed by the head coach

Question	Responses
1	• I felt comfortable with being involved in the PDMS sessions. • I was uncertain as to whether my involvement would cause some athletes to not speak or create fabricated stories.
2	• My athletes are motivated to achieve for the greater good of the team. • My athletes have been more resilient in training and matches. • My athletes have approached stressful scenarios and have tried to solve problems and deal with the emotional consequences.
3	• Being involved in PDMS sessions helped me understand my athletes more. • I have gained an understanding of my athletes that will help me tailor my support and coaching practice.
4	• I was satisfied with the delivery of the intervention. • The practitioners acted professionally and ethically at all times.
5	• I feel the intervention has been successful at producing an initial boost for the team. • I feel the intervention would benefit from continuing to work on action points identified in our initial discussions.

changes in psychological variables following PDMS sessions resulted in changes in team performance. However, in our context, athletes were only competing in ad hoc pre-season matches, which made it difficult to link psychological changes to potential performance change. The idea of linking psychological change to performance change continues to be an ongoing challenge for applied practitioner psychologists (Barker, Mellalieu, McCarthy, Jones, & Moran, 2013).

Attributing changes in psychological variables to our PDMS intervention is influenced by a range of threats to validity. For example, our intervention programme reflects a one-group pretest-posttest design with no control group, which is a typical design employed by PDMS researchers (e.g., Windsor et al., 2011). Additionally, changes in team identification (for example) could be caused by maturation effects as the team began to get to know each other outside of our PDMS intervention. Ruling out rival hypotheses in scenarios where practitioners have been approached to work with one group remains a significant challenge for applied psychology practitioners (e.g., Barker et al., 2014).

Based on social validation data (and our previous research and applied practice experiences), PDMS was an emotional experience for our athletes. For many athletes, PDMS activities serve as the first opportunity to share personal thoughts, feelings, and experiences with teammates, which appears therapeutic for athletes and has been suggested by researchers as contributing to driving PDMS benefits (Barker et al., 2014). We also found that PDMS was an emotional experience for us as practitioners. Although we are experienced at delivering PDMS interventions, we were taken aback when hearing athletes mutually share deeply personal and sometimes sensitive information. In our experiences, we find that athletes and practitioners are constantly surprised by the PDMS process and outcomes. For instance, while athletes can feel apprehensive prior to PDMS sessions (e.g., Barker et al.) or perceive PDMS to serve no purpose (Evans et al., 2019), athletes typically feel pleased with PDMS sessions following their completion and generally experience positive PDMS outcomes (e.g., Barker et al; Evans et al., 2013). Like any practitioner, it would never have been our intention to create any discomfort during our intervention programme. Nevertheless, practitioners should be aware that there is always the potential that athletes can experience discomfort or distress in relation to PDMS activities because of the nature of the PDMS experience and the sensitivity of information that might be shared. In such an event, we advise that practitioners refer distressed athletes to an appropriate professional (e.g., a club's Welfare Officer). Supporting athletes and implementing referral procedures are ethically important to help address any negative responses arising within PDMS interventions (see Evans et al., 2019).

We were concerned about the lack of rapport we had with our athletes prior to our intervention programme given that PDMS requires athletes to share previously unknown and potentially deeply personal and sensitive information and/or stories (Dunn & Holt, 2004). In particular, we felt it was important for our athletes to trust and respect us and our intervention so that they felt comfortable enough to engage with it and open-up to others, which was vital if athletes were to experience potential PDMS outcomes. Under conditions where rapport is difficult to build as a practitioner, it might be useful to include other individuals (e.g., coaches) who have rapport with athletes to help secure practitioner buy-in. Indeed, researchers have suggested that PDMS interventions can still be effective when rapport is limited between practitioners and athletes (Evans et al., 2019). This reflection in particular highlights that practitioners can deviate in their delivery of PDMS interventions and that such deviations are likely given variations in contextual factors and athlete needs that PDMS practitioners will encounter in applied settings (Evans et al., 2013).

Summary and Conclusions

During this chapter, we have provided a brief introduction into the potential value of PDMS in soccer, outlined theories, and reviewed research relating to the four forms of PDMS documented in applied sport psychology literature. We have also outlined our hypothetical use of a PDMS intervention programme with an academy soccer team at an English Premier League soccer club to provide an example of implementing key PDMS procedures and methods of evaluation as part of an intervention programme. Our hypothetical use of a PDMS intervention programme also provided key case-study reflections that highlight some prominent challenges, dilemmas, and solutions facing PDMS practitioners. To conclude, we would like to emphasise that practitioners should appraise the suitability of using PDMS before administering a PDMS intervention. Of equal importance, practitioners should ensure appropriate referral and support procedures are in place for the possibility that an athlete discloses information that is deeply personal, involves illegal acts, highlights physical or mental abuse, or compromises teammates. Accordingly, it is crucial that sport psychology practitioners create a safe environment for athletes to enable them to feel comfortable in the content of their speeches and their possible emotional reactions (Holt & Dunn, 2006; Steptoe, Barker, & Harwood, 2013). As practitioners, we may never know what athletes will say during a PDMS session, but we should be prepared for how we react to athlete disclosures.

Key Messages and Further Reading

1. Stemming from counselling settings, PDMS interventions involve athletes preparing and later sharing previously unknown information and/or personal stories to members of a group or team.
2. PDMS interventions are theorised to benefit psychological variables by providing athletes with greater empathetic understanding of one another and providing a safe and therapeutic environment where athletes give and receive social support.
3. PDMS was introduced into applied sport psychology literature as a team-building intervention, but research has since highlighted that PDMS can be used to address a diverse range of psychological needs. Specifically, the effects and athlete perceptions of participating in four forms of PDMS have been documented in applied sport psychology literature.
4. Researchers have commonly included a single PDMS activity as part of a PDMS intervention which appears to stimulate short-term but not long-term changes in psychological variables.
5. PDMS interventions are challenging to conduct as a practitioner and participate in as an athlete based on several contextual factors, meaning that the delivery of PDMS interventions can be flexible. That said, conducting initial needs analyses, determining PDMS suitability, introducing PDMS to athletes, administering a PDMS session, and implementing support and referral procedures should be consistent features of a PDMS intervention programme.

There are undoubtedly several other potentially useful applications and forms of PDMS than those documented in extant literature given the many psychological needs that athletes and teams can present (e.g., poor quality coach–athlete relationships) and the diverse range of topics (e.g., retirement) that athletes could talk about during PDMS activities. A key area for future research would therefore involve exploring other applications of PDMS or forms of PDMS yet to be developed and delivered to athlete populations. Practitioners would benefit from future researchers documenting their reflections of applying PDMS to new cases and delivering novel forms of PDMS to athlete groups. A common theme in extant literature has been for one group/team of athletes to participate in a PDMS intervention with quantitative and/or qualitative assessment methods taken to evaluate the effectiveness of the intervention (e.g., Evans et al., 2013). To overcome threats to validity, future researchers could adopt a single-case research design where the delivery of PDMS activities is staggered across multiple PDMS groups (see Evans et al., 2019). Alternatively, future researchers could use a crossover design by randomly assigning groups of athletes to a PDMS intervention or alternative intervention(s) which would enable the efficacy of PDMS against alternate intervention methods to be compared (see Evans et al., 2019). Recent research has used PDMS activities to elicit further changes in target psychological variables (e.g., Turner & Davis, 2018). Yet no research has explored how short-term changes in psychological variables stimulated by PDMS activities could be maintained or further developed through follow-up psychoeducation or intervention strategies. For example, Evans et al. (2019) could have delivered psychoeducation workshops following on from their COPDMS session to develop coping resources athletes communicated as being important for dealing with the prospect of being released from their soccer academy or being awarded with a professional contract.

Barker, J. B., Evans, A. L., Coffee, P., Slater, M. J., & McCarthy, P. J. (2014). Consulting on tour: A dual-phase Personal-Disclosure Mutual-Sharing intervention and group functioning in elite youth cricket. *The Sport Psychologist*, 28(2), 186–197. doi:10.1123/tsp.2013-0042

Dryden, W. (2006). *Counselling in a nutshell*. London: Sage Publications.

Dunn, J. G. H., & Holt, N. L. (2004). A qualitative investigation of a Personal-Disclosure Mutual-Sharing team building activity. *The Sport Psychologist*, *18*(4), 363–380. doi:10.1123/tsp.18.4.363

Evans, A. L., Morris, R., Barker, J. B., Johnson, T., Brenan, Z., & Warner, B. (2019). Athlete and practitioner insights regarding a novel Coping Oriented Personal-Disclosure Mutual-Sharing (COPDMS) intervention in youth soccer. *The Sport Psychologist*, *33*(1), 64–74. doi:10.1123/tsp.2017-0125

Evans, A. L., Slater, M. J., Turner, M. J., & Barker, J. B. (2013). Using Personal-Disclosure Mutual-Sharing to enhance group functioning in a professional soccer academy. *The Sport Psychologist*, *27*(3), 233–243. doi:10.1123/tsp.27.3.233

References

Bandura, A. (1997). *Self-efficacy: The exercise of control*. New York, NY: Freeman.

Barker, J. B., McCarthy, P. J., Jones, M. V., & Moran, A. (2011). *Single-case research methods in sport and exercise psychology*. London: Routledge.

Barker, J. B., Mellalieu, S. D., McCarthy, P. J., Jones, M. V., & Moran, A. (2013). A review of single-case research in sport psychology 1997–2012: Research trends and future directions. *Journal of Applied Sport Psychology*, *25*(1), 4–32. doi:10.1080/10413200.2012.709579

BBC Sport. (September 10, 2014). England: Wayne Rooney calls player meetings to help team gel. Retrieved from www.bbc.co.uk/sport/football/29138379

BBC Sport. (March 9, 2016). Theo Walcott reveals Arsenal's player-only meeting. Retrieved from www.bbc.co.uk/sport/football/35765289

Crace, R. K., & Hardy, C. J. (1997). Individual values in the team building process. *Journal of Applied Sport Psychology*, *9*(1), 41–60. doi:10.1080/10413209708415383

DeSimone, J. A., Harms, P. D., Vanhove, A. J., & Herian, M. N. (2017). Development and validation of the five-by-five resilience scale. *Assessment*, *24*(6), 778–797. doi:10.1177/1073191115625803

Evans, A. L., Slater, M. J., & Turner, M. J. (in press). Using Personal-Disclosure Mutual-Sharing with first year undergraduate students transitioning into higher education in England.

Furmack, T., Tillfors, M., Everz, P. O., Marteinsdottir, I., Gefvert, O., & Fredrikson, M. (1999). Social phobia in the general population: Prevalence and sociodemographic profile. *Social Psychiatry and Psychiatric Epidemiology*, *34*(8), 416–424. doi:10.1007/s001270050163

Haslam, S. A., Eggins, R. A., & Reynolds, K. J. (2003). The ASPIRe model: Actualizing social and personal identity resources to enhance organizational outcomes. *Journal of Occupational and Organizational Psychology*, *76*(1), 83–113. doi:10.1348/096317903321208907

Holt, N. L., & Dunn, J. G. H. (2006). Guidelines for delivering personal-disclosure mutual-sharing team building interventions. *The Sport Psychologist*, *20*(3), 348–367. doi:10.1123/tsp.20.3.348

Jones, M. V., Meijen, C., McCarthy, P. J., & Sheffield, D. (2009). A theory of challenge and threat states in athletes. *International Review of Sport and Exercise Psychology*, *2*(2), 161–180. doi:10.1080/17509840902829331

Kahler, K. (December 1, 2017). The crying hour: In an unorthodox team-building exercise, Bills players share their life stories. Retrieved from www.si.com/nfl/2017/12/01/buffalo-bills-sean-mcdermott-team-building-through-storytelling

Kowalski, K. C., & Crocker, P. R. E. (2001). Development and validation of the coping function questionnaire for adolescents in sport. *Journal of Sport & Exercise Psychology*, *23*(3), 136–155. doi:10.1123/jsep.23.2.136

Lazarus, R. S. (1999). *Stress and emotion: A new synthesis*. New York, NY: Springer Publishing Company.

Mellalieu, S. D. (2017). Sport psychology consulting in professional rugby union in the United Kingdom. *Journal of Sport Psychology in Action*, *8*(2), 109–120. doi:10.1080/21520704.2017.1299061

Olarte, S. W. (2003). Personal-disclosure revisited. *The Journal of the American Academy of Psychoanalysis and Dynamic Psychiatry*, *31*(4), 599–607. doi:10.1521/jaap.31.4.599.23003

Page, J., & Thelwell, R. (2013). The value of social validation in single-case methods in sport and exercise psychology. *Journal of Applied Sport Psychology*, *25*(1), 61–71. doi:10.1080/10413200.2012.663859

Pain, M., & Harwood, C. (2009). Team building through mutual-sharing and open discussion of team functioning. *The Sport Psychologist, 23*(4), 523–542. doi:10.1123.tsp.23.4.523

Postmes, T., Haslam, S. A., & Jans, L. (2013). A single-item measure of social identification: Reliability, validity, and utility. *British Journal of Social Psychology, 52*(4), 597–617. doi:10.1111/bjso.12006

Rogers, C. R. (1951). *Client-centered therapy: Its current practice, implications and theory*. London: Constable.

Steptoe, K., Barker, J. B., & Harwood, C. (2013). Enhancing the performance of individual athletes and teams: Considerations and challenges for the delivery of sport psychology services. In J. G. Cremades & L. S. Tashman (Eds.), *Becoming a sport, exercise, and performance psychology professional: A global perspective* (pp. 77–84). London: Psychology Press.

Turner, M. J., & Barker, J. B. (2014). Using Rational-Emotive Behavior Therapy with athletes. *The Sport Psychologist, 28*(1), 75–90. doi:10.1123/tsp.2013-0012

Turner, M. J., & Davis, H. S. (2018). Exploring the effects of rational emotive behavior therapy on the irrational beliefs and self-determined motivation of triathletes. *Journal of Applied Sport Psychology*. doi:10.1080/10413200.2018.1446472

Vertopoulos, E., & Turner, M. J. (2017). Examining the effectiveness of a rational emotive personal-disclosure mutual-sharing (REPDMS) intervention on the irrational beliefs and rational beliefs of Greek adolescent athletes. *The Sport Psychologist*. doi:10.1123/tsp.2016-0071

Windsor, P. M., Barker, J. B., & McCarthy, P. J. (2011). Doing sport psychology: Personal-disclosure mutual-sharing in professional soccer. *The Sport Psychologist, 25*(1), 94–114. doi:10.1123/tsp.25.1.94

Yukleson, D. (1997). Principles of effective team building interventions in sport: A direct services approach at Penn State University. *Journal of Applied Sport Psychology, 9*(1), 73–96. doi:10.1080/10413209708415385

9
THE ROLE OF PARENTS IN DEVELOPING ELITE SOCCER PLAYERS

Camilla J. Knight and Rachael A. Newport

Introduction and Literature Review

On 8 August 2017, *The Sun* (a tabloid newspaper in the United Kingdom) published an article entitled "'I want the mansion and car.' These lads want to be top footballers—and their mums are just as determined to score them a Premier League salary" (Culley & Walters, 2017). The article detailed the stories of four mothers, each of whom had an eight-year-old son who had signed with, or been scouted by, a soccer academy. Although each story varied slightly, the overall message was consistent; these mothers were committing extensively to ensuring their sons would achieve a professional contract in soccer so that they, as their mothers, would ultimately reap the (financial) rewards of success. Through their framing, Culley and Walters presented a particularly damming illustration of parental involvement in soccer, characterised by shouting from the sidelines, excessive expectations, and a required return on their investment.

As researchers and practitioners with years of experience working with parents and learning about parental involvement in various sports, including soccer, such articles are incredibly frustrating. Through our research and experience, we are acutely aware of the negative impact such stories have on general perceptions of soccer parents, the subsequent involvement (or lack thereof) of parents within their children's sporting lives, and the desire of coaches and organisations to engage and work with parents. The sharing of such stories, which we must remember represents the minority of parents, does untold damage to perceptions of youth soccer, parents, and, most critically, the experiences and development of young players.

For children to be able to participate in soccer, have opportunities to gain the range of physical, psychological, and social benefits associated with participation, and reach their potential, which for a small percentage (<2% of children) will be an elite level, it is advantageous for parents[1] to be involved (Harwood & Knight, 2015; Knight, Berrow, & Harwood, 2017). However, the ways in which parents are involved, as well as the support they received from coaches, clubs, academies, and psychology practitioners, will dictate the extent to which they can positively and optimally contribute to their child's soccer development (Clarke & Harwood, 2014; Knight & Newport, 2017). In this chapter we will provide insights into the role parents play in facilitating the development of elite players and the types of parental involvement that are associated with the most positive outcomes for players. Next, based on an accumulation of different experiences, we provide details of a hypothetical case regarding parental involvement in a soccer academy, along with reflections on an attempted intervention in the situation. Finally, we conclude by sharing some key messages that underpin our work with parents and which we hope will stimulate honest and valuable reflection among practitioners and coaches alike.

Parents' Experiences and Roles Within Soccer

On reading Culley and Walters' (2017) article through a different lens, one focused on understanding parents' experiences, it actually provides many useful insights into the sacrifices parents make to enable their children to participate in soccer. Such sacrifices are increasingly recognised by researchers and practitioners, who have realised that parenting children involved in sport is anything but easy or straightforward (e.g., Dorsch, Smith, & McDonough, 2015; Knight et al., 2017; Thrower, Harwood, & Spray, 2016). In fact, having a child involved in sport, particularly at more elite youth levels, can result in parents facing a range of demands and challenges, often ones they did not anticipate (e.g., Harwood, Drew, & Knight, 2010; Harwood & Knight, 2009a, 2009b).

For instance, Harwood, and colleagues (2010) conducted focus groups with parents of children involved in soccer academies and identified that parents experience stressors arising from numerous sources. These included watching their children compete; navigating certain academy processes (e.g., signing and release process); a lack of understanding and communication from the academy; time, financial, work, and family time sacrifices required to facilitate soccer involvement; and managing children's education alongside their soccer commitments. Extending this earlier work, Clarke and Harwood (2014) subsequently sought to gain an in-depth understanding of parents' early experiences within elite soccer academies. Such experiences were characterised by a transition period of socialisation, during which parents recognised their changing role in their child's soccer life, negotiated relationships with coaches, and navigated the, at times, difficult yet important parent–parent relationships. This period of transition could be challenging, particularly as parents experienced enhanced feelings of responsibility to ensure they were doing the best they could to facilitate their child's development while also protecting their child from potential negative experiences (such as sacrificing their social lives and being physically tired from training)

Despite such challenges, parents recognise a range of benefits, both for their child and themselves, associated with youth sport participation (e.g., Clarke & Harwood, 2014; Holt, Kingsley, Tink, & Scherer, 2011; Wiersma & Fifer, 2008). And, clearly, as is evidenced by the millions of children who participate in soccer around the world, parents continue to encourage and support their children's participation. Such encouragement and support for children's initial participation in soccer is perhaps the most important role parents play in the development of elite soccer players (cf. Harwood & Knight, 2015). Given the young age at which most children initiate their involvement, it is usually parents who make the decision to enrol children within soccer (e.g., Côté, 1999; Knight, Dorsch, Osai, Haderlie, & Sellars, 2016).

Having selected a programme, parents subsequently make the financial commitment to pay for sessions, uniforms, and equipment, as well as committing time to transporting children to training sessions and matches and ensuring children have access to appropriate nutrition (e.g., Baxter-Jones & Maffulli, 2003; Côté, 1999; Wolfenden & Holt, 2005). At this early stage in their soccer journey, children will also be heavily influenced by their parents' feedback, particularly in relation to the value of participating in soccer, competence levels, and expectations for success (Eccles & Harold, 1991; Wigfield & Eccles, 2000). This early feedback from parents, often based on their own beliefs, goals, and attitudes towards sport and sporting success (Eccles, Wigfield, & Schiefele, 1998; Knight et al., 2016), will be internalised by their child over time and subsequently continue to influence their perceptions as they progress into adolescence and potentially even adulthood (Eccles & Harold, 1991).

As children progress and increasingly commit their time and energy to soccer training and matches (i.e., enter the specialising stage of sport development; Côté & Hay, 2002), the required commitment from parents also increases. For instance, parents will increasingly provide tangible support in the form of time and money (Holt & Dunn, 2004; Gledhill & Harwood, 2014; Gledhill, Harwood, & Forsdyke, 2017). Such a commitment may come at the detriment to their own working, personal, or family life (Harwood & Knight, 2009a; Harwood et al., 2010). However, beyond tangible support, as children increase their involvement in training and competitions (and also start to negotiate the various transitions associated with adolescents such as changing schools and increasing importance of peer relationships; Wylleman & Lavallee, 2004) parents will be increasingly valuable sources of emotional support (Gledhill & Harwood, 2014; Holt & Dunn, 2004).

The most visible provision of emotional support is through the comments that parents make during and following matches—that is, the gestures, comments, and feedback parents display in response to their child's successful or unsuccessful performances (cf., Elliott & Drummond, 2017; Holt, Tamminen, Black, Sehn, & Wall, 2008). However, emotional support from parents is not limited to matches. Rather, emotional support from parents, particularly as players progress further along the elite pathway, is increasingly required to help players manage off-pitch issues such as team selections, injuries, contracts, and (dis)continuing education (cf., Holt & Dunn, 2004; Gledhill & Harwood, 2014; Knight, Harwood, & Sellars, 2018). The provision of emotional support can be particularly challenging for parents as they themselves are facing their own emotional rollercoster (cf. Harwood & Knight, 2015). Whether it's standing on the sidelines watching their child become frustrated and despondent during a poor performance or seeing their child's happiness following the renewal of a contract or a particularly good outcome, parents will empathise with their child and share their experiences vicariously (cf. Holt et al., 2008).

Parents often take a step back as coaches (as well as agents, peers, teammates, partners, etc.; Wylleman & Lavallee, 2004) become increasingly important in an elite player's life. However, the guidance parents provide relating to sport and broader life decisions will be substantial (cf. Holt & Dunn, 2004; Holt & Mitchell, 2006; Wolfenden & Holt, 2005), but it can be a source of stress for parents (Harwood & Knight, 2009a). Overall, it is important to remember that, within the current youth sport/soccer environment, children are very heavily reliant upon their parents to even be able to participate, and, thus, parents will *always* be involved in the journey.

Optimising Parental Involvement in Soccer

Although parents will always be involved in their child's soccer journey, the ways in which they are involved can vary substantially. In the previous section, we have detailed the basic roles parents fulfil to allow their children to participate and, hopefully, progress in soccer. However, effective sport parenting is far more complex and intricate than simply providing tangible and emotional support; it necessitates, for instance, parents successfully negotiating relationships with coaches and other parents, accurately reading and assessing their child's mood after matches and responding with appropriate comments, ensuring they adapt their involvement to their child's ever-changing needs, and managing the various emotional demands that are an inherent part of youth sport (Harwood & Knight, 2015; Knight et al., 2017). When parents are able to successfully manage these range of challenges, and most particularly remain involved in the ways that are desired by their individual child (Knight & Holt, 2014), they will be able to facilitate their children's sporting and psychosocial development (Knight et al., 2017).

In 2015, drawing on the literature available at the time, Harwood and Knight proposed six postulates of sport parenting expertise. Based on these postulates, as well as soccer-specific studies on each of these areas, it is possible to identify the types of involvement we many want to see and encourage from parents.

Select Appropriate Soccer Opportunities and Provide Appropriate Types of Support

As detailed previously, the selection of the "right" soccer programme—one that is developmentally appropriate, focused on fun and enjoyment and deliberate play rather than structured practice, among others (Côté & Hay, 2002; Keegan & Knight, 2017)—lays the pathway for all subsequent engagement in soccer (Gledhill et al., 2017). Such decisions are extremely important, and as a result, perhaps unsurprisingly, choosing programmes and providing support can become a stressor for parents (Harwood & Knight, 2009a). As practitioners we can play an important role both in helping parents to make these decisions and also in supporting coaches and clubs to create such developmentally appropriate opportunities available (cf., Keegan & Knight, 2017). Once developmentally appropriate opportunities have been selected, parents must also be supported to provide feedback to their children that aligns with this developmental approach (e.g., self-improvement and effort rather than winning; Gledhill et al., 2017). Unfortunately, the professionalised, win-focused youth sport culture, combined with parents' desires to protect their children and empathise with their disappointment, can impact on the types of comments and feedback parents provide (Dorsch, Smith, Wilson, & McDonough, 2015; Holt et al., 2008). Currently, many parents only learn what to say or do through trial and error (Burgess, Knight, & Mellalieu, 2016; Knight et al., 2016). Given the large impact parents have on children's earliest soccer experiences, providing parents with information and guidance regarding the types of comments and behaviours that may facilitate performance and psychosocial development early in their children's sporting journey is pertinent.

Adopt an Authoritative or Autonomy-Supportive Parenting Style

The influence parents have on their children is not limited to the opportunities they provide or the comments they make. Rather, the overall emotional climate that parents create (i.e., their parenting style) will also impact upon children's soccer development (cf., Holt et al., 2009; Knight & Holt, 2014). There is limited research in this area, and the research that is available must be considered with caution due to a lack of diversity in the research populations considered (Holt & Knight, 2014). Nevertheless, the research that is available indicates that adopting an autonomy-supportive or authoritative parenting style is most beneficial (Harwood & Knight, 2015). For instance, research by Sapieja, Dunn, and Holt (2011) indicated that authoritative parenting was associated with more "adaptive" styles of perfectionism. Such a parenting style is characterised by both high demands from parents and high levels of responsiveness and understanding (Darling & Steinberg, 1993). However, given the limited research in this area, it may be most beneficial for practitioners to adapt this suggestion and instead encourage parents to consider not only how their engagement with their children at competitions may be impacting upon their development but also the influence of their broader involvement in the home and around training.

Appropriately Manage the Emotions Experienced at Competitions

Watching children compete in youth soccer matches and competitions is emotional (Holt et al., 2008) and can be challenging (Harwood et al., 2010). Nevertheless, it is in such environments that parents are required to provide much of their emotional support to their children, and, as such, parents need to be able to manage their own emotions and respond appropriately to their children (Harwood & Knight, 2015). The management of such emotions is not an easy task for parents (cf. Harwood et al., 2010), and research within soccer has indicated that the emotions parents experience may be a contributing factor to negative or inappropriate comments from the sidelines (Holt et al., 2008). Recognising that their comments can negatively impact on their children, parents report concerns regarding the appropriateness of their sideline and post-match comments (particularly if their child is disappointed or perceives that they have performed poorly; Harwood & Knight, 2009a, 2009b; Tamminen, Poucher, & Povilaitis, 2017). Given such concerns, practitioners may find it useful to work with parents to help them understand the objectives of different matches, anticipate the emotions they may experience while watching, and help them develop their own coping strategies to use on the sidelines.

Develop Effective Relationships with Others in the Soccer Environment

When children engage in sport and subsequently enter a talent development pathway (i.e., a soccer academy or equivalent), they will interact with a growing number of individuals from coaches, physiotherapists, and sport scientists to teammates and other parents. Consequently, parents will also engage with these individuals and the extent to which they can develop open, honest, and effective relationships will impact not only on their experience but also their child's (cf. Gledhill & Harwood, 2014; Gledhill et al., 2017). As Clarke and Harwood (2014) identified, negotiating the distribution of power and responsibilities with coaches and forming friendships with, and managing cliques among, other parents are just two of the challenges parents may face here. Nevertheless, it is increasingly recognised that access to social support from within and beyond their family (cf., Burgess et al., 2016) as well as frequent communication with coaches (Knight & Holt, 2014; Knight & Newport, 2017) is necessary for parents to optimise their involvement. Through facilitating parent support networks and encouraging opportunities for parents and coaches to get to know each other and work together, practitioners play an important role here.

Cope with the Demands Associated with Youth Soccer

The demands that parents face when their children make a commitment to soccer are substantial and can impact upon parents' working and family life (Harwood et al., 2010). Such demands can result in feelings of pressure and stress, which may subsequently be translated into pressuring behaviours and high expectations (e.g., Dorsch et al., 2015; Knight et al., 2017). Unfortunately, if the youth soccer context remains as it currently is, it is unlikely that these demands are going to change. Thus, developing strategies to cope with these demands and prevent them from impacting on behaviours is important for parents. Practitioners can help here by providing opportunities for parents to learn from more experienced parents regarding the types of strategies that they have found useful (e.g., Burgess et al., 2016), teaching specific coping strategies, and also giving parents a clear picture of what is to come at the outset of their journey.

Change Involvement to Align with Their Child's Needs at Each Stage of Development

As outlined previously, the roles parents fulfil in their children's soccer careers change over time. When parents enter a soccer club or academy, they often do not know what to expect or what is expected of them (cf., Clarke & Harwood, 2014; Harwood et al., 2010). Consequently, parents will benefit from being provided information early and subsequently being supported through this transition (Knight & Newport, 2017), by, for instance, having opportunities to discuss their experiences with parents of older children. Supporting parents to understand and appreciate the challenges that talented youth soccer players experience may also help them to understand the increasing need for emotional support as their children progress. This is particularly true for older players as the demands of managing school work, pressure to perform, and maintaining social relationships increase (Elliott, Drummond, & Knight, 2018). Providing opportunities for parents to engage in constructive and honest conversations with their children regarding their goals, demands, and experiences can be particularly useful (cf., Knight & Holt, 2014).

Creating a Parent-Positive Culture in Soccer: A Case Study

As detailed above, there are types of parental involvement that are generally associated with more positive outcomes for children (Holt & Knight, 2014). However, based on our experiences, the ability of parents to engage in such manners and to demonstrate "optimal involvement" is largely influenced by the culture of clubs and academies in which parents and players are located. Specifically, the perception coaches have of parents is critical in producing, what we term, a "parent-positive" culture. Based on an accumulation of many different cases and experiences both within and beyond soccer, the following case study illustrates why such a parent-positive culture is important and how practitioners may go about helping to develop one.

Background and Context

We were working with a youth soccer team (aged 10 and under) to provide them with some basic psychological skills, as well as supporting parents to optimise their involvement. The team was made up of select players from across the region and, as is the case with most 10-year-old children, they all thought they had a chance of being a professional player. When their children were selected for this team, the children's parents were implicitly told that their children were better than others (i.e., those who had not been selected) and explicitly informed that their children were talented. The coaches, who were employed part-time with the team, sought to adopt a developmental approach to coaching and focus on the children's improvement, but they could not escape their own desire for their team to be successful and win.

A new season had started, with a number of new players joining the team. Included within this group was one player who has left his local club, where he was coached by his father and at which he had played for the last three years with his school friends. This player, and his parents, had now committed to travelling approximately an hour each way three times a week for training, as well as giving up approximately three weekends a month for matches and tournaments.

Presenting Issue(s)

A few weeks into the season the team were due to travel to a tournament some distance away and the coaches had requested that parents did not attend. This request was a result of some previous issues with parents being perceived to interfere at matches, as well as the coaches' desire for the children to begin to develop their independence. The parent of the player mentioned previously was extremely unhappy about this situation, perceiving that his son was too young to travel alone to a match without him and disappointed that he was going to miss one of his son's matches. The son was worried about the weekend and was not sure that he wanted to travel without his father. The father tried to speak to the coaches about the situation, but they did not want to engage with him. Consequently, the father decided that he would attend his son's match anyway, despite the coaches' request. On arrival at the tournament, the coaches realised that the father had attended and were extremely annoyed (to put it lightly!). As a consequence, they decided to limit the child's playing time and to subsequently review his place within the team.

Parent Perspective

The father was used to being a, if not the, key member of his child's soccer life. He had never missed a match and knew that his son liked him to be in attendance. He believed that 9 years old was too young for children to travel without their parents for matches, particularly given the importance of ensuring children have not only enjoyable but also safe sporting experiences, and he did not trust that the coaches would give his son the care and attention he was used to. As a parent he felt that he had a right to attend the match, particularly as he committed large amounts of time, money, and emotional energy to facilitating his son's soccer.

Coach Perspective

The coaches had been coaching young soccer players for many years and had spent a great deal of time deciding if the players were ready to attend a match without their parents. Based on their past experiences they were confident that the players would perform better without their parents in attendance as they would be less concerned about what they might say or think. They also thought it would be nice for the parents to have a weekend off from matches and could not understand why this father was making such a fuss. They were frustrated that this father was questioning their decision and doubting their ability as coaches. They felt they were wasting time dealing with this one "pushy" parent to the detriment of the rest of the team, because time spent responding to his emails was eating into their time to prepare sessions.

Player Perspective

The player was used to his father being present at matches, and he liked hearing his feedback. He and his father had worked out what types of comments helped him to perform better in matches, and he felt confident knowing his father was there to help. However, he was also excited at the thought of going away with his new friends, and he wanted to be the same as them, which meant no father in attendance. He also wanted to please his new coaches and did not want them and his father to argue.

The Intervention/Work Conducted

In response to this situation, the specific intervention conducted with the father, coach, and player focused upon three key activities:

- *Managing the coaches' frustrations and responses*: This comprised simply being available for the coaches to offload their frustrations regarding the situation. The coaches needed opportunities to vent to minimise the chance for their anger to impact on the team or the club more than it already had. After a few days, once the coaches had calmed down, informal conversations were held with the coaches to help them think through the possible consequences of different actions and to consider the impact of their decisions on the child. These meetings subtly and implicitly sought to help the coach see the situation from the parent and child's perspectives as well as their own. This informal approach was successful but did take time and required a relatively constant presence to prevent the coach from engaging in an action that was not thought through (e.g., angrily responding to the parent without due consideration).
- *Facilitating conflict resolution between the parent and the coach*: Formal meetings were organised between the coaches and the father, which were facilitated by us. These meetings sought to focus on the airing of grievances on both sides and an opportunity for both parties to share their perceptions of the situation. Ground rules regarding how parties should address each other, the importance of focusing only on this one situation, and a desire to come to a workable agreement for the future were implemented. Both the father and the coaches were encouraged *not* to discuss the situation with anyone else so as not to aggravate the situation further. However, it was clear that this was not adhered to by either party.
- *Talking with the player regarding his feelings about the situation*: Recognising the potential impact on the player, we wanted to arrange to meet formally with the player to discuss his feelings. However, the father was not keen on this because he was worried that it would focus negatively on his behaviour. Nevertheless, given the importance of ensuring the player was provided with appropriate support and an opportunity to share their feelings, we knew that we needed to work directly with him. Consequently, we took time to walk with the player to the pitch when he was training and tried to check-in through casual chats and "opportunistic" meets around the club. The player appeared to be coping well with the situation, but it was hard to get a true picture without formal meetings. However, we made it clear that the player could approach either of us at any time to share his feelings and that we would always have time to speak to him.

Although these steps were all necessary to address short-term issues, it quickly became clear that if longer-term changes and interventions were not introduced, this or similar situations would occur repeatedly. This was particularly apparent because, through our conversations with the coaches, it became clear that they had little time or respect for parents, highlighting them as a challenge or issue to be managed. They shared numerous negative stories about problem parents and, although implying they were joking, frequently talked about how nice it would be to coach a team without parents. The coaches indicated that this feeling was shared throughout the club. At the same time, it became clear from talking with the father that parents did not feel that they were valued or welcomed within the club. They thought that the coaches should have been more open to their opinions and knowledge, particularly in relation to their own children and that the club did not recognise the sacrifices that they made. Given these concerns, we believed that a more substantial culture change was needed, but we also recognised that this would require substantial time. To begin to facilitate a culture change, we engaged in numerous steps, including:

- Ensuring we always talked positively about parents, highlighting why their involvement was important, and subtly reminding coaches that parents were a part of the broader team.
- Having informal conversations with coaches regarding the amount of time they felt they "wasted" with parents when issues arose to encourage them to see that time spent early on talking with parents might ultimately save them time in the future.
- Actively challenged coaches when they engaged in "parent-bashing" (i.e., listing all the issues parents were creating) and encouraged them to consider the cause of the issues.
- Facilitating opportunities for parents and coaches to get to know each other and learn about the demands that both parties face within their roles.
- Sought every opportunity to speak with parents so that they knew there was someone within the environment they could speak with and who valued their thoughts and opinions.
- Reinforced to parents and coaches, at every opportunity, why they needed to work together to enhance children's soccer development and also ensure children were enjoying their soccer in a physically and psychologically safe environment.

Key Messages and Further Reading

As a result of our years working with parents, coaches, and organisations, we have learnt (and continue to learn) many things regarding how to produce a parent-positive culture. Our five key messages are:

1. **Language matters:** In our experience, the first step to changing attitudes and approaches to parents is to change the language that is used. For instance, *dealing with* or *managing* parents implies that parents are a challenge that must be overcome or a problem to minimise, while *working* with parents recognises parents as valuable contributors to children's soccer experiences and part of the broader team supporting children. Reflecting on the language used to

frame parental involvement (i.e., does it imply parents are detrimental or positive contributors) will quite quickly provide insights into the type of culture being created in relation to parents.

Further reading: Knight, C. J., & Newport, R. A. (2017). Understanding and working with parents of young athletes. In C. J. Knight, C. G. Harwood & D. Gould (Eds.), *Sport psychology for young athletes* (pp. 303–314). Abingdon, Oxon: Routledge.

2. **Focus on the small things:** We all respond more positively and with greater enthusiasm when we feel valued and welcome. Parents commit extensive amounts of time, money, and emotional energy to enabling their children to participate in sport, and it often comes at the detriment to their own working, social, and family lives. Small tokens of appreciation or recognition, such as thanking parents for bringing children to training and matches, asking for parents' feedback, and including parents within discussions about changes in the club, are simple ways of showing parents that you appreciate their sacrifices. When we truly acknowledge and value parents' involvement, they are much more likely to buy-in to and support the activities of coaches, clubs, and academies.

Further reading: Clarke, N. J., & Harwood, C. G. (2014). Parenting experiences in elite youth football: A phenomenological study. *Psychology of Sport and Exercise, 15*, 528–537.

3. **Early engagement is key:** It is easy to assume that parents will know what to expect and what is expected of them, but this is not always the case—particularly if parents have not played soccer themselves. Committing time early in the season to get to know parents, explain the club and coaching philosophies, and outline roles and expectations for the season ensures that everyone involved in players' lives are starting from the same place. Time committed up front to develop effective relationships with parents will pay dividends as the season progresses.

Further reading: Knight, C. J., & Gould, D. (2016). The coach-parent interaction: support or distraction? In R. Thelwell, C. Harwood & I. Greenlees (Eds.), *The psychology of sports coaching: Research and practice* (pp. 84–98). Abingdon, Oxon: Routledge.

4. **Encourage continual communication:** Although early communication with parents is key, this alone will be insufficient. For parents to be able to most effectively support and facilitate their child's development, it is important to encourage and provide opportunities for regular communication between parents and coaches and also between parents and their child(ren). The more parents and coaches can communicate, the more consistency there is likely to be in the messages that are transmitted to players. For instance, letting parents know what children have been working on or what their goals are for a match will enable parents to tailor their feedback appropriately. Similarly, regular conversations between parents and children regarding, for instance, goals for the season and perceptions of parents' behaviours will ensure parents can make any necessary changes to their involvement before it causes any issues.

Further reading: Clarke, N. J., Harwood, C. G., & Cushion, C. J. (2016). A phenomenological interpretation of the parent-child relationship in elite youth football. *Sport, Exercise, and Performance Psychology, 5*, 125–143.

5. **Promote peer-to-peer support among parents**: Supporting children in soccer, particularly those on an elite pathway, can be very demanding for parents. Moreover, being in

competitive sport environments can change how parents think, feel, and behave. Encouraging parents to draw on each other for tangible support (i.e., lift sharing), informational support (e.g., key training and match information), and emotional support (e.g., when a player is injured or struggling to perform) will help parents to manage the varying demands they face and also remind them that they are not alone on this journey.

Further reading: Dorsch, T. E., Smith, A. L., & McDonough, M. H. (2015). Early socialization of parents through organized youth sport. *Sport, Exercise, and Performance Psychology, 4*, 3–18.

Conclusion

Parents have an important role to play in the development of elite soccer players. Parents experience the highs, lows, and challenges alongside their child and learn along the journey with them. They are there for children to celebrate the exciting moments, but also to pick up the pieces when setbacks occur. However, for parents to be able to provide optimal support, they need to be supported in a culture that values their role. The environment should appreciate the demands and challenges parents encounter, while encouraging them to provide support that meets the needs of their child.

Note

1 Throughout this chapter the term "parents" is used to account for parents, step-parents, guardians, and carers.

References

Baxter-Jones, A. D., & Maffulli, N. (2003). Parental influence on sport participation in elite young athletes. *Journal of Sports Medicine and Physical Fitness, 43*, 250–255.

Burgess, N. S., Knight, C. J., & Mellalieu, S. D. (2016). Parental stress and coping in elite youth gymnastics: An interpretative phenomenological analysis. *Qualitative Research in Sport, Exercise, and Health, 8*, 237–256.

Côté, J (1999). The influence of the family in the development of talent in sport. *The Sport Psychologist, 13*(4), 395–417.

Côté, J., & Hay, J. (2002). Children's involvement in sport: A developmental perspective. In J. M. Silva & D. E. Stevens (Eds.), *Psychological foundations of sport* (pp. 484–502). Boston, MA: Allyn & Bacon.

Culley, G., & Walters, I. (2017). I want the mansion and car: These lads want to be top footballers - and their mums are just as determined to score them a Premier League salary. Retrieved from www.thesun.co.uk/living/4200882/mums-sons-footballer-premier-league-salary/

Darling, N., & Steinberg, L. (1993). Parenting style as context: An integrative model. *Psychological Bulletin, 113*(3), 487–496.

Dorsch, T. E., Smith, A. L., & McDonough, M. H. (2015). Early socialization of parents through organized youth sport. *Sport, Exercise, and Performance Psychology, 4*(1), 3–18.

Eccles, J. S., & Harold, R. D. (1991). Gender differences in sport involvement: Applying the Eccles' expectancy-value model. *Journal of Applied Sport Psychology, 3*, 7–35.

Eccles, J. S., Wigfield, A., & Schiefele, U. (1998). Motivation. In N. Eisenberg (Ed.), *Handbook of child psychology* (Vol. 3, 5th ed., pp. 1017–1095). New York, NY: John Wiley & Sons.

Elliott, S. K., & Drummond, M. J. N. (2017). During play, the break, and the drive home: The meaning of parental verbal behavior in youth sport. *Leisure Studies, 36*(5), 645–656.

Elliott, S. K., Drummond, M. J. N., & Knight, C. J. (2018). The experiences of being a talented youth athlete: Lesson for parents. *Journal of Applied Sport Psychology*, 1–19.

Gledhill, A., & Harwood, C. G. (2014). Developmental experiences of elite female youth soccer players. *International Journal of Sport and Exercise Psychology, 12*, 150–165.

Gledhill, A., Harwood, C. G., & Forsdyke, D. (2017). Psychosocial factors associated with talent development in football: A systematic review. *Psychology of Sport and Exercise, 31,* 93–112.

Harwood, C. G., Drew, A., & Knight, C. J. (2010). Parental stressors in professional youth football academies: A qualitative investigation of specialising stage parents. *Qualitative Research in Sport and Exercise, 2,* 39–55.

Harwood, C. G., & Knight, C. J. (2009a). Stress in youth sport: A developmental investigation of tennis parents. *Psychology of Sport and Exercise, 10,* 447–456.

Harwood, C. G., & Knight, C. J. (2009b). Understanding parental stressors: An investigation of British tennis-parents. *Journal of Sports Sciences, 27,* 339–351.

Harwood, C. G., & Knight, C. J. (2015). Parenting in youth sport: A position paper on parenting expertise. *Psychology of Sport & Exercise, 16,* 24–35.

Holt, N. L., & Dunn, J. G. H. (2004). Toward a grounded theory of the psychosocial competencies and environmental conditions associated with soccer success. *Journal of Applied Sport Psychology, 3*(1), 99–219.

Holt, N. L., Kingsley, B. C., Tink, L. N., & Scherer, J. (2011). Benefits and challenges associated with sport participation by children and parents from low-income families. *Psychology of Sport and Exercise, 12,* 490–499.

Holt, N. L., & Mitchell, T. (2006). Talent development in English professional soccer. *International Journal of Sport Psychology, 3,* 77–98.

Holt, N. L., Tamminen, K. A., Black, D. E., Mandigo, J. L., & Fox, K. R. (2009). Youth sport parenting styles and practices. *Journal of Sport & Exercise, Psychology, 3,* 37–59.

Holt, N. L., Tamminen, K. A., Black, D. E., Sehn, Z. L., & Wall, M. P. (2008). Parental involvement in competitive youth sport settings. *Psychology of Sport and Exercise, 9,* 663–685.

Keegan, R. J., & Knight, C. J. (2017). Initiating involvement and building foundations for the future: Sampling, physical literacy, and intrinsic motivation. In C. J. Knight, C. G. Harwood & D. Gould (Eds.), *Sport psychology for young athletes* (pp. 57–76). Abingdon, Oxon: Routledge.

Knight, C. J., Dorsch, T. E., Osai, K. V., Haderlie, K. L., & Sellars, P. A. (2016). Parents' experiences, expectations, and involvement in organized youth sport. *Sport, Exercise, and Performance Psychology, 5,* 161–178.

Knight, C. J., Harwood, C. G., & Berrow, S. R. (2017). Parenting in sport. *Current Opinion in Psychology, 16,* 93–97.

Knight, C. J., Harwood, C. G., & Sellars, P. A. (2018). Supporting adolescent athletes' dual careers: The role of an athlete's social support network. *Psychology of Sport and Exercise, 38,* 137–147.

Knight, C. J., & Holt, N. L. (2014). Parenting in youth tennis: Understanding and enhancing children's experiences. *Psychology of Sport and Exercise, 15,* 155–164.

Knight, C. J., & Newport, R. A. (2017). Understanding and working with parents of young athletes. In C. J. Knight, C. G. Harwood, & D. Gould (Eds.), *Sport psychology for young athletes* (pp. 303–314). Abingdon, Oxon: Routledge.

Sapieja, K. M., Dunn, J. G. H., & Holt, N. L. (2011). Perfectionism and perceptions of parenting styles in male youth soccer. *Journal of Sport & Exercise Psychology, 33,* 20–39.

Tamminen, K. A., Poucher, Z. A., & Povilaitis, V. (2017). The car ride home: An interpretive examination of parent-athlete sport conversations. *Sport, Exercise, and Performance Psychology,* 1–15.

Thrower, S. N., Harwood, C. G., & Spray, C. M. (2016). Educating and supporting tennis parents: A grounded theory of parents' needs during childhood and early adolescence. *Sport, Exercise, and Performance Psychology, 5,* 107–124.

Wiersma, L. D., & Fifer, A. M. (2008). The schedule has been tough but we think it's worth it: The joys, challenges, and recommendations of youth sport parents. *Journal of Leisure Research, 40,* 505–530.

Wigfield, A., & Eccles, J. S. (2000). Expectancy-value theory of achievement motivation. *Contemporary Educational Psychology, 1,* 68–81.

Wolfenden, L. E., & Holt, N. L. (2005). Talent development in elite junior tennis: Perceptions of players, parents, and coaches. *Journal of Applied Sport Psychology, 17,* 108–126.

Wylleman, P., & Lavallee, D. (2004). A developmental perspective on transitions faced by Athletes. In M. R. Weiss (Ed.), *Developmental sport and exercise psychology: A lifespan perspective* (pp. 503–523). Morgantown, WV: Fitness Information Technology.

10
ENHANCING COACHING EFFICACY IN YOUTH SOCCER

Richard Anderson and Chris G. Harwood

Introduction

A youth academy coach discussed how the intentional application of psychology-related coaching behaviour aided his confidence (taken from Harwood, 2008, p. 126):

> It's the fact that you are actually initiating a child to specifically improve their commitment, or communication, or concentration etc that was different. The kids are actually doing some of this stuff already, but you don't recognize it or appreciate it naturally. Just an actual recognition that you are working on commitment makes a difference. We can now apply the strategies that will help that quality in a session.

Today's soccer coaches are faced with an ever more complex set of responsibilities as they work to effectively nurture the future players of tomorrow. Whereas coaches may have placed a primary focus on developing and fostering young players' physical, technical, and tactical development (Richardson, Relvas, & Littlewood, 2013), they now need to consider the complete interaction between the whole player, the task, and the environment for effective talent development (e.g., Hackfort, 2006; Martindale, Collins, & Daubney, 2005; Wylleman & Lavallee, 2004). Coaches are being challenged to carefully consider maximising personal development experiences in young soccer players, one element of which is nurturing the psychological and social qualities most associated with performance enhancement (Johnston, Harwood, & Minniti, 2013; Holt & Dunn, 2004).

As the psychological and social processes of talent development and the training of positive developmental outcomes for young athletes continue to receive wide attention from researchers (e.g., Harwood, 2008; Harwood, Barker, & Anderson, 2015; MacNamara, Button, & Collins, 2010), so does the need to support and educate youth coaches. To achieve these outcomes requires a coach to possess an extensive degree of confidence in their coaching ability: an intrapersonal concept referred to as coaching efficacy (Feltz, Chase, Moritz, & Sullivan, 1999). It is therefore vital that to build this specific coaching efficacy, the sport psychologist practitioner and coach become valuable allies to one another if they are to positively shape a youth player's psychosocial responses and behaviours.

Coaches are often highly influential in shaping the thoughts, feelings, and behaviours of their players. While they form only part of an ever increasingly complex social-environmental system (Bronfenbrenner, 1999), the sport-specific time, credibility, and respect that they have built with their players best positions them to deliver and reinforce key psychological messages (Harwood & Johnston, 2016).

With this in mind, our chapter focuses on how sport psychology practitioners who work alongside coaches might support and help to develop coaching efficacy through the application of psychological principles in soccer. We first examine the current literature to identify the antecedents and outcomes of coaching efficacy, before discussing applied research in this area, specifically conducted within soccer. Following on from this we present a case-study intervention conducted within a professional soccer club youth academy, whereby the first author worked with the coaches to enhance their confidence in influencing key psychosocial factors associated with player development. Finally, we will draw the chapter together with our reflections and conclusions before summarising the key messages that we present within this chapter.

Review of Literature

The concept of coaching efficacy has been defined as the extent to which coaches believe they have the capacity to influence the learning and performance of their athletes (Feltz et al., 1999). Traditionally, the construct of coaching efficacy has been multidimensional, consisting of technique, motivation, game strategy, character building "efficacies," and assessed via the coaching efficacy scale (CES; Feltz et al., 1999). In a subsequent revision of the CES for use with high school team sports, Myers, Feltz, Chase, Reckase, and Hancock (2008) introduced a fifth dimension and subscale of physical conditioning "efficacy."

Research on coaching efficacy has often sought to explain how these dimensions of coaching efficacy information influenced beliefs which, in turn, predict coach, athlete, and team outcomes (see Figure 10.1). Coaching experience or preparation, prior success, the perceived skill of athletes and social support from parents, administrators, and the community have also been posited as antecedents of coaching efficacy beliefs (Chase & Martin, 2012).

Several studies have explored the impact of coaches' engagement in coach education programmes on coaching efficacy beliefs. For example, Malete and Feltz (2000) noted positive

Sources of coaching efficacy information	Coaching efficacy dimensions	Outcomes
• Extent of coaching experience/preparation • Prior success (win/loss record) • Perceived skill level of the athletes • School/community support	• Game strategy • Motivation • Technique • Character building	• Coaching behaviour • Player/team satisfaction • Player/team performance • Player/team efficacy

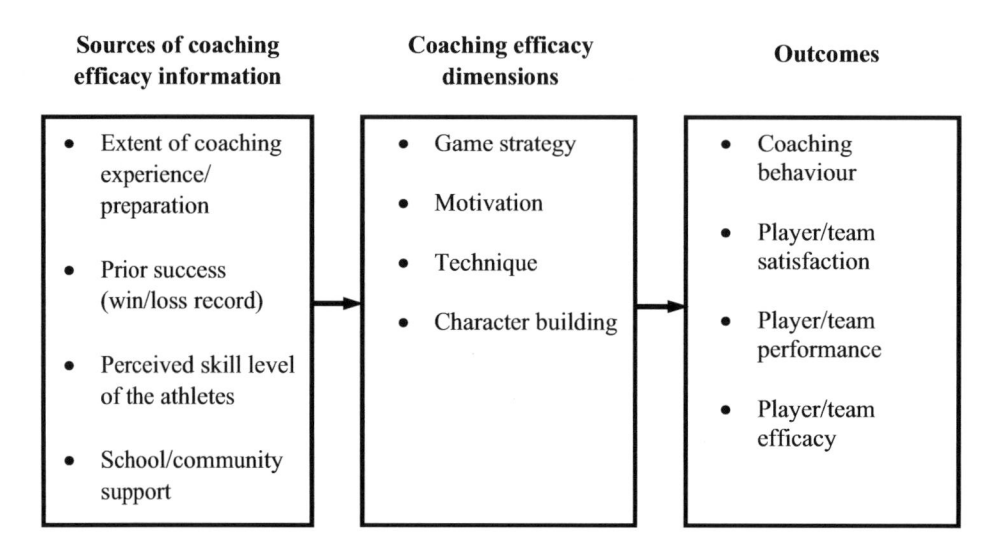

FIGURE 10.1 Feltz and colleagues' (1999) conceptual model of coaching efficacy

differences in coaching efficacy between those coaches who participated in a short-term coach education programme compared to non-participants. The greatest gains were observed in game strategy and technique efficacy. Coaches in the experimental group attended two six-hour educational sessions, one week apart, through the Program for Athletic Coach Education (PACE; Seefeldt & Brown, 1990). These sessions included attention to the role of the coach in respect to motivational, psychological, and social skills and reinforcing the benefits of structured coach education programmes on perceived efficacy levels.

Similar findings have emerged when examining groups of certified coaches versus non-certified coaches (Lee, Malete, & Feltz, 2002; Campbell & Sullivan, 2005; Malete & Sullivan, 2009). Research has also been generally supportive of a positive relationship between experience (years of coaching) and coaching efficacy (Fung, 2002). For example, Marback, S. E. Short, M. W. Short, and Sullivan (2005) noted the influence of experience on the efficacy beliefs of coaches across several individual and team sports. Specifically, they found that greater coaching experience significantly corresponded to higher motivation, game strategy, and character-building efficacies.

Further research has examined the influence of coaching efficacy beliefs on coach and athlete outcomes. Examples of such outcomes include leadership style (coaching behaviour), player and/or team satisfaction and performance, as well as player and team efficacy beliefs. Collectively, the findings here suggest that where coaches are more confident in their roles as educators and motivators, the more they engage in behaviours that are closer to their perceived ideal leadership style, with respect to the amount of praise and encouragement and appropriate levels of training and instruction (Smith, Smoll, & Hunt, 1977; Sullivan & Kent, 2003).

Greater perceptions of athlete and team satisfaction have been reported in response to coaches who reported higher coaching efficacy levels (Myers, Vargas-Tonsing, & Feltz, 2005). This relationship appears to hold for team performance with respect to links between higher coaching efficacy and better team results. Myers and colleagues (2005) also noted how the efficacy dimensions of motivation and character building were mostly associated with higher winning records, while also predicting athlete's perceptions of team efficacy (Vargas-Tonsing, Warners, & Feltz, 2003).

More recent research conducted by Boardley, Kavussanu, and Ring (2008) using a modified version of the CES indicated several key relationships between the original four efficacy dimensions and athlete outcomes. Specifically, they reported that athletes' evaluations of their coach's motivation effectiveness predicted athlete effort, commitment, and enjoyment; their perceptions of their coach's technique effectiveness predicted their own levels of self-efficacy; and their evaluation of the coach's character-building effectiveness predicted their own self-reported prosocial behaviour. Therefore, it is important that coaches are made aware of their potentially influential role on these key aspects of athletes' psychological functioning and understand that through their behaviour they can substantially affect the quality of the athletic experience.

Taken in their entirety, the implications are that coaches need to invest time on building their experiences, while reinforcing the important role of motivation, technique, and character-building efficacy. Further, where coaches (or athletes) possess the belief in their ability to influence athletes in positive psychological and social manners, positive athlete/team perceptions, experiences, and outcomes may follow. Practitioners can support this process through well-structured and informative coach education programmes.

Coaching Efficacy From a Psychological and Social Perspective

The vast majority of coaching efficacy research focused on the coaching efficacy model has been quantitative and cross-sectional in nature with a focus on examining model predictions and improving measurement scales for specific sport populations (e.g., Myers, Chase, Pierce, & Martin, 2011; Myers et al., 2008). There still remains limited field-based intervention research that targets situation-specific confidence in integrating particular skills or influencing specific athlete behaviours, responses, or outcomes in training sessions.

One such specific coaching efficacy lies in a coach's development of psychological and social (or psychosocial) factors, qualities, or characteristics in their athletes (e.g., *commitment*, Holt and Dunn, 2004; *character*, Lerner, Fisher, & Weinberg, 2000; *emotional control*, Harwood, 2008). The term "psychosocial" can be defined as pertaining to the interrelation of individual psychological characteristics with social influences and to the ways in which these may shape or guide behaviours (Gledhill, Harwood, & Forsdyke, 2017).

Research conducted by Holt and Dunn (2004), among others, offers support to the idea that psychosocial factors can differentiate between performance levels in soccer or are positively associated with career progression to a senior elite level. They identified commitment, resilience, and discipline as psychosocial competencies and social support as a key environmental condition. These assets are thought to play protective, enhancing, and resilience-based roles. Arguably, it is important for coaches to support and nurture these competencies in order to successfully aid a young player's transition through an academy soccer setting, targeting them at early stages of development.

Longitudinal fieldwork is also lacking whereby interventions track improvements in coaching efficacy over time as a result of ongoing education, support, practice, and self-reflection. The limitation of a short, intensive bout of formal education has been acknowledged by Malete and Feltz (2000), who proposed that

> a longer program could have greater effects . . . and could also include more time for mastery experiences for coaches, where they could have opportunities for practicing positive feedback techniques, effective instruction of a skill, or maintaining control during a simulated practice.
>
> *(p. 416)*

Steptoe, King, and Harwood (2019) described the steps they took in developing a programme aimed at supporting the development of psychosocial assets in young soccer players within a professional academy over three seasons. They noted at the beginning of the process how there was an incongruence between the perceived importance of psychological competencies and coach, or player, engagement in specific long-term psychological training programmes. Coaches noted the value of psychological skills in being able to achieve high performance in soccer but appeared unable to operationalise knowledge about psychological performance in a meaningful way that affected positive change within their youth players.

Gould, Damarjian, and Medbery's (1999) research presented evidence as to why coaches weren't integrating mental skills effectively with their players. In the context of tennis, the coaches noted insufficient content information, salience, and knowledge of psychological skills, as well as a lack of user-friendly examples and limited concrete, hands-on resources. In essence, they disclosed their discomfort with the process of integrating psychology without having a clear knowledge base and tools to apply the discipline confidently within their coaching. Therefore, while it can be seen that coaches often acknowledge the important role psychological development plays, they often require a systematic structure that is empowering in terms of content, strong on user-friendly ideas, and high on consultant support.

Research by Harwood (2008) supports the utility of promoting longitudinal adaptive training and supportive environments through education programmes in successfully increasing coach efficacy in the development of players' psychosocial competencies. Based on a 5Cs framework, the programme targeted ways that a group of professional soccer academy coaches could shape positive psychosocial responses in players (i.e., commitment, communication, concentration, (emotional) control, and confidence). Drawing from the PYD literature (see Schulman & Davies, 2007; Holt, Deal, & Smyth, 2016; Harwood & Johnston, 2016), each C was introduced in separate 90-minute coach workshops where awareness was raised around core theoretical principles and involved coach-led discussion on the coaching strategies and interactions that would help the player to demonstrate and develop the player-related behaviours and responses that coaches agreed were positive representations of each C (e.g., effortful persistence after setbacks indicative of *Commitment*).

Following each workshop, coaches then practiced the application of these coaching strategies in normal training sessions with their players. After five sessions, coaches' levels of efficacy in influencing players' 5Cs were reassessed prior to commencing the educational workshop on the next C in the series. This cycle of education–application–evaluation continued until the principles, practices, and behaviours associated with each C had been covered.

Harwood's (2008) findings demonstrated gains in coaching efficacy across all coaches, which were also associated with corresponding elevations in perceived squad behaviour around the 5Cs. In particular, "commitment" and "communication" coaching were seen as particularly influential on the confidence of coaches. In addition, the influence of C-related education and practice wasn't limited solely to the target C, and crossover effects across the Cs were evident. Captured social validation data did, however, indicate some coach's uncertainty in implementing more advanced psychological skill techniques (i.e., attentional and emotional control techniques such as imagery, breathing, relaxation). Collectively, these findings highlighted the strategic role of the coach in facilitating psychosocial outcomes for young athletes (Côté & Fraser-Thomas, 2007; Gould & Carson, 2010; Camiré, Forneris, Trudel, & Bernard, 2011), particularly where coaches represent significant figures in a young athlete's microsystem.

In follow-up research, Harwood et al. (2015) collected data on players' self-perceptions, coach perceptions, and parent perceptions of the players' 5C behaviours in training situations. The coach received sequential education in the principles of each C subsequent to integrating relevant strategies in their coaching sessions. During the five intervention phases, players completed assessments of their behavioural engagement in training associated with each C, triangulated with observation-based assessments by the coach and the players' parents. Results indicated cumulative increases in positive psychosocial responses across the intervention for selected players. Such changes in self-reported player behaviour were also corroborated by parent and coach data in conjunction with post-intervention interviews. The study adds to the growing evidence showing the value of sport psychologist practitioners working with coaches as conduits for the psychological development of young athletes.

While this latter study did not assess levels or changes in coaching efficacy per se, the social validation data collected from this study and Harwood (2008) suggested that coaches who were motivated to learn about optimising their psychological role benefitted greatly in terms of practical knowledge and the opportunity to practice the integration of such knowledge in a naturalistic setting. In this respect, the creation of an optimal learning and performance environment that exerts an influence on player behaviour may be dependent on the confidence a coach has on utilising coach-to-player and peer-to-player education and feedback opportunities related to basic, fundamental psychosocial qualities.

In the following section, I (the first author) will present a case study based upon work I conducted within a professional soccer club academy in England. While my work within the academy was multifaceted, a key element was to work with and educate the coaches to develop the confidence they possessed in applying coaching strategies and behaviours that would influence key psychosocial behaviours in their players—in other words, targeting psychosocial coaching efficacy. In this way the academy was striving to bring the domains of psychology and social skills outside onto the training pitch so that they were given equal prominence with the technical, tactical, and physical coaching. Influenced by continued collaborations with the second author and drawing from the extant literature, I will outline the background to the coach efficacy programmes and the work conducted through a series of coach education workshops and provide examples of some of the materials used and support provided for the coaches. The section will conclude with an overview of the experiences and feedback I received from the coaches, supporting data collected over the season and some personal reflections around the programme, working with the coaches and possible future directions.

Practical Applications—Case Study

Background and Context

Using Harwood's (2008) 5C framework as the foundation, the developed coaching efficacy programme was similarly built around cycles of (i) awareness and knowledge building of the theoretical underpinnings for each C (e.g., the "commitment" coaching phase focused on the principles of Achievement Goal Theory (AGT; Elliot, 1999; Nicholls, 1989) and Self Determination Theory (SDT; Deci & Ryan, 1985), (ii) application and developing confidence in implementing strategies that influence the Cs, and (iii) evaluation and reflection. The by-product of the initiative was ultimately to improve the psychosocial development of the young players in the academy. Recent research (e.g., Gould & Carson, 2010; Camiré et al., 2011; Zakrajsek, Lauer, & Bodey, 2017) has focused on the role of the coach as the instrument to achieve athlete psychosocial development, without deviating away from the technical coaching curriculum operated by a soccer club academy. This stemmed from the belief that the academy coaches would be best placed to influence the psychosocial development of their players, due to the high degree of sport-specific contact time they have with them (Steptoe et al., 2019).

A central component of this process was coach education in-service support sessions delivered on a six-weekly basis to fit in with the academy in-service support programme. Previous research has highlighted the need and desire from coaches for psychosocial-related coach education alongside more performance and technical content (Santos, Camiré, & MacDonald, 2017). Therefore, one introductory support session and five C-focused support sessions (totalling six sessions in total) were delivered throughout a 42-week season, each lasting a minimum of two hours. An additional practical session was also conducted on the pitch to demonstrate how psychosocial returns can be gained within practical sessions (Harwood et al., 2015; Pierce, Kendellen, Camiré, & Gould, 2018).

As with Harwood's (2008) programme, this initiative progressed from an examination of motivational and interpersonal attributes through to self-regulatory qualities and concluded with principles underpinning the development of self-efficacy in players. In sum, the in-service session order was (1) introduction and overview, (2) commitment, (3) communication, (4) concentration, (5) (emotional) control, and (6) confidence.

The Work Conducted

Introducing the Framework: In-Service Session One

The first coaching support session took place in the second week of the academy's coaching curriculum, during the pre-season period. The session served as the first opportunity to introduce the coaches to the idea of shaping a young player's psychosocial development, the role the coaches play within this, and to outline the 5C framework before narrowing in on one C in subsequent sessions (Harwood et al., 2015). To this end, the session had the following aims: (1) to enhance the coach's knowledge about the 5Cs and what to expect from their players; (2) to identify key 5C skills, behaviours, and responses in youth players; and (3) to discuss applications of the 5Cs and how to integrate them into the coach's own coaching practice.

To begin with, the coaches were introduced to the underpinning principles behind the 5Cs. It was explained why the 5Cs was the model being adopted by the academy and the important role that the coaches will play in influencing psychosocial behaviours and responses in their players through the 5Cs (Steptoe et al., 2019). Specific reference was given to how they can achieve this on the training pitch (e.g., the creation of a task involving an autonomy-supportive coaching climate), to ensure that theoretical knowledge was framed within a practical context (Mesquita, Ribeiro, Santos, & Morgan, 2014).

The coaches were then taken through a scenario-based activity aimed at unpacking the Cs (Harwood & Anderson, 2015). In groups the coaches were provided with a C-related training, or match, situation that required the coaches to define their C and the behaviours and responses they might hear, see, or notice from their players if they were/were not demonstrating that C (see Figure 10.2). This was used to spark discussion about the individual nature of the 5Cs, what they may look like, how they (as coaches) might approach these, or similar situations in the future and to highlight that the coaches already possess a degree of "psychosocial awareness." Next, each C was taken in turn and defined, identifying their core soccer behaviours. Examples of actions and responses profiling a player demonstrating each C were also highlighted (Higham, Harwood, & Cale, 2005; Harwood & Anderson, 2015).

Following this awareness-raising and knowledge-building section of the in-service support session, the focus switched towards how the coaches can encourage the development of the 5C behaviours in training sessions. Once more in groups, the coaches were tasked with imagining they were planning their next training session and seeking to integrate one of the Cs (e.g., concentration) into the session. Using pre-recorded training footage, the coaches were asked to pick out situations, behaviours, or actions that they observed whereby they believed that, if they were delivering that session live, they would use it as an opportunity to highlight their chosen C

Coach scenario task

You are working on improving your team's attacking play in the final third to help you score more goals. Your 'C' of focus is confidence.

Your task is to:

- Define what you think confidence is and how it relates to soccer performance
- Describe what you would see, hear, or notice from your players if they were <u>not</u> demonstrating confidence
- Describe what you would see, hear, or notice from your players if they <u>were</u> showing confidence

Example behaviours and responses of players showing confidence

- Drive forward on or off the ball
- Demand the ball from teammates and involve themselves to receive the ball under pressure
- Shoot when they see the option without fear of any negative evaluation or criticism

Example behaviours and responses of players <u>not</u> showing confidence

- Hide from the game, or be out of position and unavailable to pass to
- Not call for the ball or not want the ball
- Want to offload the ball quickly and often backwards

FIGURE 10.2 Example of coach-based scenario activity aimed at defining the Cs and identifying behaviours relating to that C as part of building psychosocial coaching efficacy

behaviours and reinforce, or challenge, their players' use of the C. Each group would then feedback their observations.

The take-home messages from this task was that any practice can have a mental skills outcome or a "psychological return" (Fraser-Thomas, Côté, & Deakin, 2005; Gould, Collins, Lauer, & Chung, 2007). The same practice can also have multiple psychological returns, so it is not the practice per se that is important but the coaches' planned behaviours and responses. These mental skill outcomes or returns do not have to be at the expense of technical, or tactical, coaching but can supplement and support them (Harwood, 2008).

P.R.O.G.R.E.S.S.

The practical component of the in-service session focused on introducing the concept of "PROGRESS" (see Figure 10.3). PROGRESS (Harwood & Anderson, 2015) is an acronym of eight coaching behaviour guidelines that encourage the development of an optimal learning environment for all coaching sessions. These management and behavioural strategies were relevant to incorporate in coaching segments at the start of a session (i.e., pre-session brief), throughout the session, and at the end of the session (i.e., post-session debrief) to gain maximum impact on the players with respect to each C. PROGRESS was outlined in the classroom before taking to the pitch to practically demonstrate.

Using one of the academy age group teams, the coaches were taken through how each of the coaching behaviours could be implemented. The demonstration consisted of examples of the pre-during-post session process. At the conclusion of the practical, the coaches were given the opportunity to share their reflections and ask questions before being challenged with integrating behavioural coaching techniques (Smoll & Smith, 2006) related to PROGRESS into their upcoming training sessions. For the next workshop, the coaches were also asked to be psychologically and socially aware of the behaviours and responses of each of their players. In this way they would build up a picture of the needs of their age group to feedback and discuss in future support sessions.

Progressing Through the Framework: C-Specific In-Service Support

Subsequent in-service support sessions that focused specifically on an individual C followed a very similar format of awareness-raising, knowledge-building, and application (Harwood et al., 2015). In addition to this, these in-service sessions would begin with a recap and provide an opportunity for the coaches to share their experiences and reflections of strategies, behaviours, and promoted squad interactions (Mesquita et al., 2014) employed with their age groups over the previous six weeks.

The application portion of the session focused specifically on helping the coaches to develop a "toolbox" of potential strategies that could be used to integrate the C into their coaching practice (Zakrajsek et al., 2017). From this, the coaches were tasked with planning and sharing a group-developed training practice that built in, or integrated, behaviours and responses related to the C (see Figure 10.4). In addition, the coaches were taken through a "best practice" C coaching demonstration on the pitch (i.e., pre-session brief, followed by the main session, and concluding with a post-session debrief). During the practical segment, the coaches were provided with an observation task to guide their attention within the session, and from which to provide feedback at the end of the demonstration.

For the final C (confidence) the coaches were split into small groups to deliver a planned practice out on the pitch (10–15 minutes duration).

> **Promote the 'C'** in the same way that you would introduce and value a technical or tactical skill. Draw out what it means and how important it is to soccer.
>
> **Role-Model the 'C'**, bringing its meaning to life by demonstrating or referring to excellent examples, versus bad examples from soccer, or other sports.
>
> **Ownership of their learning.** Involve players in decisions within the session about how they can demonstrate a 'C'; allow them options to work at their own pace and to benefit from favourite drills and practice that showcase their strengths.
>
> **Grow the 'C'** by providing players with opportunities to practice the 'C', and then to train it in more open game situations when 'pressure' can be added to test players.
>
> **Reinforce the 'C'** by praising those players who respond by demonstrating the chosen 'C' skill or behaviour, and by making courageous decisions.
>
> **Empower peer support** by encouraging players to praise each other for positive efforts related to each 'C' in order to build individual and collective confidence.
>
> **Support the supporter** by acknowledging those players when they achieve the above, thereby closing the loop on a supportive environment around each of the 'Cs'.
>
> **Self-review and responsiveness.** Check-in with players on their levels of the 'C' and empower them to keep working hard; use monitors to review collective efforts and apply the 'golden minutes' of 'reviewing your learning' at the end of the session.

FIGURE 10.3 Guidelines for making PROGRESS with the 5Cs in coaching (from Harwood & Anderson, 2015)

Supporting the Coaches

Following each workshop, the academy coaches would deliver training sessions that paid attention to strategies that shaped and influenced the C of focus for the next six weeks (e.g., coaching "communication"). The academy operated with two coaches per age group, giving each coach a minimum of nine sessions with which to lead a session and practice incorporating a C (based on three sessions per week), and sought to attain the greater positive effects, as posited by Malete and Feltz (2000), by coaches engaging in a longer practice and education process. Coaches would plan how they intended to influence key behaviours and responses as part of their normal session planning and reflect on how well they achieved this, their strategy

Strategy 1: Silent soccer

Introduce a phase of the game where nobody is allowed to talk. Draw the player's attention to the other ways they communicate with their teammates through non-verbal means. For example, pointing to where they want a pass to go, applauding a teammate's intent, and the body language they present.

Strategy 2: Silent vs. Vibrant soccer

After a couple of minutes of the 'silent soccer' condition, allow one player per team to talk. Gradually increase the number of players who can talk per team until everyone is allowed to communicate. It is likely the pitch will be far more vibrant than at the start of the practice, therefore it is important to draw the player's attention to this. You may also wish to try playing one team that can communicate verbally against one team that must stay silent.

Strategy 3: Communication confidence booster

To develop and help the player feel comfortable giving and receiving praise, build into the practice that the only communication allowed is praise or encouragement.

FIGURE 10.4 Example of u13 coach's training practice with strategies aimed at building communication into the practice (from Harwood & Anderson, 2015)

use, and success in promoting squad interactions as part of their session evaluation (i.e., how well they made P.R.O.G.R.E.S.S. within the session).

Previous research by Mesquita et al. (2014) with Portuguese coaches emphasised the importance of reflecting and engaging with a variety of learning experiences. As a consequence, I implemented a support programme that incorporated individual coach observations, feedback, and self-reflection mechanisms to supplement the work conducted with the six-weekly workshops.

Where logistics permitted (i.e., coach availability, matches replacing training, cancelled sessions) each coach was observed twice within a six-week period. The observations took in the pre-session briefing, the main session, and the post-session debrief. In order to help guide my analysis I created an assessment sheet to help evaluate the coaches' use of PROGRESS in shaping the C across the session, how well they encouraged and influenced the associated positive behaviours and responses for that C, and how well they recognised and used "teachable" moments, either with individuals or with the team. Each element on the observation sheet (e.g., "How well did the coach give equal recognition to players for successful outcomes and for high effort?" as part of the commitment observation) was graded in order to help the coach identify areas they may wish to focus on and as a means for tracking improvement from one observation to the next (for example templates, see Harwood & Anderson, 2015). Feedback was then provided to the coach at the next training session.

As the season progressed investment in the academy allowed us to film training sessions on a regular basis. This access to training footage allowed me to support the written observation and feedback with tangible examples from the session. It became apparent from coach feedback, however, that example footage was seen as more beneficial to the coaches in helping them to build psychosocial coaching efficacy. By seeing themselves positively influencing their players behaviours and responses, it acted as a driver for coaches to make continued progress (Bandura, 1977).

As a consequence, and in collaboration with the academy performance analyst, I developed a bespoke 5C analysis framework to categorise psychosocially directed coach behaviours and subsequent player responses from the training footage. For example, if a coach had promoted the importance of peer reinforcement, or implemented a condition in a training drill that required peer reinforcement, this would be coded and "clipped" to show the coach. It would then be cut together with examples of the players reinforcing each other and with any coach reinforcement of player reinforcement to complete the loop. Where the coach personalised this information, the footage would cut together the coach's information to the player, the player's responses, and coach-personalised reinforcement of this. Therefore, I was able to provide the coaches with more tangible feedback of the sessions, showing both positive examples and demonstrating areas whereby the coaches could make further progress.

This approach helped to foster a supportive climate between coaches who valued the role of core psychological principles in player development, and such support has been noted as a factor contributing towards coaching efficacy (Feltz et al., 1999). A clear sign of the growing confidence the coaches had influencing psychosocial competencies was seen in how the coaches would actively seek to "see their clips" following filmed training sessions. The coaches often shared their footage with other coaches and discussed novel ways they could continue to PROGRESS each C in their training.

The final element of the support programme was to introduce a 5Cs component to the coach's session evaluations. Self-reflection, or reflective practice, has regularly been cited as a means through which to improve coaching practice (e.g., Ghaye, 2001). Therefore, a 5C component was added to the coach's session evaluations to encourage self-reflection. The coaches were asked to reflect on the confidence they possessed to employ coaching strategies and behaviours to help their players exhibit the 5Cs, using a seven-point scale from "not at all confident" to "extremely confident." The coaches were also asked to consider the responses they saw from their players, how they went about promoting social interaction, and any future changes they may want to make next time to the session.

Case-Study Reflections

The purpose of the coaching intervention was the enhancement of coaches' beliefs in their capability in employing sport psychology and interpersonal principles in an intentional and deliberate manner. This was based upon the belief that a coach's intentional establishment of a wider psychological-skill climate is a responsibility to be encouraged (Harwood, 2008; Harwood & Johnston, 2016). It is, however, predicated on how much coaches have the confidence and belief in influencing such factors (Feltz et al., 1999; Myers et al., 2008). Inevitably, this will only be possible if psychological and interpersonal skills are allocated the same importance and identity as technical skills, tactical understanding, and physical development (Holt & Dunn, 2004; MacNamara et al., 2010; Johnston et al., 2013). In this particular academy, support from the academy manager was pivotal in fostering a culture that valued the inherent importance of psychology.

At the end of season, the coaches were invited to feedback their thoughts and experiences about the support programme. All coaches expressed feelings of improved confidence due to perceived increases in process knowledge, related to how they could influence psychological and interpersonal responses of players in training sessions. For some, simply having a heightened awareness was enough to feel more able to influence and generate more adaptive and prosocial behaviours.

Coaches also noted they felt capable of confidently employing the eight coaching-behaviour directives of PROGRESS. They believed that by having a framework from which to guide their integration of key behaviours and responses, helped them to gain a real sense of coaching efficacy in shaping a session that had a psychosocial outcome. As previously noted, the use of recorded training session footage was also a powerful tool in refining the use of PROGRESS, particularly in helping the coaches to "G-row" and "R-einforce" the C throughout the session.

It has been noted in previous studies (e.g., Harwood, 2008; Steptoe et al., 2019) that often coaches lack a depth of training in techniques to develop psychological skills (e.g., imagery and emotional awareness) that would be implemented by sport psychologists in an applied setting. To overcome this, workshops on concentration and control were tailored more towards specific educational sessions pertaining to more traditional mental skill training. Coach feedback suggested that in the time available for the workshops, too much information may have been provided in an attempt to arm the coaches with knowledge and a variety of strategies. Going forwards I intended to provide supplementary sessions throughout the six-week block for psychological skills "drop-in" sessions. In this way I hoped that the coaches wouldn't feel overwhelmed by the amount of information and psychological-specific content, which may serve as a hindrance to a coach's confidence in employing psychosocial principles.

Collectively, the message received from the coach's feedback suggested that they found value in theoretical knowledge that was framed within a practical context and that was also reinforced through "best practice" on the pitch examples. The coaches further identified the importance in having a varied set of user-friendly ideas and strategies from which to draw from to assist in their own practice.

The anecdotal feedback from the coaching staff was also reflected in the data collected throughout the season from the coach's session evaluation scoring (see Figure 10.5). Positive increases in psychosocial coaching efficacy were noted across all psychosocial principles related to the 5Cs. As has been reported in previous studies (Harwood, 2008; Harwood et al., 2015), there was also an observable crossover effect as a result of the education sessions, follow-up support, and personal practice. In other words, their influence was not solely limited to efficacy increases in the targeted psychosocial principle (e.g., communication), and progressive increases in a coach's confidence appeared to occur cumulatively from one "C" to the next.

Improvements in coaching efficacy also corresponded with the players' improved beliefs of their own psychosocial related behaviours and responses (see Figure 10.6). As part of the wider 5C strategy within the academy, each player was issued with a training diary, of which one element was to assess and record their perceived 5C weekly performance. Across each of the age groups the players deemed themselves to have made improvements in their 5C performance. This aligned similarly to the perception of their coaches, namely that "commitment" and "communication" coaching saw the largest increases and evidence of use, while "confidence" increased as a consequence of focus on each of the other 4Cs. Not only did this give an indication of the impact of the coaching efficacy programme, it provided a more impartial measure of coach behaviour and supported the decision to influence the psychosocial development of the academy players through the coaches.

Finally, the regularity and variety of education, practice, and support during each phase throughout the season was crucial in helping coaches attain more mastery experience (Mesquita et al., 2014). Further, by building in coach reflection practices, the coaches were continually reconsidering or reinforcing ideas and strategies to strengthen their belief in their ability to influence psychosocial behaviours (Ghaye, 2001). This continuous educational support allied with shared group coaching experiences may have fostered a greater sense of social and peer support, a factor deemed important within the coaching efficacy model (Feltz et al., 1999).

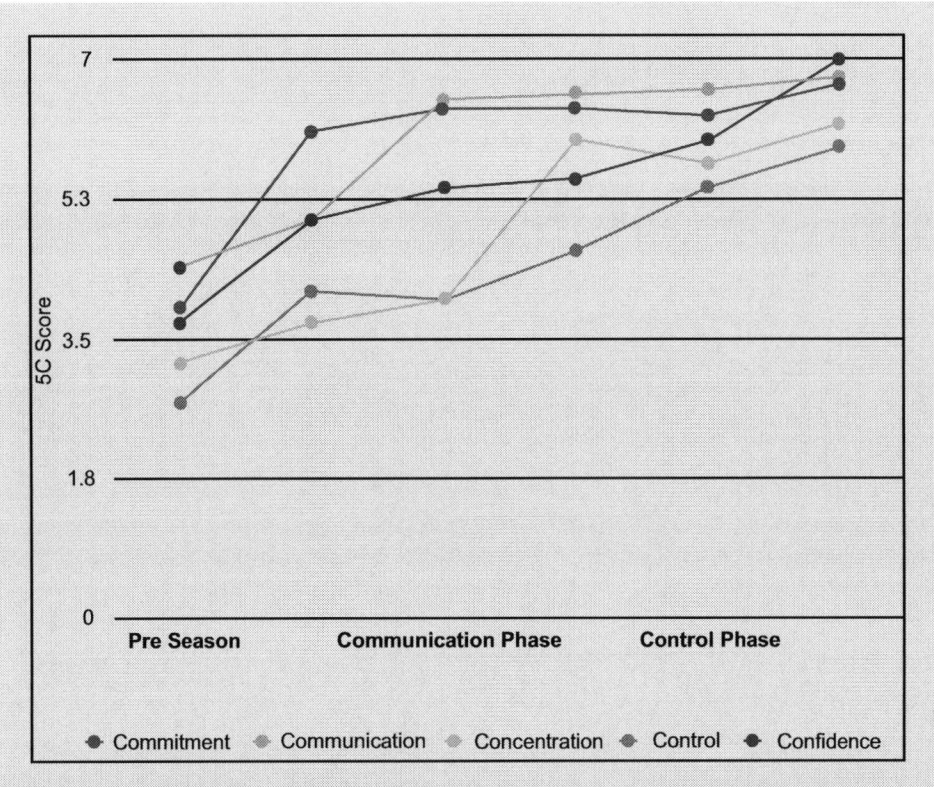

FIGURE 10.5 Combined u14 coaches' 5C scoring on the confidence they possessed to use strategies and behaviours to help their players exhibit the 5Cs

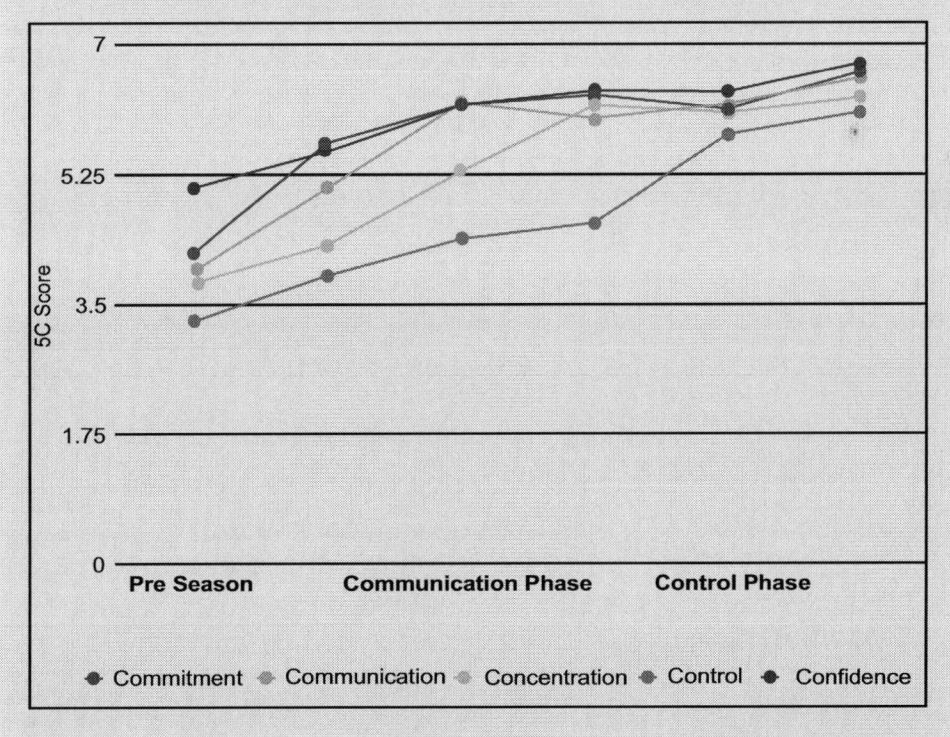

FIGURE 10.6 Combined u14 player perceptions of their 5C use taken from the players' training diaries

Summary and Conclusions

Coaching efficacy is undoubtedly an important construct in the psychology of coaching. While the receptiveness of the coach is a key factor, past research has noted that coaches repeatedly benefit from applied knowledge as they seek to become comfortable with processes of integration that help them to overcome uncertainty in influencing psychological and social competencies (Gould et al., 1999; Harwood, 2008).

The need to influence a young player's psychosocial development has been highlighted as relevant to an academy soccer player in striving to meet the demands of a highly competitive and elite-level environment (Holt & Dunn, 2004). The coach has been identified as having a key strategic role to play in facilitating these outcomes for young athletes (Côté & Fraser-Thomas, 2007). Coaches therefore need to consider how they maximise the development opportunities for young athletes.

These wider development goals can only be achieved by providing constant support for coaches. The sport psychologist practitioner therefore must see a pivotal part of their role being to build rapport, educate, and provide practical ideas to build coach confidence in structure and reinforce practices that offer psychosocial returns for player development.

The case study outlined in this chapter focused on ways in which I (first author) sought to intentionally build psychosocial coaching efficacy to foster psychological skill development through coach–player interactions, specifically in the context of a training session (before-during-after). This is obviously only part of the coaching domain. Match day (before-during-after) is another key context in which this specific form of coaching efficacy can be applied. All the good work with coaches to facilitate their confidence on the training pitch can easily be undone on match days should coaches not feel their work is translating or they feel they are not capable of implementing strategies to support psychosocial integration in this unique context.

Further, in keeping with Fraser-Thomas et al.'s (2005) emphasis on a coherent, supportive environment, such work with coaches should not exist in a vacuum. Any psychological and social development programme needs to be allied with other stakeholders in the soccer club, to build confidence in facilitating psychosocial competencies, reinforce the same value messages, and create a community of practice. Opportunities to influence and acknowledge performance and progression across these core psychosocial behaviours exist at all times and from all members of staff working towards elite performance. The multidisciplinary approach that soccer clubs now operate means that player development is no longer isolated to the training pitch and no longer the sole purview of coaches. It is important to consider how transferable identified psychosocial behaviours and responses are across different environments. This, therefore, requires applied sport psychology practitioners to consider the extent to which their psychosocial education caters for all stakeholders that support a young player's development.

Key Messages and Further Reading

1. Coaches may be best positioned to influence psychosocial development in their youth players due to a high degree of sport-specific contact time. Therefore, a coach's intentional establishment of a wider psychosocial climate is a responsibility to be encouraged by applied sport psychologists.
2. Establishing a wider psychosocial climate requires coaches to possess confidence in their ability to influence a player's psychosocial responses and behaviours. The applied sport psychology practitioner must become a valuable ally of the coach and work together to positively shape these competencies.

3. Long-term coach education programmes that are empowering in terms of educational content, strong on user-friendly ideas and strategies, and high on practitioner support are an effective means of developing a coach's confidence in influencing psychosocial competencies.
4. Coach education workshops have consistently been shown to improve coaching efficacy. These workshops should meet the need for theoretical knowledge to be framed in practical contexts and provide coaches with the opportunity to share and reflect their own and others' experiences to develop learning.
5. Planned coach behaviours and responses are important to facilitate mental skill outcomes alongside technical, tactical, and physical training practice outcomes. The applied sport psychologist practitioner can support the coach to help refine their practice through structured observation, feedback, and encouragement of reflective practice.

Feltz, D. L., Chase, M. A., Moritz, S. A., & Sullivan, P. J. (1999). A conceptual model of coaching efficacy: Preliminary investigation and instrument development. *Journal of Educational Psychology, 91*, 765–776.

Harwood, C. G. (2008). Developmental consulting in a professional football academy: The 5Cs coaching efficacy program. *The Sport Psychologist, 22*, 109–133.

Harwood, C. G., & Anderson, R. (2015). *Coaching psychological skills in youth football: Developing the 5Cs*. London: Bennion-Kearny.

Harwood, C. G., Barker, J. B., & Anderson, R. (2015). Psychosocial development in youth soccer players: Assessing the effectiveness of the 5Cs intervention program. *The Sport Psychologist, 29*, 319–334.

Steptoe, K., King, T., & Harwood, C. G. (2019). The consistent psycho-social development of young footballers: Implementing the 5C's as a vehicle for interdisciplinary cohesion. In E. Konter, J. Beckmann & T. Loughead (Eds.), *Football psychology: From theory to practice*. London: Routledge/Psychology Press.

References

Bandura, A. (1977). Self-efficacy: Toward a unified theory of behavioral change. *Psychological Review, 84*, 191–215.

Boardley, I. D., Kavussanu, M., & Ring, C. (2008). Athletes' perceptions of coaching effectiveness and athlete-related outcomes in rugby union: An investigation based on the coaching efficacy model. *The Sport Psychologist, 22*, 269–287.

Bronfenbrenner, U. (1999). Environments in developmental perspective: Theoretical and operational models. In S. L. Friedman & T. D. Wachs (Eds.), *Measuring environment across the life span: Emerging methods and concepts* (pp. 3–28). Washington, DC: American Psychological Association.

Camiré, M., Forneris, T., Trudel, P., & Bernard, D. (2011). Strategies for helping coaches facilitate positive youth development through sport. *Journal of Sport Psychology in Action, 2*, 92–99.

Campbell, T., & Sullivan, P (2005). The effect of a standardized coaching education program on the efficacy of novice coaches. *Avante, 11*, 38–45.

Chase, M. A., & Martin, E. (2012). Coaching efficacy beliefs. In J. Dennison, P. Potrac & W. Gilbert (Eds.), *Handbook of sports coaching*. London: Routledge.

Côté, J., & Fraser-Thomas, J. (2007). Youth involvement in sport. In P. Crocker (Ed.), *Sport psychology: A Canadian perspective* (pp. 270–298). Toronto: Pearson.

Deci, E. L., & Ryan, R. M. (1985). *Intrinsic motivation and self-determination in human behavior*. New York, NY: Plenum Press.

Elliot, A. J. (1999). Approach and avoidance motivation and achievement goals. *Educational Psychologist, 34*, 169–189.

Fraser-Thomas, J., Côté, J., & Deakin, J. (2005). Youth sport programs: An avenue to foster positive youth development. *Physical Education and Sport Pedagogy, 10,* 19–40.

Fung, L. (2002). Task familiarity and task efficacy: A study of sports coaches. *Perceptual and Motor Skills, 95,* 367–372.

Ghaye, T. (2001). Reflective practice. *Faster Higher Stronger, 10,* 9–12.

Gledhill, A., Harwood, C., & Forsdyke, D. (2017). Psychosocial factors associated with talent development in football: A systematic review, *Psychology of Sport & Exercise, 31,* 93–112.

Gould, D., & Carson, S. (2010). Coaching behaviours and developmental benefits of high school sports participation. *Hellenic Journal of Psychology, 7,* 298–314.

Gould, D., Collins, K., Lauer, L., & Chung, Y. (2007). Coaching life skills through football: A study of award winning high school coaches. *Journal of Applied Sport Psychology, 19,* 16–37.

Gould, D., Damarjian, N., & Medbery, R. (1999). An examination of mental skills training in junior tennis coaches. *The Sport Psychologist, 13,* 127–143.

Hackfort, D. (2006). A conceptual framework and fundamental issues investigating the development of peak performance in sports. In D. Hackfort & G. Tenenbaum (Eds.), *Essential processes for attaining peak performance* (pp. 10–25). Oxford: Meyer & Meyer.

Harwood, C., & Johnston, J. (2016). Positive youth development and talent development. In N. L. Holt (Ed.), *Positive youth development through sport* (pp. 113–125). London: Routledge.

Higham, A., Harwood, C. G., & Cale, A. (2005). *Momentum in soccer: Controlling the game.* Leeds: Coachwise/1st for Sport Publications.

Holt, N. L., Deal, C. J., & Smyth, C. (2016). Future directions for positive youth development through sport. In N. L. Holt (Ed.), *Positive youth development through sport* (2nd ed., pp. 229–240). London: Routledge.

Holt, N. L., & Dunn, J. G. H. (2004). Toward a grounded theory of the psychosocial competencies and environmental conditions associated with soccer success. *Journal of Applied Sport Psychology, 16,* 199–219.

Johnston, J., Harwood, C., & Minniti, A. M. (2013). Positive youth development in swimming: Clarification and consensus of key psychosocial assets. *Journal of Applied Sport Psychology, 25,* 392–411.

Lee, K. S., Malete, L., & Feltz, D. L. (2002). The strength of coaching efficacy between certified and noncertified Singapore coaches. *International Journal of Applied Sports Sciences, 14,* 55–67.

Lerner, R. M., Fisher, C. B., & Weinberg, R. A. (2000). Toward a science for and of the people: Promoting civil society through the application of developmental science. *Child Development, 71,* 11–20.

MacNamara, A., Button, A., & Collins, D. (2010). The role of psychological characteristics in facilitating the pathway to elite performance: Part 1: Identifying mental skills and behaviours. *The Sport Psychologist, 24,* 52–73.

Malete, L., & Feltz, D. L. (2000). The effect of a coaching education program on coaching efficacy. *The Sport Psychologist, 14,* 410–417.

Malete, L., & Sullivan, P. J. (2009). Sources of coaching efficacy in coaches in Botswana. *International Journal of Coaching Science, 3,* 17–28.

Marback, T. L., Short, S. E., Short, M. W., & Sullivan, P. J. (2005). Coaching confidence: An exploratory investigation of sources and gender differences. *Journal of Sport Behavior, 28,* 18–34.

Martindale, R., Collins, D., & Daubney, J. (2005). Talent development: A guide for practice and research within sport. *Quest, 57,* 353–375.

Mesquita, I., Ribeiro, J., Santos, S., & Morgan, K. (2014). Coach learning and coach education: Portuguese expert coaches' perspective. *The Sport Psychologist, 28,* 124–136.

Myers, N. D., Chase, M. A., Pierce, S. W., & Martin, E. (2011). Coaching efficacy and exploratory structural modeling: A substantive-methodological synergy. *Journal of Sport & Exercise Psychology, 33,* 779–806.

Myers, N. D., Feltz, D. L., Chase, M. A., Reckase, M. D., & Hancock, G. R. (2008). The coaching efficacy scale II-High school teams. *Educational and Psychological Measurement, 68,* 1059–1076.

Myers, N. D., Vargas-Tonsing, T. M., & Feltz, D. L. (2005). Coaching efficacy in collegiate coaches: Sources, coaching behavior, and team variables. *Psychology of Sport and Exercise, 6,* 129–143.

Nicholls, J. G. (1989). *The competitive ethos and democratic education.* Cambridge, MA: Harvard University Press.

Pierce, S., Kendellen, K., Camiré, M., & Gould, D. (2018). Strategies for coaching for life skills transfer. *Journal of Sport Psychology in Action, 9,* 11–20.

Richardson, D., Relvas, H., & Littlewood, M. (2013). Sociological and cultural influences on player development. In A. M. Williams (Ed.), *Science and soccer: Developing elite performers* (3rd ed., pp. 139–153). London: Routledge.

Santos, F., Camiré, M., & MacDonald, D. J. (2017). Youth sport coaches' perspective on positive youth development and its worth in mainstream coach education courses. *International Sport Coaching Journal, 4*, 38–46.

Schulman, S., & Davies, T. (2007). *Evidence of the impact of the "Youth Development Model" on outcomes for young people: A literature review.* London: The National Youth Agency: Information and Research.

Seefeldt, V., & Brown, E. (1990). *Program for athletic coach education (PACE).* Carmel, IN: Benchmark Press.

Smith, R. E., Smoll, F. L., & Hunt, E. B. (1977). A system for the behavioral assessment of athletic coaches. *Research Quarterly, 48*, 401–407.

Smoll, F. L., & Smith, R. E. (2006). Development and implementation of coach-training programs: Cognitive-behavioral principles and techniques. In J. M. Williams (Ed.), *Applied sport psychology: Personal growth to peak performance* (5th ed., pp. 458–480). Boston, MA: McGraw-Hill.

Sullivan, P. J., & Kent, A. (2003). Coaching efficacy as a predictor of leadership style in intercollegiate athletics. *Journal of Applied Sport Psychology, 15*, 1–11.

Vargas-Tonsing, T. M., Warners, A. L., & Feltz, D. L. (2003). The predictability of coaching efficacy on team efficacy and player efficacy in volleyball. *Journal of Sport Behavior, 26*, 396–407.

Wylleman, P., & Lavallee, D. (2004). A developmental perspective on transitions faced by athletes. In M. R. Weiss (Ed.), *Developmental sport and exercise psychology: A lifespan perspective* (pp. 503–523). Morgantown, WV: Fitness Information Technology.

Zakrajsek, R. A., Lauer, E. E., & Bodey, K. J. (2017). Integrating mental skills and strategies into youth sport training: A tool for coaches. *International Sport Coaching Journal, 4*, 76–89.

PART III
Working in the Environment

11

ECOLOGY AND CULTURE IN TALENT DEVELOPMENT—A FOUR-STEP INTERVENTION TOWARDS CULTURAL LEADERSHIP IN KEY STAKEHOLDERS IN A DANISH SOCCER ACADEMY

Jonas Vestergaard Jensen and Pætur Smith Clementsen

Brief Introduction and Literature Review

"It takes a village to raise a child." This African proverb means that everyone in the child's environment influences it and is important to its upbringing. This point of view is our basis for this chapter and is illustrated in a soccer talent development context.

In recent decades, in addition to major investments in senior elite male soccer, large sums of money and resources have been invested in talent development (Lovett, 2018). Talent has the interest of professionals and practitioners alike, which is also currently the case in Denmark (De Bosscher, Shibli, Westerbeek, & van Bottenburg, 2015; Storm, Nielsen, & Thomsen, 2016), with Team Danmark being the leading elite sport organisation. Team Danmark's purpose is to create a fruitful setting to produce elite athletes by establishing an optimal approach to talent development in Denmark. Furthermore, the Danish Football Association (Danish FA) has in recent years invested significantly in developing clubs to improve the conditions necessary to develop the players of the future. Denmark is a country with relatively few soccer players (about 350,000; (Fester & Gottlieb, 2018)) compared to the bigger nations, and therefore a structured and dedicated talent development work is necessary to compete among the best nations in the world.

Within modern soccer, the essential developmental characteristics are often termed "environmental," "psychological," "sociological," "physiological," "technical," and "tactical" attributes (Sarmento, Anguera, Pereira, & Araújo, 2018). Moreover, sport psychology is perceived as one of the factors that is essential to peak performance in sport (Johnson, Andersson, & Fallby, 2011), as well as it is widely recognised that young talented athletes do not develop when isolated and without influential relationships (Henriksen & Stambulova, 2017; Henriksen, Storm, & Larsen, 2018; Larsen, 2013). Moreover, over the last decade this perspective has led to an increased interest in research of the environment in which the athlete develops and what characterises successful environments (e.g., Henriksen, 2010; Martindale & Mortimer, 2011; Wagstaff, Fletcher, & Hanton, 2012).

A successful talent development environment (TDE) can be defined as having a high track record of producing senior elite athletes (Henriksen & Stambulova, 2017). Presently, a study was undertaken of a successful soccer TDE, based on a qualitative case-study design and with the purpose of examining factors influencing the environment's success in developing future elite players. The key point in the study was that the successful soccer TDE was characterised by a strong and cohesive organisational culture based on values, focusing on long-term development and on being concerned about the balance of the players' daily lives (Larsen, Alfermann, Henriksen, & Christensen, 2013). Similar findings were presented in an interview study of ten elite soccer coaches, which highlighted the importance of building a strong and dynamic organisational culture, where developing trusting relationships with key stakeholders and player welfare were essential for a successful TDE in soccer (Mills, Butt, Maynard, & Harwood, 2014). In practice, this means, for example, that successful TDEs, who explicitly value long-term development, also "walk the talk" by valuing athletes' developmental progress more than winning the upcoming match. The importance of environmental factors in talent development has been shown in different areas. To illustrate, organisational structure is essential for successful transitions from youth to senior (e.g., having a club strategy for integrating youth players to the senior team; Morris, Tod, & Oliver, 2015). Optimal player development is also the result of the interplay between many different factors within the environment, such as the coach–athlete relationship and a coherent organisational culture (Aalberg & Sæther, 2016; Mills et al., 2014). Moreover, the literature highlights the importance of examining the structures and relationships that exist within a TDE, and it indicates that the culture within the development environment is crucial for successful talent development (Henriksen & Stambulova, 2017; Henriksen et al., 2018; Maitland, Hills, & Rhind, 2015).

To summarise, to be a successful TDE, environmental factors, such as organisational culture and relationships within the TDE, seem to be essential to successful player development. Thus, when working as a sport psychology consultant (SPC) on developing psychological skills in players, it is necessary to work with the organisational culture. To achieve this, the SPC must start with examining the structures and reciprocal interactions within the TDE.

In the following chapter, we will present a hypothetical intervention based on case-study research that we conducted in a talent development academy in a high-level Danish soccer club (Jensen & Clementsen, 2016), combined with our own experiences as SPCs. The main purpose of this chapter is to provide the reader with an example of how to analyse a TDE and how to work deliberately from a sport psychological perspective towards establishing functional talent development culture through the creation of cultural leadership in key stakeholders.

Practical Applications—Case study

Background and Context

To conduct a theoretical-guided case-study intervention, we were inspired by the holistic ecological approach (HEA). The HEA underlines the interactions of the athlete and the sporting and non-sporting environment as a key factor for talent development, both in sport in general (Henriksen & Roessler, 2011; Henriksen, Stambulova, & Roessler, 2010b; Larsen et al., 2013; Storm, Henriksen, Larsen, & Christensen, 2014) and also in soccer more specifically (Aalberg & Sæther, 2016; Christensen, Laursena, & Sørensen, 2011; Grossmann & Lames, 2015; Larsen et al., 2013; Mills et al., 2014; Morris et al., 2015). HEA is based on ecological system theory (Bronfenbrenner, 1979), cultural psychology (Greenfield & Keller, 2004), and organisational psychology (Schein, 2010). The HEA is ecological in the way that it emphasises players' development in a context and that every component (e.g., persons, club, school system) influences the players' development. The HEA is holistic in the sense that it focuses on both the athletic and non-athletic environment and thus points out the importance of working with the athletes as whole persons (Henriksen & Stambulova, 2017). The HEA forms the base for the two working models, Athletic Talent Development Environment (ATDE) model and Environment Success Factor (ESF) model, which we used as theoretical foundation for the following intervention's methodology. In short, the ATDE model considers the player's microenvironment, such as family, club, and school, and macroenvironment, which includes components that players do not engage with directly, such as sport federation, school system in general, and national and youth culture. Moreover, the ATDE model is divided into the sport and non-sport domain.

The sport domain is comprised of components that are directly related to sport (e.g., club, teammates, coaches, sport federation), while the non-sport domain contains components that are related to the player's life outside of sport (e.g., school, friends outside of sport, family, youth culture).

The ESF model is an explanatory model which highlights several important factors that are crucial for creating a successful TDE (Henriksen & Stambulova, 2017). The model starts with the preconditions (i.e., the human, material and financial conditions) provided by the club. Next are the daily routines and processes, such as training, camps, and matches, which create three outcomes: individual development and achievement (athletic and psychosocial skills), team development, and organisational and cultural development. Culture is a core component in the ESF model. It is based on Schein's (2010) understanding of organisational culture at three levels: artefacts, espoused values, and basic assumptions. The premise of the ESF model is that the TDE success is a result of the interplay between preconditions, individual and team development, with the organisational culture as the fulcrum that ties elements together and promotes (or inhibits) the process (see Henriksen & Stambulova, 2017). Additionally, empirical research supporting the validation of the HEA has been done in successful TDEs in kayaking (Henriksen & Roessler, 2011), track and field (Henriksen et al., 2010b), sailing (Henriksen, Stambulova, & Roessler, 2010a), and soccer (Aalberg & Sæther, 2016; Larsen et al., 2013).

The HEA has also been used as framework for sport psychology interventions in soccer (Larsen, Alfermann, & Christensen, 2012; Larsen et al., 2013). An intervention conducted in a Danish youth soccer academy proved beneficial when establishing talent development culture where players develop the skills required to succeed at a professional level (Larsen et al., 2012). After a thorough analysis of the environment, the SPC worked with the organisation at different levels to create a common practice for development of psychosocial skills in the players. The HEA as framework for sport psychological interventions has shown to be beneficial when the aim is to create a coherent organisational culture for developing sport-specific psychological skills in a TDE (Henriksen, 2015; Larsen, 2018; Larsen, Henriksen, & Alfermann, 2014).

Studies of organisational culture are described as one of the most diverse areas in elite sport research due to the complexity of interactions and the structures of power in the organisation (Frontiera, 2010; Mcdougall, Nesti, Richardson, & Littlewood,

2017). Working in this domain as an SPC is highly difficult and complex (Eubank, Nesti, & Cruickshank, 2014) and requires sufficient time to get a comprehensive understanding of the environment. Therefore, we find that a thorough analysis of the organisational culture within the environment is crucial to create a successful and sustainable outcome of the intervention.

In summary, even though the HEA has been used as an analytical approach to understand talent development, research into using the HEA as a framework for sport psychological interventions in soccer is presently scant (Henriksen & Stambulova, 2017). In the following sections, we present some postulations for how sport psychologists can develop interventions aimed at developing the TDE.

Presenting Issue(s)

The following case takes place in the youth academy of a professional club in Denmark, which regularly competed for the national championship, as well as participated in European competitions. The purpose of the youth academy was to produce future elite players for the club. The manager of the youth academy first contacted us, as he saw the recruitment of SPCs as a natural next step in the further development of the club's youth academy. He wanted us to focus on the environment in and around the U15 and U17 teams, as he explained these age groups to be very eager to learn and be receptive to new initiatives. The manager wanted us to examine the organisation of the youth academy and, if necessary, direct an intervention with the purpose of optimising the talent development to produce elite players, as the club expects the academy to deliver high-quality youth players to the highest national and international elite level.

The Intervention/Work Conducted

Based on the issue presented by the club's manager, we decided to use the HEA approach as framework for a four-step intervention (see Table 11.1). The first step

TABLE 11.1 Four-step intervention overview

1. *Analysing the environment and culture*	2. *Creating organisational awareness*	3. *Creating coherent organisational behaviours*	4. *Implementing behaviours and ongoing evaluation*
Three weeks analysing the environment and culture based on the ATDE model and ESF model	Findings from the analysis were presented and discussed with stakeholders	Workshop with manager and two head coaches elaborating on which behaviours were required to create a coherent TDE and culture	Implementing the behaviours from previous step on the pitch and evaluating these continuously

was to analyse the TDE and the culture in the club. We called the second step "organisational awareness." It consisted of a session in which we presented and highlighted our findings from the analysis and discussed these with the stakeholders. In the third step we conducted a workshop called "coherent organisational behaviours," where the manager and two head coaches elaborated on which behaviours were required to create a coherent TDE and culture. Finally, the fourth step was aimed at implementing the agreed behaviours and evaluating them continuously. Understanding the environment and culture of the organisation is crucial when working as an SPC (Eubank et al., 2014), and focusing on coach behaviours has proven beneficial when working with organisational culture development in elite sport, because coaches are the direct link between the organisation's values and the players' immediate learning environment (Henriksen, 2015; Schroeder, 2010).

In the following description of the TDE, the most significant elements of the intervention's four steps are described.

Step 1—Analysing the Club's TDE and Culture

After a kick-off meeting with the manager on the first day, we were introduced to the entire youth academy staff. We presented ourselves and informed the staff that we were hired to work with the entire environment surrounding the U15 and U17 teams in order to support the talent development work. We further told them that we, in the beginning, would only be trying to get to know the organisation, so they should not worry about us interfering with them, the players, or the organisation in general. After the staff meeting, we were introduced to the players.

As previously mentioned, we work on the assumption that successful talent development relies on a coherent talent development organisation (Henriksen & Stambulova, 2017). However, knowing that every environment is unique and that every group creates its own unique culture (Bronfenbrenner, 1979; Greenfield & Keller, 2004; Henriksen, 2010; Schein, 2010), we wanted to create a holistic picture of the environment. First, we adopted a qualitative case-study design (Stake, 1995). To perform a comprehensive, structured, and systematic analysis, we created an observation guide (Spradley, 1980) and semi-structured interview guide (Kvale & Brinkmann, 2009) based on the two aforementioned working models: the ATDE model and the ESF model (Henriksen, 2010). Throughout our observations, we registered what we saw and heard along with our reflection on what we experienced. The interview guide was used to explore how the interviewees experienced the environment.

Throughout the first three weeks, we attended all the U15 and U17 teams' practices and matches as well as staff meetings. We looked at the interactions between coaches, experts, other staff members, and players, as well as the cultural footprints in the everyday language and behaviours (Greenfield & Keller, 2004). For example, their daily jargon consisted of many in-house expressions, such as "we will *develop players for number 10*," meaning developing players for the senior team, which was located in building number 10. In addition to these observations and informal talks, we performed interviews with two players, two coaches, and two parents of players.

160 Jonas Vestergaard Jensen and Pætur Smith Clementsen

The aim of these was to obtain different perspectives on the TDE that they were a part of and how they experienced the relations between the different people. The interview information was used to support and differentiate our overall findings.

Step 2—Organisational Awareness

After approximately six weeks in the environment, we invited the manager to a meeting, where we presented our findings in the form of two empirical models (see Figures 11.1 and 11.2). Figure 11.1 is the empirical version of the ATDE model (Henriksen et al., 2010a) adapted to depict our particular case. The dotted lines illustrate a weaker and occasional relation between the different actors, while a full drawn line

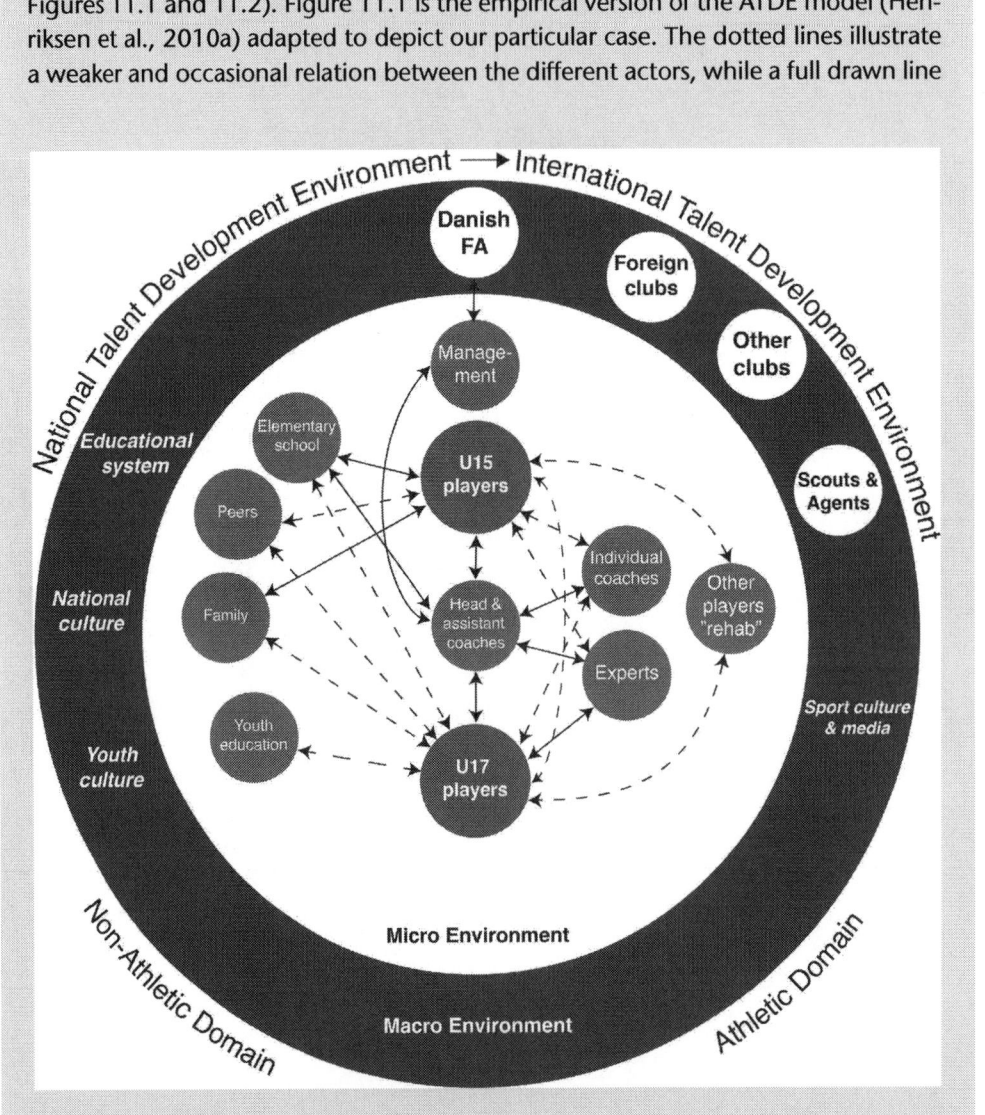

FIGURE 11.1 ATDE model. A simplistic description of actors present in the TDE and how they interacted

Source: Note. Empirical model adapted from the Henriksen, Stambulova, & Roessler (2010a) ATDE working model

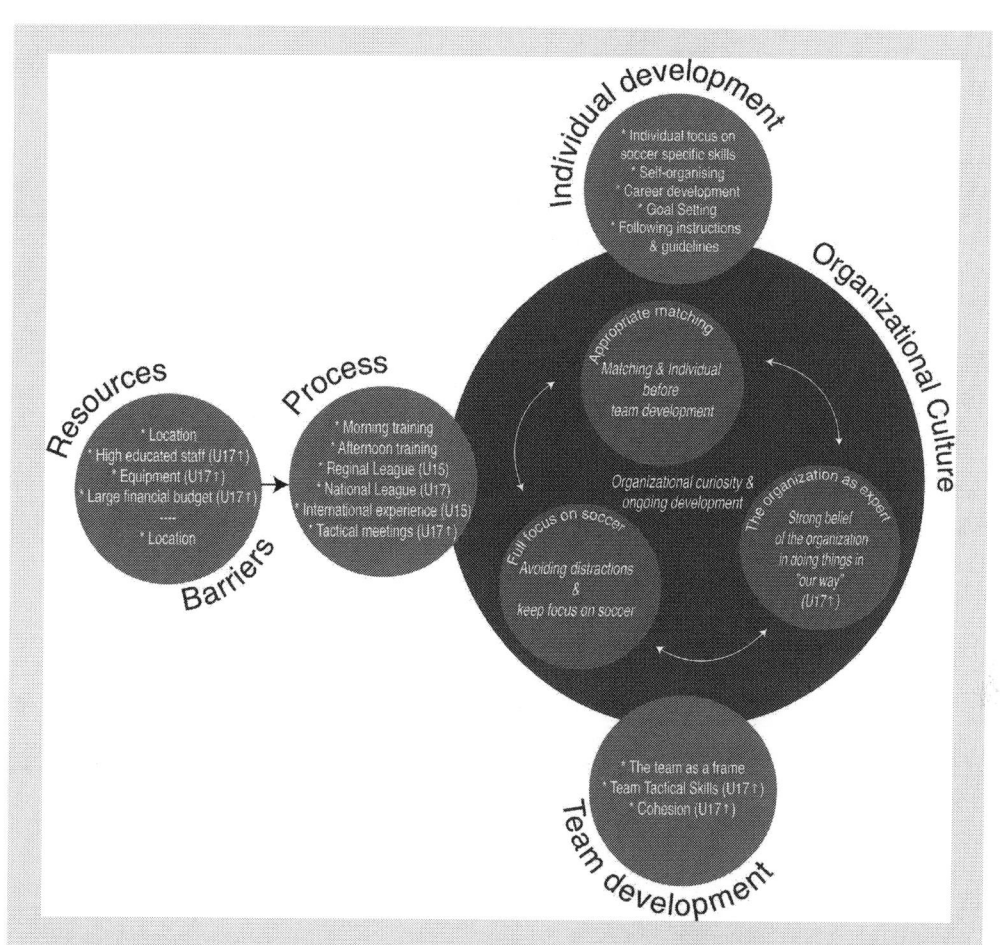

FIGURE 11.2 ESF model. A simplistic description of the most important factors in each category of the talent development environment

Source: Note. Empirical model adapted from the Henriksen, Stambulova, & Roessler (2010a) ESF working model

illustrates a closer and more regular relation. The idea was to visualise the different interactions in the TDE and to create an awareness of how the different components could potentially affect the players' development.

At the centre of the athletic domain in the microenvironment were the U15 and U17 players, coaches, and the administration. This illustrates that these were most prominent in the environment. There was a strong and proximal connection between the head coach, the assistant coaches, and the players, as the coaches played a significant role in the players' development. The coaches spent a lot of time with the players both on and off the training pitch, and they functioned as role models to some of the players. In contrast, the administration mostly had an indirect influence on the players' development by establishing conditions and guidelines for the coaches to follow. The experts cooperated closely with the head coaches as well as some of the players (e.g., injured players working with the physiotherapist).

In the non-athletic domain of the microenvironment, we found that there was a close relationship between elementary schools, especially the private school which the club had a formal collaboration with, and both head coaches. Moreover, there was a close relationship between the elementary schools and the players, which mainly concerned the U15 team. At the U17 team, there were both players who attended elementary schools and youth education. Family represents an integral part of the players' lives. However, even though the non-athletic and athletic domains graphically seemed balanced, the athletic domain was dominant in that family holidays and social activities outside sport were mostly planned in consideration to the soccer calendar. Thus, the club had the players at their disposal at any time. On the other hand, this could create internal conflicts in families, as the activity of one child was more dominant. This created a dilemma for the players, trying to live up to expectations on different arenas.

The macroenvironment consisted of cultural components and other tangible organisations. The most prominent was the Danish FA, which was the macro component with the strongest influence on the environment, as the Danish FA was responsible for tournament structure and selection of players to participate in talent centres and national teams.

Aside from the descriptive analysis of the environment, we also collected qualitative data based on the ESF model (see Figure 11.2). Figure 11.2 is the empirical version of the ESF model (Henriksen et al., 2010a) adapted to depict our particular case. The model is a simplistic description, and it portrays the most important factors in each category of the ESF model. Moreover, the model describes the factors of the entire environment, which represents both the U15 and U17 teams. Differences within the environment are highlighted in brackets. The arrows in the brackets indicate an upgrade of the factor compared to the other team.

The preconditions include being located in a large city with access to a lot of players and staff. A relatively large budget offered possibility to hire highly educated staff and to have all the necessary training equipment. This setup especially favoured the U17 team, which had more coaches and experts attached compared to the U15 team. The location was also a barrier, as there were no possibilities for expansion and limited access to training pitches outside of the usual training time, effectively restricting the players' possibilities for self-organised training, which is described as a critical factor in successful TDEs (Henriksen & Roessler, 2011; Henriksen et al., 2010b, 2010a).

As for the team development and achievement, the teams mostly functioned as frameworks for individual development. However, the teams did develop their tactical abilities and cohesion, but this was more prominent in the U17 team. We observed that the U17 team spent more time on video meetings and tactical training sessions as preparation for upcoming matches.

Through a deductive qualitative data triangulation based on Schein's (2010) theory of organisational culture, it emerged from our observations, interviews, and document analysis that the organisational culture was characterised by three basic assumptions: "appropriate matching," which represents the club's belief in individual development rather than team development and, in particular, appropriate challenges for the players; "full focus on soccer" means avoiding distractions and concerns to achieve optimal preparation; and, the third assumption, "the organisation as expert" highlights the club's strong belief in doing things their own way and the importance of the coaches' abilities.

Regarding individual development, we noticed an individual focus on soccer-specific skills on both teams, where the "appropriate matching" assumption was evident. Players were placed in different training groups, so they could be challenged appropriately, and the club participated in international tournaments to accommodate the matching issue. Moreover, the development of psychosocial skills, such as self-organisation, career development, and goal-setting, was often a theme in coach meetings, and was frequently brought up in informal conversations among the coaching staff, and therefore seemed to be highly valued by the club. In contrast, the planning of the players' day into small details, along with the players' minimal influence on the training programme, developed the players' ability to follow instructions and guidelines. Another issue in regard to the basic assumption "full focus on soccer" appears in a notable study of 124 American college athletes in which it was concluded that identifying exclusively with the athlete role and failing to explore alternative roles was associated with delayed career development (Murphy, Petitpas, & Brewer, 1996). Furthermore, it was found that especially male athletes participating in revenue-producing sport are at risk of not acquiring sufficient career decision-making skills. Moreover, athletic identity foreclosure is suggested to be associated with, for example, substance abuse, low level of career maturity, burn-out, and drop out (Brewer & Petitpas, 2017). Thus, the assumption "full focus on soccer" might have the opposite effect than originally intended. It could even be the opposite of adapting a whole-person perspective on player development, which over time could lead to delayed career development or even drop out.

In regard to the assumption "the organisation as expert," our findings are in line with other studies indicating that youth soccer coaches adopt a coach-centred approach and mainly use instructional behaviours as coaching strategy during practice (Cushion & Jones, 2001; Ford, Yates, & Williams, 2010). To illustrate, a study conducted by Cushion and Jones (2001) analysed the coaches' awareness of their actual behaviours and found that the coaches barely are aware of their instructional behaviours. In line with our findings, it seems that there is an overall basic assumption in soccer that an authoritarian character, which has a pervasive and influential effect on coaching and coach behaviour, should be present (Cushion, Ford, & Williams, 2012; Cushion & Jones, 2006). In the analysis of our data, the basic assumption, "the organization as expert," became evident in one of the club's statement papers: "Optimizing player education by a tighter structure and more control." This, together with another description from the club's statement papers, ". . . the higher the competence in the head coaches' group, the more likely the possibility of success," gave us the impression of a coach expertise discourse, where the coach is seen as a knowledge-giver and the athlete as a knowledge-receiver. This is a well-known tendency in sports coaching (Cassidy, Jones, & Potrac, 2009). Additionally, and interestingly, the players in both the U15 and U17 teams were assisted in several areas, for example by having their training clothes washed every day and getting breakfast prepared after each morning training, which did not correspond to the desire to let players take responsibility and handle their own daily lives.

Overall, the club's TDE had a broad focus on creating players who possessed the necessary skills and competencies to become elite players, as well as preparing them to make good decisions outside the world of soccer. Theoretically, an athlete-centred approach is beneficial in regard to creating reflectiveness, where the athletes are involved in the decision-making process and feel ownership, acceptance, trust, and autonomy in their development (Nelson, Cushion, Potrac, & Groom, 2014). However, there often seems to be a gap between actual coaching behaviours and theoretically recommended coaching strategies (Cushion et al., 2012). It can be argued that this was the case in certain situations in this TDE as illustrated previously. This could be inhibitory to the coach influencing the players in the intended direction and ultimately developing less autonomous players.

After the presentation, we invited the manager to discuss and reflect upon our findings before giving the U15 and U17 coaches a lighter version to discuss and reflect upon.

Step 3—Coherent Organisational Behaviours

After discussing our findings with the manager and the two head coaches, we invited the three stakeholders to a workshop aimed at creating awareness about what the staff wanted the players to be characterised by and to align the organisational and staff behaviours to these characteristics. The underlying assumptions in this workshop was based on the ABC model (Antecedence-Behaviour-Consequence; MacNamara, 2011) and value-based cultural leadership (Schein, 2010). Through the workshop, we developed an overview summarising the preferred player characteristics and behaviours, as well as the corresponding requirements for the organisation and coaches (see Table 11.2). The stakeholders were presented with a sequence of questions: (1) What should characterise the players of your TDE? (2) Which player behaviours correspond to these characteristics? (3) What are the requirements for the organisation in order to encourage these behaviours? (4) Which behaviours should the coaches have in order to encourage these behaviours? In short, the overall premise was to ask the stakeholders how to promote the desired player behaviour and how to make it possible for the players to carry out these behaviours.

The identified objects are presented in Table 11.2. In the following description, we have sought to give the reader an impression of how the intervention progressed, but with respect of the extent of this chapter, we report one of the agreed characteristics.

To describe what should characterise the club's players, we encouraged the staff to think about holistic characteristics that were suitable both inside and outside the world of soccer. In the end, the staff narrowed it down to four characteristics: self-awareness, decision-making, courage, and accountability.

We found that "buzzwords" were often used to describe the characteristics without a shared meaning to the staff and the organisation. Thus, question two was crucial to engage the participants in an open-minded reflection of which meaning they attached to each characteristic and create a shared cultural understanding (Greenfield & Keller, 2004). With that ambition, we asked the staff to discuss how a self-aware player would behave. First, we encouraged them to brainstorm and list a range of desired behaviours in a prioritised order. In this process, it was interesting to observe how colleagues who were working relatively close together had an entirely different understanding of which actual behaviours corresponded to the agreed characteristics. One of the coaches believed that players who "asked well-qualified questions to the coaches" had a fundamental behaviour of self-awareness, while another coach believed that a player who was "evaluating himself at home alone" was self-aware.

After finding and qualifying a list of actual behaviours, we then changed the perspective towards the question "what are the requirements for the organisation in order to encourage these behaviours?" Again, a very crucial part at this point was to be concrete. One example involved physical training programmes for the players, which were normally prepared by the physical coach. Now, the staff asked themselves whether it would be beneficial to let the players develop their own physical training programmes, making the players more involved in their own development and hence more self-aware in the long term.

Finally, we asked the staff to turn the spotlight towards their own behaviours. The overall question was "which behaviours should the coaches have in order to encourage these behaviours?" The aim was to list staff behaviours that could stimulate the desired player behaviours, hence facilitating the staff to take on the role as cultural leaders of the environment.

We asked the coaches to what extent they were able to create an environment which facilitated the players to think for themselves. We offered an example from our observations, where we had often seen the coaches address the players with a lot of feedback during breaks in the training sessions. This initiated a reflection about the coaches' eagerness to provide meaningful feedback to the players. The coaches agreed that a mandatory part of a player's training sessions should be to choose one key point that they wanted feedback on during or after the session. This approach should lead to players who fully engage in this self-awareness activity, receive better feedback, and, as a result, become better players.

Step 4—Implementation of Behaviours and Ongoing Evaluation

The fourth step of the intervention was to start working on implementing the desired behaviours and secure ongoing evaluation and adjustment.

At this stage, we asked the coaches to prioritise and choose one characteristic that they wanted to foster in their players over a two-week period (see Harwood, 2008). The coaches mainly focused on their own behaviour and how this could influence the players' behaviours in the desired direction. For example, to foster self-awareness in players, one coach chose to focus on how to facilitate player peer-to-peer feedback during training sessions.

Once every two weeks, we met with the manager and the coaches to evaluate how things were progressing. We asked the coaches to bring a video sequence with examples of themselves conducting both the desired and the inexpedient coaching behaviour (Harwood & Steptoe, 2013). From this, the coaches would discuss, become aware of, and further develop their coaching behaviour in accordance with the specific objectives. As an example, the above-mentioned coach brought a video sequence, where he paused an exercise and asked the players to pair up to reflect on and evaluate their performance. Regarding our role in the implementation phase, we regularly observed training sessions and shared our experiences with the coaches at the evaluation meetings.

Outcome Analysis

The success criteria of our intervention were a change in talent development culture through changes in coach behaviours. This was rooted in the assumption that the coaches' behaviours influenced the culture of the TDE (Cushion et al., 2012; MacNamara, 2011; Schein, 2010) and thus the players' abilities to develop desired skills. To form an adequate picture of the intervention's effect, we chose to rely on two different effectiveness indicators (Anderson, Mahoney, Miles, & Robinson, 2002). In line with our overall qualitative case-study design, we used both qualitative interviews and observations of coach behaviours as we were interested in the coaches' and manager's experiences of the intervention and its perceived effect, as well as observable changes in coach behaviours. As observation guide, we used the desired coach behaviours in Table 11.2 developed by the coaches themselves.

We found it crucial for the long-term effect and sustainability of our intervention that the coaches and the manager were actively involved in an ongoing evaluation process. At each meeting, we asked them how they experienced the effectiveness of the intervention so far. Furthermore, we regularly observed training sessions to determine whether we could observe changes in behaviour. The coaches reported some challenges in the early stages of the video evaluations, but along the way, the process became more comfortable and rewarding. In addition, the coaches found the video evaluation sessions, along with peer discussions with colleagues, very useful to becoming more aware of their own behaviours. These statements were complemented by our observations, which, over time, showed more consistent coach behaviours, in line with the desired coach behaviours in Table 11.2.

In general, and in line with the way of thinking in cultural leadership (Henriksen et al., 2018), it was crucial for us that the coaches themselves were able to develop self-awareness, if they wanted their players to develop the same skill. The coaches and manager were motivated to put in the necessary long-term work to further develop the entire TDE. The successful development of the TDE required effort over time, which was something the manager and coaches embraced.

Case-Study Reflections

Some would argue that soccer is a somewhat conservative environment, characterised by routines and sceptical towards the use of scientific methods (Cushion et al.,

TABLE 11.2 Schematic representation of the workshop for the characteristic of self-awareness

Characteristics	Desired player behaviours	Demands of the organization	Desired Coach behaviours
Self-awareness	– Asking questions – Studying from home – Evaluating himself constructively – Evaluating the team's performance constructively (both matches and practices) – Goal-setting; with concerns of the outside world (school, peers, family, etc.) – Preparing own physical training programme – Relate critically/ constructively to his preferred future	– Open door to the coach's office – Available examples of physical training programs – Short practical lectures about physical training – Short practical lectures about goal-setting and constructive evaluation – Coaches available in online chat forum to give feedback – Establishing school homework-café before practices – Appointing U17 mentors who would help U15 players with homework and preparing physical training programs	– Asking before giving feedback – Giving feedback to players who use the online video software – Monthly appointments with the player who has evaluated his own videos the most – Asking players about their progress in their physical training – Participate in the homework-café once a week

2012; Ford et al., 2010) such as sport psychology. More specifically, studies indicate that this conservative culture towards the integration of sport psychology is dominated by coaches' sceptical attitude (Harwood & Steptoe, 2013; Pain & Harwood, 2004). For example, a study of Swedish coaches' experiences with SPC noted that some coaches had ". . . a distorted prior knowledge about the potential of sport psychology services, such as perceiving it as 'mumbo jumbo' or just about relaxation training in the locker room" (Johnson et al., 2011). However, this was not something we found to be particularly evident in this club, which had highly qualified, well-educated people, who were curious about ways to improve the environment. However, we quickly discovered that an overuse of academic language would not benefit us, as the club staff was practically orientated and seemed to question our expertise if we moved too far away from their everyday language (Williams & Kendall, 2007). Thus, we had to master the coaches' jargon to be accepted as trusted colleagues, which is a typical challenge in the work of a consultant (Larsen, 2017). Another main challenge was to convince the coaches to give each other feedback on coaching behaviour. It seemed that the coaches were quite used to giving players feedback, but they were not comfortable giving, and in particular receiving, feedback on their own behaviour. Indeed, the importance of SPC–athlete relationship in regard to a successful intervention has received attention in research (Henriksen, Storm, Stambulova, Pyrdol, & Larsen, 2019), but research into the importance of the SPC–coach relationship has been limited (Harwood & Anderson, 2012). We

> recommend consultants to spend time with the participants in the beginning to become familiar with the culture of the environment; however, one should be aware that some coaches may experience the analysis phase as monitoring of their work. Therefore, it is important that the SPC has cultural sensitivity to achieve a true understanding of the workspace and its surrounding landscape (Eubank et al., 2014), to create constructive relationships with the coaches involved. As our work was based on the assumption that the coaches and manager were key stakeholders in the talent development environment, we therefore aimed our intervention towards them as cultural leaders (Henriksen et al., 2018).

Summary and Conclusions

Cultural change takes time and effort, but it can drive a sport organisation forward to greatness (Cruickshank & Collins, 2012; Henriksen et al., 2018). We conducted a four-step intervention starting with a thorough analysis of the environment; second, a presentation of our findings to the manager and head coaches; third, workshops aimed at the manager and coaches as cultural leaders; and, finally, implementation and ongoing evaluation of the behaviours in regard to cultural leadership. Our work demonstrates the importance of working long-term to create sustainable changes in culture and, more specifically, cultural markers such as behaviours. In our work, focus was on involving the head coaches of the relevant teams and gaining the trust and respect from the key stakeholders, which was crucial for successful and credible relationships with all staff and players.

In conclusion, the two most important elements in the work of cultural interventions are time and relationships with key stakeholders. First, we believe that it is crucial for practitioners to spend time on an in-depth analysis and not to rush things. Second, we cannot stress the importance of establishing a trusting and credible relationship with the key stakeholders in the environment enough. These kinds of sport psychological interventions are not a quick fix but rather a long haul, which requires continuous effort over time. Regarding practical implications for practitioners, they first must be willing to spend a lot of time in the environment under study, as well as being able to convince the club in undergoing this long-term process. Additionally, the practitioner must possess the necessary social competences to develop good relationships with the key stakeholders in the environment.

To be able to deliver a more efficient and evidence-based work as SPC, further research in applied sport psychology using HEA as intervention framework is needed, especially considering the limited number of interventions performed in a talent development context in soccer.

Key Messages and Further Reading

1. Take time to get to know the environment, the culture, and the people.
2. Invest in trusting relationships with key stakeholders. Without trust and cooperation with the leaders, you do not stand a chance.
3. Working with sport psychology through the environment and cultural leaders has the potential to be more sustainable compared to classic one-on-one or group sport psychology sessions.
4. To empower clients/key stakeholder of the environment, make sure to involve them in developing the intervention evaluation criteria.

5. A TDE characterised by a tight and controlling structure might have a potential disadvantage when working with players' self-awareness.

We have highlighted the five most pertinent further reading resources below:

> Cruickshank, A., Collins, D., & Minten, S. (2014). Driving and sustaining culture change in Olympic sport performance teams: A first exploration and grounded theory. *Journal of Sport & Exercise Psychology, 36*(1), 107–120. https://doi.org/10.1123/jsep.2013-0133
> Henriksen, K., & Stambulova, N. (2017). Creating optimal environments for talent development: A holistic ecological approach. In J. Baker, S. Cobley, J. Schorer & N. Wattie (Eds.), *Routledge handbook of talent identification and development in sport* (1st ed., pp. 271–284). London: Routledge.
> Jensen, J. V., & Clementsen, P. S. (2016). *Characteristics of a Danish football talent development environment: A constructivist case study of FCK School of Excellence*. Master thesis. University of Copenhagen. Retrieved from https://doi.org/10.13140/RG.2.1.2887.9607
> Maitland, A., Hills, L. A., & Rhind, D. J. (2015). Organisational culture in sport: A systematic review. *Sport Management Review, 18*(4), 501–516. https://doi.org/10.1016/j.smr.2014.11.004
> Schein, E. H. (2010). *Organizational culture and leadership* (4th ed.). San Francisco, CA: Jossey-Bass.

References

Aalberg, R. R., & Sæther, S. A. (2016). The talent development environment in a Norwegian top-level football club. *Sport Science Review, 25*(3–4), 159–182. https://doi.org/10.1515/ssr-2016-0009

Anderson, A. G., Mahoney, C., Miles, A., & Robinson, P. (2002). Evaluating the effectiveness of applied sport psychology practice: Making the case for a case study approach. *The Sport Psychologist, 16*(4), 432–453. https://doi.org/10.1123/tsp.16.4.432

Brewer, B. W., & Petitpas, A. J. (2017). Athletic identity foreclosure. *Current Opinion in Psychology, 16*, 118–122. https://doi.org/10.1016/j.copsyc.2017.05.004

Bronfenbrenner, U. (1979). *The ecology of human development: Experiments by nature and design*. Cambridge, MA: Harvard University Press.

Cassidy, T., Jones, R. L., & Potrac, P. (2009). The discourses of coaching. In T. Cassidy, R. Jones & P. Portrac (Eds.), *Understanding sports coaching: The social, cultural and pedagogical foundation of coaching practice* (2nd ed., pp. 115–125). London: Routledge.

Christensen, M. K., Laursena, D. N., & Sørensen, J. K. (2011). Situated learning in youth elite football: A Danish case study among talented male under-18 football players. *Physical Education and Sport Pedagogy, 16*(2), 163–178. https://doi.org/10.1080/17408989.2010.532782

Cruickshank, A., & Collins, D. (2012). Culture change in elite sport performance teams: Examining and advancing effectiveness in the new era. *Journal of Applied Sport Psychology, 24*(3), 338–355. https://doi.org/10.1080/10413200.2011.650819

Cushion, C., Ford, P. R., & Williams, A. M. (2012). Coach behaviours and practice structures in youth soccer: Implications for talent development. *Journal of Sports Sciences, 30*(15), 1631–1641. https://doi.org/10.1080/02640414.2012.721930

Cushion, C., & Jones, R. (2001). A systematic observation of professional top-level youth soccer coaches. *Journal of Sport Behavior, 24*(4), 354–376. http://search.ebscohost.com/login.aspx?direct=true&profile=ehost&scope=site&authtype=crawler&jrnl=01627341&AN=5483713&h=mWDod9N5G64Qqd40N0M7l6PKfdJBLpJTwRMEPtKSXcZOqWLbN1NfspAL2CBw0ltJuXjMQP3r2GQxhy9c4904JA==&crl=c

Cushion, C., & Jones, R. L. (2006). Power, discourse, and symbolic violence in professional youth soccer: The case of Albion football club. *Sociology of Sport Journal, 23*(142), 142–161.

De Bosscher, V., Shibli, S., Westerbeek, H., & van Bottenburg, M. (2015). *Successful elite sport policies: An international comparison of the sports policy factors leading to international sporting success (Spliss 2.0) in 15 nations*. Aachen: Meyer & Meyer. Retrieved from http://www.m-m-sports.com/succesful-elite.sport-policies-978178550761.html

Eubank, M., Nesti, M., & Cruickshank, A. (2014). Understanding high performance sport environments: Impact for the professional training and supervision of sport psychologists. *Sport and Exercise Psychology Review, 10*(2), 30–37.

Fester, M., & Gottlieb, P. (2018). Idrætten i tal 2017 — Status på foreningsidrætten i Danmark (Sport in numbers 2017: Status of sports participation in Denmark). Retrieved from www.dif.dk/da/politik/vi-er/medlemstal

Ford, P. R., Yates, I., & Williams, A. M. (2010). An analysis of practice activities and instructional behaviours used by youth soccer coaches during practice: Exploring the link between science and application. *Journal of Sports Sciences, 28*(5), 483–495. https://doi.org/10.1080/02640410903582750

Frontiera, J. (2010). Leadership and organizational culture transformation in professional sport. *Journal of Leadership and Organizational Studies, 17*(1), 71–86. https://doi.org/10.1177/1548051809345253

Greenfield, P. M., & Keller, H. (2004). Cultural psychology. In C. D. Spielberger (Ed.), *Encyclopedia of applied psychology* (1st ed., Vol. 1, pp. 545–553). Oxford; Boston, MA: Elsevier Academic Press.

Grossmann, B., & Lames, M. (2015). From talent to professional football: Youthism in German football. *International Journal of Sports Science & Coaching, 10*(6), 1103–1113. https://doi.org/10.1260/1747-9541.10.6.1103Harwood, C. G. (2008). Developmental consulting in a professional football academy. The 5Cs coaching efficacy program. *The Sport Psychologist, 22*, 109–133.

Harwood, C. G., & Anderson, R. (2012). Professional practice issues when working with team sports. In S. Hanton & S. D. Mellalieu (Eds.), *Professional practice in sport psychology: A review* (pp. 79–106). Abingdon, Oxon; New York, NY: Routledge.

Harwood, C. G., & Steptoe, K. (2013). The integration of single case designs in coaching contexts: A commentary for applied sport psychologists. *Journal of Applied Sport Psychology, 25*(1), 167–174. https://doi.org/10.1080/10413200.2012.690361

Henriksen, K. (2010). *The ecology of talent development in sports*. Odense, Denmark: University of Southern Denmark. Retrieved from https://doi.org/10.1038/332676b0

Henriksen, K. (2015). Developing a high-performance culture: A sport psychology intervention from an ecological perspective in elite orienteering. *Journal of Sport Psychology in Action, 6*(3), 141–153. https://doi.org/10.1080/21520704.2015.1084961

Henriksen, K., & Roessler, K. K. (2011). Riding the wave of an expert : A successful talent development environment in kayaking. *The Sport Psychologist, 25*, 341–362.

Henriksen, K., Stambulova, N., & Roessler, K. K. (2010a). Holistic approach to athletic talent development environments: A successful sailing milieu. *Psychology of Sport and Exercise, 11*(3), 212–222. https://doi.org/10.1016/j.psychsport.2009.10.005

Henriksen, K., Stambulova, N., & Roessler, K. K. (2010b). Successful talent development in track and field: Considering the role of environment. *Scandinavian Journal of Medicine and Science in Sports, 20*, 122–132. https://doi.org/10.1111/j.1600-0838.2010.01187.x

Henriksen, K., Storm, L. K., & Larsen, C. H. (2018). Organisational culture and influence on developing athletes. In C. J. Knight, C. G. Harwood & D. Gould (Eds.), *Sport psychology for young athletes* (1st ed., pp. 216–227). London: Routledge.

Henriksen, K., Storm, L. K., Stambulova, N., Pyrdol, N., & Larsen, C. H. (2019). Successful and less successful interventions with youth and senior athletes: Insights from expert sport psychology practitioners. *Journal of Clinical Sport Psychology, 13*(1), 72–94. https://doi.org/10.1123/jcsp.2017-0005

Johnson, U., Andersson, K., & Fallby, J. (2011). Sport psychology consulting among Swedish premier soccer coaches. *International Journal of Sport and Exercise Psychology, 9*(4), 308–322. https://doi.org/10.1080/1612197X.2011.623455

Kvale, S., & Brinkmann, S. (2009). *InterView: Introduktion til et håndværk* (2nd ed.). Købehavn: Hans Reitzels Forlag.

Larsen, C. H. (2013). *"Made in Denmark": Ecological perspectives on applied sport psychology and talent development in Danish professional football*. Odense, Denmark: University of Southern Denmark.

Larsen, C. H. (2017). Bringing a knife to a gunfight: A coherent consulting philosophy might not be enough to be effective in professional soccer. *Journal of Sport Psychology in Action*, 1–10. https://doi.org/10.1080/21520704.2017.1287142

Larsen, C. H. (2018). Working in Danish ice hockey: Psychological services derived from the context Carsten. *Journal of Sport Psychology in Action, 9*(2), 121–131.

Larsen, C. H., Alfermann, D., & Christensen, M. K. (2012). Psychosocial skills in a youth soccer academy: A holistic ecological perspective. *Sport Science Review, XXI*(3–4), 51–74. https://doi.org/10.2478/v10237-012-0010-x

Larsen, C. H., Alfermann, D., Henriksen, K., & Christensen, M. K. (2013). Successful talent development in soccer: The characteristics of the environment. *Sport, Exercise, and Performance Psychology, 2*(3), 190–206. https://doi.org/10.1037/a0031958

Larsen, C. H., Henriksen, K., & Alfermann, D. (2014). Preparing footballers for the next step : An intervention program from an ecological perspective. *The Sport Psychologist, 28*, 91–102. https://doi.org/10.1123/pes.2013-0015

Lovett, G. (2018). World football report. Retrieved from https://doi.org/www.sponsorreport.nl/download.php?id=113

MacNamara, Á. (2011). Psychological characteristics of developing excellence. In D. Collins, A. Abbott & H. Richard (Eds.), *Performance psychology: A practitioner's guide* (pp. 47–64). London: Elsevier. Retrieved from https://doi.org/10.1016/B978-0-443-06734-1.00004-3

Martindale, R., & Mortimer, P. (2011). Talent development environments: Key considerations for effective practice. In D. Collins, A. Abbott & H. Richard (Eds.), *Performance psychology: A practitioner's guide* (pp. 65–84). London: Elsevier. Retrieved from https://doi.org/10.1016/B978-0-443-06734-1.00005-5

Mcdougall, M., Nesti, M., Richardson, D., & Littlewood, M. (2017). Emphasising the culture in culture change: Examining current perspectives of culture and offering some alternative ones. *Sport & Exercise Psychology Review, 13*(1), 47–62. https://doi.org/https://doi.org/10.1016/j.jcorpfin.2010.10.004

Mills, A., Butt, J., Maynard, I., & Harwood, C. G. (2014). Toward an understanding of optimal development environments within elite English soccer academies. *The Sport Psychologist, 28*, 137–150. https://doi.org/10.1123/tsp.2013-0018

Morris, R., Tod, D., & Oliver, E. (2015). An analysis of organizational structure and transition outcomes in the youth-to-senior professional soccer transition. *Journal of Applied Sport Psychology, 27*(2), 216–234. https://doi.org/10.1080/10413200.2014.980015

Murphy, G. M., Petitpas, A. J., & Brewer, B. W. (1996). Identity foreclosure, athletic identity, and career maturity in intercollegiate athletes. *The Sport Psychologist, 10*, 239–246.

Nelson, L., Cushion, C., Potrac, P., & Groom, R. (2014). Carl Rogers, learning and educational practice: critical considerations and applications in sports coaching. *Sport, Education and Society, 19*(5), 513–531. https://doi.org/10.1080/13573322.2012.689256

Pain, M. A., & Harwood, C. G. (2004). Knowledge and perceptions of sport psychology within English soccer. *Journal of Sports Sciences, 22*(9), 813–826. https://doi.org/10.1080/02640410410001716670

Sarmento, H., Anguera, M. T., Pereira, A., & Araújo, D. (2018). Talent identification and development in male football: A systematic review. *Sports Medicine, 48*(4), 907–931. https://doi.org/10.1007/s40279-017-0851-7

Schroeder, P. J. (2010). Changing team culture: The perspectives of ten successful head coaches. *Journal of Sport Behavior, 33*(1), 63–88.

Spradley, J. P. (1980). *Participant observation*. Independence, KY: Thomson Learning, Inc.

Stake, R. E. (1995). *The art of case study research*. Thousand Oaks, CA: Sage Publications.

Storm, L. K., Henriksen, K., Larsen, C. H., & Christensen, M. K. (2014). Influential relationships as contexts of learning and becoming elite: Athletes' retrospective interpretations. *International Journal of Sports Science and Coaching, 9*(6), 1341–1356.

Storm, R. K., Nielsen, K., & Thomsen, F. (2016). Can a small nation be competitive in the global sporting arms race? The case of Denmark. *Managing Sport and Leisure, 21*(4), 181–202. https://doi.org/https://doi.org/10.1080/23750472.2016.1243993

Wagstaff, C. R. D., Fletcher, D., & Hanton, S. (2012). Positive organizational psychology in sport. *International Review of Sport and Exercise Psychology, 5*(2), 87–103. https://doi.org/10.1080/1750984X.2011.634920

Williams, S. J., & Kendall, L. (2007). Perceptions of elite coaches and sports scientists of the research needs for elite coaching practice. *Journal of Sports Sciences, 25*(14), 1577–1586. https://doi.org/10.1080/02640410701245550

12
APPLIED PSYCHOLOGY IN ACADEMY SOCCER SETTINGS

A Systems-Led Approach

Cherrie Daley, Chin Wei Ong, and Philippa McGregor

Brief Introduction and Review of Literature

In this chapter, we provide commentary on the evolving landscape of psychology provision within English soccer academy settings; recognising the wide range of existing approaches to delivery within such contexts, we explore the potential benefits and challenges associated with a systems-led approach to integration of the discipline in such settings. Recognising that it is less common for theory and real-world reflections to be coupled in the literature, we share a case-study example of a core project, underpinned by a systems-led approach. Somewhat uniquely, we offer a potential "how to" guide for practitioners to adapt and utilise as appropriate within their own applied contexts.

A Background to Applied Psychology in English Academy Soccer

The positive influence of psychology in elite soccer environments has been championed by both researchers and practitioners for more than a decade (Gilbourne & Richardson, 2005; Nesti, 2010; Pain & Harwood, 2009). These calls for a more integrative outlook to player development that included an emphasis on psychology were formalised institutionally, through the launch of the Football Association's (FA) four-corner model (i.e., technical/tactical, physical, social, and psychological; The FA, 2001). Specifically, the emphasis on psychology was aimed at developing future English players with psychological skills and strategies that would shape winning cultures and mentalities. Following the introduction of the four-corner model, the FA launched the "Psychology for Football" course in 2002 (The FA, 2002). This course was created to achieve the FA's strategic aim to provide better education and service to players and coaches around psychology, uniting them with qualified psychology professionals (Cale, 2004). Nonetheless, in comparison to the technical, tactical, and physical corners of soccer, the discipline of psychology continues to be plagued by challenges in its acceptance and integration into academy programmes (Pain & Harwood, 2004).

In an effort to improve the quality of and increase the opportunities for psychological work in English soccer academies, a long-term strategy for youth development in soccer was conceived by the Premier League in collaboration with other key stakeholders (Steptoe, Barker, & Harwood, 2016). Known as the Elite Player Performance Plan (EPPP), it details the processes and criteria necessary to create a world-leading academy system (The Premier League, 2011). The objectives of the EPPP are to (1) increase the number and quality of home-grown players;

(2) create more time for players to play and be coached; (3) improve coaching provision; (4) implement a system of effective measurement and quality assurance; (5) positively influence strategic investment into the academy system; and (6) seek to implement significant gains in every aspect of player development (Steptoe et al., 2016). To ensure close monitoring and adherence to the EPPP, an audit system was established on the criteria covering all four corners of soccer development. Specifically, academies are audited regularly and are awarded a category status ranging from 1 (highest award) to 4 (lowest award). Funding received by academies is contingent on the audit outcome, consequently incentivising academies to promote more holistic development programmes. Relative to the previous closed-minded industry towards psychology (Pain & Harwood, 2004), the introduction of the EPPP has certainly sparked a renewed focus on effective psychology provision in English soccer academies.

Organisational Structures of Applied Psychology

In comparison to Olympic, Paralympic, and other professional/elite environments (Durand-Bush, & Salmela, 2002; Gould, Eklund, & Jackson, 1992; Jones, Hanton, & Connaughton, 2002), psychology provision in soccer has been historically less accepted and embedded. As far as we are aware, EPPP academy staffing guidelines presently include no stipulated requirements to employ specialist psychological support staff within soccer academy programmes. Category 1 and 2 academies are required at the minimum to have a full-time Welfare and Safeguarding position to cover psychological wellbeing support, while Category 3 and 4 clubs may use their Head of Education to fulfil this role. The staffing specifications for other disciplines that require domain expertise (e.g., sport science) are defined with greater clarity, which raises some concerns around discipline and role expertise for promoting and supporting the psychological corner of development and wellbeing in soccer academies (Jones, 2018). Although there are a number of professional clubs and academies now integrating psychology into their programmes from a staffing perspective, they have done so using varied provision models. Depending on an academy's organisational structure and/or availability of resources, programmes could be led by academic institutions with a number of practitioners or trainee practitioners involved or rely on a single psychologist either employed as a member of staff or as an independent consultant.

As we have discussed so far, the challenge of integrating psychology is likely a consequence of (a) not having specialist support in place at all for psychology or having the psychology corner covered by other departments, (b) the psychology corner being overly academic rather than driven by applied expertise, and (c) having limited resource (single person or part-time/consultant-based positions). Further, it is not difficult to see how these conditions are associated with some of the reported challenges such as the lack of clarity, negative perceptions of players and staff towards psychology, delivery not being specific to the context and demands of the academy environment, content being overly academic and/or theoretical, and problems with psychology staff "fitting in" to the environment (Pain & Harwood, 2004). To illustrate, Harwood (2008) reported only after working in a professional soccer club as an applied practitioner for an extended period did the appreciation for the extensive scope, needs, and untapped potential of psychology services emerge. To date there remains a limited number of full-time psychology support staff in soccer academies and even fewer teams of psychology staff compared to other discipline areas (e.g., sport science and physiotherapy).

Psychology provision in academy soccer has been similar to other youth sport settings, traditionally as group-based educational workshops and individual one-to-one sessions, guided by welfare principles (i.e., "Children are not mini-adults"; Cale, 2004; Cotterill, 2012; Visek, Harris, & Blom, 2009). Delivery tends to be purposefully designed for player, coach, performance staff, and parent groups (Cotterill, 2012; Steptoe et al., 2016) and often takes place in a classroom-based environment. The content delivered is usually informed by the wealth of youth sport psychology literature available, which the psychology practitioner uses to define, craft, and deliver the sessions (Côté, 1999; Côté & Hancock, 2016; Harwood, 2005; MacNamara, Button, & Collins, 2010). The provision of pre-designed frameworks for applied practitioners to utilise (e.g., 5Cs and PCDEs) helps manage the all-too familiar challenge of limited time either at the club itself or within the academy schedule. Utilising such frameworks enables psychology practitioners to be able to "hit the ground running" in regard to areas of delivery.

Underlying Psychological Models/Frameworks to Optimise Youth Development

Sport facilitates positive youth development (The National Research Council and Institute of Medicine, 2002) by promoting aspects such as psychological safety, supportive relationships, opportunities to belong, and support for efficacy that are important features of programme design. Although these features are not specific to youth sporting environments, they are considered to be important foundations when building youth programme content (Côté & Abernethy, 2012). Further, Harwood (2005) provided the 5Cs model of soccer: commitment, communication, concentration, control, and confidence. Such psychological factors served to identify key motivational, self-regulatory, and interpersonal attributes that had previously informed psychology educational interventions, as well as developmental assets deemed important for youth soccer (Holt & Dunn, 2004). The 5Cs model has been utilised in several research studies in academy soccer, lending itself to presentations, logbook, parent, and coach education sessions (Harwood, 2008; Harwood, Barker, & Anderson, 2015; Higham, Harwood, & Cale, 2005; Pain, Harwood, & Anderson, 2015). Although success has been achieved utilising this model, research has consistently reported the benefit of using the 5Cs to support those with greater access to players (e.g., coaches) in becoming more confident with sport psychology and its potential to be integrated into different discipline areas (Harwood, 2008; Harwood et al., 2015).

With talent development as a focal point, MacNamara et al. (2010) identified a range of psychological factors that are key to maximising potential and maintaining excellence: competitiveness, commitment, vision of what it takes to succeed, imagery, importance of working on weaknesses, coping under pressure, game awareness, and self-belief. This research is built upon talent development work conducted earlier in music (MacNamara, Holmes, & Collins, 2006), which identified motivation, commitment, goal-setting, quality practice, imagery, realistic performance evaluations, coping under pressure, and social skills as psychological factors for talent transitions to occur. Coined as the psychological characteristics of developing excellence (PCDEs), these identified psychological factors incorporated psychological skills, attitudes, emotions, and desires needed to successfully realise potential, with considerable overlap established between sport and music environments. Nonetheless, MacNamara et al. (2010) acknowledged that consideration should be given to any list of PCDEs based on stage of development and performance domains. This suggests that although pre-defined psychological models and frameworks are useful in helping to provide an evidence-informed starting point for psychology support programmes, practitioners should consider tailoring the content to the specific environment and sporting context in which they operate.

Linked to the recommendation of developmentally appropriate programme design, the Developmental Model of Sport Participation (DMSP; Côté, 1999; Côté, Baker, & Abernethy, 2007) has also been influential in informing youth sport systems aiming to provide quality experiences. The DMSP presents concepts about athlete development that are considered quantifiable and testable yet targeted at performance, participation, and personal development (Côté & Hancock, 2016). Considerations made by the DMSP included diversity and deliberate play considered at various stages of development (sampling years 6–12; recreational participation or specialising years 13–15; investment years 16+) as well as early specialisation. The key processes of deliberate play, diversification, and the environment in which the processes occur (the influence of coaches, peers and parents) were deemed to facilitate the integration of performance, participation, and personal development in youth sport. Overly structured, competitive, and adult-driven sporting environments were identified as leading to negative outcomes during childhood. However, post-adolescence, intensive, sport-specific, competitive, success-focused programmes were recommended if the intended outcome is to produce elite performers (Côté & Hancock, 2016). In line with previous research it was suggested youth sport programmes should use a holistic and integrated approach (Côté et al., 2007). For example, coach-led/delivered psychological programmes can often be more effective than those delivered solely by psychologists (Brown & Fletcher, 2017).

Despite the growing body of research and applied practice within academy soccer, the number of empirical and practical resources available to practitioners is relatively limited. From our collective experiences within such environments, we recognise that soccer academies present a somewhat unique version of long-term player development. Players can sign with academies' Foundation Phase from as young as 8, before progressing into the Youth Development Phase where some will be offered places on the full-time training model. At the age of 16 players then enter the Professional Development Phase and are offered scholarships and, in some cases, professional contracts. Given the potential age of initial recruitment, there emerges a substantial accumulation of years during childhood and adolescence that young people can spend in an academy system. Additionally, the unfavourable statistics on young players progressing through the academies to the first team only serve to highlight the higher obligation soccer academies have to their young players. Beyond developing players to prepare them for professional careers in the game, academies must also take responsibility for the development of the person, equipping them with skills and attributes that not only complement their soccer performance but also their personal development (Harwood, 2008).

Acknowledging and evidencing the relevant research in the field of youth sport and academy soccer, we set out on our mission of being able to shape, design, and build an approach to psychology that is contextualised to academy soccer. This approach to psychology would span across ten academy teams and allows us to use our resources as efficiently as possible without compromising on quality and impact. However, even the best programmes require craft in integration. Informed by our collective applied experience, we avoided creating the impression of psychology being "owned" by the psychologist, because such an approach often leads to a lack of integration and consequently short-lived impact (Brown & Fletcher, 2017). Instead, we believe that a systems-led approach where psychological concepts are owned and driven by a wide range of coaching and multidisciplinary staff will have a stronger chance of success.

Practical Applications—Case study

Background and Context

Integration of Applied Psychology Through a Systems-Led Approach

Talent development within soccer academies has been informed significantly by the theories and empirical research on the psychological aspect of talent development in sport (e.g., the 5Cs model, PCDEs, and the DMSP). While the creation of new knowledge has positively influenced perspectives towards psychology in the domain of talent development, most of the literature has focused narrowly on psychology and less so on how psychology impacts development in tandem with the other "corners of development" (e.g., technical, tactical and physical; Arthur, Callow, Roberts, & Glendinning, 2019; Brown & Fletcher, 2017; Harwood, 2008). Without a broad-based insight to talent development, and the role psychology plays in it, it is unsurprising that various challenges around effective integration of psychology (both in terms of practice and knowledge) still persist. An example of this lack of integration is reflected in the underlying belief in soccer that talent (especially the psychological aspect) is binary. Despite the aforementioned theoretical and empirical models such as the 5Cs, PCDEs, and the DMSP, supporting the idea that psychological characteristics conducive for talent development can be cultivated among young athletes, the soccer world can still sometimes operate around the consensus that a young player either has "it" or not. Evidently, the recognition of psychology as an important component of understanding talent is only part of the process; there is still work to be done in soccer to integrate psychology and shift thinking.

We believe the challenges in integration are largely due to peoples' natural tendencies to focus narrowly when thinking about cause and effect. Indeed, such perspectives are evident in sport, where a "myth of individualism"—the fallacy of sporting success or failure being determined by the individual, or the sum of individual parts in teams (Wagstaff, 2017)—is purported to prevail. The susceptibility of isolated thinking is more pronounced in high-performance environments where there is pressure and preoccupation over results. A consequence of a results-oriented outlook is the narrow and short-term focus on the psychology of the performer(s), which has probably perpetuated a practice model that is aimed at working directly with the performer(s). Although popular and very relevant, relying solely on a performer centric model of practice might not be optimising the impact psychology can have on performance and/or development in soccer academies. For example, a focus on developing psychological preparedness during competition is important, but it might not be addressing the anxieties that stem from broader aspects such as team (un)selection and scholarships. Further, the professionalisation and modernisation of sport at the elite level has led to increasingly complex organisational structures in sport becoming commonplace (e.g., Cruickshank, Collins, & Minten, 2013). Indeed, several English soccer academies have evolved complex organisational structures that typically comprise interconnected clusters of specialised teams (e.g., sport science, coaching, education, and welfare) that are coordinated centrally via a structure of hierarchy (e.g., performance/technical directors, heads of department). To this end, there is benefit for applied practitioners within soccer academies to engage in a *systems-led approach*, so that a broader sense of what constitutes cause and effect can be attained. Having a broader view enhances the ability of psychologists to understand the multiple influences of behaviours, how these influencing factors are interlinked, and consequently the opportunities that are available to positively impact these behaviours.

A Systems-Led Approach

When encountering an applied challenge, a typical response from practitioners would be to break down this challenge into smaller, more manageable chunks and then examining each component in detail. Such an approach essentially permits us to figure out cause and effect without the influence of confounding factors, which has led to impressive advances in knowledge, most evidently in scientific research. However, studying only the cause and effect of core components often means that it ignores the integrative and dynamic characteristics of complex systems, which could make proposed solutions to problems unsuited to the intended context in the real world (Pawson & Tilley, 2014). Indeed, real-world challenges are often greater than the sum of their parts, therefore attempting to address applied challenges by reducing problems into isolated concepts is likely to be ineffective. For example, the reasons behind challenging behaviours displayed by adolescent players in a soccer academy might not always be confined to the academy but can be influenced by situations/events occurring outside of soccer, such as at home or in school (Ong, McGregor, & Daley, 2018).

Recognising a soccer academy as a system—an organised collection of elements interconnected in a pattern that produces a characteristic set of behaviours over time, often classified as "purpose" (Meadows, 2008)—positions applied practice closer to the real world. Three key aspects make up a system: elements, interconnections between them, and purpose. Elements can be things within the system that are tangible and visible, as well as intangible and more difficult to pinpoint. In a system such as a soccer academy, tangible elements could be the building, the pitches, staff, and players, while intangible ones could be the nurturing demeanour of staff, the collective pride in the achievements of players from the academy, and the prevailing attitudes towards the provision of psychology. Interconnections are the links that hold elements together. In the soccer academy, these could comprise the multidimensional development programmes for players, interactions among people like meetings and gossip, and the translation of knowledge to application—or learning—which presumably is the purpose for soccer academies. A systems-led approach would encourage applied practitioners to see not only the "big picture" of how soccer academies function, but also appreciate their unique intricacies and nuances. For example, it helps us to make sense of seemingly more implicit but important factors such as, "What it means to players and staff to be part of a soccer academy?" or "What is the definition of success to players and staff in the academy?" Such insight would help psychologists to cultivate greater agility in supporting players and staff under varying contexts.

A Systems-Led Approach to Applied Practice

The goal of applying a systems-led approach is to enable psychologists to effectively comprehend and manage complexity that is reflective of their real-world environment. Characteristics of high functioning systems are resilience, self-organisation, and hierarchy. A resilient system is one that has the capacity to withstand or restore itself from the effect of stressors under variable circumstances. Developing a resilient system requires a rich network of consistent behaviours that will serve to withstand or restore the system back to its original state. Therefore, building up a collection of consistent behaviours towards psychology could be a key aim for a psychologist within any soccer academy. This can be achieved by creating a unique academy-branded shared model to guide the practice of psychology. This shared model of practice is based on principles of participation and mutual learning among staff that allows for the democratisation of psychology to take place organically. The consultative and supportive roles of the psychologist with this approach promotes a shared ownership of a unique academy-led brand of psychology (Arthur et al., 2019), as opposed to perspectives of psychology being a specialist area that is "owned" by psychologists. The litmus test of a resilient system, would be when psychology is integrated with other disciplines of work in the academy (e.g., coaching) and is confidently and sustainably being applied without the direct intervention of the psychologist.

Enabling staff to drive psychology-based interventions also encourages systems to be self-organising—that is the system's ability to learn, diversify, complexify, and evolve (Meadows, 2008). Creating a shared model of practice inevitably invites a diversification of ideas, which helps to shape, complexify and evolve the academy's unique brand of applied psychology. A potential risk of self-organisation is the inherent uncertainty of creating something new and more complex, which could be frightening to some individuals who prefer doing things in ways they are used to. Self-organising behaviour can also threaten power structures and could face resistance. One example of increasing self-organisation is the use of diverse language to describe certain psychological concepts observed in soccer; it causes confusion if left unchecked. For instance, terms like "courage," "bravery," and "self-belief" are common terms used in the soccer context to describe what is essentially known in the psychology literature as "confidence." Without attempts to establish a shared language for psychology within the soccer context, confusion is bound to take place. Thus, self-organisation needs to be directed in a way so that shared outcomes are realised. An example of this in a soccer academy is the group case formulation approach to making sense of challenging player behaviours, which aims to safeguard players' mental wellbeing. This was a self-organising initiative in terms of inviting diverse input from multiple parties in the sense-making process, which complexified the process, but was guided effectively by the underpinning City PASS framework to achieve the intended purpose (Ong et al., 2018). Self-organising behaviour is a hallmark of an evolving system which can bring about both value and chaos. To fully harness the value of a self-organising system, a careful balance of providing guidance and promoting autonomy is required by the applied practitioner.

The Paradox of Language: The Source of Confusion and Clarity

Language is key to the communication of information and ideas, without which systems cannot thrive. To facilitate clear information streams, language needs to be precise and meaningful, so that confusion is avoided, especially when systems become more complex (e.g., this is what we mean when we describe a player as being confident). When systems evolve, the language used to convey information also needs to be consistent across the breadth of the system (e.g., Is being confident on the pitch the same as that off the pitch? If not, how do we distinguish them?). As mentioned earlier, there is a lack of clarity and consensus in the language/terms used to describe psychological characteristics in self-organising systems, which has created conceptual confusion and inconsistent language within the discipline. This lack of clarity and consensus is compounded by the lack of clarity within the research literature as well (e.g., mental toughness—Hardy, Bell, & Beattie, 2014; resilience—Thelwell, Weston, & Greenlees, 2005). Indeed, previous commentary on the use of language in psychology proposed that language could be the source of misunderstandings that led some to draw hasty and misleading conclusions about psychological concepts (Lindsay, Pitt, & Thomas, 2014). Further, the authors elaborated that there is a susceptibility in psychology to confuse verbs with nouns, which could be innocuous but has led to the mistaken belief certain psychological characteristics are "had" rather than "done." A good example is the one shared earlier on the tendency for people in soccer to engage in binary thinking when describing talent. Thus, it is important when devising a shared model of practice that language is carefully crafted to convey as accurately as possible its intended meaning, so as not to confuse and mislead.

When considering language, it should also be recognised that the vocabulary used is inherent and unique to specific cultures. Indeed, in soccer there are certain types of language that are more commonly used and their meanings sometimes implicitly understood by only insiders of the sport. For any model, intervention or strategy to work, it is imperative that it is sensitive to the idiosyncrasies of language that are specific to a particular culture. For example, "courage" could be used in soccer to describe what is essentially known as "confidence" in the psychology literature, so using the former in the soccer context would be more suitable. Involving a diverse group of members in the soccer academy in the process of creating this shared model of practice enabled us to capture a wide bandwidth of language that is unique to (academy) soccer, which we subsequently used to craft this shared model of practice for psychology. Utilising language that is familiar to the soccer lexicon helps with creating "stickiness" that would promote greater receptiveness and therefore ownership of the model, aid understanding and communication of concepts, and ultimately a model that members feel confident about and can rely upon to integrate psychological principles in their own specialised fields of work (Gladwell, 2000). Crafting a shared model of practice that is sensitive to the language commonly used in a given system promotes a "shared language" of psychology in the academy, thereby opening up information streams for people to communicate effectively and for ideas to flow.

A soccer academy is a dynamic system composed of interconnected elements that strives to evolve, complexify and organise itself in order to achieve a common purpose. Crafting a shared model of psychology that is guided by a systems-led approach enhances the capacity to integrate with other disciplines of work. The integrative process is also facilitated by the emphasis on establishing a common language for psychology within the shared model, achieved through enhanced communication and information streams.

Presenting Issue(s)

Crafting a Systems-Led Approach to Applied Psychology

We propose that a fundamental tenet of the systems-led approach is acceptance that the individual psychologist or team of psychology practitioners cannot wholly "own" psychology in the context. By very definition, this approach aims to integrate the discipline into "how it is around here"—the everyday language, frameworks, and common practices of the academy. Broadening the sense of involvement and ownership of psychology concepts and projects to include coaching, support, and operational staff has the potential to create great gains in terms of integration of the discipline (Arthur et al., 2019; Lindsay et al., 2014) but it is not without challenges. The skill sets required to effectively educate staff to co-create and employ various projects are critical, as is an ability to drop our own sense of ego in relation to the discipline. If we can embed core concepts so effectively that staff across the system begin to speak comfortably and confidently about them, referencing themselves and the broader academy as architects and owners of these initiatives then we have, to some degree, achieved a key outcome.

For the psychologist, this may well feel very challenging, because sharing ownership and direction of key projects with staff outside the discipline can mean more work and less control (than in more traditional MST approaches). The dynamic (often described as "self-organizing") nature of any system can create a sense of almost constant flux. Psychologists are not immune to the sense of evaluation regarding the front facing aspects of our roles and are of course keen to deliver impact against the backdrop of a less tangible and relatively young discipline in the sport; these can add to the discomfort we may experience when relinquishing total control of "our work" in an unpredictable environment. The temptation to retreat in to "telling" what psychology should look like from the comfort of an "expert" position may well be great, however the authors maintain that the richness and longevity that may be achieved through collaborative initiatives is worth that sacrifice. A further temptation or pressure that will likely occur in such settings is the drive (from ourselves or others) to focus in a more reactive manner on the "here and now" delivery, for example to provide support to the most talented older players or to teams reaching key stages in various youth competitions. In our experience, the innately competitive nature of coaching staff (even in a talent development environment) will serve to exacerbate that pressure to focus on short-term gains; this is why a strong understanding of the drivers for key stakeholders is important. We recommend seeking an appropriate balance between some immediate support (particularly around any instances of risk or wellbeing concerns), while maintaining an investment in the future coherence of psychology services through a commitment to the systems-led approach.

More specifically, this approach is based on the belief that an in-depth and evolving understanding of the system, combined with a flexible and low-ego approach to engagement, will pay dividends. Striking a balance between inclusivity in project design and providing clear and well-informed guidelines for those collaborative sessions is most critical. Indeed, a clear strategy and the development of a strong model for the project should allow more flexibility and comfort later on. If the co-creation occurs within your clear model, then it is easier to adopt a "less is more" approach to your direct input in sessions, having the confidence to guide other staff through this model and the humility to understand that they may hold many of the answers that you don't is most critical. The inherent engagement, flexibility, and coherence that are required to do so effectively have led us to refer to these applications as "craft" rather than "delivery"; it is a highly challenging but potentially fruitful enterprise.

As referenced previously, the reductionist approach in scientific examination is incompatible with the interactionist reality of an applied practice setting. The most effective integration of the discipline must harness both scientific underpinning and expertly crafted application in order to maximise impact. At the heart of this approach (and the effective integration of wider staff groups) is the translation of concepts in to easily digestible, "snappy," and impactful projects that can be co-created, launched, and maintained by a wider group of staff. To help us stay focused on this integrative approach, we return repeatedly to the question—"How long would this project/approach/concept live if I/we left the environment?" Sharing ownership allows us to generate a sense of shared pride around something and to avoid the possibility of psychology existing as a potentially alien and isolated concept.

Practically speaking, we would recommend the below as a good starting point either when first initiating work in this setting or before starting a new chapter; given the dynamic nature of any system, we recommend revisiting this on an ongoing basis as even subtle changes in the context can be influential. While holding true to the overarching strategy, the psychologist/s should have clear project aims and then set out to capture all the things they know (or can discover) about the academy context:

- Who are the key stakeholders? (who will have touching points with this in any way?)
- Identify the "gatekeepers" (who might "champion" or "kill" this project/concept?)
- What projects have been launched before in this space?
- What has worked well and not so well and why?
- What are the contextual realities? (e.g., are key staff new or long-serving appointments, is there a sense of concern in terms of job stability that could be impactful? Who might this project create more "work" for in their day to day practice? How might this project impact on something staff are accountable for?)
- What are the perspectives and preferences of those key staff?
- What are the key staff most concerned or fearful about?
- What are the practical implications of achieving the strategic aims here? (e.g., how are we constrained by contact time, existing models, staffing levels and other resource related factors?)

(see Cotterill, 2012, for relevant learnings related to this)

Once the aforementioned has been considered, the psychologist/s should have a stable platform to build a framework for the project before launching into the engagement piece with wider staff. Once the project begins to take shape, we can then begin to think about the most appropriate way to "wrap" each element of the project for maximum impact (we refer to this approach as "packaging") and create a clear, realistic, and time-bound plan for launching various elements of the project over time (we borrow from the world of marketing and refer to these as "activations"). It is reasonable to expect that you may need to package the project in different ways for end-user groups (e.g., staff, players, parents) and that a wide variety of "activations" may be required in order to create the desired integration and impact over time.

When you take a systems-led approach you can aim to harness a common "in house" approach to psychology which brings some coherence. In reality, this may share the same theoretical underpinning as many other approaches but, done well, it will be crafted in the best manner to suit the system and its stage of maturity in terms of psychology integration. Of course, most applied psychologists will already integrate some systems thinking in their approach, regardless of their preferred working model. For example, when we work 1–1 with a player but start to consider their support network as a possible area of intervention, we are effectively acknowledging that the performance of a player not as an isolated occurrence, but one that is part of a wider system. We are always clear not to discredit any other models and approaches; there are many ways to approach our practice and a systems-led approach is just one. It is important to anticipate that practitioners (particularly coaches) will likely have a view of psychology developed through their own experience, interest, reading and/or through content within their structured coach education "badges" or other training which may not fit well with the framework you propose. Therefore, be prepared when coaches or others challenge a particular approach or feel more comfortable with a model they have employed previously (e.g., the 5Cs approach or PCDE model, both of which are well-grounded and widely utilised within the United Kingdom). It has been our experience that some coaches have, over time, even designed their own individual philosophies which include the "Mental" aspects of player development. This can be one of the most challenging things you will face when launching a new "in house" model of psychology, as such philosophies may not be as well-underpinned and could likely contrast with the shared model. You might expect to encounter strong resistance (overt or otherwise) to a new shared model and so it is worth spending time during the early scoping phases to spot these challenges and plan contingencies. It isn't necessary to harshly critique other approaches, not least since many of them are intuitively good, but it is essential to have a clear rationale for why the club may design and integrate their own. One of the easiest approaches here could be to liken the debate to soccer playing philosophy and compare the need for each club to know and articulate their own soccer style.

We wish to emphasise that simplifying psychology and creating "sticky" concepts is not about "dumbing down" but "opening up" knowledge and perspectives that can serve the system well. In our projects we have repeatedly tested psychology practitioners to learn new concepts and about a variety of disciplines to give us the best chance of threading the projects through the wider system. For example, staff could upskill themselves in performance analysis software to give them the best chance of creating strong activations with that team. These activations have reinforced the projects more broadly and can applied readily to discussions on soccer performance.

Intervention/Work Conducted

We propose that a great starting point in any development environment is to create a shared framework and common language for psychology, and to do that in a collaborative manner.

In many academy environments there may have been earlier approaches to psychology delivery, or there may have been no inclusion of psychology—either way, some degree of change will be required, so this is something you should scope and consider before proceeding. You may want to do this at the same time as identifying key stakeholders and some of the other considerations referenced above, and you can request time with a wide variety of individuals to get their sense about what has been done before and what could be done moving forward. This could be invaluable as staff may reveal significant insight into previous interventions or constraints

CREATE a sense of urgency

INSTITUTE change

BUILD a guiding coalition

SUSTAIN acceleration

the big opportunity

FORM a strategic vision and initiatives

GENERATE short-term wins

ENLIST a volunteer army

ENABLE action by removing barriers

FIGURE 12.1 Kotter's (2014) eight-step model for leading change
Source: (Reprinted with permission)

TABLE 12.1 Kotter's (2014) eight-step model—illustrated against our case study

Step 1—Create a sense of urgency

Without being overtly critical of any work that has preceded this approach, it's important to generate a clear reason why change is required and why it is needed now—what will happen if we don't change it now? What are the benefits if we do? In terms of stakeholders, can you align the benefits of this change with their key drivers or the risks of not changing with their fears or concerns? In our project, we conducted a piece of work with coaches and scouts which captured the wide range of terms and definitions they were employing when defining and describing the "Mental" aspects of players. From this we built a compelling case (upwards and on the ground) for the importance of this work (by playing out the risks if we didn't address this) and gained support to invest in it.

***Step 2*—Build a guiding coalition**

Ensure that the right people are on-board with this and can play a part in guiding the process. Soccer can be incredibly hierarchical so it is important to include (or certainly keep appraised) people in positions of power or influence as well as ensuring that coaching and other disciplines are represented. If there are some people within your system who you feel could be resistant or undermine the project then target them early and try to get them in to the coalition as "first followers" of the concepts, harness the energy of others and give some ownership to key individuals.

Step 3—Form a strategic vision

A wider long-term strategy for psychology would be a key component of any systems-based approach, but individual projects such as this should also have them. What is the broader objective here? How can you capture and articulate that clearly and consistently? What is appealing about this vision? Remember that change can feel challenging or risky. This is your opportunity to link the project with the key drivers of people within the organisation. How will this project be delivered in a time-bounded and realistic manner? Our experience (the typical "planning fallacy") is that every step takes longer than you anticipate and so you should give yourself plenty of time to design and launch the work.

***Step 4*—Enlist a volunteer army**

For us this meant combining a strong group of psychology practitioners (with clear roles and responsibilities in the project) with a wider group within the other disciplines. These practitioners need to be brought in, able to see and articulate to others the value and potential impact of the project. From the outset you should consider how these people will be involved (in a safe environment) and (importantly) credited for their input?

***Step 5*—Enable action by removing barriers**

We refer to this above but "clearing the path" in terms of previous models/approaches that may linger is key. You must work to understand how staff feel about current or previous approaches and how they are currently "living" in the environment. You need to ensure that the space exists for the project to grow and get traction. For example, you could go through an entire piece of change management, build a new model, launch and run it for a year before finding that coaches were still employing an earlier model in all of their session planning—simply because they are used to it and the printed sheets that they have to complete still feature the "boxes" or "headings" that relate to the previous model! You might also find that existing coach education programmes and academy evaluations are referring specifically to other models. To "clear the path" you must put in the work which will make it at least as easy, if not easier, to adopt the new common model. In our project we took steps to embed the shared language in to the day-to-day evaluation and planning tools for coaches, medics included aspects from the model within their rehabilitation planning templates, and so on.

*Step 6—***Generate short-term wins**

Taking a truly systems-led approach and launching a shared model/language is not a short-term task. For that reason, this approach may be better suited to academy/youth development environments than first-team performance equivalents. Within the longer-term strategy for the project it is critical to identify shorter term "milestones" and opportunities to achieve and celebrate success—particularly to maintain the enthusiasm and momentum with the volunteer army. Expect setbacks along the way; it might even be worth identifying the potential of some of these at the outset and doing some contingency planning, but ensure that you visibly celebrate successes of the project.

*Step 7—***Sustain acceleration**

We would probably refer to this as "maintaining momentum," and it is critical to the delivery of change. It is critical that we don't work very hard to launch a "shiny" new approach only to falter when it comes to embedding that into every day working approaches. It is particularly important to think about this even as a project enjoys success. This relates strongly to the core project planning work and central project strategy; how would you plan out the broader impact plan and how will you anticipate when things could slow or become stale? Done well, the systems-led approach needs to be dynamic, flexing as the system evolves, and a core project like this must do the same. You should expect that the initial launch might be successful but that, unless we are mindful, the project could stall. Plan ways to continue to evolve and integrate the shared model, "refreshing" and adapting it over time where required.

*Step 8—***Institute Change**

This is about ensuring that the model "lives" in the academy environment. Although this is Step 8, these aspects should have been considered and integrated throughout every step of the plan, what will take this model off the page, out of the "classroom" and on to the pitch, into the team talk and the treatment room? One very deliberate action within our approach was to make the shared model highly behavioural—it is a collection of things that are not just "said" but "done." In employing that approach, we were able to thread the model through every discipline, providing a platform and simple language through which coaches and support staff can have consistent conversations with players about behaviours in the performance context. The model increased the consistency and alignment of those conversations with players as they progress through the pathway age groups; therefore, the project managed to largely replace the varied beliefs and practices that staff previously adhered to.

that it would be difficult for you to spot at the outset and therefore your plan for implementing change (to whatever degree is required) will benefit from that input.

When seeking the required change to design, launch, and embed a shared framework for psychogym we have borrowed from the well-known "eight-step model for leading change" (Kotter, 2014).

Case-Study Reflections

i. Have a clear strategic plan for psychology and aims for each project you deliver—these don't need to be shared more widely but should guide your work.
ii. Be patient, do not underestimate the time required to bring about change in such dynamic systems. Ensure you manage the expectations of key stakeholders around what is required to do this well (and the benefits of that).

iii. A core part of the "craft" required here revolves around sharing ownership of these projects. We invested heavily in the integration of "member checking" style procedures during design (reverting back to staff as the framework developed to get their feedback on whether it represented their input and the "real-world" requirements) to ensure that staff felt a sense of ownership—this aided the creation of first followers.

iv. The benefit of having a psychology team to check and challenge each other during the process was clear. If you are operating as a lone practitioner in an academy then it might be worth finding some "critical friends" from the discipline to perform this role for you.

Summary and Conclusions

As structures within academy soccer continue to evolve and modernise, the conditions that drive performance or talent development become more complex. For psychology to enable young people to fulfil their potential in these complex and dynamic environments, we propose a systems-led approach to the discipline. We acknowledge that such an approach might not be the most straightforward to implement and may not be suitable under certain conditions, but if done well, it is a highly effective approach to achieving enduring integration of psychology within an academy environment.

Key Messages and Further Reading

1. We can learn from, yet not be restricted by, how psychology has been "done" in other elite sporting environments for implementation in academy soccer settings.
2. The integration and delivery of psychology within academy soccer varies across clubs, with no right or wrong ways established or prescribed. Scoping what has come before and what the current needs and demands are could be useful initial steps.
3. Acknowledging the integrated nature of psychology across allied disciplines and departments when building it into soccer academy programmes.
4. A systems-led approach is a good complement to individual/team focused approaches to applied practice.
5. It is important to consider the use of language when developing shared models of practice.

We have highlighted the five most pertinent further reading resources below:

Arthur, R. A., Callow, N., Roberts, R., & Glendinning, F. (2019). Coaches coaching psychological skills: Why not? A framework and questionnaire development. *Journal of Sport & Exercise Psychology*, *41*, 10–23.

Lindsay, P., Pitt, T., & Thomas, O. (2014). Bewitched by our words: Wittgenstein, language-games, and the pictures that hold sport psychology captive. *Sport & Exercise Psychology Review*, *10*, 41–54.

Meadows, D. H. (2008). *Thinking in systems: A primer*. White River Junction, VT: Chelsea Green Publishing.

Ong, C. W., McGregor, P., & Daley, C. (2018). The boy behind the bravado: Player advanced safety and support in a professional football academy setting. *Sport & Exercise Psychology Review*, *14*, 65–79.

Steptoe, K., Barker, J. B., & Harwood, C. (2016). Psychological service provision to the elite football performance network: Supporting coaches, players, parents, and teams. In J. G. Cremades & L. S. Tashman (Eds.), *Global practices and training in applied, sport, exercise, and psychology: A case study approach* (pp. 79–87). London: Routledge.

Acknowledgements

"Alone we can do so little. Together we can do so much."

Helen Keller.

We would like to acknowledge the contributions of our sport psychology team members—Lorraine O'Malley, Jennie Killilea, Luke Dennison and Cassie Wood—who have been instrumental in implementing the systems-led approach described in this chapter.

References

Brown, D. J., & Fletcher, D. (2017). Effects of psychological and psychosocial interventions on sport performance: A meta-analysis. *Sports Medicine, 47,* 77–99.
Cale, A. (2004). *Psychology for football: The official FA guide to success on and off the pitch.* London: FA Learning.
Côté, J. (1999). The influence of the family in the development of talent in sport. *The Sport Psychologist, 13,* 395–417.
Côté, J., & Abernethy, B. (2012). A developmental approach to sport expertise. In S. M. Murphy (Ed.), *The Oxford handbook of sport and performance psychology* (3rd ed., pp. 435–447). New York, NY: Oxford University Press.
Côté, J., Baker, J., & Abernethy, B. (2007). Practice and play in the development of sport expertise. In G. Tenenbaum & R. C. Eklund (Eds.), *Handbook of sport psychology* (pp. 184–202). New York, NY: John Wiley & Sons.
Côté, J., & Hancock, D. J. (2016). Evidence-based policies for youth sport programmes. *International Journal of Sport Policy and Politics, 8,* 51–65.
Cotterill, S. (2012). Experience of working in an elite sports academy: A case study in professional cricket. *Sport & Exercise Psychology Review, 8,* 45–53.
Cruickshank, A., Collins, D., & Minten, S. (2013). Culture change in a professional sports team: Shaping environmental contexts and regulating power. *International Journal of Sports Science & Coaching, 8,* 271–290.
Durand-Bush, N., & Salmela, J. H. (2002). The development and maintenance of expert athletic performance: Perceptions of World and Olympic champions. *Journal of Applied Sport Psychology, 14,* 154–171.
The Football Association. (2001). The future England player: Skills and attributes. Retrieved May 14, 2019, from www.thefa.com/learning/england-dna/the-future-england-player/attributes-and-skills
The Football Association. (2002). The FA psychology award level 1. Retrieved May 14, 2019, from https://learning.thefa.com/totara/program/view.php?id=160
Gilbourne, D., & Richardson, D. (2005). A practitioner-focused approach to the provision of psychological support in soccer: Adopting action research themes and processes. *Journal of Sports Sciences, 23,* 651–658.
Gladwell, M. (2000). *The tipping point: How little things can make a big difference.* New York, NY: Back Bay Books.
Gould, D., Eklund, R. C., & Jackson, S. A. (1992). 1988 U.S. Olympic wrestling excellence: I: Mental preparation, precompetitive cognition, and affect. *The Sport Psychologist, 6,* 358–382.
Hardy, L., Bell, J., & Beattie, S. (2014). A neuropsychological model of mentally tough behavior. *Journal of Personality, 82,* 69–81.
Harwood, C. G. (2005). Goals: More than just the score. In S. Murphy (Ed.), *The sport psych handbook* (pp. 19–36). Champaign, IL: Human Kinetics.
Harwood, C. G. (2008). Developmental consulting in a professional football academy: The 5Cs coaching efficacy program. *The Sport Psychologist, 22,* 109–133.

Harwood, C. G., Barker, J. B., & Anderson, R. (2015). Psychosocial development in youth soccer players: Assessing the effectiveness of the 5Cs intervention program. *The Sport Psychologist, 29,* 319–334.

Higham, A., Harwood, C., & Cale, A. (2005). *Momentum in soccer: Controlling the game.* Leeds: Coachwise Publications.

Holt, N. L., & Dunn, J. G. H. (2004). Toward a grounded theory of the psychosocial competencies and environmental conditions associated with soccer success. *Journal of Applied Sport Psychology, 16,* 199–219.

Jones, G., Hanton, S., & Connaughton, D. (2002). What is this thing called mental toughness? An investigation of elite sport performers. *Journal of Sport & Exercise Psychology, 14,* 205–218.

Jones, S. (2018). How well are the elite players performance plan (EPPP) supporting young players with psychological welfare? *Journal of Psychology and Clinical Psychiatry, 9,* 237–314.

Kotter, J. P. (2014). *Accelerate: Building strategic ability for a faster-moving world.* Boston, MA: Harvard Business Review Press.

MacNamara, Á., Button, A., & Collins, D. (2010). The role of psychological characteristics in facilitating the pathway to elite performance: Part 1: Identifying mental skills and behaviours. *The Sport Psychologist, 24,* 52–73.

MacNamara, Á., Holmes, P., & Collins, D. (2006). The pathway to excellence: The role of psychological characteristics in negotiating the challenges of musical development. *British Journal of Music Education, 23,* 80–98.

National Research Council and Institute of Medicine. (2002). *Community programs to promote community development.* Washington, DC: National Academy Press.

Nesti, M. (2010). *Psychology in professional football: Working with elite and professional players.* London: Routledge.

Pain, M. A., & Harwood, C. G. (2004). Knowledge and perceptions of sport psychology within English soccer. *Journal of Sports Sciences, 22,* 813–826.

Pain, M. A., & Harwood, C. G. (2009). Team building through mutual sharing and open discussion of team functioning. *The Sport Psychologist, 23,* 523–542.

Pain, M. A., Harwood, C. G., & Anderson, R. (2015). Developing the 5Cs over the season planning for psychological development. *The Boot Room, 13,* 56–61.

Pawson, R., & Tilley, N. (2014). *Realistic evaluation.* London: Sage Publications.

The Premier League. (2011). The elite player performance plan. Retrieved May 14, 2019, from https://www.premierleague.com/youth/EPPP

Thelwell, R., Weston, N., & Greenlees, I. (2005). Defining and understanding mental toughness within soccer. *Journal of Applied Sport Psychology, 17,* 326–332.

Visek, A., Harris, B. S., & Blom, L. S. (2016). Doing sport psychology: A youth sport consulting model for practitioners. *The Sport Psychologist, 23,* 271–291.

Wagstaff, C. R. D. (2017). Organizational psychology in sport: An introduction. In C. R. D. Wagstaff (Ed.), *The organizational psychology of sport: Key issues and practical applications* (pp. 1–7). Abingdon, Oxon: Routledge.

13

A CHALLENGE CULTURE

Reflections on Implementing a Psychological Skills Programme in Elite Youth Soccer

Joseph G. Dixon and Marc V. Jones

Brief Introduction and Review of Literature

> "We have to concentrate on our own football, playing in the style we have throughout the tournament, and playing with the same mentality. We have to show the resilience and the freedom we've played with up to this point. I want the players to continue to attack the tournament as we have. That shouldn't change in the knockout stage. We should feel freer, if anything, because these are the sort of matches you want to be involved in. The lads have the chance to write their own stories now."
>
> (England First-Team Manager Gareth Southgate prior to the 2018 World Cup knockout game against Colombia)

During the world's biggest international soccer tournament, the England men's national team manager responded to media questions about the team's biggest game up to that point with a clear focus on what positive traits his players had demonstrated thus far, what they could control, and what the group could achieve moving forward. All these factors are fundamental in promoting a challenge mindset which is central to success in sport.

A motivated performance situation is one in which an individual is required to perform instrumental responses to reach an important or self-relevant goal. As discussed across the resilience literature, such situations could emerge across different contexts and could include such tasks as undertaking a test, competing in an event, public speaking, or interacting with others (see Galli & Gonzalez, 2015; Hase, O'Brien, Moore, & Freeman, 2018; Sarkar & Fletcher, 2014, for reviews). One of the most commonly experienced motivated performance situations is that of participation within sport. The importance of such situations is emphasised by Seery (2011), who highlighted how they have meaningful consequences to those involved and are likely to occur in some form for most individuals on a regular basis. For instance, there are those which will form part of an individual's everyday existence, such as embarrassment and being accepted socially, and those which are less frequent, such as attending job interviews or finding romantic partners. Performing in a sporting event is another such situation which is likely to have meaningful consequences for an individual. Thus, with the presence of consequences, it becomes apparent as to why motivated performance situations can be potentially stressful, individual goals can be achieved or lost, and the potential success of the situation is likely to be uncertain for the individual. However, such characteristics do not always create a negatively stressful experience for the individual concerned (Turner & Jones, 2018). Not everyone will experience similar situations in the same way; in fact, some may experience the same situation with intense excitement whereas others would experience sheer terror (e.g., undertaking a bungee jump). It is purported across the literature that a positive response to a motivated performance situation is likely to increase the likelihood of successful performance (Blascovich & Mendes, 2000; Blascovich & Tomaka, 1996; Dixon, Jones, & Turner, 2019).

The concept of challenge and threat has emerged as a way to conceptualise resilience in individuals; challenge and threat states are two distinct ways that an individual can respond to a perceived stressor (Jones, Meijen, McCarthy, & Sheffield, 2009). Evidence from researchers studying challenge and threat has demonstrated that challenge is a positive energising state that is associated with effective coping and the perception of sufficient resources (e.g., Mendes, Reis, Seery, & Blascovich, 2003).

The Theory of Challenge and Threat States in Athletes (TCTSA; Jones et al., 2009) draws on prominent transactional appraisal theories of stress and emotion, predominantly the biopsychosocial model (BPSM) of challenge and threat states (Blascovich & Mendes, 2000), but also others (Lazarus & Folkman, 1984; Dienstbier, 1989; Jones, 1995; Skinner & Brewer, 2002). A challenge state is seen as effective at facilitating improved decision-making, effective cognitive functioning, decreased likelihood of reinvestment, efficient self-regulation, and increased anaerobic power, with all these factors likely to contribute to successful competitive performance (Jones et al., 2009). In a threat-state cardiovascular (CV) reactivity pattern, pituitary adreno-corticol activity is thought to temper sympathetic adreno-medullary activity; therefore, compared with a challenge CV reactivity pattern, efficient energy delivery to the brain and muscles does not occur (Dienstbier, 1989, 1992). Thus, a threat state is proposed to lead to ineffective decision-making and cognitive functioning, increased likelihood of reinvestment, inefficient self-regulation, and decreased anaerobic power compared with what is experienced in a challenge state. This adverse impact on psychophysiological functioning is therefore likely to increase the chances of unsuccessful competitive performance (Jones et al., 2009). For example, a soccer player in a threat state may struggle to choose and execute the optimal pass available to them, they may feel "leggy" and lethargic during performance, and they may "overthink" in certain in-play situations such as executing a free-kick.

In the TCTSA it is proposed that a unique combination of psychological constructs (self-efficacy, perceived control, and an approach focus) interact to determine challenge and threat states. Specifically, in a challenge state an individual has high self-efficacy, high perceived control, and an approach focus. In a threat state, however, there is low self-efficacy, low perceived control, and an avoidance focus. Previous researchers using the TCTSA have predominantly focused on individual responses to motivated performance situations in the form of psychophysiological testing (e.g., Dixon et al., 2019; Turner, Jones, Sheffield, & Cross, 2012; Turner, Jones, Sheffield, Slater et al., 2013). In these studies, netballers, cricketers, and soccer players were tested immediately prior to performance to investigate the presence of challenge and threat states and with all demonstrating consistently that challenge states are associated with better performance. Such research demonstrated that imminent performance can be predicted by challenge and threat CV reactivity.

It is not just the performance aspect of sport that can be stressful for those involved; professional sport environments have been shown to incorporate a number of perceived organisational stressors (Arnold & Fletcher, 2012; Arnold, Fletcher, & Daniels, 2017; Woodman & Hardy, 2001). However, presently no research has explored the application of TCTSA principles in a professional sport organisation. Consequently, there presented an opportunity to focus on the work conducted by, and with, the coaches, support staff, and athletes in their sporting environment.

This enabled investigation into the factors that impact on the culture of the organisation and the stress responses demonstrated across the working environment. As such, in this chapter we aim to provide the reader with an overview and impact of the work delivered by the first author as an applied practitioner working in professional football, focusing on how a theoretical framework underpins the sport psychology programme. The following case study investigates this through the implementation of a psychological skills programme within a Category 1 Academy of a Premier League Soccer Club. In delivering the consultancy the TCTSA (Jones et al., 2009) was used as a guiding framework for the applied work, providing the core concepts around which the design and delivery of a psychology education programme within academy soccer took place.

Practical Applications—Case Study on Developing a Challenge Culture

Background and Context

The following case study draws on applied ethnographic methodology. Ethnographic research is based on the belief that there are multiple truths and multiple ways of seeing and interpreting things (Angrosino & Mays de Perez, 2000). An ethnographic approach refers to the process of collecting information about a specific group or culture, and the product that draws together events, understandings, and behaviours into a meaningful portrait (Krane & Baird, 2005). Applied ethnography can be used for evaluating applied sport psychology interventions, problem-solving in sport, or enhancing multicultural understanding and there has been a growing focus on ethnographical work undertaken in sport with an increasing output of research using this methodology (Hughson & Hallinan, 2001).

The professional soccer club where the work was being undertaken was granted Academy status by the FA Premier League in 1999. Prior to the 2013/14 soccer season the academy had used the services of sport psychologists from a local university to provide educational workshops and psychological support on a consultancy basis. However, based on the continued growth of the academy, the recognition of the need for further psychological support and education and the requirement of providing such support in order to meet the Premier League requirements for a Category 1 (elite) status academy, the role of Academy Psychologist was created, and in September 2013 I (first author) began my work as the first individual holding this position at the soccer club. The initial scope of the role was fairly broad, and as I (first author) was the first full-time psychologist to work at the soccer club I was afforded a high level of autonomy with regard to designing and implementing a psychology programme.

Presenting Issue(s)

During the initial introduction phase into the role I did find that there were a range of expectations as to what a psychologist does in a soccer environment and varying perceptions of the need for a psychologist in the academy. This confusion is not uncommon and has been highlighted as a challenge that regularly faces sport psychology practitioners (Aoyagi & Poczwardowsk, 2011; Pain & Harwood, 2004). However, the majority of individuals were extremely positive and welcoming; I was actually surprised about the level of enthusiasm and openness I was afforded on commencing the role. Due to the ranges of experience, personalities, and skill sets across the coaches and staff I looked to interact with each one individually to explain my role, build rapport, and understand where, if possible, I could support them. I feel that my approach helped me to deal with range of responses and openness to me during my early stages in the job; initially I listened to the range of issues they presented, including any potential reluctance or misconceptions associated with engaging with myself. I was fully aware that I was going to be working in the environment full-time, so rather than trying to address and solve all challenges straight away I was mindful to take my time to truly understand the environment and individuals in it. I chose to work with the most receptive people first (alongside any specific priorities); these were typically the staff members who were receptive, inquisitive, and engaged with me. From this I looked to demonstrate impact and build acceptance through my work and the influence I was able to make. This approach included delivering and obtaining regular feedback from staff, referencing examples of the work being undertaken to a wider audience in multidisciplinary meetings, and being mindful to regularly approach and offering my support to those staff that I had not yet worked with.

The Challenge Culture Intervention

On beginning the role, my line manager, the Head of Academy Sport Science, ensured the weekly timetable included time slots for me to conduct team workshops and one-to-one sessions with individual players. I designed a psychology-specific education programme for the different age groups to fit around this schedule. The initial curriculum drew on the TCTSA (such as delivering team workshops focusing on potential performance impacts of challenge and threat states), while using other approaches such as the 5Cs framework (Harwood & Anderson, 2015), to provide the theoretical basis of the work. The programme has continued to evolve using the TCTSA as the main framework, and based on evaluation of the work being done, feedback from players and staff and the evolution of my own role at the club. Also, it is important to note that there was recognition that the curriculum should not be constrained by the TCTSA, and if required could incorporate other ideas and theory that would support individuals within the environment.

Initially, the education sessions were predominantly classroom-based workshops lasting approximately one hour and focusing on a specific topic related to sport psychology and performance. The Foundation Phase teams (U8s-U11s age groups) had one education workshop per cycle (every six weeks), the Youth Development Phase teams (U12s-U16s age groups) had one education workshop per week, and the Professional Development Phase teams (U18s and U21s age groups) had one education workshop every two weeks. The curriculum evolved with a growing focus on the TCTSA; the six cycle themes were identified as Confidence, Emotional Control,

Teamwork, Concentration, Communication, and Challenge Mindset. At this stage the concepts of "challenge mindset" and "challenge environment" were also emerging from the work being undertaken as areas that link the TCTSA to the culture and behaviours across the academy, so much so that one of the themes was named "challenge mindset." Initially it was thought that each cycle theme would incorporate one or two elements of the TCTSA (and social support). For instance, it was expected that the cycle theme of emotional control would incorporate control, confidence would incorporate self-efficacy, teamwork would incorporate social support, and so forth. However, it became apparent as the work was being delivered that all elements of the theory were regularly referenced during each cycle theme and overlap of the TCTSA constructs was frequent. For instance, self-efficacy is associated with perceived control because individuals need to believe that they are in control, and can intentionally execute their actions, for self-efficacy to develop (Bandura, 1997). Thus, it was decided that a challenge mindset cycle theme would be required to help consolidate the learnings from the other five cycle themes relating back to this theory.

Each cycle theme was designed with a mixture of classroom-based education, practical elements, information delivered to coaches, and with a focus on the language and strategies associated with the TCTSA. Thus, by the third season the curriculum had evolved to include more integrated work with coaches across the various sessions conducted with players throughout their weekly schedule. For example, developing leadership behaviours was identified by coaches as an area of required focus (e.g., Price & Weiss, 2011, 2013). Consequently, leadership groups were implemented in the Professional Development Phase teams, comprising 4–5 players voted for by their peers to represent them, promote the team values, and be a link between players and staff. This is a practice that has been used in other soccer teams and across other sports (e.g., Rugby) and was suggested following regular references and comments by coaches and staff as to the lack of leaders in youth soccer.

As the curriculum evolved at the Youth Development Phase age groups, education workshops were reduced from weekly to every other week, with the aim of the psychologist being able to spend more time with coaches and looking to integrate the psychological concepts across other areas of the programme (e.g., in training sessions, during match analysis sessions). At this stage the Foundation Phase programme became predominantly practical-based, delivered by the psychologist alongside coaches. Initially the classroom-based sessions had been well-received by players and coaches based on verbal feedback and programme evaluation forms completed by the players; however, it was deemed easier in terms of learning transfer to conduct the session in a practical pitch-based setting with the coach present. As such, players would get early exposure to psychological concepts during their training sessions, providing a base-level understanding of some of the ideas that would be introduced in more depth when they progress to Youth Development Phase level.

The following reflections directly focus on the resource aspects of the TCTSA (Jones et al., 2009), which constituted the underpinning framework of the psychology curriculum and hence will be discussed in-turn.

Self-Efficacy (Confidence)

The importance of promoting self-efficacy and its associated concepts (confidence, self-belief, self-assurance) is highlighted across the applied psychology literature (e.g., Donaldson, Csikszentmihalyi, & Nakamura, 2011; Lomas, Hefferon, & Ivtzan, 2014). Further, it was consistently referenced by players, coaches, staff, and parents during the work conducted across the programme. Notably, this was often attributed as a causal factor for players not performing well. Workshops were delivered to players across the different age groups focused on educating players on the concept of self-efficacy, understanding their own sources of self-efficacy, and developing strategies for maintaining and improving this area in themselves. Self-efficacy was also a topic that was regularly raised in the one-to-one consultation with players that took place across the three-year period. Situations varied from players highlighting a temporary drop in confidence (caused by things such as poor performances, mistakes, being dropped from the starting line-up, and negative feedback), to more long-term issues where players constantly experienced low levels of self-efficacy while in the environment. One of the more common occurrences that impacted confidence levels was when a new player was brought in from another club (usually one viewed as smaller and of a lower level), and sometimes from another country (e.g., Richardson, Littlewood, Nesti, & Benstead, 2012). Supporting the integration of the player in this adaptation was important to help them settle into a new environment and culture to provide the best possible opportunity for them to perform at their best. Part of this process was helping them understand, draw on, and re-appraise the resources they had available to themselves (e.g., Sammy et al., 2017). Intervention work varied depending on the individual and the outcome of the respective needs analysis undertaken (e.g., Keegan, 2015). For example, for one particular new player an intervention focused on reducing their anxiety through addressing their ability to interpret the positive feedback they were receiving as evidence that they were integrating successfully into the team and environment.

Work was done to help players develop an awareness of or improve self-efficacy itself, including workshops educating players on the concept of confidence, focusing on players' understanding of their own strengths, and giving players opportunities to provide positive feedback to each other. Observations highlighted that players across age groups were quick to criticise and moan at teammates during matches when they were perceived to have made a mistake, things weren't going well, or they weren't being passed to. Discussions with the players revealed that this was a behaviour that would regularly cause a negative impact on confidence levels in them. Furthermore, it was frequently observed that players were reluctant to engage in group environments and did not feel comfortable speaking in front of their team and staff (e.g., Beekes, 2006). Subsequently, initiatives were put in place to provide players with opportunities to do so, along with guidance and feedback to help them develop in this area. One such strategy was players preparing and delivering a presentation at their performance review to coaches and parents. Furthermore, the psychology education workshops would regularly focus on getting players to present and answer questions in front of their peers and coaches would be encouraged to build more interactive strategies into their sessions to help promote player self-efficacy in speaking in front of the group.

Control

It was apparent early on during my work in the academy that the area of control associated with the TCTSA would require specific focus across all age groups and coaches in the academy. Through speaking to individuals and observing behaviours across the environment there would often be a focus on factors outside of their control (e.g., Biddle, 1999). Often through observation of training sessions or matches it was apparent that players were becoming distracted by things that were not likely to support effective performance. During the programme there was a mixture of work, both planned and reactive, focused on promoting the importance of perceived control and supporting individuals to develop and improve skills to do so (e.g., Ajzen, 2002). In one-to-one discussions players and coaches would often reference and be overly focused on things that were likely to diminish feelings of perceived control, namely things that they had little or no control over. So, my language and intervention work would look to promote feelings of perceived control (e.g., Butler, Chapman, Forman, & Beck, 2006; McArdle & Moore, 2012). A lot of the work conducted with players (in individuals and as teams) and coaches would focus on educating them on their locus of control (e.g., Ajzen, 2002), breaking down the things they can control, what they can influence, and the things they have no impact on. These individuals would then be challenged to understand and reflect on their own locus of control using real-life soccer scenarios that were likely to be faced during performance.

Workshops were implemented for players to promote understanding of such thought processes, the associated impact and strategies to help promote move effective cognitions to support a challenge state (Jones et al., 2009). The classroom-based workshops were delivered across the programme to all playing age groups with the aim of explaining the importance of perceived control in developing an effective psychophysiological state prior to performance. The workshops would give simple explanations, examples, and strategies at the younger age groups and would become increasingly more complex as individuals developed their understanding as they progressed through the age groups. Constant repetition of these ideas (by myself, coaches, staff, and teammates) was promoted, combined with individual and team feedback. Also, where required, one-to-one intervention work was utilised to support players in this area. Players' personal development plan "key areas" frequently featured on constructs to do with resilience, body language, emotional control, confidence, and concentration. During the individual work conducted with players focusing on their respective psychological key areas they would often cite that they would focus on things that impact negatively on perceptions of control, notably these were often things that they had no control over and therefore presenting an opportunity to work on this construct with them (e.g., Hermansson & Hodge, 2012).

Approach Focus

The most common observations that were made regarding the approach focus element of the TCTSA were regarding the language (verbal and physical) demonstrated by players and coaches. Avoidance language was observed in coach, staff, and players at times, denoting a fear of failure (e.g., Sagar, Lavallee, & Spray, 2009).

Team talks, meetings, and individual one-to-one work with players could regularly provide phrases and sentences, including the words "shouldn't," "don't," "can't," "mustn't," followed by references to the opposition, making mistakes, losing, and other negative outcomes. Again, the initial observation of such behaviours presented a need which was addressed through promoting awareness and understanding of the potential negative impact. Workshops with players and coaches were delivered to introduce the idea of approach versus avoidance and the associated benefits of using approach language and behaviours (over avoidance ones; e.g., Lochbaum & Gottardy, 2015).

Social Support

The TCTSA does not explicitly reference the importance of the support of significant others in helping to promote a challenge state in individuals. However, interviews conducted at the club with coaches and staff from across the environment and other contemporary research focusing on stress and resilience in performance environments have highlighted the importance of social support (e.g., Fletcher & Sarkar, 2012; Galli & Vealey, 2008; Gustafsson, Hassmen, Kenta, & Johansson, 2008; Rees, Hardy, & Freeman, 2007). During the work conducted within the academy there were regular opportunities to observe and listen to situations that provided evidence to support the findings demonstrated on contemporary research. In one-to-one consultations players would consistently reference the importance of friends and family helping them with demanding situations and discuss the benefits of support being received by teammates, coaches, and staff. Teams that performed well in the academy often referenced the "togetherness" they felt among the group and, conversely, those that did not perform as well regularly highlighted not being particularly close as a factor contributing to negative performance outcomes (e.g., Slater, 2019). Consequently, at the Professional Development Phase there was a focus on driving the social identity and values of the specific teams alongside the coaches, areas that have been highlighted as important to support team cohesion and on-field performance (e.g., Slater, Coffee, Barker, & Evans, 2014). Consequently, sessions were conducted with players and staff to design and implement team values, behaviours, and targets. The outcomes of these sessions were drawn on throughout the season in meetings, team-talks, and in one-to-one work with the aim of improving cohesion and togetherness among the squads. The importance of effective leadership within sporting teams is another area that has received focus in recent research (e.g., Price & Weiss, 2011, 2013).

Outcome Analysis

Measuring the impact of interventions is something I was conscious of exploring, developing, and improving for the benefit of the academy programme and for my own personal development as a practitioner. In a results-focused environment such as elite sport, quantification of success is often required, and the need for effective evaluation within sport psychology is no different (e.g., Haberl & McCann, 2012; Martindale & Collins, 2007). There were three main ways on which I evaluated the work that I did. First, I obtained psychophysiological measures of challenge and threat states in Professional Development Phase players which gave an indication of individual stress responses to games and an understanding of the overall group response (Dixon et al., 2019). Broadly, these data supported the notion that a challenge response is helpful for performance. I also obtained detailed interviews from three staff members and three players on the development and evaluation of the programmes. Again, the data suggested a positive response to the work done around developing a challenge mindset and culture.

Second, I also conducted a number of ongoing observations as part of my work. As such I had the opportunity to see whether the behaviours discussed when referencing the TCTSA are displayed. I have also used these observations to evaluate effectiveness of interventions and as another method to help develop my own technical and tactical understanding of the sport. During these observations, I would either consciously undertake them with a plan of focusing on specific things (e.g., a player, a coach, a period of the game), or wait for things to emerge. I would take notes during the game or training of anything I deemed worthy of recording (e.g., behaviour, language, a pattern of incidents) using a pen and paper. For instance, a coach requested specific feedback on whether he was being overly verbose in the time he took to deliver his messages pre-match and during half-time, and I used the observations as evidence to support the intervention work with players looking to improve communication, concentration, and emotional control performance issues. I also used the evidence obtained to draw individuals' attention to certain things that I believed could be improved or addressed, such as one player's reactions being somewhat delayed after a transition in possession or a coach's body language after his team lost the ball. I would type the notes up within a day and use them for the relevant work following this (e.g., one-to-one feedback to an individual, referencing it in a team match analysis, discussing with the coach). I would regularly look to feedback observations to coaches, staff, and players; sometimes this would be during a break in training or at half-time during games if it was deemed relevant to support the individual at that moment. Alternatively, I would look for a suitable time (e.g., after training or within a couple of days of a match) to speak to the individuals involved and deliver my feedback. During the programme I have been able to conduct many observations, covering different formats (e.g., games, training, match analysis, gym sessions, team talks, pre-season trips) and purposes (e.g., focusing on specific area, coach, team, player, colleague, scenario). My own reflections are that I feel being present and visible allowed me first-hand some of the areas that I would discuss with coaches, staff, and players; such evidence proved extremely valuable in contextualising issues. Also, coaches and players knowing that I had been present would approach me and look for my opinion, which initiated several specific pieces of work. Observing the players and coaches in their sporting environment helped me to understand and relate to their individual circumstances (e.g., McKenzie & van der Mars, 2015) and in conjunction with other assessment and data collection methods (e.g., one-to-one consultation) was a valuable methodology for identifying areas of work that the individual may not have had an awareness that there was a need for potential work to support them.

Case-Study Reflections

Sporting environments are complex entities that present a number of potential challenges for practising sport psychologists (Chandler, Eubank, Nesti, Tod, & Cable, 2014), including building relationships, demonstrating credibility, handling sensitive information, dealing with interpersonal disagreements and conflict, and maintaining effectiveness when working within volatile and unpredictable environments (McDougall, Nesti, & Richardson, 2015). Entering into a professional sporting environment for my first full-time applied role (in sport) felt a little daunting, particularly coming face-to-face with ex-professional players whom I had watched while growing up. I was initially unsure as to whether I would have the necessary experience and skill set to support a type of colleague (professional athletes, coaches and support staff), whom I had limited exposure to in my previous work. I also did not know how individuals in the environment would react to having a full-time psychologist working with them (something that they were likely not to be used to). I believe I may also have been influenced by some of the negative stereotypes that have remained regarding soccer culture; according to Parker (2006), English soccer comprised a masculine working-class culture that included abusive language, personal criticism, scornful humour, and all-male banter. Research has indicated that sport psychology consultants can place themselves under significant pressure entering new and unfamiliar environments (Barker & Winter, 2014); to challenge these trepidations I did look to reflect on my previous experiences of working with senior leaders of global organisations and delivering workshops to high performing individuals and teams in business to allow me to feel confident that I could apply my skill set successfully in this environment. This type of work was similar in that I would regularly be working with experts in fields where I had significantly less knowledge and experience of the daily tasks they perform, and where I had to demonstrate my ability to understand them and have an impact in the work I undertake. Over time I found even the most sceptical, challenging or aloof individuals would seek me out, ask me questions, and look for my input to support them. I believe that this was supported by demonstrating impact and trust with the other staff members, players and teams. To break down these initial barriers and "win individuals over" gave me great satisfaction, to the point where from having very little input with one coach to him asking me to contribute to a significant part of his pre-match meeting to his players (focusing on a psychological area of performance), felt extremely rewarding.

On reflection, there was possibly an initial naivety from myself in assuming that I could potentially change or shift a culture completely. Different soccer clubs possess their own individual sub-culture, reflecting its social world, values, traditions and working practices (Relvas, Littlewood, Nesti, Gilbourne, & Richardson, 2010). One person trying to change the habits of many players and staff is extremely challenging and I would be honest to say that I have yet to embed the challenge and threat framework as deeply as I would have liked. I would like for players and staff to be using the language and demonstrating the behaviours of a Challenge Mindset and make a more concerted effort to drive each other in terms of developing a Challenge Culture. However, I also need to be realistic with regards to implementing concepts that have evolved during the work undertaken to-date; I feel the next stage of the psychology programme in the academy will be important in further developing and implementing these ideas. There have been many positives which I have highlighted, yet I would have liked for coaches to be proactively looking to embed the concepts in their on-field training sessions more (without requiring prompting), and to be using the TCTSA (challenge mindset language) more consistently (rather than sporadically and interspersing it with other broad psychological phrases). However, I feel there are significant reasons for this which I have identified and learnt from as my role has developed.

A theme that was observed in my work across the academy was a lack of praise and positive feedback delivered to players at times. In their enthusiasm to develop their players it was noticed that there could at times be a focus on constructive feedback by coaches rather than positive recognition. Occasionally it was also inferred that coaches believed that the players should know what they are good at, are operating in an elite environment and therefore, they seemed to feel that the best way to help them was to tell them what to improve on. This was not just observed in coaches but also staff and occasionally in some parents. Thus, a mixture of individual and group-based work was conducted (drawing on the TCTSA concepts), over the programme with coaches and staff, (and group-based sessions with parents). Where there was threat-based language it was illustrated how this can impact negatively on the player's psychophysiological state based on the research that has been undertaken (e.g., Turner et al., 2012;, Turner et al., 2013).

At times, I noticed that there were patterns of push-back or challenges to points made in the meetings that related to players being treated too "softly" by staff compared to what previous generations of players may have experienced and that such perceived "mollycoddling" (overindulgence) was not helping them to develop the skills required to succeed at the top level in the game. Furthermore, coaches would occasionally question if the other support disciplines were getting in the way of the actual soccer in terms of the time spent away from the soccer pitches or restrictions placed on the amount and type of load (physical work) players should be exposed to. Sometimes such challenges could be taken personally by individuals and viewed as a criticism of their work. However, I did feel that to help drive a culture of healthy debate, and questioning, the challenging of each other in a respectful way is necessary to facilitate improvement and push the academy forward (e.g., Reid, Stewart, & Thorne, 2004). As the coaches are on the front-line in terms of developing the players, making the difficult final decisions regarding retaining or releasing them, and typically being the staff that spend the most time with them, I was conscious to listen to and see things from their perspective, particularly when they voiced concerns about overprotecting players to their detriment developmentally. At times, psychology can be perceived as a discipline that facilitates such "softness" because of the focus on talking and therapy which, is not viewed as a traditionally masculine thing to do when dealing with problems. Such negative perceptions of sport psychology have been addressed in the literature (Ravizza, 1988), and specifically within soccer (Pain & Harwood, 2004). Therefore, I was mindful to highlight the aims of the psychology programme at such times; reminding staff and coaches that the focus was to ensure that players can deal with the demands of elite-level soccer and that

> we were looking to equip players with the skill sets to succeed in elite soccer, including having the resilience to deal with challenges. I would draw on the TCTSA (Jones et al., 2009) language to highlight how we are looking to develop players who are confident, focused on things that they can control and are focused on what they can achieve, in order for them to embrace challenge. I also highlighted the benefits of players addressing and discussing issues rather than bottling them up and emphasising the courage required to do so, rather than it actually being "soft." I did in fact, at times, find myself in agreement with coaches and some of their concerns; I do see the point that players have the potential to become institutionalised, over-sanitised, and comfortable in the modern environment of an elite academy, and if they do have to go out on loan to a lower league club with basic facilities and much less in the way of support, they may not be properly equipped to do so. However, part of the work being undertaken through the psychology programme was about educating the coaches and staff that being challenged is about having the ability to cope with difficult circumstances and thus the work being conducted was equipping them with such skills.

Summary and Conclusions

When making conclusions about the implementation of the academy's first psychology programme and the research that accompanied this process, I can reference a number of positive outcomes. Being the first full-time sport psychologist in the academy, I was unsure as to how the discipline and work would be received; however, from the start of the programme until now psychology has developed into an accepted and valuable part of the academy curriculum. Players, coaches, staff, and parents have utilised the support available and reference the benefits of the work undertaken with them. Processes (e.g., psychology-based curriculum, individual interventions based on development needs, on-field interventions through coaches) have been implemented that support the development of the players and staff. Consequently, there has been an ongoing focus on demonstrating measurable impact of this work to not only highlight the value of the discipline but to support the ongoing development of the psychology curriculum within the academy. This included post-cycle (every six weeks) reviews of the work conducted, undertaking personal reflections, having appraisals with my line manager, obtaining feedback from coaches and players in informal discussions, conducting formal end-of-season (confidential) programme evaluations, to building-in observable key performance indicators to utilise behavioural measures of the work implemented, drawing on agreed measures of progress with individuals in one-to-one work, and reviewing with staff in player development plan meetings. However, I feel there are still improvements to be made in terms of how the work conducted can be measured and tracked, particularly the impact of the TCTSA demands and resources on challenge and threat states. Though logistically it was sometimes challenging and time-consuming, there are potentially significant benefits to be gained from conducting psychophysiological measurement of all players and coaches moving forward. Obtaining such data would provide insights and markers to trigger intervention work to support their stress response to motivated performance situations. My conclusions of the work conducted as a full-time applied psychologist over a period of three years immersed in an elite youth sporting environment must focus on the overall success I feel the psychological programme has been in this time. The discipline is now seen as an important integrated part of the player's learning; the coaches and staff utilise the support available to them, and embrace ideas and suggestions that they can incorporate into their own work. The TCTSA (Jones et al., 2009) has been an effective framework that seems to have connected with individuals in terms of relatable concepts and language that can be linked to on-field performance. I have felt myself develop as a practitioner, and my reflections have identified where I feel I continue to develop the programme across all ages and disciplines within the academy.

Key Messages and Further Reading

Five key messages/critical learning points:

1. The TCTSA provides a strong theoretical basis when designing and implementing a psychological skills programme in academy-level soccer.
2. The concepts of demands and resources (e.g., confidence, control, and approach focus), align well with language used by soccer coaches and can be integrated in on-field work with players.
3. Social support appears to be an important resource in addition to those referenced in the TCTSA to help staff and players manage the demands of academy-level soccer.
4. When working as a practitioner in professional sport there can be a broad range of expectations as to the work delivered by a psychologist; developing role clarity is likely to be a significant factor in helping succeed in a role.
5. A psychological skills programme is likely to evolve over time based on your experiences and learnings and needs to adapt with the changing nature of the environment you are working in.

Directions and suggestions for future researchers:

- Further psychophysiological research of soccer players in pre-performance situations to provide greater evidence.
- Research into the extent to which social support acts as a resource/buffer to stress in soccer players.
- Ongoing development of measuring impact and effectiveness of practice as psychologists working in professional sporting environments.
- Integration of the TCTSA into psychological programmes within other sports and sporting environments (e.g., rugby, cricket, athletics).
- Explore the balance in an academy environment between testing players for selection and future contracts while simultaneously looking to support and develop them.

We have highlighted the five most pertinent further reading resources below:

Dixon, J., Jones, M. V., & Turner, M. J. (2019). A challenge mind-set on match day: Investigating cardiovascular reactivity in professional academy footballers. *European Journal of Sports Sciences*. doi:10.1080/17461391.2019.1629179

Epel, E. S., Crosswell, A. D., Mayer, S. E., Prather, A. A., Slavich, G. M., Puterman, E., & Mendes, W. B. (2018). More than a feeling: A unified view of stress measurement for population science. *Frontiers in Neuroendocrinology, 49*, 146–169.

Jones, M. V., Meijen, C., McCarthy, P. J., & Sheffield, D. (2009). A theory of challenge and threat states in athletes. *International Review of Sport and Exercise Psychology, 2*(1), 61–180.

Turner, M. J., & Jones, M. V. (2018). Arousal control in sport. *Oxford Research Encyclopedia of Psychology*. doi:10.1093/acrefore/9780190236557.013.155

Turner, M. J., Jones, M. V., Sheffield, D., Barker, J. B., & Coffee, P. (2014). Manipulating cardiovascular indices of challenge and threat using resource appraisals. *International Journal of Psychophysiology, 94*, 9–18.

References

Ajzen, I. (2002). Perceived behavioral control, self-efficacy, locus of control, and the theory of planned behavior. *Journal of Applied Social Psychology, 32*, 665–683.

Angrosino, M. V., & Mays de Perez, K. A. (2000). Rethinking observation: From method to context. In N. K. Denzin & Y. S. Lincoln (Eds.), *Handbook of qualitative research* (2nd ed., pp. 673–702). Thousand Oaks, CA: Sage Publications.

Aoyagi, M. W., & Poczwardowski, A. (2011). Models of sport psychology practice and delivery: A review. In S. D. Mellalieu & S. Hanton (Eds.), *Professional practice in sport psychology: A review* (pp. 5–30). London: Routledge.

Arnold, R., & Fletcher, D. (2012). A research synthesis and taxonomic classification of the organizational stressors encountered by sport performers. *Journal of Sport and Exercise Psychology, 34*, 397–429.

Arnold, R., Fletcher, D., & Daniels, K. (2017). Organizational stressors, coping, and outcomes in competitive sport. *Journal of Sports Sciences, 35*, 694–703.

Bandura, A. (1997). *Self-efficacy: The exercise of control*. New York, NY: W.H. Freeman.

Barker, S., & Winter, S. (2014). The practice of sport psychology: A youth coaches' perspective. *International Journal of Sports Science & Coaching, 9*, 379–392.

Beekes, W. A. (2006). The "Millionaire" method for encouraging participation. *Active Learning in Higher Education, 7*, 25–36.

Biddle, S. J. H. (1999). Motivation and perceptions of control: Tracing its development and plotting its future in exercise and sport psychology. *Journal of Sport & Exercise Psychology, 21*, 1–23.

Blascovich, J., & Mendes, W. B. (2000). Challenge and threat appraisals: The role of affective cues. In J. P. Forgas (Ed.), *Feeling and thinking: The role of affect in social cognition* (pp. 59–82). Paris: Cambridge University Press.

Blascovich, J., & Tomaka, J. (1996). The biopsychosocial model of arousal regulation. *Advances in Experimental Social Psychology, 28*, 1–51.

Butler, A. C., Chapman, J. E., Forman, E. M., & Beck, A. T. (2006). The empirical status of cognitive-behavioral therapy: A review of meta-analyses. *Clinical Psychology Review, 26*, 17–31.

Chandler, C., Eubank, M. R., Nesti, M. S., Tod, D., & Cable, T. (2014). Personal qualities of effective sport psychologists. *International Journal of Sport Psychology, 47*, 297–317.

Dienstbier, R. A. (1989). Arousal and physiological toughness: Implications for mental and physical health. *Psychological Review, 96*, 84–100.

Dienstbier, R. A. (1992). Mutual impacts of toughening on crises and losses. In L. Montada, S.-H. Filipp & M. J. Lerner (Eds.), *Life crises and experience of loss in adulthood* (pp. 367–384). Hillsdale, NJ: Lawrence Erlbaum.

Donaldson, S. I., Csikszentmihalyi, M., & Nakamura, J. (Eds.). (2011). *Applied positive psychology: Improving everyday life, health, schools, work, and society*. London: Routledge Academic.

Fletcher, D., & Sarkar, M. (2012). A grounded theory of psychological resilience in Olympic champions. *Psychology of Sport and Exercise, 13*, 669–678.

Galli, N., & Gonzalez, S. P. (2015). Psychological resilience in sport: A review of the literature and implications for research and practice. *International Journal of Sport and Exercise Psychology, 13*, 243–257.

Galli, N., & Vealey, R. S. (2008). "Bouncing back" from adversity: Athletes' experience of resilience. *Sport Psychologist, 22*, 316–335.

Gustafsson, H., Hassmen, P., Kenta, G., & Johansson, M. (2008). A qualitative analysis of burnout in elite Swedish athletes. *Psychology of Sport and Exercise, 9*, 800–816.

Haberl, P., & McCann, S. (2012). Evaluating USOC sport psychology consultant effectiveness: A philosophical and practical imperative at the Olympic games. *Journal of Sport Psychology in Action, 3*, 65–76.

Harwood, C. G., & Anderson, R. (2015). *Coaching psychological skills in youth 24 football: Developing the 5Cs*. London: Bennion-Kearny.

Hase, A., O'Brien, J., Moore, L., & Freeman, P. (2018). The relationship between challenge and threat states and performance: A systematic review. *Sport, Exercise, and Performance Psychology*. doi:10.1037/spy0000132

Hermansson, G., & Hodge, K. (2012). Uncontrollable outcomes: Managing expectations at the Olympics. *Journal of Sport Psychology in Action, 3*, 127–138.

Hughson, J. E., & Hallinan, C. J. (2001). *Sporting tales: Ethnographic fieldwork experiences*. Sydney: ASSH, Inc.

Jones, G. (1995). More than just a game: Research developments and issues in competitive anxiety in sport. *British Journal of Psychology, 86*, 449–478.

Keegan, R. J. (2015). A model of the applied sport psychology consulting process: A system for understanding and evaluating practice. *Journal of Science and Medicine in Sport, 19*, 49.

Krane, V., & Baird, S. M. (2005). Using ethnography in applied sport psychology. *Journal of Applied Sport Psychology, 17*, 87–107.

Lazarus, R. S., & Folkman, S. (1984). *Stress, appraisal, and coping*. New York, NY: Springer Publishing Company.

Lochbaum, M., & Gottardy, J. (2015). A meta-analytic review of the approach-avoidance achievement goals and performance relationships in the sport psychology literature. *Journal of Sport and Health Science, 4*, 164–173.

Lomas, T., Hefferon, K., & Ivtzan, I. (2014). *Applied positive psychology: Integrated positive practice*. Thousand Oaks, CA: Sage Publications, Inc.

Martindale, A., & Collins, D. (2007). Enhancing the evaluation of effectiveness with professional judgment and decision making. *The Sport Psychologist, 21*, 458–474.

McArdle, S., & Moore, P. (2012). Applying evidence-based principles from CBT to sport psychology. *Sport Psychologist, 26*, 299–310.

McDougall, M., Nesti, M., & Richardson, D. (2015). The challenges of sport psychology delivery in elite and professional sport: Reflections from experienced sport psychologists. *The Sport Psychologist, 29*, 265–277.

McKenzie, T. L., & van der Mars, H. (2015). Top 10 research questions related to assessing physical activity and its contexts using systematic observation. *Research Quarterly for Exercise and Sport, 86*, 13–29.

Mendes, W. B., Reis, H. T., Seery, M. D., & Blascovich, J. (2003). Cardiovascular correlates of emotional expression and suppression: Do content and gender context matter? *Journal of Personality & Social Psychology, 84*, 771–792.

Pain, M. A., & Harwood, C. G. (2004). Knowledge and perceptions of sport psychology within English soccer. *Journal of Sports Sciences, 22*, 813–826.

Parker, A. (2006). Gender, class and "race" in lifelong learning. *British Educational Research Journal, 32*, 687–701.

Price, M. S., & Weiss, M. R. (2011). Peer leadership in sport: Relationships among personal characteristics, leader behaviors, and team outcomes. *Journal of Applied Sport Psychology, 23*, 49–64.

Price, M. S., & Weiss, M. R. (2013). Relationships among coach leadership, peer leadership, and adolescent athletes' psychosocial and team outcomes: A test of transformational leadership theory. *Journal of Applied Sport Psychology, 25*, 265–279.

Ravizza, K. (1988). Gaining entry with athletic personnel for season long consulting. *The Sport Psychologist, 4*, 330–340.

Rees, T., Hardy, L., & Freeman, P. (2007). Stressors, social support and effects upon performance in golf. *Journal of Sports Sciences, 25*, 33–42.

Reid, C., Stewart, E., & Thorne, G. (2004). Multidisciplinary sport science teams in elite sport: Comprehensive servicing or conflict and confusion? *The Sport Psychologist, 18*, 204–217.

Relvas, H., Littlewood, M., Nesti, M., Gilbourne, D., & Richardson, D. (2010). Organizational structures and working practices in elite European professional football clubs: Understanding the relationship between youth and professional domains. *European Sport Management Quarterly, 10*, 165–187.

Richardson, D., Littlewood, M., Nesti, M., & Benstead, L. (2012). An examination of the migratory transition of elite young European soccer players to the English Premier League. *Journal of Sports Sciences, 30*, 37–41.

Sagar, S., Lavallee, D., & Spray, C. M. (2009). Coping with the effects of fear of failure: A preliminary investigation of young elite athletes. *Journal of Clinical Sports Psychology, 3,* 73–98.

Sammy, N., Anstiss, P., Moore, L., Freeman, P., Wilson, M., & Vine, S. (2017). The effects of arousal reappraisal on stress responses, performance, and attention. *Anxiety Stress and Coping, 30,* 1–20.

Sarkar, M., & Fletcher, D. (2014). Psychological resilience in sport performers: A review of stressors and protective factors. *Journal of Sports Sciences, 32,* 1419–1434.

Seery, M. D. (2011). Challenge or threat? Cardiovascular indexes of resilience and vulnerability to potential stress in humans. *Neuroscience and Biobehavioral Reviews, 35,* 1603–1610.

Skinner, N., & Brewer, N. (2002). The dynamics of threat and challenge appraisals prior to stressful achievement events. *Journal of Personality and Social Psychology, 83,* 678–692.

Slater, M. (2019). *Togetherness: How to build a winning team.* Oakamoor: Bennion Kearny.

Slater, M., Coffee, P., Barker, J., & Evans A. L. (2014). Promoting shared meanings in group memberships: A social identity approach to leadership in sport. *Reflective Practice, 15,* 672–685.

Turner, M. J., Jones, M.V., Sheffield, D., & Cross, S. L. (2012). Cardiovascular indices of challenge and threat states predict performance under stress in cognitive and motor tasks. *International Journal of Psychophysiology, 86,* 48–57.

Turner, M. J., Jones, M.V., Sheffield, D., Slater, M. J., Barker, J. B., & Bell, J. J. (2013). Who thrives under pressure? Predicting the performance of elite academy cricketers using the cardiovascular indicators of challenges and threat states. *Journal of Sport & Exercise Psychology, 35,* 387–397.

Woodman, T., & Hardy, L. (2001). A case study of organizational stress in elite sport. *Journal of Applied Sport Psychology, 13,* 207–238.

14
UNDERSTANDING THE EFFECTS OF ORGANISATIONAL CHANGE IN PROFESSIONAL SOCCER

Christopher R. D. Wagstaff and Richard C. Thelwell

Brief Introduction and Review of Literature

According to the League Managers' Association (LMA), during the 2017–2018 football season there were 65 manager movements in the English Football League (EFL), comprising 54 dismissals and 11 resignations. A record high of 15 dismissals occurred in the Premier League, which comprises just 20 teams. These statistics are somewhat alarming, yet there is potential cause for encouragement; the managers dismissed in 2017–2018 were in post for an average of 1.18 years, up slightly on the 2016–2017 record low of 1.16 years for the average tenure of dismissed managers (League Managers' Association, 2018). Alas, despite this minor reverse in tenure length, the overall managerial turnover statistics in elite English football provide a bleak picture.

The statistical trends in managerial change noted in the opening paragraph are an important consideration for performance psychologists seeking to support football organisations. That is, some scholars have argued that there is a natural time for a change in sport (see Tena & Forrest, 2007), such as the end of an annual (e.g., the end of a season) or quadrennial (e.g., the end of an Olympiad) cycle. Yet, while there might be a logical time for leadership change in elite sport, many organisations change leaders at unconventional and, in some cases, illogical times. Indeed, scholars (e.g., Dobson & Goddard, 2011) have noted that a growing trend has emerged of dismissing sport leaders in-season in an attempt to improve performance, with other researchers noting that the role of the professional manager in sport is one of chronic insecurity (Audas, Dobson, & Goddard, 2002; Bruinshoofd & ter Weel, 2003; Day, Gordon, & Fink, 2012; Flores, Forrest, & Tena, 2012). Moreover, recent research has begun to shed light on the human and organisational implications of managerial turnover in elite sport, with data demonstrating that such events are often volatile and leave those remaining in the organisation vulnerable to changes of climate, culture, and working practices (Wagstaff, Gilmore, & Thelwell, 2015, 2016). In this chapter, the research on the prevalence and influence of managerial change is reviewed. We then detail a case study of leader succession-related organisational change before unpacking this from coach, player, and practitioner perspectives.

Leadership Succession Events

Leadership change is commonly referred to in the general management literature as a "succession event" (Karg, McDonald, & Schoenberg, 2015, p. 31), and the term is adopted here for consistency across academic literatures. While many succession events are "owned" by executive boards, a succession event refers to the departure and replacement of a leader regardless of whether the leader was dismissed or resigned and whether the successor was internal or external to the organisation. Therefore, succession is a process of changing leaders that involves at least two distinct succession actions within a cycle—the removal of one leader and the appointment of another. These two actions can happen simultaneously, with a new leader immediately replacing the outgoing leader, or separately where there is a gap between the departure of one leader and the appointment of another (see Karg et al., 2015).

As alluded to previously, although succession can be a natural, logical, "clean" process, this is uncommon in elite sport, and such events can have implications across the entire sport organisation. Hence, leadership succession events are viewed here as a form of organisational change (see Wagstaff et al., 2015; Wagstaff, 2016), which is defined as "a deliberately planned change in an organization's formal structure, systems, processes, or product-market domain intended to improve the attainment of one or more organizational objectives" (Lines, 2005, pp. 9–10). When change is "owned" or initiated by executive boards, owners, or CEOs (hereafter referred to collectively as "senior management"), it is the employees located at multiple levels of the organisation's hierarchy who are tasked with implementing and coping with the change (Porras & Robertson, 1992). Unsurprisingly, the emotional and attitudinal responses of those change recipients are likely to influence their behaviour during that process and thus play a significant role in determining the effectiveness of the overall outcome of change (e.g., Liu & Perrewe, 2005; Paterson & Hartel, 2002). The key change recipients influenced by leader succession-related organisational change will likely be those in the performance (e.g., players, coaches) and performance support (e.g., science, medicine, technological support staff) departments.

Leadership Succession Prevalence

While the statistics on football manager turnover presented at the beginning of this chapter might appear bleak, the hiring and firing of elite sport leaders is a commonplace occurrence. Karg et al. (2015) recently reported that less than 5% of managers across the four major US professional leagues (Major League Baseball (MLB), the National Basketball Association (NBA), the National Football League (NFL), and the National Hockey League (NHL)) had tenures longer than a decade, while less than 10% of managers in the entire English football league had a tenure of longer than four years. A number of previous studies relating to leader succession in the sporting context date back as far as the 1960s. Some of these have focused on the major American sports industries such as the NBA (e.g., Giambatista, 2004), NHL (e.g., Rowe, Cannella, Rankin, & Gorman, 2005), MLB (e.g., Grusky, 1963; McTeer, White, & Persad, 1995), and the NFL (e.g., Brown, 1982). Others have focused on football in European leagues, such as the English Premier League (EPL), Dutch Eredivisie, German Bundesliga, Spanish La Liga, and Italian Serie A (Audas et al., 2002; Bell, Brooks, & Markham, 2013; Bruinshoofd & ter Weel, 2003; De Paola & Scoppa, 2011; Frick & Simmons, 2008; González-Gómez, Picazo-Tadeo, & García-Rubio, 2011; Koning, 2003; Tena & Forrest, 2007; ter Weel, 2011). For example, Audas et al. examined data for all English Football League and EPL fixtures completed during the 28 seasons between 1972–1973 and 1999–2000. During this period 1,138 separate managerial spells occurred, of which 1,058 spells terminated during the observation period. While Audas et al. did not distinguish between manager and head coach roles, an increasing trend of leader turnover was clear, driven mainly by a rise in involuntary departures. While voluntary departures have remained roughly constant, 736 (69.6%) of the 1,058 departures took place within-season and only 322 (30.4%) during the close-season. Only 12.9% of the 736 within-season departures were voluntary, while 27.3% of the 322 close-season departures were voluntary. Both the number of involuntary departures and the total departures vary inversely with divisional status. The high degree of leader turnover observed by Audas et al. has been mirrored in other countries. For instance, based on 22 years of data, Frick, Barros, and Prinz (2010) reported that, on average, 35% of managers in Germany's Bundesliga are fired each year. In Argentina, based on a similar period of 20 years, the incidence of sackings is more than one per season per club (Flores et al., 2012).

Leadership Succession and Performance

The research examining the influence of leadership succession events on performance in the United States has produced mixed findings. To elaborate, in the MLB, Grusky (1963) found a negative relationship between managerial change and performance that created a vicious circle of continual decline, whereby poor performance triggered a succession event that intensified poor performance. This spiral led to a perpetual cycle of decline driven by increased organisational instability brought on by a leadership change. Brown (1982) drew similar conclusions in the NFL and proposed that organisational effectiveness and performance do not increase following managerial change. McTeer et al. (1995) concluded that there was no improvement in performance in the full season after a leadership succession event yet did notice a fleeting minor increase in performance immediately after the change. More recently, Rowe et al. (2005) suggested that giving managers more time leads to better performance in the NHL. Rowe et al. added that this improvement occurs because new managers need time to lead organisational reconstruction and implement the right initiatives to achieve their goals.

Beyond the North American context, research from Dutch football (e.g., Bruinshoofd & ter Weel, 2003; Koning, 2003; ter Weel, 2011) has found that club performance did not improve when a manager was fired and that new managers performed worse than their fired predecessors in several instances. Also using data from Dutch football, Koning (2003) found that team performance decreased following 11 of the 28 manager changes made by Dutch Eredivisie clubs during the seasons 1993–1994 to 1997–1998. De Paola and Scoppa (2011) drew similar conclusions in relation to data from Italian football, where the results of a four-year study indicated that changing a manager does not improve club performance.

Researchers have recently examined the influence of mid-season managerial change, also noting disruptions to performance rather than improvements (Giambatista, 2004). Nevertheless, converse findings were reported by González-Gómez et al. (2011), who reviewed the influence of mid-season succession events on sporting performance in Spanish first-division football clubs. Their league standing, but not their final league position, was worse than comparable teams that had not changed managers during the season. González-Gómez et al. (2011) concluded that changing managers mid-season can be effective when the team is not performing well but recommended that club executives should plan the season well beforehand to avoid the necessity for such change (González-Gómez et al., 2011). Unfortunately, it is evident that the majority of club executives do not subscribe to this advice and change manager during the season in response to a poor run of results—a short-term decision, occasionally at the cost of long-term cultural and climatic stability.

In one of the most rigorous examinations to date, ter Weel (2011) used difference-in-difference estimates and a two-stage least squares (2SLS) regression analysis strategy to model the influence of leadership succession on team performance using information from the Dutch soccer league in the period 1986–2004. Ter Weel's analyses indicated that the strongest determinants of forced manager turnover include manager investments (measured by the number of players bought) and remaining contract length at the time of a performance dip. That is, when managers have invested more money on player resources, they are more likely to be sacked during performance dips but less likely to be fired when they have a longer period left on their current contract. This is likely to be due, in part, to the substantial compensation required when manager contracts are terminated or boards still having trust in the manager. Ter Weel also highlighted that tenure had a small effect on forced managerial turnover, with more experienced managers having a lower probability to be fired. Ter Weel also observed a brief, one game, performance increase following managerial turnover. Ter Weel proposed that this effect was a "shock effect" influenced by popular media and expectation of the team members to perform better to justify the sacking of the previous manager. Nevertheless, this effect did not last long, and those teams with new managers performed worse compared to control groups for the next three periods (i.e., games). The medium- and long-term effects indicated an unclear, but largely negative, picture. Moreover, manager quality (measured by the manager's previous achievements as a player, years of managerial experience, and number of spells) did not significantly matter for predicting turnover and did not explain performance variation after departure. In interpreting these findings, ter Weel argued, "manager quality does not matter in predicting manager turnover and success... [and is] generally not able to influence firm outcomes and only play a role in the process of mean reversion after a performance dip" (p. 291). These findings largely support those using data from other countries (Audas et al., 2002; Frick & Simmons, 2008).

Leadership Succession and Organisational Functioning

In addition to the research that has examined the performance outcomes associated with leadership succession events, there has been a growing body of research examining the psychosocial consequences of such change for other stakeholders within sport organisations. For example, in a study of an EPL football club, Gilmore and Sillince (2014) illustrated how science and medicine practices that were previously embedded within coaching were deinstitutionalised within a six-month period following managerial change. Further, the authors noted that leadership change disrupted working practices and routines and challenged coach philosophy.

Recently, Wagstaff et al. (2015) presented findings from a programme of research exploring the change experiences of individuals employed within elite sport organisation performance departments. Specifically, using a two-year longitudinal design, data were collected in three temporally defined phases via 49 semi-structured interviews with 20 sport medics and scientists employed by three organisations competing in the top tiers of English football and cricket. Findings highlighted four distinct stages of change: anticipation and uncertainty, upheaval and realisation, integration and experimentation, normalisation and learning. Anticipation and uncertainty was defined as the process of attempting to gather information to understand the change and was characterised by a climate of sensitivity, rumour, speculation, and gossip. Upheaval and realisation was defined as the process of confirming assumptions and gaining perspective regarding the implications of change for extant practice and was characterised by a focus on past practices, varyingly resulting in resistance to new practices, opportunism, and behaviours. Integration and experimentation was defined as the process by which assumptions regarding change were challenged and new practices developed and was characterised by a focus on assimilating previous and current practices. Normalisation and learning was defined as the process of establishing norms that align with emerging practices and reflecting on the change as a past event and was characterised by a focus on translating one's knowledge, skills, and abilities to relevant others. In their conclusion, Wagstaff et al. drew attention to salient emotional, behavioural, and attitudinal employee experiences, the existence of poor employment practices, and direct and indirect implications for on-field performance associated with organisational change.

Wagstaff et al. (2016) recently extended the psychosocial research on leadership succession by exploring employees' responses to *recurrent* change events as opposed to a single event. Given the infancy of repeated change research, the authors adopted an exploratory approach to investigate employees' responses to repeated leadership succession events. Data were gathered via 20 semi-structured interviews with employees from two organisations competing in the EPL. Ten employees from each organisation were sampled. All of the participants were paid employees of their respective organisation and fulfilled roles as medical practitioners (e.g., doctor, physiotherapist), sport scientists (e.g., psychologist, performance analyst), coaches whose work was densely infused by sport science activities (e.g., strength and conditioning) or training practices (e.g., technical coaches), and athletes (e.g., players). At the time of data collection, the organisations from which the participants were sampled had both made five managerial changes within the preceding four-year period ($M^{\text{tenure}} = 12.28$ months, $SD = 9.27$). These figures were comparable to the EFL average at the time for managerial tenure of 1.4 years. The participants had encountered an average of 4.2 ($SD = 0.89$) managerial changes in their current position. The results indicated that employees responded to recurrent leadership succession events in positive (namely resilience, learning, performance, challenge appraisals, and autonomy) and negative (namely trust, cynicism, organisational development, motivation, turnover, engagement, and commitment) emotional, behavioural, and attitudinal ways. Specifically, the data not only indicated increasingly deteriorating employee attitudes across succession events but also highlighted the important role of cognitive appraisal in influencing responses to each succession event.

While the research reviewed previously has examined the immediate influence of leadership succession on organisational stakeholders inside the performance department, Karg et al. (2015) examined the influence of such events on those *outside* of the performance department. In a study of season ticket holder (STH) attitudes (i.e., satisfaction and renewal intentions), Karg et al. interpreted their data as showing that appointing a new coach (used interchangeably with manager) was met with increases in positive attitudes towards almost every aspect of the STH experience, whereas removing a coach had no meaningful influence on attitudes. The authors argued that their findings support the view that leadership succession is a multiple-phase process including distinct stages of removal and replacement. While it is the desire for improved performance that often motivates coach succession, Karg et al.'s data indicate that the influence of succession activities on fans is more wide-ranging.

In reflecting on the emerging responses to leadership succession research, Wagstaff (2016) voiced his concern regarding the emotional impact of employment volatility on the wellbeing of those working in sport performance departments. In doing so, he drew attention to the high turnover, satisfaction, and effectiveness of performance department staff (i.e., players, coaches, sport scientist, and medical staff) and suggested that the precariousness of employment is not simply experienced by traditional "players" (i.e., athletes and managers) but is now witnessed across the performance and support departments.

Elsewhere, in work examining the lived professional life of a performance psychologist in the EPL, Gilmore, Wagstaff, and Smith (2018) recently noted the precarity of employment in this domain. In presenting the narrative of one such professional, Gilmore et al. noted:

> When managers change, everyone's thinking "what does this mean for me?" There's no consideration for each other among the staff; there's no "Right, we've been here three years as a group and this is how we're going to approach it". So it becomes a very volatile and unpleasant environment. Some people know they're going to be pushed out because the new manager's worked with the same fitness coach for 15 years; you're the incumbent fitness coach so your world's changing significantly. . . . The precariousness of it does

impact how you approach it and that's a reflection on the industry. In most jobs, you've got a line manager who is there to support you, but in football your line manager's in exactly the same position as you and just trying to hang on to his job. I've had five managers in five years. This brings fear and uncertainty because any time there's change you don't know whether your face is going to fit.... All of this adds to the precarious nature of the work. You do the best you can to survive and hopefully thrive as well. Just try and apply what you're capable of doing and hopefully you can create enough goodwill, respect or credibility to (a) stay in the job and (b) hopefully *do* a good job.

The narrative provided by Gilmore et al. (2018) demonstrates the inherent precarity of working in an elite football performance support department as a performance psychologist and provides glimpses into a shared experience among other performance staff, particularly at times of organisational change. Such observations signal the broad impact of leader succession on the individuals, practices, and processes of various stakeholder groups across a football organisation.

Collectively, this body of work provides an insight into the employment realities within sport organisations' performance and performance support departments during change. Performance psychologists must be aware that leadership succession is unlikely to positively influence performance and will likely negatively affect support staff, athlete, and coach effectiveness and influence fan attitudes, for a short period of time, nominally between 16 matches and six months (see Audas et al., 2002; ter Weel, 2011; Wagstaff et al., 2015), regardless of any short-term, "honeymoon" improvement in performance.

Practical Applications—Case Study

Background and Context

The case reflects that of a football club in the EFL. The club has a history of competing for the top six positions in the Premier League and a rich cultural history for attacking football which is an identity fiercely protected by many fans. The club has a global reach with many millions of fans around the world. In recent years there have been several leadership succession events, with the board of directors appointing and firing five managers in the last five years. These changes have been characterised by several managers imposing contrasting styles of play, each recruiting several expensive players to fit their preferred tactics. This has resulted in an expensive squad that lacks cohesion and "fit" for the type of attacking play the club is generally known for. Fans have recently voiced their dissatisfaction and attendance and season-ticket sales have been poor. There are six games of the season left and qualification for the Champions' League is dependent on other teams losing points. Given the fixtures ahead for rivals, qualification is possible, but unlikely, and this would mean a rare season without a trophy or prospects of elite European football next season. The poor results, rumbling rumours of changing room conflict, and fan dissatisfaction has prompted the owners to notify the current manager that this season—his first at the club after a successful career in Italy and Spain—will be his last. It was not the intention to notify the media of the leadership succession, but the news has been leaked. Although aware of fan dissatisfaction and rumours, had not been formally notified of the owners' decision, so the media reports of the change were the first they knew. There is much rumour, discussion, and uncertainty among the performance and performance support staff, with some openly discussing whether they expect to be at the club next season.

Presenting Issue(s)

The Coaches' Perspective

In this context, the title "coach" is taken to reflect a variety of roles within both the performance (e.g., assistant coach, goalkeeping coach) and the performance support (e.g., strength and conditioning coach) departments. While the roles and responsibilities of these coaches will vary, all individuals who hold a coaching-related position are likely to be influenced by the arrival of a new manager. Indeed, this perspective will likely differ from the perspective of the player. Considering the case material from a coaches' perspective is important due to the stage-based experiences of employees in Wagstaff et al. (2015, 2016) research. That is, it is likely that the coaches currently employed by the club in the case material will experience an assortment of anticipation and uncertainty, upheaval and realisation, integration and experimentation, normalisation and learning, perhaps in a largely linear order.

For those coaches who are closely aligned with the outgoing manager, such as an assistant coach or strength and conditioning coach, they are likely to experience heightened levels of job insecurity and uncertainty regarding their future employment as they anticipate and "game" their next steps. As a core member of the outgoing manager's backroom staff, it is unlikely that they will retain their current position. Should the outgoing manager gain immediate reemployment, they might be offered an opportunity to join them, which may or may not suit them or their personal circumstances. Alternatively, a period of redeployment in a more junior role and for reduced remuneration, perhaps in the academy, or a period of unemployment is likely. For those coaches who are less fundamental or openly aligned with the outgoing manager's backroom staff, and hold a performance support coaching role, such as a performance analysis coach, it is possible that their role will be less at risk, yet this depends on the incoming manager's integration of their skill set. For instance, some managers have preferred science and medicine support disciplines and this leads to potential change in the integration of certain skill sets and individuals (see Gilmore & Sillince, 2014).

Performance psychologists must proactively prepare coaches and support staff for the inevitable change that they will experience. Much work can be done through education and interventions aimed at creating a psychologically safe culture. By ensuring coaches are educated regarding the precarity of jobs in elite football, there may be less novelty and unpredictability perceived in the challenges associated with managerial change. This education might be delivered throughout qualification, during employee intake, and sporadically throughout employment, such as during professional development and reviews.

From a more reactive perspective, as change is impending or recently announced, the coaches within the performance and performance support departments will almost certainly, but with varying degrees of intensity, experience anticipation and uncertainty. This will lead to a search for information to understand the change and how it might impact them. At such times, coaches might be more sensitive, and engage in rumour, speculation, and gossip. It is important that performance psychologists offer coaches an opportunity to voice their concerns and dedicate suitable time and sensitively selected space and location for this. While rumour might not necessarily be a negative influence, this can be toxic to an environment and should be monitored and potentially handled by the performance psychologist.

Once a new manager arrives, it may lead to several coaches experiencing upheaval as the new regime and "ways of doing things" are discussed and implemented. For some coaches this might trigger a realisation and confirmation of their assumptions regarding the implications of change for their current practice. At this time, coaches might benefit from reactive emotion regulation support, as well as problem-solving and conflict management reflection facilitation. For instance, where a new manager has new ideas for how science and medicine practice is integrated into the daily training of the team, this might lead coaches to ruminate about past regimes and processes and resistance to new practices. Alternatively, coaches might feel emancipated from the change and experience opportunism and a freedom to propose new and better ways of doing things. The nature of the relationship between the incoming manager and head of science and medicine will likely set the tone for the outcomes of this period of upheaval and the performance psychologist can proactively seek to optimise relationships and facilitate opportunities for reflection, mutual sharing and personal disclosure, and general information sharing.

Regardless of the relationships between incoming manager and coaches, there will likely be a period of integration and experimentation, whereby assumptions regarding change are challenged and new practices formally developed. Here the performance psychologist can help coaches to overcome resistance to change and seek to assimilate previous and current practices in a culturally and historically sensitive manner to enable faster normalisation and learning. Specifically, developing a culture of openness, collaboration, and regular communication between senior performance and performance support staff is pivotal to the effective integration of these departments following leader succession. The performance psychologist is excellently placed to facilitate such processes given their knowledge of creating psychologically informed performance systems. In supporting coaches and the incoming manager on behalf of the football organisation, performance psychologists must remain cognisant that elite football managers are expected to instantly and consistently deliver success, and therefore may enter this process with a well-established modus operandi, and some resistance to change. Hence, it will require skill on the behalf of the psychologist to help stakeholders to communicate and translate their knowledge, preferences, and previous and current practices, while also assisting with the "scene-setting" regarding the cultural, climatic, and historical context of the organisation into which the incoming manager and their backroom staff have entered.

The Players' Perspective

While a leadership succession is likely to cause uncertainty for players (i.e., "will I fit the new manager's plans or might I be sold?"), there are several reasons why this may not be intensely felt by all players in the squad. It is likely that the length remaining on a player's contract, it's value, their influence and leadership, age, form, and fit with the incoming manager's style of play, will all influence the extent an athlete might experience uncertainty. Performance psychologists should identify those at risk depending on their individual profile. For instance, players close to transitions (e.g., established, but aging and expensive player, or an unestablished young or rookie player, yet to consolidate a position in the squad) might feel more intensely the uncertainty that managerial change might bring. By first identifying at risk players, the performance psychologist can target reactive support for these individuals. Moreover, it is possible that experienced players will have encountered several leader succession events already and may be able to mentor or support others through this period. The psychologist should be careful to monitor the influence of senior players at such times, given the observation that recurrent leadership change can lead to cynicism and a weakened psychological contract (see Wagstaff et al., 2016). Hence, efforts by the performance psychologist to support organisational identity might benefit players during the remaining games of the season for the case study organisation. Athlete leadership representatives could help maintain consistency and communication in the interim period and work closely with the incoming manager to ease transition. The performance psychologist is well-placed to instigate and guide such processes. Elsewhere, the proactive education of academy players regarding the typical experiences of leadership succession is an obvious potential gain for performance psychologists. The development of psychosocial resources to better cope with future demands during organisational change will also likely benefit footballers.

The Intervention/Work Conducted

The Practitioner's Perspective

There is perhaps an irony associated with encouraging performance psychologists to help others during a period of uncertainty and upheaval, when they may also be personally experiencing job insecurity or cynicism towards their employers. Unfortunately, in the absence of professional body lobbying or employment support, there is a very real precarity for performance support staff operating in elite sport (cf. Gilmore et al., 2018). Hence, the personal and professional precarity experienced by the practitioner requires self-reflection, self-awareness and self-care to navigate the potential pitfalls of "working on two fronts." If the personal and professional challenges experienced by a performance psychologist aiming to support an organisation while concerned for their own security can be personally monitored and managed, or assuaged by reassurance from senior leaders, then the opportunities for engaged and valuable support can be realised. From the psychologist's perspective, there is not an off-the-shelf intervention that can be provided throughout leader succession. This inability is due to the personal (e.g., personnel and personal preferences) and systemic (e.g., culture, history, size and nature of the organisation) characteristics of the elite sport context. In the absence of an off-the-shelf intervention in the sport psychology literature, practitioners might acquaint themselves with the recent change experience work (e.g., Wagstaff et al., 2015, 2016) and the general change management models (e.g., Bridges, 2009; Kotter, 1995).

To better assist senior leaders and managers to understand the typical responses of those around them to leader succession, performance psychologists might consider the use of Wagstaff et al. (2015) stage-based process model of organisation-change experiences. It is likely that progress across each stage can be expedited with appropriate interventions that might be developed in collaboration between the psychologist, senior leaders, and the incoming manager. Such interventions might also assist the remaining coaches and athletes to better understand the experiences of their "sea of relationships" to promote effective practice during the change process and foster psychosocial capital (see Wagstaff, Hanton, & Fletcher, 2013).

A second model that practitioners might use in conjunction with Wagstaff et al. (2015) stage-based general response model is the exit, voice, loyalty, and neglect (EVLN; see Rusbult, Farrell, Rogers, & Mainous, 1988). EVLN offers a typology of four specific behavioural responses that employees might exhibit during adversity: to leave the organisation, speak up, patiently and confidently hope for a better future, or be lax and disregardful. Hirschman originally conceived of his seminal exit, voice, and loyalty model to explain customers' and employees' responses to "lapses from efficient, rational, law-abiding, virtuous, or otherwise functional organizational behaviour" (1970, p. 1). Hirschman's account has made its way into various research areas, such as comparative politics, labour economics, marketing, political sciences, and social and even intimate relationships, to capture and structure the various ways in which individuals might respond to adverse circumstances. In the general organisational literature, it has acquired a position as a model that allows for and differentiates a variety of employees' responses to adverse conditions in the workplace (Farrell, 1983; Rusbult et al., 1988; Turnley & Feldman, 1999).

The performance psychologist might seek to use their observations and competence as a facilitator to "steady the ship" in an emotionally intelligent manner (see Wagstaff et al., 2013), particularly where there is significant uncertainty and upheaval among stakeholders. Both Wagstaff et al.'s (2015) stage-based and the EVLN model offer an insight into the possible emotional, attitudinal, and behavioural responses of sport performers or those they rely on for optimal performance and how they might change over time. In turn, practitioners and coaches might use such information to develop tailored culture change (see Cruickshank, Collins, & Minten, 2013) or emotion ability and regulation strategy interventions (see Wagstaff et al., 2013) to promote organisational functioning during periods of change.

As alternatives to the sport-based models for understanding and supporting individuals' responses to leader succession, practitioners might look to management change models for guiding frameworks. For instance, Bridges' (2009) transition model focuses on transition rather than change. In doing so, this approach distinguishes the way that change management is approached. Rather than attempting to assist change that happens *to* people, which can lead to cynicism and helplessness, performance psychologists might seek to assist organisations by encouraging a focus on any leader succession as a journey over time, towards organisational goals, rather than an abrupt, intrusive shift. That is, Bridges' transition model might help practitioners guide sport organisation stakeholders through the reactions and emotions they will encounter when encountering change. To do so, Bridges advises three stages of transition, each of which the employee must be guided through for the change to be successful: ending, losing, and letting go; the neutral zone, and; the new beginnings. While a full overview of the available models is beyond the scope of this chapter, there is a wealth of literature available for the interested reader.

Outcome Analysis and Reflections

Conclusion

It would appear logical for performance psychologists to offer their services and skill set to football organisations to limit the negative impact of manager leader succession events. In doing so, practitioners might help develop and sustain a robust performance *system* that integrates playing, coaching, and science and medicine expertise, into which the football organisation hires individuals to the position of manager who holds appropriate capabilities and knowledge of such performance systems and a willingness to adapt their modus operandi to the cultural and historical context into which they are entering. When managers do not possess such skills, a performance director might be recruited to help coordinate commercial and operational responsibilities, enabling the manager to act in the role more aligned with a Head Coach. The working practices of the robust performance system should remain intact regardless of managerial change. This systemic approach could be developed in alignment with the culture, history, goals, and practices of the organisation, providing stability during change and reducing the uncertainty and upheaval currently observed in research on managerial change in elite sport.

Despite the apparent logic outlined above regarding performance systems in organisations, two things appear evident from the preceding review and case material. First, managers get fired at an alarming rate at unpredictable times. Second, performance psychologists might, but currently rarely do, assist organisations during times of leadership succession. Taking the first point, employees in performance and performance support departments (i.e., coaches, performance support staff, athletes) typically become increasingly frustrated and disenchanted with their work when exposed to repeated leadership succession events (see Wagstaff et al., 2015, 2016). At such times, the extant research indicates that these individuals—who have both direct and indirect influences on performance—also look for opportunities for self-expression, self-fulfilment, and self-progression and, therefore, respond to succession event circumstances in various ways. These responses occur in tandem with reduced effectiveness and performance for an extended period until working practices, culture, and responsibilities are routinised. Further, the research indicates that these decrements are associated with a weakening psychological contract and increasing cynicism towards the employing organisations that must be addressed by the incoming manager and any remaining personnel (see Wagstaff et al., 2015, 2016).

Turning to the second conclusion, that performance psychologists can assist organisations during times of leadership succession. There is a need to move beyond the distinction between and support of siloed coach, performance support staff, and athlete groups and to see these various stakeholders as intertwined collectives. The shared culture and climate of the football club, the actions of the senior leaders, and the implications of these, will impact on this collective in a multitude of ways. Nevertheless, these influences will in turn be communicated among colleagues across the football club (e.g., via EVLN). Performance psychologists are particularly well-placed to observe and advise on the impact of organisational change on the day-to-day behaviours, emotions, and attitudes of the collective stakeholders in football clubs due to their proximal yet out-group position and interdependent working relations such individuals have with athletes, coaches, and performance support staff. Moreover, athletes commonly share information with physiotherapists and psychologists that they might wish to hide from coaches or managers, with whom they regularly engage in impression management (cf. Collins, Moore, Mitchell, & Alpress, 1999). It also follows that performance psychologists should seek to develop among senior leaders a foundational understanding of how organisational change events or other organisation-wide issues are experienced by those that operate within an elite sport environment. From an educational perspective, individuals in football clubs must understand that leadership succession events are an inevitable but complex facet of elite sport. Developing an awareness among all stakeholders regarding the nature of elite sport will likely provide the most valuable starting point for implementing proactive and reactive support and engaging in authentic and transparent conversations with the manager and team during any change process.

To conclude, the acquisition of the right manager is likely to be integral to a sport organisation's success as they are responsible for selecting the players and the style in which they play, ultimately leading to success or failure. If failure persists, the club owners might feel they have little option but to dismiss the manager in a "scapegoat" reaction. Yet, the appointment and subsequent dismissal of the wrong manager can be extremely costly across performance (see ter Weel, 2011), financial (see Bell et al., 2013), and employee wellbeing (see Wagstaff et al., 2015, 2016) indicators. Moreover, there are encouraging signs that performance psychologists are developing a body of knowledge and competence to advise on and support leader succession events in elite sport.

Key Messages and Further Reading

- There is a managerial merry-go-round that occurs in elite sport when head coaches or managers leave their role. Such leader succession events lead to substantial upheaval and uncertainty to the working lives of individuals within football organisations with direct and indirect implications for performance and wellbeing.

- Senior leaders should pay close attention to and carefully consider the impact of leader succession on all departments within the organisation and prepare for subsequent exit, voice, loyalty, and neglect among their stakeholders. These negative effects might last six months and therefore have an unintended influence on the sociocultural environment of the organisation during subsequent managerial tenures.
- Repeated experience of leader succession events can have numerous positive (e.g., resilience, learning, performance, challenge appraisals, and autonomy) and negative (e.g., trust, cynicism, organisational development, motivation, turnover, engagement, and commitment) emotional, behavioural, and attitudinal ways.
- Performance psychologists should develop knowledge of organisational and systems working and develop associated service provision competence. This will require psychologists to work outside of the science and medicine team and at various levels of the hierarchy of a football organisation. Organisational and systems psychology expertise would be particularly valuable during periods of change, such as during and after a leader succession event.
- An organisational sport psychology approach can help practitioners develop a psychologically informed performance system that is cognisant of the culture, history, goals, and practices of the organisation. One aim of this work would be to foster stability during periods of substantial change using cultural and linguistic artefacts as symbols and frames to guide progress towards the desired future of the organisation.

Future research is required to develop robust but adaptive organisational competence frameworks for intervention and to undertake systematic research investigations to better understand the efficacy and effectiveness of various forms of intervention and support.

Pertinent References

Day, D. V., Gordon, S., & Fink, C. (2012). The sporting life: Exploring organizations through the lens of sport. *The Academy of Management Annals*, 6(1), 397–433.

Gilmore, S., & Sillince, J. (2014). Institutional theory and change: The deinstitutionalisation of sports science at Club X. *Journal of Organizational Change Management*, 27(2), 314–330.

Gilmore, S., Wagstaff, C., & Smith, J. (2018). Sports psychology in the English Premier League: "It feels precarious and is precarious." *Work, Employment and Society*, 32(2), 426–435.

Wagstaff, C. R. D., Gilmore, S., & Thelwell, R. C. (2015). Sport medicine and sport science practitioners' experiences of organizational change. *Scandinavian Journal of Medicine and Science in Sports*, 25(5), 685–698.

Wagstaff, C. R. D., Gilmore, S., & Thelwell, R. C. (2016). When the show must go on: Investigating repeated organizational change in elite sport. *Journal of Change Management*, 16(1), 1–7.

References

Audas, R., Dobson, S., & Goddard, J. (2002). The impact of managerial change on team performance in professional sports. *Journal of Economics and Business*, 54(6), 633–650.

Bell, A., Brooks, C., & Markham, T. (2013). The performance of football club managers: Skill or luck? *Economics and Finance Research*, 1(1), 19–30.

Bridges, W. (2009). *Managing transitions: Making the most of change* (3rd ed.). Philadelphia, PA: De Capo Press.

Brown, M. C. (1982). Administrative succession and organizational performance: The succession effect. *Administrative Science Quarterly*, 27, 1–16.

Bruinshoofd, A., & ter Weel, B. (2003). Manager to go? Performance dips reconsidered with evidence from Dutch football. *European Journal of Operational Research*, *148*(2), 233–246.

Collins, D., Moore, P., Mitchell, D., & Alpress, F. (1999). Role conflict and confidentiality in multidisciplinary athlete support programmes. *British Journal of Sports Medicine*, *33*(3), 208–211.

Cruickshank, A., Collins, D., & Minten, S. (2013). Culture change in a professional sports team: Shaping environmental contexts and regulating power. *International Journal of Sports Science and Coaching*, *8*, 271–290.

Day, D. V., Gordon, S., & Fink, C. (2012). The sporting life: Exploring organizations through the lens of sport. *The Academy of Management Annals*, *6*(1), 397–433.

De Paola, M., & Scoppa, V. (2011). The effects of managerial turnover: Evidence from coach dismissals in Italian soccer teams. *Journal of Sports Economics*, *13*, 152–268.

Dobson, S., & Goddard, J. (2011). *The economics of football*. Cambridge: Cambridge University Press.

Farrell, D. (1983). Exit, voice, loyalty, and neglect as responses to job dissatisfaction: A multidimensional scaling study. *Academy of Management Journal*, *26*(4), 596–607.

Flores, R., Forrest, D., & Tena, J. D. D. (2012). Decision taking under pressure: Evidence on football manager dismissals in Argentina and their consequences. *European Journal of Operational Research*, *222*(3), 653–662.

Frick, B., Barros, C. P., & Prinz, J. (2010). Analysing head coach dismissals in the German "Bundesliga" with a mixed logit approach. *European Journal of Operational Research*, *200*, 151–159.

Frick, B., & Simmons, R. (2008). The impact of managerial quality on organizational performance: Evidence from German soccer. *Managerial and Decision Economics*, *29*(7), 593–600.

Giambatista, R. C. (2004). Jumping through hoops: A longitudinal study of leader life cycles in the NBA. *The Leadership Quarterly*, *15*(5), 607–624.

Gilmore, S., & Sillince, J. (2014). Institutional theory and change: The deinstitutionalisation of sports science at Club X. *Journal of Organizational Change Management*, *27*(2), 314–330.

Gilmore, S., Wagstaff, C., & Smith, J. (2018). Sports psychology in the English Premier League: "It feels precarious and is precarious." *Work, Employment and Society*, *32*(2), 426–435.

González-Gómez, F., Picazo-Tadeo, A. J., & García-Rubio, M. Á. (2011). The impact of a mid-season change of manager on sporting performance. *Sport, Business and Management: An International Journal*, *1*(1), 28–42.

Grusky, O. (1963). Managerial succession and organizational effectiveness. *American Journal of Sociology*, *69*, 21–31.

Karg, A., McDonald, H., & Schoenberg, G. (2015). The immediate impact of coach succession events on season ticket holder attitudes. *Sport Marketing Quarterly*, *24*(1), 30–42.

Koning, R. H. (2003). An econometric evaluation of the effect of firing a coach on team performance. *Applied Economics*, *35*(5), 555–564.

Kotter, J. P. (1995). Leading change why transformation efforts fail. *Harvard Business Review*, *73*, 59–67.

League Managers' Association. (2018). End of season manager statistics: Report by the League Managers Association. Retrieved January 2019, from www.leaguemanagers.com/news/lma-latest/lma-end-season-report-and-statistics-2017-18/

Lines, R. (2005). The structure and function of attitudes toward organizational change. *Human Resource Development Review*, *4*(1), 8–32.

Liu, Y., & Perrewe, P. L. (2005). Another look at the role of emotion in the organizational change: A process model. *Human Resource Management Review*, *15*(4), 263–280.

McTeer, W., White, P. G., & Persad, S. (1995). Manager/coach mid-season replacement and team performance in professional team sport. *Journal of Sport Behavior*, *18*(1), 58–68.

Paterson, J. M., & Härtel, C. E. J. (2002). An integrated affective and cognitive model to explain employees' responses to downsizing. In N. M. Ashkanasy, C. E. J. Härtel, & W. J. Zerbe (Eds.), *Managing emotions in a changing workplace* (pp. 25–44). Armonk, NY: M.E. Sharpe.

Porras, J. I., & Robertson, P. J. (1992). *Organizational development: Theory, practice, and research*. Palo Alto, CA: Consulting Psychologists Press.

Rowe, W. G., Cannella, A. A., Rankin, D., & Gorman, D. (2005). Leader succession and organizational performance: Integrating the common-sense, ritual scapegoating, and vicious-circle succession theories. *The Leadership Quarterly*, *16*(2), 197–219.

Rusbult, C. E., Farrell, D., Rogers, G., & Mainous, A. G. (1988). Impact of exchange variables on exit, voice, loyalty, and neglect: An integrative model of responses to declining job satisfaction. *Academy of Management Journal, 31*(3), 599–627.

Tena, J. de Dios, & Forrest, D. (2007). Within-season dismissal of football coaches: Statistical analysis of causes and consequences. *European Journal of Operational Research, 181*(1), 362–373.

ter Weel, B. (2011). Does manager turnover improve firm performance? Evidence from Dutch soccer, 1986–2004. *De Economist, 159*(3), 279–303.

Turnley, W. H., & Feldman, D. C. (1999). The impact of psychological contract violations on exit, voice, loyalty, and neglect. *Human Relations, 52*(7), 895–922.

Wagstaff, C. R. D. (2016). Coaching through organizational change: The influence of leadership succession events. In R. C. Thelwell, C. Harwood & I. Greenlees (Eds.), *The psychology of sports coaching* (pp. 68–83). London: Routledge.

Wagstaff, C. R. D., Gilmore, S., & Thelwell, R. C. (2015). Sport medicine and sport science practitioners' experiences of organizational change. *Scandinavian Journal of Medicine and Science in Sports, 25*(5), 685–698.

Wagstaff, C. R. D., Gilmore, S., & Thelwell, R. C. (2016). When the show must go on: Investigating repeated organizational change in elite sport. *Journal of Change Management, 16*(1), 1–7.

Wagstaff, C. R. D., Hanton, S., & Fletcher, D. (2013). Developing emotion abilities and regulation strategies in a sport organization: An action research intervention. *Psychology of Sport and Exercise, 14*(4), 476–487.

15
UNDERSTANDING THE ROLE OF ENVIRONMENT AND CULTURE WHEN DELIVERING SPORT PSYCHOLOGY SERVICES IN ELITE WOMEN'S INTERNATIONAL SOCCER

Jenn Gandhi and Peter Schneider

> Culture is a complex phenomenon. It is about behaviours, beliefs, values, habits and expectations. Living relationships working toward a shared goal. Culture is both fluid and dynamic, continually evolving through time. Culture is not something you are. It's something you do.

Theoretical Background

Creating effective team cultures within business has been increasingly important to upper management at businesses throughout the modern world. The idea of effective and positive team cohesion in sport, however, has been around for even longer. In the sport of soccer, this emphasis on effective team cohesion can be taken to the extreme—where more skilled individuals are passed upon for the good of the team collective. A classic example of this in German soccer culture is the oft-repeated quote "Elf Freunde müsst ihr sein" (You must be eleven friends). Friendships aside, the ability to work together on a daily basis (Carron & Eys, 2012), to put the team before one's personal ego or goal (Benson, Eys, Surya, Dawson, & Schneider, 2013), and to function under pressure when there's something to win or lose (Wergin, Zimanyi, Mesagno, & Beckmann, 2018) has become the focus of many coaching staffs, and specifically their team psychologists.

Perhaps there is no place this unity or cohesion has more focus within soccer teams than during the international matches played leading up to and during competitions such as the UEFA European Championship, CONCAF Championship, Africa Cup of Nations, the Asia Cup, or, the biggest of all, the World Cup. The best players of a country are brought together, usually after a hard-fought season where they are required to be leaders in their respected club teams and expected to perform at their highest level against the best of the world with teammates who share a minimum of one commonality—a passport. Various international coaches have tried a range of strategies to unite their rosters into performing teams as quickly as possible; however, one method seems to slowly have transformed the approach international staffs are taking: holistic ecological approaches focusing on developing a collective culture among a group of individuals.

We have seen these ecological and holistic approaches popping up in sport psychological literature at an increasing rate in recent years. Modern holistic approaches include cultural-specific psychological theories (Henriksen, 2010; Henriksen & Stambulova, 2017), where three aspects of a team or club are considered. These include the interpersonal relationships between the coaches and players as well as among the players themselves (Mallett & Rynne, 2015; Eys, Loughead, & Godfrey, 2017), contextual factors, such as the city and/or federation providing opportunities in the sport (Côté, MacDonald, Baker, & Abernethy, 2006), and finally the greater cultural environment, where national identity and norms can effect behaviour (Si & Lee, 2007).

Henriksen and colleagues (2010a) sought to combine all of these factors, using the bio-ecological model (Bronfenbrenner, 2005), and developed working models to identify both components of effective athletic talent develop environments (ATDE) and, perhaps more importantly, the environmental success factors (ESF), at whose core is the cultural paradigm producing results. This cultural paradigm can be further divided and is comprised of three factors: cultural artefacts, espoused values, and basic assumptions (Schein, 1990).

A summary of three studies (Henriksen et al., 2010a, 2010b, 2011); Henriksen (2010) revealed eight characteristics of effective talent development environments:

> 1) training groups with supportive relationships, 2) proximal role models, 3) support of sporting goals by the wider environment, 4) support for the development of psychosocial skills, 5) training that allows for diversification, 6) focus on long-term development, 7) strong and coherent organizational culture, and 8) integrations of efforts.

Larsen and colleagues (2013) investigated these characteristics in a soccer context, to demonstrate if the same environmental factors could be demonstrated in a team sport. They found the following factors played a pivotal role in the development of an elite Under-17 soccer team: (1) preconditions—the club's location, prestige, coaches; (2) process—five to six highly organised training sessions per week; (3) a clear cultural paradigm, including trophies, posters, and knowledge of true legends of the club; (4) a strong family feeling—close core of players, coaches, managers; (5) preference for less talent, more hard work—celebrating a "blue-collar" mentality throughout the organisation; (6) a focus on education and development—balancing winning and learning in soccer; and lastly (7) a holistic approach towards education, emotional, and soccer-related development.

This study's findings are in line with others that echo the importance of a close-knit and family like environment (Bruner, Munroe-Chandler, & Spink, 2008) as well as findings from Martindale, Collins, and Daubney (2005), who explain the importance of high levels of organisational culture within successful clubs. In addition, the empirical models resulting from the environmental studies (Henriksen et al., 2010a, 2010b, 2011; Larsen et al., 2013) have been repeated again in a Norwegian soccer environment as well as women's handball (Aalberg & Sæther, 2016; Storm, 2015), reiterating the importance of a cohesive environment and culture to produce effective results, for both individuals and the team.

In the application of these ecological and cultural theories, there is only some evidence that gender plays a role in the creation of a successful environment. For example, it has been shown that in such environments there are increased pressures on female athletes, who tend to put a greater emphasis on school and have stricter societal expectations regarding appearance (Henriksen et al., 2010b). Moreover, Holt and Morley (2004) found that women regard enjoyment as a motive to compete in sport at a much greater level than their male counterparts, likely influencing their decision to stay involved in a particular club or team.

A similar finding has emerged in regard to long-term athletic development. It has been argued that social roles and factors, gender included, can have a large impact on the development of athletes (Gill, 2001). For example, due to the lack of female role models (Norman, 2014), a difference in life priorities, or a lack of financial resources, many women have either discontinued sport or been unable to reach their full potential (Coakley & White, 1992). These greater societal and cultural influences cannot be ignored in a truly ecological and holistic intervention. However, due to the grandiose nature of some of these issues, it can often be beyond the capacity of the applied practitioner to address them directly. Therefore, it is logical when conducting such interventions that one is aware of and embraces the role gender can play in the team environment, even while not being able to 100% influence all factors.

In an example of an ecological intervention in soccer, Larsen and colleagues (2014) held seminars at an elite academy including a range of topics. The intervention began with seven months of observations, gaining the trust of the staff and players, after which three methods to improve the psychosocial development of players were put into place: (1) workshops spread over four months, (2) ongoing one-on-one sessions with the head coach, and (3) numerous psychological training sessions on the training field intended to incorporate the workshop topics. The results of the intervention were positive, and young athletes felt a greater understanding of the psychological requirements to becoming a professional player. In a summary of their work the authors stated that four factors are necessary when conducting ecological interventions: (1) stimulating relationships inside an environment are time-consuming but significant, (2) the coach's acceptance and support are vital to the process, (3) sport psychology should be conducted in the athlete's environment, and (4) professional players' narratives can stimulate reflection and learning among younger players.

This three-step process involving the four critical factors suggested by Larsen, Henriksen, Alfermann, Christensen (2014) of an ecological intervention can also be found in Daniel Coyle's (2018) most recent publication *The Culture Code: The Secrets of Highly Successful Groups*, in which he describes empirical evidence from a variety of high-performance teams and groups around the world. These groups and teams range from the highly successful San Antonio Spurs to the development of the US Navy's SEAL Team Six and even reasons for the effectiveness of outstanding jewellery robbers. Coyle states that for all these groups there are three major hurdles to achieve a healthy culture and produce thereby a powerful performing group: (1) build safety, (2) share vulnerability, and (3) establish purpose.

Build Safety

In the first step towards developing an effective culture, humans need to feel they belong to the group. The moment we are unsure of our place in the hierarchy among others or our value to a team, our brains naturally sound the survival alarm bells, telling us to withhold possible information and resources from the group (Lieberman, 2013). It is only after we have established our firm connection to the group through clear communication and double-sided recognition that we begin to feel safe enough to share without hesitation.

Share Vulnerability

Although vulnerability is a concept traditionally avoided by elite performers in the athletic world (Brown, 2006), the second step to greater culture in Coyle's description involves persuading leaders to admit their weaknesses or lack of knowledge, and by doing so, they empower others in the group to do the same. Vulnerability can create acute stressful situations among team members, releasing the prosocial hormone oxytocin, thereby encouraging group members to work together and build trust (Neumann, Krömer, Toschi, & Ebner, 2000; Donaldson & Young, 2008; Dawans, Fischbacher, Kirschbaum, Fehr, & Heinrichs, 2012). Further support for this can be found in Adam Grant's book *Give and Take* (2013), where multiple examples are presented of highly successful leaders who give first, demonstrate vulnerability, and are able to create powerful connections thereafter. Other examples have demonstrated that showing vulnerability can lead to greater psychological strength (Hägglund, Kenttä, Thelwell, & Wagstaff, 2019) and the development of psychologically safe environments (Edmondson, 2018).

Establish Purpose

The final step involves cooperatively developing a higher goal or shared purpose for the team. No group, even one with great trust, will stay highly productive without concrete direction and intention. This part of the process involves ranking priorities, creating specific phrases or a working language, and consistently setting and measuring goals which are of significance to group members. Additionally, an established and accepted purpose has been shown to influence group members' behaviours to match this aspired narrative. It has been known by psychologists for over 50 years that if humans believe we are destined for a specific goal, we will be more likely to change our behaviour to achieve it (Rosenthal & Jacobson, 1966). Furthermore, we are even more likely to continue to be motivated if we can connect our efforts to the greater benefit of the group (Grant et al., 2007).

Adapted and empirical examples of the aforementioned process of cultural and ecological interventions can be found in boys soccer (Larsen et al., 2014), women's handball (Storm, 2015), and women's soccer (Schneider, in press); however, such interventions are never entirely alike and there is no "cookbook recipe" which can be delivered off the shelf. If it were so, then each and every group could be highly productive and sport psychologists would not be required in the field. In the following section we hope to provide an additional idiosyncratic example of the complexities involved in applying an intervention embracing the presented research within the high-pressure context of elite international soccer and in conclusion a reflection as to how this context-dependent example can be used to expand sport psychology's knowledge of ecological intervention strategies.

Practical Applications—Case Study

Background and Context

Soccer is without a doubt the much-loved national sport of many nations. However, traditionally stereotyped as a man's game, there has been an evident lack of identity and sense of shared purpose for international female players. On joining a woman's national team prior to a World Cup, the legacy of women being sidelined from the sport, struggling to be taken seriously, and, most significantly, being demoted to amateur obscurity for five decades were still raw in the language and stories of group members. Indeed several female players have reported shaving their heads in attempts to pass as male players and therefore be rewarded the right to play the game they love so passionately (Oxenham, 2017). Despite increased focus on women's soccer throughout the most recent World Cup, this year sees only the 8th female World Cup compared to no less than 21 in the men's game. Hence, on taking up the role of psychologist within such a team, it was imperative to first seek a deeper level of understanding of the team culture and identity, as existing within the broader culture of the women's national pathway and the organisation as a whole.

Finally, with the rapid growth of the women's game and also of society today, recognition towards the diversity of national players was also important, a facet not properly considered when it comes to understanding the make-up of collective culture.

At their very core, teams are comprised of groups of humans awarded different roles: players, coaches, and supporting staff, all of whom depend on achieving an inner sense of belonging to survive. Indeed, humans need to belong to something bigger than the self, to a community, in order to feel safe, to be able to trust, and to have and give protection to others. Having a collective, shared identity within a team can strengthen belonging (Coyle, 2018). When it comes to the achievement of performance goals, wellbeing, and the ability to bring one's best self to an environment, establishing a feeling of belonging through identity is fundamental. It drives confidence and focus and increases intrinsic motivation and selflessness (Larsen et al., 2014), ultimately promoting competitive advantage.

In today's evolving society young people adopt a relatively fluid sense of identity, influenced greatly by their environment, social media, and the many external groups they might belong to. With divided loyalties among players between club and country, challenges of creating a shared identity are many. Indeed players and staff alike come together only for international duty for a matter of days or weeks at a time, often as few as eight times per year (with the exception of international competition). Entering the current environment, the absence of belonging to something shared and greater than the self, compounded by expectation-driven anxiety, self-protection, and general disconnect, not surprisingly underperformance had been the result. In essence, the team expressed no sense of "this is who we are, this is what we belong to" and "this is how we do things round here" qualities the best high-performing teams rely on under pressure (Schein, 1990).

Presenting Issue(s)

Following an extensive period of immersion in the team's environment, including getting to know key stakeholders, players, staff, and in particular the head coach of the team, it was concluded that the main presenting issues were grounded in a lack of interpersonal relationships between and within both the player group and staff, a facet evidenced as fundamental to achieving a healthy, safe performance culture (Eys et al., 2017). There was also little sign of leadership within the whole group, and conflict as well as fear of conflict (e.g., lack of willingness to challenge or engage in difficult but necessary conversations) was present in the majority of interactions. There was also a distinct lack of role clarity and consistency of staff performance, exacerbated by sometimes conflicting personal values and motivations, all at the detriment to collaboration, trust, and empowerment, qualities previously highlighted integral for success (Larsen et al., 2013). Suffice to say the feeling of shared purpose, belonging, and safety was amiss. Subgroups were operating throughout the system and became increasingly disruptive when challenged and tested against the pressure of major tournaments, when there was something to win or lose.

The initial purpose of this intervention was to build collective identity and belonging through safety, shared vulnerability, and a sense of purpose and subsequently to develop a winning culture within an international women's soccer team, facilitating performance on the world stage.

The following section presents an outline of work completed over the course of 18 months in the build-up to a World Cup and European championship. It should be noted that the authors' initial introduction to the current team was as a part of a larger operating team of psychologists working across several of the other national teams.

The Intervention

The first stage of the intervention involved delving into the existing culture to better understand individuals' lived experience within the team. The nature of international soccer both favours and hinders the ability to do this effectively, with teams coming together only once every four to six weeks to compete and train. Furthermore, each of these blocks is heavily loaded with delivery both on and off the field across multiple disciplines (e.g., technical, tactical, physical, nutritional, social, and psychological). Perhaps unsurprisingly therefore, building relationships and gaining trust from the team were extremely challenging. Entering an environment where psychological safety was amiss, the presence of a supporting psychologist was also extremely new and understandably for some quite unnerving, feared, and resisted. Furthermore, past traumatic experiences associated to heavy performance losses, career-ending injuries, and both shared and personal grievances had left many of the team with a residue of bitterness, resentment, and unhelpful beliefs that perpetuated current behaviour and thinking, blinding the perceiver to the true nature of their current existence. Thus, in line with a strong body of research, building safety within the group was vital (Brown, 2012; Coyle, 2018), also achieving leadership role clarity and understanding individual identities. It is believed that once an individual establishes security in their place of belonging, they are more open to experience vulnerability and present fewer defensive behaviours (Brown, 2012; Edmondson, 2018).

What was most prevalent in the language, behaviour, emotion, and thought was the past. A previous, painful defeat as a group, which had by all accounts been individually and collectively suppressed, was still alive and burning at the very heart of the team. Driven by this and the need for resolve, a pivotal group session was conducted early on in the intervention that involved gathering players and staff together to share their vulnerabilities, anxieties, and hurt with courage, humility, and compassion (Brown, 2012; 2017). Over the course of three hours, players and staff sat in a closed circle and reflected on their emotions, feelings, and thoughts about the past, of themselves and each other's. Pain of the past, bitterness, guilt, hatred, anger, and resentment all reared their heads in the first passionate display of raw emotion the group had ever shared. It was crucial for this experience that the boundaries of confidentiality were contractually agreed upon as a group and that there was no time limit on this session. As such, individuals expressed compassion, loving kindness, and a huge level of acceptance towards themselves and each other. Vulnerability was expertly role modelled by the head coach, who was the first to share her feelings, closely followed by the team captain. This was vital for establishing a sense of safety, trust, and openness among the team. By the end of the night the group had all but exhausted themselves, leaving with a visibly lighter, freer sense of optimistic excitement towards the future. Hägglund et al. (2019) support that allowing oneself to be fully open to experience vulnerability in this way may be a crucial stage in achieving sustainable high performance. Further supported by Brown (2012), *"vulnerability is uncertainty, risk, and emotional exposure, but it is also the birthplace of courage, creativity and change."* Suffice to say this experience had offered a crucial turning point for the team.

With the continuation of private self-reflection and informal group sharing (initially driven by the introduction of daily journaling and facilitated sharing of reflections to better understand one's own and others' internal experience of the world), what emerged in the following days was a more connected team. For example, they demonstrated increased expression of emotion on and off the pitch, improved awareness of inner experiencing, and willingness to share personal stories, also supporting each other to dig deeper in training and focusing on their future legacy as one team excited to set their own vision, define their shared sense of purpose, and, most importantly, develop a greater sense of "this is who we are."

Away from the formal camp environment, three full-day sessions were held with all key members of the team's staff. The purpose of these were threefold: (1) to understand the current culture as experienced through personal feelings, emotions, values, beliefs, and stories shared, and on an articulated surface level according to goals, aspirations, objectives, and rules; (2) to understand individual character preferences and needs within the team and how these played out in the dynamic unpredictability of real-world soccer; and (3) to discover a true shared vision complete with values, behaviours, and attitudes for the team, to which all members could authentically and honestly connect. Specifically, the full staff team met for three separate days at locations away from the familiar soccer environment with the intention of developing culture. On the first of these days the psychologist facilitated an in-depth analysis of existing culture, initially identifying visible processes, goals, objectives, and structures, before understanding the individual's real life, internal experiencing of these facets. This process involved discussing the various stories, behaviours, language, beliefs, and habits (both helpful and unhelpful) that perpetuated group norms at the very heart of the team's culture. All individuals also took part in psychometric reporting through which they learned about their own and each other's preferences towards communication style, behaviour, feedback, and management of emotion. Using this information, group dynamics were explored as well as the significance of this in association with lived, current challenges. Finally, the team gathered together to share their personal hopes, fears, and concerns as to what they would like to achieve as a collective both during and beyond the World Cup. They also identified collective values, beliefs, and behaviours that were important to live through as a team. As Coyle (2018) identified, establishing and defining purpose in this way can in itself initiate change in behaviour and increase motivation and belonging.

Once a clear vision had emerged, conversations followed to create a season-goal tree outlining every major performance milestone, opportunity, and process required for success along each stage of the onward journey. A crucial part of this involved the psychologist facilitating discussion during which all individuals outlined their unique contribution to success.

This process of identifying and defining team vision, values, and goals was then delivered with the players in a series of small group discussions and whole group workshops taking place over a couple of hours. A key aspect of the whole group session involved all individuals physically walking a marked pathway from current to future state and in doing so connecting internally to the emotions, thoughts, feelings, and behaviours that each stage triggered for them. It was important that all staff members were involved in this and that it was, unlike the staff session that was led by the psychologist, primarily led by the head coach. This lent to further strengthen the silent existence of supportive leadership and togetherness. A key component of this stage involved players and staff writing personal and shared stories about their imagined legacy that in time future youth would look upon with inspiration. Freedom was awarded to this exercise with regard to how stories were presented to ensure all players could be expressive in their preferred way, through words, images, songs, or film. This increased connection to shared purpose, sense of belonging, responsibility, and also motivation. Sharing in the exploration and discovery of shared purpose provided incredible connection between individual members of the team, ensuring values were not merely a series of words printed on walls but shared, believed in, and lived.

The team's identity continued to strengthen and evolve over the ensuing weeks as a result of deliberate action, frequent individual and group reflection, and purposeful growth. Discussions took place about the importance of the little things, habits, behaviours, rituals, and standards. Awareness of cultural norms was broadened through education, visits from the games iconic players, and celebration of the nations most honoured traditions. Rituals led by the team captain were embedded to induct new members of the team to our sacred values. With the support of specialist experts, versed in the history of women's football we learned more about our ancestors, shared our journey with colleagues, the organisation, and later the nation, collectively recognising the hardship, tribulations, and celebrations that had been achieved by something far greater than one individual team, the movement to thrive as female soccer players. By strengthening relationships with other national age group teams across the pathway, players were also able to interpersonally connect with those that came before them and waited in line as their successors.

Storytelling, man's most natural gift, became a significant part of the team's culture. Sharing individual highs, lows, personal journeys, aspirations, hopes, and fears gave everyone the opportunity to connect on a deeper level, and talk authentically in what was fast becoming a much safer environment in which vulnerability was not only supported but celebrated. It was important that individual disclosures connected to past experience and personal heritage were linked in some way to the team's shared identity and the internal sacred values that bound everyone together—one in which vulnerability was increasingly demonstrated. A significant aspect of this involved recognising the diversity within the team. Indeed, we have one of the most diverse teams of young soccer players in the world, something of a gift and major factor in our future success (it already is). Dual nationalities either become all of who you are or they're not embraced at all. I was immensely aware that the human desire to belong might lead to a minimising of difference and misalignment of *"who we are,*" causing disconnect between different groups and players who might otherwise represent other nations or are closer to home at other clubs. Hence to ensure our collective identity captured and embraced the unique qualities brought by all of us, we spent time sharing stories about native cultures, backgrounds, and understanding the multiple roles, strengths, values, and passions. One particularly momentous session facilitated by the psychologist involved drawing representations of family connections on boots signifying family ties and writing names on shirts identifying each other's immediate support networks.

It was not long before the team faced their first major test in a European championship tournament. It was then soon realised that the team behind the scenes was only as durable as the demands imposed behind the scenes, something perhaps overlooked in training opportunities to that point. How true was the connection to who we are? Was it truly greater than the self, or did selfish misguided behaviour leak out when emotions were high and fear disabling, when there was something to win or lose?

Indeed, this first major test of character for the team caused small cracks and the exposure of weak areas within the team. For example, inter-group conflicts broke out among the playing team, causing devastating divides within the group. Fatigue from long working hours under immense pressure led to mismanagement of emotions and communication breakdowns among staff and players. On occasion, individuals lost focus of shared objectives, acting selfishly in pursuit of personal reward. Previously agreed behaviours were not always adhered to, for example tardiness crept in, mess and reduced training efforts. Collaboration and inter-department (i.e., medical team: technical team) communications all but ceased with subgroups forming to work in separate spaces. Furthermore, there was an evident lack of within-team leadership that might have enabled the required level of challenge and focus. This all provided quality guidance for what became the next phase of the intervention.

During the next block of time together as a team, increased emphasis was focused on defining leadership roles within the staff and player groups. This not only empowered individuals to become the directors of their journey (Larsen, Alfermann, & Christensen, 2012) but also allowed for a more effective means of driving standards, maintaining focus, and ensuring whole group togetherness continued to grow. Leaders demonstrated positive deviances from unhelpful group behaviours and norms (e.g., tardiness, mess and negative language) towards behaviours consistent with the vision and values of the team. This is supported by Wagstaff, Fletcher, and Hanton (2012), who argued that leadership attitude is hugely positive for prosocial group behaviour, cohesion, and collective efficacy.

Arguably one of the most significant turning points for the whole team was experienced in the immediate approach to the World Cup, when the team took part in a three-day immersion experience with one of the world's leading armed forces—an elite organisation with a superbly strong mindset and deep-rooted sense of belonging. This was by far the most extraordinary challenge the team had ever faced, the result of which was equally extraordinary and undoubtedly momentous. Over the course of three days, the whole team of staff and players were identifiable only by name. Hierarchy and roles were diminished, together with uniforms and all forms of communication with the outside world. One team. One identity. No distraction. Embarking on one immensely challenging but collective experience. In the face of mental, emotional, and physical exhaustion individuals showed courage, bravery, composure, and fearlessness as one team. Transferrable skills in leadership, communication, and resilience were all tested and strengthened. No one was ever left behind. No one was ever left unsupported. One team emerged stronger, leaving behind all traces of disconnect, uncertainty, half-heartedness, or question. Together. Belonging. Trusting. Safe. At the end of the three days the team conducted a full debrief led by the psychologist. Individuals offered personal reflections, feedback between one another, and collective recognition as to how the experience would shape their team, and ultimately their performances moving forward.

In the final phase of preparation, storytelling was again used as players and staff learned, reflected, and shared their personal experiences of stress, best performances, preferred means of communication, and needs for energy management and emotional wellbeing. Throughout these discussions frequent references were made to their most recent experience with the armed forces. Using the months that had led up to this point, individuals revealed themselves as human, in suffering and triumph, building safety and belonging together, so that when the heat began to rise they themselves would be key to their individual and therefore collective success. A result of this process and supported by the aforementioned use of psychometrics, staff and players were able to better understand themselves, and consequently each other, empowered with knowing how to get the best out of each other when it really mattered most.

As previously highlighted, the end goal of all the work outlined above was the World Cup. The team's performance throughout which was remarkable, leading them to finishing third in the world—an accolade never before achieved in the history of the national pathway. It is without a doubt that several factors not discussed above contributed to this success, for example technical and tactical work, physical development, and nutritional and medical expertise. While it is impossible to determine the exact contribution provided by individual aspects of the intervention, it goes without saying that the changes, growth, and shifting of culture observed during the course of two years with the team would not have been achieved without such work. The detail invested in planning, reviewing, reflecting, and building at each stage was vital.

Feedback from the head coach, staff team, and players supports both the performance impact and, perhaps most notably, the positive impact on something far greater than one moment but one team. Reflecting on the two years one player stated: "We're all joined together and we will support each other through any struggle it's what we do." While another said: "You don't go through the journey us lot have been through and not come out stronger. Us lot are a family now. These girls are my family. They're my sisters. No-one will ever come between that." On returning from the World Cup one of the teams' leaders shared her thoughts: "It's life or death but we're in it together. We've got each other's backs and we'd fight to the death for each other. We trust each other."

A senior representative of the governing body who experienced various moments in the team's journey provided the following reflection when asked about the team's journey: "You've shown far more than talent and skill on the ball. What you have shown has been remarkable. Courage, bravery, attitude. That's a winning team." And finally, when reflecting on the team's success the head coach commented:

> From the leaders through the staff through the players. You just can't break the connection anymore, there is no difference. Something special has happened I just can't explain it in any other way than how proud I am to be a part of something so much more than me. When I was a player I never knew the history there was no identity there were no leaders. There was no story. You fought for yourself. This is something special.

Case-Study Reflections and Summary

A key enabler for all of the work carried out previously was the strength of relationship patiently built over time between myself and the head coach of the team. Building trust, mutual respect, and understanding between the two of us was fundamental (Larsen et al., 2014). Without such a bond several, if not all of the processes described, would have lost value. This relationship involved providing the coach with a confidential place of safety without judgement or discomfort, a place for safe reflection, supportive challenge towards growth, and above all to show vulnerability. As a head coach, leading a team through unfamiliar ground, change, and uncertainty promotes fear, not least so in the build up to a World Cup performance when the nation's eyes are waiting, scrutinising, expecting. Indeed, the head coach was placing a huge amount of trust in me, and nurturing our relationship was crucial to enabling healthy challenge, debate, and compassion (Edmondson, 2018).

I cannot underestimate the value in my own support network throughout this period of time. As a psychologist, when the focus of your work is towards driving culture change, while "immersed," you are primarily an external agent, overseeing the system, trusted advisor, confidant, challenger, and developer. Hence, maintaining perspective and emotional stability throughout is paramount, and frequent conversations with my psychology team, professional supervisor, and, importantly, personal confidant were instrumental (Arthur, Wagstaff, & Hardy, 2017).

Culture is a fluid, dynamic concept requiring relentless attention and effort. Continuous self-reflection, together with challenge and scrutiny from respected colleagues, was really important in ensuring every detail of the intervention was purposefully tailored to the individuals, players, and system surrounding it. Mistakes were made and, as highlighted previously, communication, behaviour, and embedded processes broke down early on when tested under pressure. Accountability and continual searching for opportunity amidst failure was hard but vital, and in time these drops in performance lessened to become all but non-existent. Identity as a concept resonated strongly with both players and staff and supported by a shared sense of purpose provided a safety net around us when the team needed it most. Knowing who you are when you are in the toughest moments of life is undeniably powerful. Perhaps the hardest thing to evolve that took courage was a true sense

> of belonging: the foundation for deep trust, selflessness and cohesion, feeling connected to the nation, to the shirt, to have a true sense of togetherness as a team. Finally, the value benefitted through storytelling really emphasised to me the power of narrative language on deep emotion, connection, and unity. The narrative we create can engineer (hard wire) the performance behaviours needed to execute a strategy, a goal, and performance. As highlighted by Wagstaff (2018), performance success is the result of interpersonal, group, and cultural factors, not individualism. This was never clearer when our shared stories became real.

Key Messages and Further Reading

- **People first.** High-performing people make high-performing teams. Humans require safety, belonging, and shared purpose. Spending time nurturing interpersonal relationships is fundamental to creating great cultures.
- **Build safety and trust through role models.** Operating under stress in high-pressure environments requires trust. Building trust through shared vulnerability, role modelling by leadership facilitates strong interpersonal connections able to withstand adversity.
- **Talk with emotion.** We are how others experience us, and deep culture is both lived and experienced by a collective of unique individuals. Recognising differences in others' experiences lessens defensive behaviour, making room for deeper connection.
- **Approach and embrace adversity.** Rather than dismiss, excuse or avoid the uncomfortable failures and hardships, recognise the strength and resilience to be gained by approaching them together.
- **Share purpose.** One man's purpose is one man's goal. High-performing teams share an identity, purpose, and vision and in doing so unite in achieving collective goals, which they as individuals could not accomplish otherwise.

Brown, B. (2012). *Daring greatly: How the courage to be vulnerable transforms the way we live, love, parent, and lead.* New York, NY: Gotham.

Coyle, D. (2018). *The culture code: The secrets of highly successful groups.* New York, NY: Bantam Books.

Edmondson, A. C. (2018). *The fearless organization: Creating psychological safety in the workplace for learning, innovation, and growth.* Hoboken, NJ: John Wiley & Sons.

Hägglund, K., Kenttä, G., Thelwell, T., & Wagstaff, C. R. D. (2019). Is there an upside of vulnerability in sport? A mindfulness approach applied in the pursuit of psychological strength. *Journal of Sport Psychology in Action.* doi:10.1080/21520704.2018.1549642

Lieberman, M. D. (2013). *Social: Why our brains are wired to connect.* New York, NY: Crown Publishers/Random House.

References

Aalberg, R. R., & Sæther, S. A. (2016). The talent development environment in a Norwegian top level football club. *Sport Science Review, 25,* 159–182.

Arthur, C. A., Wagstaff, C. R. D., & Hardy, L. (2017). Leadership in sport organizations. In C. R. D. Wagstaff (Ed.), *The organizational psychology of sport: Key issues and practical applications* (pp. 153–175). Abingdon, Oxon: Routledge.

Benson, A. J., Eys, M., Surya, M., Dawson, K., & Schneider, M. (2013). Athletes' perceptions of role acceptance in interdependent sport teams. *The Sport Psychologist, 27,* 269–280.

Bronfenbrenner, U. (2005). Bioecological theory of human development. In U. Bronfenbrenner (Ed.), *Making human beings human: Bioecological perspectives on human development* (pp. 3–15). Thousand Oaks, CA: Sage Publications.

Brown, B. (2006). Shame resilience theory: A grounded theory of women and shame. *Families in Society, 87*(1), 43–51.

Brown, B. (2017). *Braving the wilderness: The quest for true belonging and the courage to stand alone.* London: Random House.

Bruner, M. W., Munroe-Chandler, K., & Spink, K. S. (2008). Entry into elite sport: A preliminary investigation into the transition experiences of rookie athletes. *Journal of Applied Sport Psychology, 20,* 236–252.

Carron, A. V., & Eys, M. A. (2012). *Group dynamics in sport* (4th ed.). Morgantown, WV: Fitness Information Technology.

Coakley, J., & White, A. (1992). Making decisions: gender and sport participation among British adolescents. *Sociology of Sport Journal, 9,* 20–35.

Côté, J., MacDonald, D., Baker, J., & Abernethy, B. (2006). When "where" is more important than "when": Birthplace and birthdate effects on the achievement of sporting expertise. *Journal of Sport Sciences, 24,* 1065–1073.

Coyle, D. (2018). *The culture code: The secrets of highly successful groups.* New York, NY: Bantam Books.

Dawans, B. von, Fischbacher, U., Kirschbaum, C., Fehr, E., & Heinrichs, M. (2012). The social dimension of stress reactivity: Acute stress increases prosocial behavior in humans. *Psychological Science, 23,* 651–660.

Donaldson, Z. R., & Young, L. J. (2008). Oxytocin, vasopressin, and the neurogenetics of sociality. *Science, 322,* 900–904.

Edmondson, A. C. (2018). *The fearless organization: Creating psychological safety in the workplace for learning, innovation, and growth.* Hoboken, NJ: John Wiley & Sons.

Eys, M., Loughead, T. M., & Godfrey, M. (2017). Group cohesion and athletic development. In J. Baker, S. Cobley, J. Schroer & N. Wattie (Eds.), *Routledge handbook of talent identification and development in sport* (pp. 301–311). London: Routledge.

Gill, D. L. (2001). Feminist sport psychology: A guide for our journey. *The Sport Psychologist, 15,* 363–372.

Grant, A. (2013). *Give and take: Why helping others drives our success.* New York, NY: Viking.

Grant, A. M., Campbell, E. M., Chen, G., Cottone, K., Lapedis, D., & Lee, K. (2007). Impact and the art of motivation maintenance: The effects of contact with beneficiaries on persistence behavior. *Organizational Behavior and Human Decision Processes, 103,* 53–67.

Henriksen, K. (2010). *The ecology of talent development in sport: A multiple case study of successful athletic talent development environments in Scandinavia.* Doctoral dissertation. University of Southern Denmark.

Henriksen, K., & Stambulova, N. (2017). Creating optimal environments for talent development. In J. Baker, S. Cobley, J. Schroer & N. Wattie (Eds.), *Routledge handbook of talent identification and development in sport* (pp. 271–284). London: Routledge.

Henriksen, K., Stambulova, N., & Roessler, K. K. (2010a). A holistic approach to athletic talent development environments: A successful sailing milieu. *Psychology of Sport and Exercise, 11,* 212–222.

Henriksen, K., Stambulova, N., & Roessler, K. K. (2010b). Successful talent development in track and field: Considering the role of environment. *Scandinavian Journal of Medicine & Science in Sports, 20,* 122–132.

Henriksen, K., Stambulova, N., & Roessler, K. K. (2011). Riding the wave of an expert: A successful talent development environment in kayaking. *The Sport Psychologist, 25,* 341–362.

Holt, N. L., & Morley, D. (2004). Gender differences in psychosocial factors associated with athletic success during childhood. *The Sport Psychologist, 18,* 138–153.

Larsen, C. H., Alfermann, D., & Christensen, M. K. (2012). Psychosocial skills in a youth soccer academy: A holistic ecological perspective. *Sport Science Review, 21*(3–4), 51–74.

Larsen, C. H., Alfermann, D., Henriksen, K., & Christensen, M. K. (2013). Successful talent development in soccer: The characteristics of the environment. *Sport, Exercise, and Performance Psychology, 2*(3), 190–206.

Larsen, C. H., Henriksen, K., Alfermann, D., & Christensen, M. (2014). Preparing Footballers for the next step: An intervention program from an ecological perspective. *The Sport Psychologist, 28,* 91–102.

Mallett, C. J., & Rynne, S. B. (2015). Changing role of coaches across development. In J. Baker & D. Farrow (Eds.), *Routledge handbook of sport expertise* (pp. 394–403). New York, NY: Routledge.

Martindale, R. J. J., Collins, D., & Daubney, J. (2005). Talent development: A guide for practice and research within sport. *Quest, 57*, 353–375.

Neumann, I. D., Krömer, S. A., Toschi, N., & Ebner, K. (2000). Brain oxytocin inhibits the (re)activity of the hypothalamo-pituitary-adrenal axis in male rats: Involvement of hypothalamic and limbic brain regions. *Regulatory Peptides, 96*, 31–38.

Norman, L. (2014). *Gender and coaching report card for the London 2012 Olympics: Report for the international council for coaching excellence.* Leeds: Leeds Beckett University.

Oxenham, G. (2017). *Under the lights and in the dark: Untold stories of women's soccer.* London: Icon Books.

Rosenthal, R., & Jacobson, L. (1966). Teachers' expectancies: Determinates of pupils' IQ gains. *Psychological Reports, 19*, 115–118.

Schein, E. G. (1990). Organizational culture. *American Psychologist, 45*, 109–119.

Schneider, P. (in press). *A successful talent development environment in an amateur soccer club: Redefining "success" for the greater population.* Unpublished doctoral dissertation. Leipzig University.

Si, G., & Lee, H. (2007). Cross cultural issues in sport psychology research. In S. Jowett & D. Lavallee (Eds.), *Social psychology in sport* (pp. 278–334). Champaign, IL: Human Kinetics.

Storm, L. K. (2015). *"Coloured by culture": Talent development in Scandinavian elite sport as seen from a cultural perspective.* Doctoral dissertation. Institute of sport science and clinical biomechanics, University of Southern Denmark.

Wagstaff, C. R. D. (2018). Taking stock of organizational psychology in sport. *Journal of Applied Sport Psychology, 31*, 1–6.

Wagstaff, C. R. D., Fletcher, D., & Hanton, S. (2012). Exploring emotion abilities and regulation strategies in sport organizations. *Sport, Exercise and Performance Psychology, 1*, 262–282.

Wergin, V., Zimanyi, Z., Mesagno, C., & Beckmann, J. (2018). When suddenly nothing works anymore within a team: Causes of collective sport team collapse. *Frontiers in Psychology, 9*, 1–14.

16
ASSESSING THE IMPACT OF PSYCHOLOGY PROVISION IN ELITE YOUTH SOCCER

Charlotte Chandler, Karl Steptoe, and Martin Eubank

Brief Introduction and Review of Literature

The concept of practitioner effectiveness and the ability to demonstrate impact is an important aim in applied practice and an increasingly necessary objective for the sport psychologist. Effective practice typically includes *what* is effective about the practitioner and their approach (e.g., Barker, McCarthy, & Harwood, 2011; Pain & Harwood, 2004; Steptoe, Barker, & Harwood, 2014) and *how* the impact of this can be evaluated (e.g., Steptoe, King, & Harwood, 2019). Individual differences between practitioners will exist when determining one's own *what* and *how* and will be influenced by unique belief systems, professional philosophies, and personal experience. The *what* and *how* will also be shaped by the environments within which the practitioner will work, meaning that impact will ultimately be determined by how well the psychologist aligns, interacts with, and influences the existing sporting culture.

In elite soccer, the persistent drive for team success plays out in a myriad of ways, from winning matches to avoiding relegation, from generating revenue to spending vast amounts of money on talented players. The constant striving to achieve can make the elite soccer environment not only a rewarding one for all those involved in a team's performance but also challenging and unpredictable, especially when things are not going so well on the pitch. There exists an extensive evidence base from which coaches and sport psychology practitioners can draw core principles to embed within academy environments, which contribute to positive youth development and that explicitly distinguish the aims of the first-team and academy environments. However, we propose that there remains a disconnect between the "best practice" espoused in the literature and the reality of embedding these principles within an academy setting. Despite the comprehensive knowledge available, the applied and research experience of the authors suggests that there remains a challenge in meeting the desire to consistently develop psychosocial skills and promote their value to youth athletes, to the same extent of technical, tactical, and physical equivalents. There has been considerable progression in the last decade that has promoted psychological training and development to become part of the everyday conversation in elite youth sport programmes, which in turn has helped normalise training in this area for the young footballer. We caution, however, that sport psychology may only be part way through this transitional phase, with members of a players' support network "saying the right thing" but (despite best intentions) not always acting accordingly. At best this is confusing for the young player and at worst serves to dilute the true value of demonstrating positive psychosocial characteristics along the development pathway. How a sport psychologist evidences their contribution to and impact on player development in this environment and the degree to which they can remain a valued member of the support staff are important considerations for those working in such elite cultures.

In this chapter, we will provide examples of applied experiences from work undertaken in elite soccer academies, which represent what we believe effective sport psychology may look like considering the real-world constraints of practice. We challenge the reader to consider how Sport Psychologists' effectiveness is best characterised and evidenced in elite soccer environments and how these compare with evaluations of more established practitioners within the multi/interdisciplinary team (i.e., strength and conditioning, performance analysis, physiology). A strength and conditioning coach may be considered effective if they can demonstrate player improvements in power or speed and a physiotherapist by reducing the length of time a player is out injured. However, establishing what effectiveness looks like in sport psychology practice can be perceived as less tangible and more subjective compared to other disciplines. Tod and Andersen's (2005) notion of the sport psychologist as the "tool" captures the essence of this challenge; they are the means by which their work is carried out and against which their effectiveness is "measured." The concept of measurement is problematic in sport psychology in this regard; in what ways can an individual reasonably be "measured" in relation to the impact they have on others? This challenge is compounded by what appears to be a preference for measurement across all aspects of sport psychology provision, including the assessment of academy players. Not only is this difficult in an environment that lacks an established understanding of what "good psychological support" looks like, but it also presents a problem with regard to coaches' expectations of players and their psychological attributes, expectations which can be unrealistic and/or ill-informed in their judgement. Furthermore, practitioner effectiveness is considered, at least in part, to be informed by the congruence of their practice with their philosophy (Poczwardowski, Sherman, & Ravizza, 2004). There may be instances, therefore, when a practitioner's positive impact cannot be tangibly measured, regardless of coach expectations or demands, yet can be determined by an internal sense of being effective.

Through evaluation of our personal applied experience, the research data we have collected, and existing literature, we offer guidance on how one might "survive and thrive" (Nesti, 2004) in an elite soccer environment as an applied sport psychologist. We will suggest that practitioner effectiveness should be characterised and evaluated not only by what we *do* and what we *know* (and the associated "know-how" and "show-how"; Harwood, 2016) but also by what we ourselves can "*be*" and bring to the sport psychology service delivery, in terms of our personal characteristics, qualities, and identity (Tod, Hutter, & Eubank, 2017). In this way, sport psychologists can work to inform their effectiveness through personal feelings of impact, authenticity, and "doing good," but also balance this by acknowledging their skill set and how this can be used to do good work despite external constraints.

Case Study: Sport Psychology Provision in Academy Soccer

Background and Context

The Elite Player Performance Plan (EPPP) was introduced by the Premier League in 2012, which brought increased opportunities for sport psychology delivery within soccer academies. The EPPP introduced formal requirements for psychological support across all phases of development that are designed to develop, for example, player psychosocial skills to meet the demands of academy soccer and to work with key stakeholders, including parents, peers, and coaches, to create environments that help shape and reinforce these requisite competencies. Central to the design of the academy psychology programme is the aim to ensure cumulative psychological return from learning experiences throughout the development pathway, not only for the player but also for the parent. This is achieved by specifically meeting the known demands presented at each phase and during key transitions (e.g., foundation to youth development, becoming a scholar, entering the professional game, and transitions out of the soccer club or game). The introduction of the EPPP allowed for coordinated support services within sport science and medicine and the systematic development of staff roles within a multidisciplinary team structure. The EPPP vision included a multidisciplinary approach that would be adopted and reinforced across departments, with the sport psychologist's role focused on performance enhancement and age-appropriate support for player development. Although there is often apparent, if not explicit, prioritisation in addressing the technical, tactical, and physical demands placed on the young player, the need to possess the requisite psychological skills is valued by academies.

The importance of a positive psychological foundation is evident from the language embedded within academy culture, which is commonly articulated as requiring the young player to have, for example, desire, courage, self-discipline, and a will to win as well as the need to be brave, resilient, and mentally tough. Despite this apparent clarity as to what is required to succeed, it is common for the sport psychology practitioner to encounter a lack of structure and consensus about how to assess and evaluate these important player competencies. This can present incongruence between how players' psychological attributes are assessed and then later evaluated and offers a challenge for the sport psychologist to evidence progression in this regard, as in the example of a player who is deemed by the coach to need to show greater desire or resilience to be considered for selection. The work outlined in the following attempts to encapsulate these issues in more detail and offers recommendations for how the notion of effectiveness can be addressed in such scenarios.

Presenting Issue(s): Establishing Fit and Priorities of Work

The sport psychologist was required, alongside the coaching, medical, and sport science staff, to assess player performance, from the point of player recruitment to the offer of a professional contract or player release. Once recruited into the academy, player performance was assessed against a series of benchmarks, which would then be used to inform individual learning plans and decisions on how to best support each player. This could range from short-term performance decisions, such as who will be on the bench that week, to those that ultimately would have a greater career impact, including whether to release the player from the academy programme. The challenge for the sport psychologist was the requirement to be part of, and contribute information to, the decision-making process in a success-oriented environment, where seemingly objective measures of performance and progression were valued.

This challenge was compounded for the practitioner, whose professional philosophy was oriented towards player performance *alongside* player development and wellbeing at all phases and their belief that "talent" cannot be reduced to objective measures alone. While for the practitioner this represented a congruent, authentic, and thus effective approach to practice, the context of their role and the culture of the academy and its support staff meant that in relation to decisions about players, the benchmarks used to justify decisions were not wholly aligned. A compromise was needed that not only acknowledged the complexity of psychological performance but one that also made clear the meaningful contribution that a professional assessment could provide to the overall performance picture. From such information, coaches could make decisions based on not only interdisciplinary data in its various forms but also their extensive professional experience, which we have found can often be marginalised in the pursuit of hard science. This challenge was further compounded by the psychologist's assessment that there was little consensus on what "good" looked like with regard to player psychology, and consequently, opinions relating to psychological attributes were not consistently shared among key stakeholders.

What Does Good Look Like?

The elite soccer environment has been characterised as one that demands immediate results and maintains a short-term focus (Gilmore & Gilson, 2007). It has been described by those working within it as competitive, selfish, and cut-throat and as employing those who work for personal gain rather than for the good of the organisation (Chandler, 2015). Such environments can promote a focus on objective measures of success, with the implicit suggestion that these can help demonstrate a practitioner's impact and value to the team. Such rigid parameters of effectiveness have not served, however, as a reliable marker by which to reflect on the contribution of our sport psychology work. In assessing whether it was a "good day at the office," we have to tease out the primary, secondary, and sometimes tertiary clients we come into contact with in the soccer academy and acknowledge that what we may perceive as being effective consultation with one may not address the requirements of the other. In fact, on occasions the sport psychologist may be working with a player (secondary client) on goals that may even be contrary to those held by the academy or soccer club (primary client), for example in supporting them in their desire to find a new club. The sport psychologist's perception of their best work was instead based on a personal feeling of "doing a good job" and having a "great day," which represented a deeper sense of effectiveness borne out of philosophical congruence and the desire to do what's right for the client. Nevertheless, the inherent focus on measurement was something that the practitioner needed to embrace in order to satisfy the demands placed on them in their role.

We have found there to be three predominant challenges in implementing what are perceived to be effective psychology programmes in soccer: (1) a lack of consensus regarding what good psychological performance looks like; (2) an inability of the sport psychology practitioner to incorporate the multiple staff perspectives regarding psychological intervention within a unified approach; and (3) a fixed mindset regarding the ability to develop/change psychological characteristics. When determining agreed positive psychological behaviours and responses, there is also a danger of perceiving youth athletes as "little adults" and consequently having inappropriate expectations of what the young footballer should be able to demonstrate at each phase. A central aim of the programme implemented in this case, therefore, was to create opportunities for a psychological return on the young footballers' experience at each age and phase and during the transitions into, through, and out of the academy. In this way, a player may perceive sub-optimal technical, tactical, or physical performance in a training or competitive session and yet still be able to experience positive psychological performance through the demonstration of, for example, persistence in the face of setbacks, good emotional control, or positive encouragement of teammates to influence momentum. It was felt that by equipping the young player with the requisite psychosocial skills they would not only be better able to meet the known performance and wellbeing demands of the elite academy environment but also be prepared for life outside of the game.

Work Conducted

To assist in the process of identifying positive psychological behaviours, the sport psychologist adopted the 5C framework (Harwood, 2008; Harwood, Barker, & Anderson, 2015) of Commitment, Communication, Concentration, Control, and Confidence, as this represented a flexible model and vehicle with which to promote a cohesive message at the academy regarding valued psychological characteristics. The 5Cs capture the core motivational, interpersonal, and self-regulatory skills that can be developed and showcased through the youth sport journey and provided a first opportunity to discuss and identify both good and bad examples of each of the Cs. Through an iterative process that sought input from practitioners involved in player development, three standards were determined as being core representations of each C, resulting in 15 standards. These included showing persistence despite setbacks as a standard of Commitment and maintaining composure in important moments as an important demonstration of Control. The 5Cs, in their "standards" form, remained purposefully abstract to enable interpretation across multiple domains (e.g., training pitch, gym, classroom, match days). Work progressed to make these more specific at the level of 5C "actions" that enabled the sport psychologist, together with coaching/sport science staff, to establish age-, stage-, and position-specific 5C behaviours and responses that represented targets for the player to achieve across a meso or training block. This important process provided the platform from which further intervention was tailored around each phase and with each member of the players' support network. An understanding of the constraints, challenges, and opportunities that are presented along the development pathway resulted in a focus on helping players DEMONSTRATE valued 5C responses and behaviours at the Foundation Phase—specifically, the "act" of, for example, good Concentration and an increased awareness that this psychological aspect of performance is observable. At the Youth Development Phase, attention was given to *training* and equipping the young player with the requisite psychological skills to enable consistent demonstration of positive 5C responses and behaviours. Examples of this include comprehensive goal-setting and increasing measures of success to promote Commitment or progressive muscle relaxation as part of a pre-performance routine to enhance Control. The Professional Development Phase provided an additional opportunity to shift any remaining perceptions of psychology as being relevant to only those "in need." Attention was given to players *excelling* in their demonstration of the 5Cs and highlighting these characteristics as a strength, not only of them as an individual but in terms of what they could contribute to the team performance. On reflection, this work was pivotal in gaining access to key stakeholders in player development and those best positioned to identify, shape, and reinforce adaptive psychosocial skills (i.e., recruitment team, parents, coaches, and support staff). The process also fostered a greater intrinsic motivation to progress the psychology programme, as these individuals made significant contribution to the 5C standards and, consequently, the culture, values, and identity of the academy player.

Promoting Psychology, Not the Psychologist

It can be challenging for practitioners, especially those new to the profession, to understand what they specifically bring to performance enhancement, as they will invariably witness several people seemingly working in the psychology space. It can be difficult to separate roles and responsibilities from coaches, educators, and parents and not fall into the trap of being the problem solver or only working with performance issues, which can perpetuate the negative stereotypes that remain in some elite sports. Through similar experiences we have learned to appreciate that in such cultures, emphasis should be placed on psychology and not the psychologist; this enables the sport psychologist to identify those best positioned to develop skills in this area. The 5Cs model allowed the practitioners in this case to provide education and training in the identification of behaviours and responses associated with each "C" and importantly that which we know to be associated with positive performance and wellbeing outcomes. In working with members of the recruitment team, we were able to identify the specific behaviours that may be expected at different age groups, for example, Commitment behaviours that would be aligned to changing definitions of competence between 9- and 12-year-olds (e.g., Nicholls, 1984; Conroy, Elliot, & Hofer, 2003). We were able to discuss the weighting that should be given to, for example, technical, physical, and psychological attributes when identifying players we believed would successfully navigate the demands of academy soccer. Through analysis of professional players' psychological performance and benchmarking of the 5Cs, we were able to challenge the implicit belief that good psychological performance or a player with resilience/mental strength was one that never demonstrated maladaptive responses in training or matches. Typically, this would require recruitment staff to value persistence in the face of setbacks and attempts to demonstrate creativity even if these did not always come off, for example, as clearly as being able to identify the "best player" on the pitch. These conversations were undoubtedly supported by the 5Cs framework and by several seasons spent in the academy, where we have experienced psychological factors as being evident in the slowing of a players' development. Players recruited on technical and physical ability at a young age often experienced challenges with motivation further down the pathway, as a consequence of not highlighting the quality as one that got the player into the system. We therefore suggest that these psychological attributes are ones we should give far greater attention to in player recruitment.

Throughout work in academy football we have been ever mindful of the notion that while there are difficulties that exist for the sport psychologist (as outlined in this chapter), their increasing involvement in player development programmes could also present challenges to coaching staff who may have previously seen psychology (and other disciplines) as part of their role. It was, therefore, always our intention to add value to what was already going on and further embed psychosocial skill development within sessions and match-day interactions. Based on an assessment over several seasons, a great deal of "psychological work" was taking place on a daily basis that players were not always aware of, as greater attention was given to technical and tactical proficiency. An initial aim, therefore, was to shine a greater light on the psychological aspect of the training and sensitise coaches towards the opportunities that exist in each session for 5C development. We therefore provided education around the progress model (Harwood & Anderson, 2015). The model provides a pedagogical structure that encourages coaches to promote the C of interest at the start of sessions and to then ROLE model positive demonstration of behaviours and/or engage players in consideration of professional players that typify the C. Players are then offered ownership in aspects of the session design, therefore creating opportunities for them to grow the C and differentiate between levels of, for example, Confidence behaviours. Having made the 5Cs an integral part of the session, it is imperative that coaches then reinforce their demonstration in the same way that technical skills may be acknowledged, with specificity, so that the player is clear on the behaviours and context that are valued. While most coaches were able to give attention to this part of the model, fewer were able to give full attention to the latter. This encouraged the coach to empower peer support and direct players to acknowledge desired 5C behaviours in their peers to then support the supporter offering praise for their observation and finally close the session through self review to ensure a psychological return on the session. Through this work, cross-department opportunities emerged to enable work with coach development leads and performance analysis teams to provide feedback on this area of coaching practice and to raise the coaches' awareness of their responsibility and influence in modelling the behaviours they were demanding of their players. This gave even greater attention to the design of optimal 5C climates.

Parents represent another stakeholder group who are uniquely positioned to shape the 5Cs of young footballers, and work in this area has required us to tread the delicate path of telling parents how to be parents. Parenting a child in an elite youth environment places multiple demands and requires considerable resource (Harwood & Knight, 2015). The guiding principle was to see the parent as part of the solution rather than the problem. Therefore, work with this group allowed for specific insight into their children and to provide them with additional skills to become both a 5C parent and to, in turn, positively shape the 5Cs in their child. Workshops and educational materials provided greater focus for training and match observation that enabled parents to notice and acknowledge the extent to which their child demonstrated positive 5C responses and raised awareness of how their unintended behaviours can impact the players' 5Cs. For example, parents may inappropriately model emotional control on the sidelines or find it challenging to manage their own thoughts, feelings, and concerns associated with academy life that may not positively promote the "composure in important moments" 5C (Control) standard. Conversations during the car journey to and from sessions are also an opportunity to develop adaptive 5C behaviours, but we have found interactions can often unhelpfully influence the young players' perceptions of success and competence (Commitment) through too great focus on analysing errors or the outcome of the match.

Outcome Analysis: Evaluating a Good Day at the Office

A guiding principle of the work outlined in this case was for the sport psychology practitioner to separate the value of psychology interventions *from*, while also highlighting their contribution *to*, the most embedded and valued outcomes within the culture, that is technical and tactical performance outcomes. Such an approach presented a further challenge for the sport psychologist in determining whether they had experienced a good day at the office, as it did not necessarily follow that competitive success was an acknowledgement of effective psychology work nor that defeat signalled a need for increased support. Instead, in the case outlined, the 5Cs framework enabled the sport psychologist to identify clear objectives and meaningful discipline performance indicators for work with players, coaches, parents, and the wider support network. In short, by identifying and agreeing 5C standards that pointed to valued behaviours and responses representative of good psychological performance, players were informed how they were being perceived for this aspect of performance and discrepancies between their own opinions with those of coaches and support staff were highlighted to inform training priorities. Work with coaches sought to increase their self-efficacy in being able to develop players' psychosocial skills, to embed this within existing practice and to reignite the coaches' role and responsibility in this area. Increased engagement with parents, as was evident in their attendance at workshops, individual sessions and requests for home visits, pointed to impact that is more tangible. However, the most meaningful to the sport psychologist was the ability to expand their observational repertoire, epitomised by a conversation overheard between two parents who stated that "it's great that we know what they are looking for [5Cs] now." The flexibility of the 5C framework made clear the utility and application across domains and to the multidisciplinary team and fostered a shared language regarding psychology and what constituted progress in this area.

Case-Study Reflections

The work conducted in the case study does not necessarily reflect an approach that represents the "theoretical ideal" from the sport psychologist's perspective but rather reflects the ideal approach given the constraints placed on them by the environment and key stakeholders (inadvertently or otherwise). The degree to which the sport psychologist could both address the "measurement" of players and maintain their integrity about personal feelings of impact and effectiveness is influenced by the way psychological information about players is assessed and utilised. The sport psychologist implemented what they considered the best vehicle for creating buy-in from all involved in a player's academy journey to educate them as to how best to support young footballers' psychological development. Maintaining integrity in this way can be considered a key challenge for the sport psychologist, particularly given that professional sport environments encourage staff to justify their performance impact and worth to the organisation, and subsequently they are often sceptical about sport psychology and its value (Eubank, Nesti, & Cruickshank, 2014). The challenges cited within the case study are therefore understandable and inevitable, and elite soccer will likely remain a challenging environment to work in unless there is a wider culture shift, with regard to both the nature of the sport itself and the degree to which it understands the value of (or even embraces) sport psychology. It is not as simple as changing others' perceptions when these are often engrained and validated by the environment itself. It would be remiss of us, therefore, to suggest that there is indeed a specific outcome, an ideal scenario within which conflicts are always resolved and where winning is not the only measure of success. The case study also does not intend to suggest that the coaches will routinely undervalue sport psychology, and we are not judging their approach to making decisions on players given the contextual and role-related demands of their work. We hope that any practitioner reading this chapter will recognise the necessity of, and benefit of, clearly defining and communicating each staff member's role, recognising that their jobs are interconnected and interdependent, while ensuring that they do not "get in the way" of each other.

Key to the sport psychologist's ability to survive and maintain good practice within their role is a focus on doing the "right thing" and on the process rather than, or at least as well as, the outcome. It would have been easy, for example, for the sport psychologist to be "sucked in" and adopt a measurement system that would enable them (at least in the short term) to demonstrate their effectiveness objectively. While the sport psychologist was required to adopt a performance agenda to "fit in" within an elite soccer environment and gain favour with the coaches, their practice itself was driven by the desire to care for the player and help manage the process rather than the outcome alone (Gilbourne & Richardson, 2006). The practitioner had to be comfortable with this tension between the external demands and their internal drives while maintaining an authentic approach, sufficiently congruent with their beliefs and values. In this sense, effectiveness was driven by the sport psychologist's subjective belief in themselves and their work, while still offering a tangible, understood, and accepted contribution to performance data to inform decision-making about a player's future. For sport psychologists, both neophyte and experienced, this emphasises the importance of "contextual intelligence" (Winter & Collins, 2015) to our effective practice, requiring an understanding of the culture and context the practitioner is operating within. In a professional practice sense, what follows is practitioner competence and confidence to willingly, pragmatically, and with legitimacy "flex" (not break) their philosophical position. This enables congruent and effective practice to continue and trust, respect, and credibility with other members of the support staff to be upheld. Here, adopting a rigid "thou shalt not yield" approach is not conducive to effective practice, be that the maintenance of effective working relationships with colleagues or survival in the job.

The effectiveness of the *practitioner* can be evaluated on several levels, and this is where the "be, know (know-how and show-how), do" framework referred to in the introduction to this chapter is immensely useful. In this specific case, evaluating what was done (*the "do"*) would include, for example, the standardisation of psychological attributes via the 5Cs framework to create stakeholder buy-in while remaining true to one's professional philosophy. Evaluating knowledge-informed practice (*the "know," "know-how," and "show-how"*) is represented by the ability of the practitioner to understand the theory and research surrounding player development (*the know*), the ability to deploy contextual intelligence to translate this knowledge using effective stakeholder education (*the know-how*), and training coaches in how to perceive and interpret evidence of the players' psychological attributes to accurately inform their work in developing talent (*the show-how*). Finally, evaluating the core ingredients of service delivery that allowed the practitioner to "*be*" effective includes personal characteristics and qualities relating to, for example, flexibility, trust, integrity, authenticity, courage, and congruence. Although potentially informed by many sources, that is coach and athlete feedback and observation, a practitioner must also keep themselves at the forefront of their assessment of effectiveness, as well as assessment of the impact of the work they do on the client.

Considering the discussions presented in the chapter, we argue that it is a practitioner's self-reflection and understanding of self that should contribute above all else to feelings of effectiveness, defined by their own understanding of their role and responsibilities as a sport psychologist. A practitioner's reflective practice must move beyond evaluation of objective outcomes and focus on personal perceptions of effectiveness, informed by philosophical congruence and authentic practice, and involve consideration of how one's qualities were "brought to the table." Such reflections should also account for where optimum practice is not possible and how a practitioner can reconcile with what may feel like a bad day at the office. While any employee should always endeavour to meet the requirements of the role and remain accountable for their work, external markers should alone be insufficient to demonstrate effectiveness, particularly given the significance of congruent practice with one's own philosophy. Self-reflection must therefore aid in developing practitioner understanding of "who they are," as a person and as a sport psychologist, and the interaction between this self and the context within which they work.

Summary and Conclusions

To understand how to evaluate the impact of sport psychology practice, it is first important to identify what represents effectiveness. To help answer this question, it is useful to consider the active ingredients of service delivery within a sporting organisation. In the context of elite soccer, this can broadly be represented by whatever factors allow players or other stakeholders such as coaches to benefit from the helping relationship with the psychologist. Traditionally, sport psychology literature has focused on specific factors associated with what the sport psychologist has done, which is commonly represented by the chosen intervention used and if, and how, what works ... works! The critical question we pose is whether considering only the specific factors as active ingredients in service delivery is enough to define and evaluate what makes the sport psychologist effective. It has been argued that common factors in service delivery are as, or more, important than specific factors for positive client outcomes (Nesti, 2004; Tod & Andersen, 2005). For example, in literature that has examined effective consultant characteristics (e.g., Chandler, Eubank, Nesti, & Cable, 2014; Chandler, Eubank, Nesti, Tod, & Cable, 2016), the common factors of service delivery are, arguably, a more valued feature of the player–psychologist helping relationship, which are present regardless of the intervention model adopted. The dominance of a specific-factor-focus in our literature had led to common active ingredients being de-emphasised and underestimated. As a way forward, considering effectiveness in a "be, know, do" framework (Tod et al., 2017) accommodates how the personal qualities of the psychologist as an embodiment of the core self-support an effective helping process in any sport context for players to realise their potential. This sits alongside what sport psychologists are skilled-up to "do" to help players achieve their performance goals and maintain wellbeing based on what they "know" about sport psychology theory and research that informs practice.

Delivering sport psychology services in contexts that often require the practitioner to develop their own job descriptions and key performance indicators does not only constitute additional work but can also impact the psychology of the psychologist. Without clear agreed measures of success and an understanding of the sport psychologist's role by all involved in player development, the practitioner can potentially experience reduced confidence and/or motivation if their input is not acknowledged. In an attempt to maintain self-efficacy and protect self-esteem there can be a tendency of practitioners to focus on the perceived lack of understanding of psychology that exists within the elite soccer environment. This can be frustrating for the sport psychologist who has expertise in using psychology to accurately inform decisions on, and the development of, players but finds their input usurped by coaches with less comprehension of psychology but craft knowledge that informs the creation of "fast and fixed" judgement. In order to accelerate the integration of psychology within elite soccer and the acceptance of the neophyte sport psychologist within an interdisciplinary team, we propose that the profession will be better served by taking responsibility for any perceived lack of understanding in this domain. Any deficiency should not be used as a criticism of the soccer environment but instead as a reflection on the need for all those involved in sport psychology to better disseminate roles, responsibilities, competencies, and goals of work at the outset of any new project.

What we wish to highlight within this chapter is not just that such challenges will occur and thus what the "ideal" approach to their effective management might be but that practitioners need to consider what effectiveness looks like and whether effectiveness always equates to a best possible performance outcome. This may be particularly challenging for a sport psychologist, whose remit could encompass goals towards performance enhancement, psychosocial development, and the promotion of positive player wellbeing. Not only can these responsibilities be at odds with each other, but also a focus on athlete wellbeing specifically may, as already discussed previously, conflict with the views of other practitioners and the objectives of the soccer club. Literature has highlighted the need for a sport psychology practitioner to maintain their integrity and be "authentic" within their role (Chandler et al., 2014; Friesen & Orlick, 2010; Nesti, 2004), yet the ability for a practitioner to always act authentically and with integrity can be constrained and/or compromised by the needs and culture of the environments in which they operate. From an education and training perspective, understanding the nature and culture of professional sport environments forms an important but often neglected part of practitioner development. The elite soccer examples given in the chapter provide a powerful illustration of why this is so and serve to illustrate some of the key consideration for sport psychologists who aspire to work effectively in the real-world contexts and cultures of elite sport to impact positively on the clients they support.

Key Messages and Further Reading

- Be prepared to compromise on the work done but not your philosophy or personal feelings of effectiveness and what it means to do "good work" and evaluate its impact.
- Commit to educating others as to the significance and value of sport psychology and how best to support player development of their psychological attributes.
- Be comfortable with an environment that encourages staff to adopt a performance agenda, and be prepared to demonstrate impact in this way, even if this isn't aligned with your dominant beliefs about your remit and role.

Chandler, C., Eubank, M., Nesti, M., Tod, D., & Cable, T. (2016). Personal qualities of effective sport psychologists: Coping with organisational demands in high performance sport. *International Journal of Sport Psychology, 47*, 297–317.

Harwood, C. G., Barker, J. B., & Anderson, R. (2015). Psychosocial development in youth soccer players: Assessing the effectiveness of the 5C's intervention program. *The Sport Psychologist, 29*, 319–334.

Steptoe, K., King, T., & Harwood, C. G. (2019). The consistent psycho-social development of young footballers: Implementing the 5C's as a vehicle for interdisciplinary cohesion. In E. Konter, J. Beckmann & T. Loughead (Eds.), *Football psychology: From theory to practice*. London: Routledge/Psychology Press.

Tod, D., Hutter, R. I.V., & Eubank, M. (2017). Professional development for sport psychology practice. *Current Opinions in Psychology, 16*, 134–137.

References

Barker, J. B., McCarthy, P. J., & Harwood, C. G. (2011). Reflections on consulting in elite youth male English cricket and soccer academies. *Sport and Exercise Psychology Review, 7*(2), 58–72.

Chandler, C. (2015). *Exploring the contribution of personal qualities to the effective delivery of sport psychology service provision*. Unpublished doctoral dissertation. Liverpool John Moores University, Liverpool, UK.

Chandler, C., Eubank, M., Nesti, M., & Cable, T. (2014). Personal qualities of effective sport psychologists: A sports physician perspective. *Physical Culture and Sport: Studies and Research, 61*(1), 28–38.

Conroy, D. E., Elliot, A. J., & Hofer, S. M. (2003). A 2× 2 achievement goals questionnaire for sport: Evidence for factorial invariance, temporal stability, and external validity. *Journal of Sport and Exercise Psychology, 25*(4), 456–476.

Eubank, M., Nesti, M., & Cruickshank, A. (2014). Understanding high performance sport environments: Impact for the professional training and supervision of sport psychologists. *Sport and Exercise Psychology Review, 10*, 30–37.

Friesen, A., & Orlick, T. (2010). A qualitative analysis of holistic sport psychology consultants' professional philosophies. *The Sport Psychologist, 24*, 227–244.

Gilbourne, D., & Richardson, D. (2006). Tales from the field: Personal reflections on the provision of psychological support in professional soccer. *Psychology of Sport and Exercise, 7*, 325–337.

Gilmore, S., & Gilson, C. (2007). Finding form: Elite sports and the business of change. *Journal of Organizational Change Management, 20*, 409–428.

Harwood, C. G. (2008). Developmental consulting in a professional football academy: The 5Cs coaching efficacy program. *The Sport Psychologist, 22*(1), 109–133.

Harwood, C. G. (2016). Doing sport psychology? Critical reflections of a scientist-practitioner. In M. Raab, P. Wylleman, R. Seiler, A.-M. Elbe & A. Hatzigeorgiadis (Eds.), *Sport and exercise psychology research: From theory to practice*. London: Elsevier.

Harwood, C. G., & Anderson, R. (2015). *Coaching psychological skills in youth football: Developing the 5Cs*. Oakamoor: Bennion Kearny.

Harwood, C. G., & Knight, C. J. (2015). Parenting in youth sport: A position paper on parenting expertise. *Psychology of Sport and Exercise, 16*, 24–35.

Nesti, M. (2004). *Existential psychology and sport: Implications for research and practice*. London: Routledge.

Nicholls, J. G. (1984). Achievement motivation: Conceptions of ability, subjective experience, task choice, and performance. *Psychological Review, 91*(3), 328–346.

Pain, M. A., & Harwood, C. G. (2004). Knowledge and perceptions of sport psychology within English soccer. *Journal of Sports Sciences, 22*(9), 813–826.

Poczwardowski, A., Sherman, C. P., & Ravizza, K. (2004). Professional philosophy in the sport psychology service delivery: Building on theory and practice. *The Sport Psychologist, 18*, 445–463.

Steptoe, K., Barker, J. B., & Harwood, C. G. (2014). Enhancing the performance of individual athletes and teams: Considerations and challenges for the delivery of sport psychology services. In L. Tashman & G. Cremades (Eds.), *Becoming a sport, exercise, and performance psychology professional: International perspectives*. London: Routledge/Psychology Press.

Tod, D., & Andersen, M. (2005). Success in sport psych: Effective sport psychologists. In S. Murphy (Ed.), *The sport psych handbook* (pp. 303–312). Champaign, IL: Human Kinetics.

Winter, S., & Collins, D. (2015). Where is the evidence in our sport psychology practice? A United Kingdom perspective on the underpinnings of action. *Professional Psychology: Research and Practice, 46*(3), 175–182.

PART IV
Working to Support Injury and Mental Health

17
EFFECTIVELY MANAGING ANTERIOR CRUCIATE LIGAMENT INJURY AND RETURN TO PERFORMANCE IN ELITE WOMEN'S SOCCER

Adam Gledhill, Osman Hassan Ahmed, and Dale Forsdyke

Introduction and Literature Review

US Women's National Team Player Andi Sullivan sustained an anterior cruciate ligament (ACL) rupture in 2016:

> Normally, I would know what I want to do and how I want to do it. But with this injury (ACL rupture), I don't know where I should be.... I'm in completely foreign territory.... It's scary, it's difficult, but it's also good to be outside your comfort zone.

ACL rupture is a serious injury in soccer that presents a high level of injury burden (Bahr, Clarsen, & Ekstrand, 2018). ACL injury incidence is as high as 8500 per 100,000 players per year in soccer, with female players at significantly greater risk of a primary ACL rupture than male counterparts (Waldén, Hägglund, Werner, & Ekstrand, 2011). This greater risk is both complex and multifactorial (Sugimoto, Myer, Barber Foss, & Hewett, 2015) and includes biomechanical, physiological, anatomical, and psychological components. Whereas previous understanding for this increased risk in females centred upon aspects such as the Q angle (Ireland, 2002), more recent thinking highlights the importance of neuromuscular control (Bencke, Aagaard, & Zebis, 2018) and the role the leg dominance may play (Mokhtarzadeh, Ewing, Janssen, & Yeow, 2017). A complete ACL rupture is an injury that not only has the potential for a significant, negative impact on an athlete's career (e.g., Tjong, Murnaghan, Nyhof-Young, & Ogilivie-Harris, 2014) but has also been shown to negatively impact an individual's quality of life for up to 25 years post-injury (Filbay, Culvenor, Ackerman, Russell, & Crossley, 2015).

Despite the potential for good physical functioning from either surgical or non-surgical intervention (Frobell et al., 2013), the most common form of treatment for an ACL rupture is a surgical repair. These procedures can take more than eight months to return to full sporting participation and are often rehabilitated through excellent physical programmes. Elite athletes tend to have higher return-to-participation (RTP) rates than lower-level athletes (Ekstrand, 2011), although RTP rates at pre-injury levels post-ACL reconstruction are poor (Fällstrom, Hägglund, & Kvist, 2016). Given the prognosis for post-ACL RTP despite often excellent physical rehabilitation programmes, it is evident that RTP rates can be affected by a range of cognitive, emotional, and behavioural factors (Ardern et al., 2014; Forsdyke, Smith, Jones, & Gledhill, 2016).

Within ACL research specifically, psychological readiness to RTP has been strongly associated with more positive RTP outcomes, such as a return to pre-injury performance levels (Ardern, Taylor, Feller, & Webster, 2013, Fällstrom, Hägglund, & Kvist, 2016; Webster, Nagelli, Hewett, & Feller, 2018). While psychological readiness to RTP is not clearly defined in sports injury literature, it is in part influenced by a sense of confidence in being able to perform to at least pre-injury levels, an athlete's belief in their rehabilitation programme, and a perception that they have been "healed" and that their knee is functioning (Podlog, Banham, Wadey, & Hannon, 2015; Webster et al., 2018). Athletes' perceptions of knee function are predictive of psychological readiness to RTP (Webster et al., 2018), whereas poorer perceptions of knee function are strongly associated with non-return (Ardern et al., 2014).

An injured athlete's readiness to RTP can also be influenced by their levels of motivation to behaviourally engage with progressively challenging rehabilitation and functional sport-specific activities as part of their rehabilitation programme (Ardern, Glasgow et al., 2016). Recent ACL-specific reviews have noted motivation to be a key factor in determining RTP outcomes (Ardern, Kvist, & Webster, 2016). Despite this, adherence rates to injury rehabilitation programmes can typically be low, which then negatively impacts on RTP outcomes.

The most prominent emotional factor associated with poor or non-RTP post-ACL reconstruction is fear of re-injury (Ardern et al., 2014; Forsdyke et al., 2016). Fear of re-injury is associated with non-RTP for up to seven years after ACL reconstruction (Ardern, Taylor, Feller, & Webster, 2012) and is a reason often cited for career retirement (Tjong et al., 2014). Surgery and recovery, the nature of pre-injury sport, personality traits, and other social considerations are all factors that can inform an athlete's fear of re-injury (Ross, Clifford, & Louw, 2017) and so should be considered as part of a holistic plan which supports an athlete's RTP. It has been suggested that the notion of fear of re-injury as an all-encompassing term is too simplistic and that considering non-fear-inducing anticipation and expectation of re-injury may also be an important step for practitioners (Gledhill & Forsdyke, 2018a).

More recently, the notion of sport injury–related growth (SIRG) has come to the fore. The idea here is that an athlete perceiving their injury as a positive developmental experience that provides an opportunity for growth is associated with positive progression through the RTP process (e.g., Booth, Mellalieu, & Bruton, 2018; Roy-Davis, Wadey, & Evans, 2017; Wadey, Podlog, Galli, & Mellalieu, 2015). The term "sport injury–related growth" encompasses all the perceived changes that an athlete believes aid them in reaching at least pre-injury levels of performance (Roy-Davis et al., 2017). SIRG can influence the RTP process in several ways, including increased psychological wellbeing (Booth et al., 2018), positive affect (Wadey et al., 2015), and enhanced self-efficacy (Roy-Davis et al., 2017). Theoretically, these positive developments are more likely to enhance psychological readiness to RTP, as well as reduce fear of re-injury.

While the picture regarding psychological readiness and fear is compelling, it is important to recognise that most of the research to date is cross-sectional (Ardern et al., 2013; Forsdyke et al., 2016), thus meaning that causality cannot be determined. However, with the need to adopt a best evidence synthesis approach (e.g., Gledhill, Forsdyke, & Murray, 2018) and given the prominence of psychological readiness to RTP, fear of re-injury, and their precursors, it is incumbent upon practitioners to consider ways that these can be effectively monitored as part of the RTP process. This will allow all stakeholders involved to make an informed decision about RTP (Forsdyke, Gledhill, & Arden, 2017). It is also important to consider interventions that can facilitate optimal development within these areas (Gledhill & Forsdyke, 2018a, 2018 b), particularly given that various psychological interventions are effective at reducing re-injury risk and reducing injury time loss (Gledhill et al., 2018).

RTP Decision-Making

One of the major questions with understanding RTP post-injury is "how do we make the decision?" Often, the psychological readiness to RTP is overlooked by practitioners. This is frequent not only because the requisite support is not in place or practitioners are not always appropriately trained to use this support but also because the "tools" used to measure this readiness have issues with their sensitivity and objectivity (Forsdyke et al., 2017). Despite these considerations, it is important that psychological readiness to RTP is considered as part of the decision-making process. There are three main elements that can contribute to this decision-making process:

1. **Know your athlete:** As a practitioner, getting to know your athlete will allow you to familiarise yourself with their typical behaviours in different situations. For example, a player pulling out of tackles in training or practice games, not putting full effort into sprints, or "hiding" during high-intensity tactical practices may all be indicators that they are not yet ready to RTP.
2. **Adopt a player-centred, shared decision-making approach to the RTP decision:** Ultimately, the RTP decision is the decision of the player. While this might not sit well with the world of professional sport and presents potential ethical and contractual issues at important times of the season, the player needs to be the one that gives final "sign-off." This being said, some players who are particularly keen to return to performance quickly may make an ill-timed or incorrect decision about when it is appropriate to return to performance. Equally, players who are forced or coerced into a premature RTP can significantly increase the risk of re-injury. The athlete needs appropriate informational support from key multidisciplinary team members (e.g., team doctor, physiotherapist, surgeon, coach, sport psychologist, parents) to be empowered to make the right decision for them.
3. **Use appropriate screening tools where necessary:** There are several screening tools that can be used to inform RTP decisions. As with any other "objective" measure, they need to be used under the right circumstances and by individuals who are best suited to interpreting their findings, to have the best effect. There are accepted limitations of some measures, specifically around a high risk of social desirability bias in responses if a player knows it is informing the RTP decision (Forsdyke et al., 2017); however, many available tools do still have an important role in supporting the decision-making process.

Psychological Intervention Strategies in ACL RTP

In intervention studies associated with sports injury, most of the research has focused on the "what?," "how?," and "why?" of using different intervention techniques to enhance rehabilitation or RTP. There is scant evidence that has examined the role of psychological intervention strategies post-RTP, to ensure that athletes remain injury-free and able to perform at pre-injury levels. Studies in this body of research have shown that psychological interventions (such as imagery, goal-setting, relaxation techniques counselling-based approaches) are effective at improving injury-related emotions and cognitions, as well as reducing negative injury-related outcomes (Maddison et al., 2012; Schwab Reese, Pittsinger, & Yang, 2012). Furthermore, additional studies suggest psychological intervention techniques can improve biomarkers of injury risk, such as cortisol levels (Dawson et al., 2014; Gledhill et al., 2018).

When designing applied intervention strategies for ACL patients, it is important to consider the wider potential theoretical benefits of these strategies and to include components based upon a "best-evidence" perspective (Gledhill & Forsdyke, 2018b; Gledhill et al., 2018). For example, we know that imagery can be used to enhance confidence in a variety of circumstances and can assume that effectively tailored imagery training will likely have a positive effective on injury-related confidence. Equally, by educating an athlete about their injury and the rehabilitation work that has been undertaken, we may be able to empower injured athletes in such a way that reduces their fear of re-injury through increased understanding and enhances their RTP outcomes (King, Roberts, Hard, & Ardern, 2018).

Case Study

Background and Context

Laura was a professional soccer player who suffered a non-contact ACL rupture while playing a competitive fixture. The timing of this injury and the subsequent surgical repair meant that Laura missed a summer World Cup tournament that she had been in contention for. Laura underwent a programme of physical rehabilitation and had been medically cleared to compete again approximately 12 months after her initial injury.

Despite the importance of considering psychosocial factors such as reinjury anxiety, fear of reinjury, and injury-related and soccer-specific confidence during the rehabilitation period (Forsdyke et al., 2016, 2017), Laura's psychosocial state was not directly addressed during her original rehabilitation programme or RTP decisions. She did not have access to a sport psychologist during her rehabilitation or following her original RTP, which is in keeping with injured female soccer players reporting a lack of access to sport psychology support through their club (Gledhill & Forsdyke, 2018a). Laura had been back playing for a few months when she sought help from AG (lead author). She expressed worries about re-injury and was experiencing doubts about her ability to play in games. She also had concerns about a perceived increased risk of re-injury on particular types of playing surfaces.

Presenting Issue(s)

Prior to commencing her initial needs analysis, AG discussed the limits of confidentiality with Laura (Keegan, 2015). Laura agreed to open information sharing between the multidisciplinary team (MDT), and she was happy for the coach to be informed that she was injured again and may not be available for selection (pending appropriate fitness tests). This was an important part of the consultancy process; transparency in communication increases the chances of successful rehabilitation outcomes (King et al., 2018), and higher quality communication between MDT members is associated with a lower risk of injury (Ekstrand et al., 2018).

Knowing that Laura had not received any sport psychology support during rehabilitation or after RTP, AG took the decision to discuss any experiences of sport psychology support that Laura had previously received. Given that Laura expressed some previous negative experiences and that common factors such as shared goal commitment, alliance, and empathy can have a significant impact on intervention success (Wampold, 2015), AG was keen to ensure that Laura felt valued during the consultation process.

During the needs analysis, Laura also reported being worried about the amount of tension that she felt about her injury and said that her worries would often keep her awake at night. She said that she often felt frustrated by feeling the way she did and felt that she had lost some control, but also that she constantly felt "silly" because it "isn't normal to react to injuries like this." Laura had also expressed that she was concerned about the impact that her injury was having on her personal life, as she found herself arguing with her partner a lot when they started talking about her thoughts on her soccer career.

Based on some of the emotional responses to injury that Laura had briefly reported during her initial discussion, AG completed an extended needs analysis that incorporated emotional disclosure techniques. Both written and verbal emotional disclosure can enhance mood state and promote SIRG post-injury (Mankad & Gordon, 2010; Mankad, Gordon, & Walliman, 2009; Salim & Wadey, 2018). From speaking to Laura about this, she stated that she found it easier to talk about things rather than write about them. She was therefore asked to talk about her deepest thoughts and feelings related to her sports injury experience and record these using an audio recorder.

The key presenting issues that arose from Laura's emotional disclosure was that she was both anxious and scared that she would get injured again. This escalated to the extent that she had convinced herself that she would get injured again should she play on a specific type of playing surface. She also spoke of being angry with herself for letting herself get to this stage and allowing her thoughts to continue for such a long period of time, as (in getting to this stage) she thought she was letting herself and her teammates down. She also noted that she had actively tried to avoid certain games by saying that she had little niggles and wasn't able to play.

During her needs analysis, Laura also began to talk a lot about the time she got injured, how it had been affecting her sleep, and how she kept thinking about the mechanism of injury. AG, therefore, drew on principles of critical incident debriefing (Mitchell, 1988) and asked her to verbally replay the inciting incident in as much detail as she could. In doing so, a more detailed understanding of the game's conditions arose, as well as the specific activities that she was undertaking. Importantly, this also allowed a clearer picture of the performance elements that she was most scared of to emerge, including any fear or anxiety-inducing triggers. Laura's biggest performance concern was entering a one-on-one duel with an opposition then trying to twist and sprint away with the ball, as this was the mechanism of her original injury.

As part of the needs analysis, Laura completed two measures of injury-related emotions and cognitions: the Injury-Psychological Readiness to Return to Sport questionnaire and the Re-injury Anxiety Inventory. Laura's scores from these did not pose any major concerns when she completed them while thinking about playing soccer in general. However, when asked to complete these while thinking about playing on the specific surface, her scores were such that she would not normally be cleared to RTP (due to her high re-injury anxiety on return to sport and low psychological readiness to return to sport).

The final presenting concern was that Laura stated in her needs analysis meeting that she would not play in upcoming games, due to her significant concerns regarding her injury. This presented us as an MDT with the ethical questions of "who was our client?" and "how can we meet the collective needs of all involved?" As an MDT, our collective responsibility was to work both to ensure the wellbeing of players and to maintain and enhance their levels of performance. However, this was a circumstance where meeting both of those obligations may not have been possible. Collectively, we considered Laura to be "injured" and not available for selection.

Based on all the aforementioned information, the priorities for working with this client were as follows (in order of priority):

- Improve overall sense of wellbeing;
- Improve psychological readiness to RTP and decrease fear of re-injury;
- Improve subjective assessment of knee function;
- Allow a return to the pitch in a safe manner.

The Intervention/Work Conducted

The approach to working with Laura was aligned to a person-first approach (Poczwardowski, Sherman, & Ravizza, 2004) that was supported by key stakeholders. In this, Laura's eudemonic and hedonic wellbeing were considered the paramount concern over and above her soccer career. There was a focus by AG on maintaining a "whole-person" approach that facilitated communication between key stakeholders and supported Laura within her soccer-specific progression and development planning (Gledhill & Harwood, 2019).

Recognising Laura's experience as a soccer player, she was involved in consultation decisions, offered different process options towards the same outcomes, and had the rationale for the potential courses of action outlined to her. This autonomy-supportive approach is linked to successful rehabilitation outcomes (Forsdyke et al., 2016), is an important part of developing strong relationships that can influence intervention effectiveness (Wampold, 2015), and is a positive way of engaging injured athletes in the RTP decision-making process (King et al., 2018).

Given the complex dynamics presented in Laura's case, an eclectic approach to support was adopted (Cockerill, 2002) where a range of support techniques and philosophies (e.g., humanistic, psychoeducational, CBT) were combined over time to help support her towards her desired outcome. Drawing on Laura's desired outcomes and coupled with observations from the initial case consultation meeting, the following broad programme of work was suggested by AG:

1. Exploring and understanding Laura's injury-related thoughts, using soccer-specific scenarios as a context to achieve this;
2. Understanding physiological changes that occur in her body when she starts to have negative injury-related emotions and cognitions (e.g., increased heart rate, increased breathing rate, sweating);

3. Understanding the difference between destructive thinking and smart thinking, with the emphasis on understanding when these might happen;
4. Exploring ways in which she may be able to control and manipulate her thoughts (e.g., changing destructive thoughts into smarter thoughts);
5. Development of psychological skills (e.g., imagery; self-talk) which could be used as part of match preparation
6. On-pitch support with match preparation, training support, and in-game support, to allow a re-RTP decision to be made.

Helping Laura to Understand Her Injury-Related Emotions, Cognitions, and Behaviours

Laura agreed that a preferred start point for the intervention would be to help her understand how she thought and felt about soccer and why she felt that way.

In this regard, the intervention started towards the end of the initial contact and needs assessment session. For the first two weeks, we agreed that Laura would keep descriptions of events that occurred, when they occurred, and any injury-related factors she had been thinking about in and around the events happening. During the first two weeks, we would start each of our consultancy sessions by discussing the data that Laura provided. The purpose of this was to support Laura in becoming more aware of negative thoughts, emotions, or comments (Fletcher & Sarkar, 2016), so that we could then help her to start focusing more on the processes of wellbeing and performance improvement (Ravizza, 2001). It was during these early sessions that it was discussed with Laura that it was not the injury that was creating unhelpful thoughts and emotions, rather it was the way she was interpreting her level of re-injury risk (Ellis & Dryden, 1997).

Challenging Beliefs and Cognitive Restructuring

The first stage of cognitive restructuring resulted in collaborative MDT working to replace Laura's current thoughts with more realistic, positive, and appropriate thinking (Fletcher & Sarker, 2016; Meichenbaum, 1986; Turner, 2016). This included educating Laura about the role of the ACL, her injury, the type of ACL reconstruction that she had undergone, and the reasons and evidence base behind the types of functional rehabilitation and RTP physical training activities that she had undertaken. In doing so, we were able to empower Laura to be a central aspect of her RTP decisions and were able to talk openly and transparently with her about the potential for re-injury.

An important part of her cognitive restructuring and challenging Laura's beliefs about her re-injury risk was to help her explore the impact and meaning of the language that she was using. For example, Laura noted that repeatedly telling herself: "I'm going to get injured again" had several negative cognitive, emotional, and behavioural impacts for her. However, when we asked Laura to change these statements to "I'm no more or less likely to get injured than anyone else who has had my injury, because I regularly complete the most effective injury prevention programme available today" and explore how she felt about that statement, she felt more in control of her potential for future re-injury and that she had actively worked to become a stronger athlete.

Imagery Use to Enhance Confidence and Reduce Injury-Related Performance Concerns

Due to the many benefits of imagery, including enhancing confidence (Callow, Hardy, & Hall, 2001), decreasing anxiety (Long & van Stavel, 1995), and managing unfamiliar situations (Munroe et al., 2000), imagery training was used to help Laura develop a more positive approach to her soccer performance. Drawing on recent guidance (Williams et al., 2013), AG involved Laura in the process of producing an imagery script so that she might be able to internalise the imagery experience further. An imagery script was used as it can provide temporal and situational cues that can influence the effectiveness of imagery (Williams et al., 2013). Importantly, the script included an element of recreating feelings of nervousness and apprehension that Laura was able to move past (MacNamara, 2011). An imagery checklist (Williams et al., 2013) was used to help plan the imagery script. Laura was provided with an audio file of the imagery script, so that she could listen to it on the way to training and games, to facilitate the regular practice necessary for skill development (Fletcher & Sarkar, 2016). The mutually agreed goal with Laura was that her imagery exercises would be completed up to three times per day, for no more than 3–5 minutes per session.

Laura's imagery script was produced using guidelines for designing effective imagery scripts (Williams, Cooley, Newell, Weibull, & Cumming, 2013). Within this, I (AG) and Laura considered five Ws of designing imagery scripts: who, where, when, why, and what.

In terms of the "who," as this was an individual script for a senior elite athlete, we worked to add more specific personalised content and specific detail about herself and her role. As Laura didn't have a great deal of experience using imagery, she didn't have a preference for imagery perspective and needed support to be able to integrate lots of different sensory experiences. Consequently, we produced slightly different imagery scripts, to allow her to experience these differences and explore her preferences. The script below is Laura's final preferred version.

We also considered the "when" and "where" when designing the script. We aimed to produce an imagery script that Laura could use at home, at training, and on the way to games and that would help her focus on a specific element of her performance (Williams et al., 2013).

The "why" guided the imagery script content in that the script was being produced to enhance Laura's confidence in specific aspects of performance, reduce her fear of re-injury and re-injury anxiety, and increase her readiness to return to sport. Consequently, it was important that we produced a script that had appropriate content to match these purposes and taking into account specific aspects of her injury mechanism and subsequent experiences.

The "what" is outlined below. Laura's imagery script was also supplemented with a video file. Produced collaboratively with the performance analyst, the short video file was a collection of clips that showed Laura successfully performing the key sports actions that she was most concerned about (i.e., duelling with an opponent for the ball, winning the ball, twisting away at speed). The video file included live sounds from each of the game scenarios she was watching, so that she could start to create a more "real," poly-sensorial experience in her mind. The joint decision was taken by Laura and AG to supplement her imagery script with the video file, so that she could enhance the vividness and clarity of the images, with a view to maximising the potential benefits. Laura's imagery script is below:

> I am at the ground and the game is going well. We are in control of the game and we have just started a counter-attack after a midfield regain. I am positioned near the side-line on the right wing, and the ball has come loose. I get a little nervous when this happens. My heart races a little and I feel myself shake. I take a deep breath and tell myself: "My knee is strong. I've prepared well. I'm a stronger player now." I force out the deep breath, and sprint towards the ball. It is close between me and the opposing defender. I block their attempt to win the ball, controlling the ball with my left foot and then flicking it away with the back of my right heel. I twist and power off in a strong, determined sprint. I twist back inside, beating the defender once again, before placing a perfectly timed pass through zone 14 to the centre forward, who scores.

RTP Decision-Making

Over the first month of our meetings, Laura's language use towards RTP had changed. Where she was previously stating that she was not going to play, she had now progressed to discussing feeling compelled to play ("I have to play"/ "I need to play"). While this language use was still concerning as it suggested an external regulation of potential behaviours given that these statements were often associated with not wanting to let her teammates down by not playing, it did suggest that Laura was open to the prospect of her RTP.

Given this change, AG decided to use a programme of motivational interviewing and decisional balance with Laura. Motivational interviewing is a client-centred approach to understanding factors underpinning behaviours and can foster motivation for behaviour change (Breckon, 2005; Miller & Rollnick, 2012). As well as using open-ended questions, affirmations, reflective listening, and summarising techniques (Green, 2005), a readiness ruler was used with Laura to gain an indication of her readiness to RTP. Laura indicated that she was "about a 7 or 8," which suggested that she was in the preparation stage of behaviour change (Miller & Rollnick, 2012), that is she was actively preparing to RTP, but had not yet started taking action to do so.

As Laura had indicated a greater intention to RTP, the decisional balance approach was employed to support Laura in considering the potential gains and losses associated with an RTP decision. The main gains that she reported related to a sense of control over her soccer career, being pleased that her injury hadn't beaten her, and a notion that she had worked hard to get to a point of considering playing soccer again. The only potential loss that Laura reported was that she might get injured again, but she qualified this by re-stating that she knew she was not at any greater risk of re-injury and, based on the work she had been doing, she was likely at a lower risk of re-injury.

As a result of this and after consultation with sports medicine staff who confirmed there was no greater risk of injury, Laura, AG, and the sports medicine team agreed that a goal would be to physically perform some of the activities that she was concerned about. We agreed that we would video these movements for her so that she could then watch the videos with the sports medicine staff and discuss the quality of her movements. We also agreed that Laura would undertake a pre-match fitness test to determine whether she was fit to play. This would to all intents and purposes be a typical fitness test, but the emphasis of analysis would be to determine her psychological readiness to RTP, given that her physical monitoring all indicated that she was physically able to compete. By this time, Laura's language had changed to "I want to play."

Pre-game Fitness Test

Prior to Laura's first game back, we set up a pre-game fitness test purposefully designed to mimic the circumstances of Laura's original injury. Laura completed the usual injury prevention warm-up, but this instead took place on the location of the pitch that was close to the point where she had originally got injured. This was because we had agreed it would be good for Laura to experience this part of the pitch before the game and see how she reacted. After this, a non-selected member of the squad acted as Laura's "opponent" for the functional elements of the warm-up. These were the specific sporting movements that Laura was concerned would cause a re-injury, as well as other typical ACL injury mechanisms (e.g., single leg landing into a diagonal cut). Prior to completing these activities, Laura engaged again with her imagery audio file and was offered the opportunity to debrief with AG. Laura completed her pre-game functional activities and indicated that she was confident she would be able to play and remain injury-free as much as could be practicably controlled. Collectively, we agreed that she had achieved her RTP criteria (Ardern, Glasgow et al., 2016). Laura indicated that she wanted to play and was happy to play.

Outcome Analysis

In line with the initial priorities, we can offer the following observations that suggest a successful outcome from the interventions provided:

- After her first session, Laura developed better sleep quality as evidenced by her regularly sleeping between six and eight hours per night.

- Quantitative values indicating Laura's psychological readiness to RTP and her RTP re-injury anxiety both improved significantly.
- Laura's self-reported adherence to her home-based psychological skills training and one-to-one psychological support sessions was 100%.

Her education regarding ACL injuries meant that Laura was cognisant of many of the factors relating to ACL injury and rehabilitation, as well as the fact that her rehabilitation meant she was potentially at a lower risk of injury than some players who had experienced similar injuries to hers. Laura thus became the central decision-maker in this process. As an MDT, we aimed to support her and empower her to make the decision that was correct for her but remained cognisant that we should not bias that decision by telling her whether or not she should play. Laura played the game. She did not suffer any injuries during this game and directly contributed to a successful team performance and outcome with goals and assists.

Case-Study Reflections

One of the potentially challenging decisions for a female player to make after ACL reconstruction is whether they should return to competitive soccer (Ardern & Khan, 2016). A key consideration is the potential negative risk for the future health of the female player. ACL rupture leads to a significantly increased risk of osteoarthritis (Culvenor, Cook, Collins, & Crossley, 2013). Female athletes involved in pivoting sports are also at up to six times greater risk of a second ACL injury on RTP (Paterno, Rauh, Schmidtt, Ford, & Hewett, 2014). Therefore, as a practitioner working with female athletes who have ruptured their ACL, this presents significant ethical considerations. In such instances, it is important that the athlete is presented with all the information required to make an informed decision and is supported through their decision-making process (Forsdyke et al., 2017; King et al., 2018). This will provide a greater sense of control and will increase the chances of the athlete experiencing greater long-term psychological wellbeing (Reider, 2014). As such, AG was keen to ensure that any RTP decision that Laura made was informed by all necessary information and that communication with her was completely transparent (King et al., 2018).

During this case, we deemed it important to use objective measures of re-injury anxiety, psychological readiness to return to sport, and emotional responses to injury. Despite each of these having a specific function in the consultation process, the client could easily have viewed this as being "over-assessed." By discussing the value of completing these inventories with Laura, she was willing to complete the inventories. One inventory that could have added extra value was the ACL Return to Sport After Injury Inventory. The literature supporting the predictive validity of this tool as a measure of RTP outcomes is growing (e.g., Webster et al., 2018), and it should be considered for future cases of this nature.

A third reflection is the importance of the multidisciplinary team working in this study and the importance of Laura's consent to open information sharing. These two elements combined meant that we were able to isolate, discuss, and understand

Laura's key concerns, then use these to plan physical, educational, and psychological intervention strategies aimed at improving her circumstances. Had this consent not been in place, it would have been significantly more difficult to work effectively and make player-centred decisions.

A final reflection is around the notion of evidence-informed practice. As literature in female soccer psychology is scarce (Gledhill, Harwood, & Forsdyke, 2017), much of the evidence-informed work was based on evidence from other sporting and non-sporting populations. The need to tailor the programme to Laura's personal circumstances (Sarkar, Fletcher, & Brown, 2015) meant at times a reliance intuition-in-action (Johansson & Krosmark, 2004) whereby tasks were adapted in response to the progress she was making during sessions. This experience has reinforced our view that the research and applied practice community need to invest further time with female youth soccer players, to generate a context-specific evidence base upon which practitioners can base their work.

Summary and Conclusions

Making a return to pre-injury performance levels post-ACL injury is complex and multifactorial. Screening for important psychosocial factors early after ACL injury may help practitioners to identify athletes who may be at risk of not returning to pre-injury performance levels. This screening may also identify athletes who are suffering from performance- or health-related concerns after they have made their RTP. In addition, it may be important to consider any circumstances unique to the individual player (e.g., concerns over particular playing surface, particular performance requirements, and certain opposition) as these may trigger negative psychological, emotional, or behavioural responses, even post-RTP. It is necessary to consider that athletes may need sport psychology support as part of their injury rehabilitation and RTP process, as this is a time when athletes may display lower levels of emotional integrity. As this can lead to athletes making poorer RTP decisions (e.g., trying to return too early to meet the needs of their team), it can also have long-term health and performance implications.

Key Messages and Further Reading

- Cognitive, emotional, and behavioural factors can affect the success of RTP outcomes but are not always clearly addressed through rehabilitation programmes.
- Educating an athlete about their injury will empower them to become a key stakeholder in the RTP decision-making process, as well as modulate their fear of re-injury and readiness to RTP levels.
- A player-centred, shared decision-making approach that involves all relevant key stakeholders is likely to improve the chances of a successful RTP.
- Post-RTP monitoring and support may be beneficial for some athletes, as delayed onset of re-injury anxiety and fear of re-injury may occur at times that have critical meaning for players.
- In the absence of data it is important to trust existing theory and then work hard to make sure that the evidence base grows

Ardern, C. K., Österberg, A., Tagesson, S., Gauffin, H., Webster, K., & Kvist, J. (2014). The impact of psychological readiness to return to sport and recreational activities after anterior cruciate ligament reconstruction. *British Journal of Sports Medicine, 48*, 1613–1619.

Culvenor, A. G., Cook, J. L., Collins, N. J., & Crossley, K. M. (2013). Is patellofemoral joint osteoarthritis an under-recognised outcome of anterior cruciate ligament reconstruction? A narrative literature review. *British Journal of Sports Medicine, 47*, 66–73.

Filbay, S. R., Culvenor, A. G., Ackerman, I. N., Russell, T. G., & Crossley, K. M. (2015). Quality of life in anterior cruciate ligament-deficient individuals: A systematic review and meta-analysis. *British Journal of Sports Medicine, 49*, 1033–1041.

Fletcher, D., & Sarkar, M. (2016). Mental fortitude training: An evidence-based approach to developing psychological resilience for sustained success. *Journal of Sport Psychology in Action, 7*, 135–157.

Forsdyke, D., Smith, A., Jones, M., & Gledhill, A. (2016). Psychosocial factors associated with the outcomes of sports injury rehabilitation in competitive athletes: A mixed-studies systematic review. *British Journal of Sports Medicine, 50*, 537–544.

Gledhill, A., Forsdyke, D., & Murray, E. (2018). Psychological interventions used to reduce sports injuries: A systematic review of real-world effectiveness. *British Journal of Sports Medicine, 52*, 967–971.

King, J., Roberts, C., Hard, S., & Ardern, C. (September 25, 2018). Want to improve return to sport outcomes following injury? Empower, engage, provide feedback and be transparent: 4 habits! *British Journal of Sports Medicine*. Epub ahead of print. doi:10.1136/bjsports-2018-09910925

References

Ardern, C. L., Glasgow, P., Schneiders, A., Witvrouw, E., Clarsen, B., Cools, A. . . . Bizzini, M. (2016). 2016 Consensus statement on return to sport from the first world congress in sport physical therapy, Bern. *British Journal of Sports Medicine, 50*, 853–864.

Ardern, C. L., & Khan, K. M. (2016). The old knee in the young athlete: Knowns and unknowns in the return to play conversation. *British Journal of Sports Medicine, 50*, 505–506.

Ardern, C. L., Taylor, N. F., Feller, J. A., & Webster, K. E. (2012). Fear of re-injury in people who have returned to sport following anterior cruciate ligament reconstruction surgery. *Journal of Science and Medicine in Sport, 15*, 488–495.

Ardern, C. L., Taylor, N. F., Feller, J. A., & Webster, K. E. (2013). A systematic review of the psychological factors associated with returning to sport following injury. *British Journal of Sports Medicine, 47*, 1120–1126.

Bahr, R., Clarsen, B., & Ekstrand, J. (2018). Why we should focus on the burden of injuries and illnesses, not just their incidence. *British Journal of Sports Medicine, 52*, 1018–1021.

Bencke, J., Aagaard, P., & Zebis, M. (2018). Muscle activation during ACL injury risk movements in young female athletes: A narrative review. *Frontiers in Physiology, 9*, 445.

Booth, A., Mellalieu, S., & Bruton, A. (2018). Subjective distress, sport injury-related growth, self-efficacy and wellbeing upon return to sport following injury. *Sport & Exercise Psychology Review, 14*, 23–31.

Breckon, J. (2005). Exercise motivation and adherence: The use of motivational interviewing. *The Sport and Exercise Scientist, 3*, 8–9.

Callow, N., Hardy, L., & Hall, C. (2001). The effects of motivational-general imagery intervention on the sport confidence of high-level badminton players. *Research Quarterly for Exercise and Sport, 72*, 389–400.

Cockerill, I. (2002). *Solutions in sport psychology*. Boston, MA: Cengage Learning, EMEA.

Dawson, M. A., Hamson-Utley, J. J., Hansen, R., & Olpin, M. (2014). Examining the effectiveness of psychological strategies on physiologic markers: Evidence-based suggestions for holistic care of the athlete. *Journal of Athletic Training, 49*, 331–337.

Ekstrand, J. (2011). A 94% return to elite level football after ACL surgery: A proof of possibilities with optimal caretaking or a sign of knee abuse. *Knee Surgery Sports Traumatology Arthroscopy, 19*, 1–2.

Ekstrand, J., Lundqvist, D., Davison, M., D'Hooghe, M., & Pensgaard, A.-M. (August 13, 2018). Communication quality between the medical team and the head coach/manager is associated with injury burden and player availability in elite football clubs. *British Journal of Sports Medicine*, Epub ahead of print. doi:10.1136/bjsports-2018-099411

Ellis, A., & Dryden, W. (1997). *The practice of rational-emotive behavior therapy*. New York: Springer.

Fällstrom, A., Hägglund, M., & Kvist, J. (2016). Factors associated with playing football after anterior cruciate ligament reconstruction in female football players. *Scandinavian Journal of Science and Medicine in Sport, 26*, 1342–1352.

Forsdyke, D., Gledhill, A., & Ardern, C. (2017). Psychological readiness to return to sport: Three key elements to help the practitioner decide whether the athlete is REALLY ready? *British Journal of Sports Medicine, 51*, 555–556.

Frobell, R. B., Roos, H. P., Roos, E. M., Roemer, F. W., Ranstram, J., & Lohmande, L. S. (2013). Treatment for acute anterior cruciate ligament tear: Five-year outcome of randomised trial. *British Medical Journal, 346*, f232.

Gledhill, A., & Forsdyke, D. (2018a). Sport psychology: An old idea from and old book, or the next frontier in sports injury prevention? *BASEM Today, 44*, 28–29.

Gledhill, A., & Forsdyke, D. (2018b). An ounce of prevention is better than a pound of cure: Shouldn't we be doing EVERYTHING to reduce sports injury incidence and burden? *British Journal of Sports Medicine*, Epub ahead of print [13th June 2018]. doi:10.1136/bjsports/-2018-099208

Gledhill, A., Forsdyke, D., & Murray, E. (2018). Psychological interventions used to reduce sports injuries: A systematic review of real-world effectiveness. *British Journal of Sports Medicine, 52*, 967–971.

Gledhill, A., & Harwood, C. (2019). Toward an understanding of player's perceptions of talent development environments in UK female football. *Journal of Applied Sport Psychology, 31*, 105–115.

Gledhill, A., Harwood, C., & Forsdyke, D. (2017). Psychosocial factors associated with talent development in football: A systematic review. *Psychology of Sport and Exercise, 31*, 93–112.

Green, S. (2005). Motivational interviewing: Putting key principles into practice. *The Sport and Exercise Scientist, 4*, 24.

Ireland, M. (2002). The female ACL: Why is it more prone to injury? *Orthopedic Clinics of North America, 33*, 637–651.

Johansson, T., & Krosmark, T. (2004). Teachers' intuitions-in-action: How teachers experience action. *Reflective Practice, 5*, 357–381.

Keegan, R. (2015). *Being a sport psychologist*. London: Palgrave Macmillan.

Long, B. C., & van Stavel, R. (1995). Effects of exercise training on anxiety: A meta-analysis. *Journal of Applied Sport Psychology, 7*, 167–189.

MacNamara, A. (2011). Psychological characteristics of developing excellence. In D. Collins, A. Button & H. Richards (Eds.), *Performance psychology: A practitioner's guide* (pp. 47–64). London: Churchill Livingstone.

Maddison, R., Prapavessis, H., Clatworthy, M., Hall, C., Foley, L., Harper, T. . . . Brewer, B. (2012). Guided imagery to improve functional outcomes post-anterior cruciate ligament repair: Randomized-controlled pilot trial. *Scandinavian Journal of Medicine and Science in Sports, 22*, 816–821.

Mankad, A., & Gordon, S. (2010). Psycholinguistic changes in athletes' grief response to injury after written emotional disclosure. *Journal of Sport Rehabilitation, 19*, 328–342.

Mankad, A., Gordon, S., & Walliman, K. E. (2009). Psycholinguistic analysis of emotional disclosure: A case study in sport injury. *Journal of Clinical Sports Psychology, 3*, 182–196.

Meichenbaum, D. (1986). Cognitive behaviour modification. In F. H. Kanfer & A. P. Goldstein (Eds.), *Helping people change: A textbook of methods* (pp. 346–380). New York, NY: Pergamon Press.

Miller, W. R., & Rollnick, S. (2012). *Motivational interviewing: Helping people change* (3rd ed.). London: Guildford Press.

Mitchell, J. (1988). Stress: The history and future of critical incident stress debriefings. *Journal of Emergency Medical Services*, 7–52.

Mokhtarzadeh, H., Ewing, K., Janssen, I., Yeow, C., Brown, N., & Lee, P. (2017). The effect of leg dominance and landing height on ACL loading among female athletes. *Journal of Biomechanics, 26*, 181–187.

Munroe, K., Giacobbi, P., Hall, C., & Weinberg, R. (2000). The 4Ws of imagery use: Where, when, why and what. *The Sport Psychologist, 14*, 119–137.

Paterno, M. V., Rauh, M. J., Schmidtt, L. C., Ford, K. R., & Hewett, T. E. (2014). Incidence of second ACL injuries 2 years after primary ACL reconstruction and return to sport. *American Journal of Sports Medicine, 42*, 1567–1573.

Poczwardowski, A., Sherman, C. P., & Ravizza, K. (2004). Professional philosophy in the sport psychology service delivery: Building on theory and practice. *The Sport Psychologist, 18*, 445–463.

Podlog, L. W., Banham, S., Wadey, R., & Hannon, J. (2015). Psychological readiness to return to competitive sport following injury: A qualitative study. *The Sport Psychologist, 29*, 1–14.

Ravizza, K. (2001). Increasing awareness for sport performance. In J. M. Williams (Ed.), *Applied sport psychology: Personal growth to peak performance* (pp. 179–189). Mountain View, CA: Mayfield Publishing Company.

Reider, B. (2014). Quality of life. *American Journal of Sports Medicine, 42*, 275–277.

Ross, C. A., Clifford, A., & Louw, Q. A. (2017). Factors informing fear of reinjury after anterior cruciate ligament reconstruction. *Physiotherapy Theory and Practice, 33*, 103–114.

Roy-Davis, K., Wadey, R., & Evans, L. (2017). A grounded theory in sport injury-related growth. *Sport, Exercise & Performance Psychology, 6*, 35–52.

Salim, J., & Wadey, R. (2018). Can emotional disclosure promote sport-injury related growth? *Journal of Applied Sport Psychology, 30*, 367–387.

Sarkar, M., Fletcher, D., & Brown, D. (2015). What doesn't kill me. . .: Adversity related experiences are vital to the development of superior Olympic performance. *Journal of Science and Medicine in Sport, 18*, 475–479.

Schwab Reese, L. M., Pittsinger, R., & Yang, J. (2012). Effectiveness of psychological intervention following sport injury. *Journal of Sport and Health Science, 1*, 71–79.

Sugimoto, D., Myer, G., Barber Foss, K., & Hewett, T. (2015). Specific exercise effects of preventive neuromuscular training intervention on anterior cruciate ligament injury risk reduction in young females: Meta-analysis and subgroup analysis. *British Journal of Sports Medicine, 49*, 282–289.

Tjong, V. H., Murnaghan, L., Nyhof-Young, J. M., & Ogilivie-Harris, D. J. (2014). A qualitative investigation of the decision to return to sport after anterior cruciate ligament reconstruction: To play or not to play? *American Journal of Sports Medicine, 42*, 336–342.

Turner, M. J. (2016). Proposing a rationale resilience credo for use with athletes. *Journal of Sport Psychology in Action, 7*, 170–181.

Wadey, R., Podlog, L., Galli, N., & Mellalieu, S. D. (2015). Stress-related growth following sport injury: Examining the applicability of the organismic valuing theory. *Scandinavian Journal of Medicine and Science in Sports, 26*, 1132–1139.

Waldén, M., Hägglund, M., Werner, J., & Ekstrand, J. (2011). The epidemiology of anterior cruciate ligament injury in football (soccer): A review of the literature from a gender-related perspective. *Knee Surgery, Sports Traumatology, Arthroscopy, 19*, 3–10.

Wampold, B. E. (2015). How important are the common factors in psychotherapy? An update. *World Psychiatry, 14*, 270–277.

Webster, K. E., Nagelli, C. V., Hewett, T. E., & Feller, J. A. (2018). Factors associated with psychological readiness to return to sport after anterior cruciate ligament injury. *American Journal of Sports Medicine, 46*, 1545–1550.

Williams, S. E., Cooley, S. J., Newell, E., Weibull, F., & Cumming, J. (2013). Seeing the difference: Designing effective imagery scripts for athletes. *Journal of Sport Psychology in Action, 4*, 109–121.

18

UNDERSTANDING MENTAL HEALTH AND WELLBEING ISSUES IN ELITE SOCCER PLAYERS: AN EXISTENTIAL SPORT PSYCHOLOGY APPROACH

Alan John Tonge

Brief Introduction and Literature Review

Tottenham Hotspur and England full-back Danny Rose intimated some of the demands that impact on elite soccer players in a press conference prior to a match against Belgium in the 2018 World Cup: "I wouldn't be shouting from the rooftops to recommend people's children to be a footballer. There are a lot of things that happen on a day to day basis at a football club that I wouldn't wish on anybody." Recent research has demonstrated that athletes who have reached the elite level of their profession are still susceptible to the challenges of poor mental health which can have a detrimental impact on their wellbeing (Rice et al., 2016). More specifically, elite-level global soccer players have reported a plethora of mental health-related problems, via autobiographies and media reports. These have included conditions such as stress, anxiety, depression, obsessive compulsive disorder, panic attacks, and addiction with reported poor maladaptive coping mechanisms employed, such as gambling, alcoholism, drug taking, and dietary abuse. From a neutral observational perspective, this can be potentially viewed as surprising given the associated gains from professional soccer such as fame, exposure, adulation, high financial reward, and enormous public regard and esteem. However, according to the Professional Footballer's Association (PFA website, 2019a), one in six people in the United Kingdom will experience a mental health–related problem each year. Transferring that statistic into elite-level soccer can potentially mean that out of a Premier League professional squad size of 25, at least four players could have an issue with their mental health. Out of the English Premier Leagues 20 club sides, approximately 80 players could be suffering with an undisclosed issue each season. There can be a plausible array of issues within elite-level soccer which suggest why players may suffer with negative mental health. These issues can be deselection (getting dropped, or moved on), injuries (short term and long term), poor relationships with managers, coaches, and other players, environmental change (such as loans, or joining another club), and negative media coverage following poor performances or form.

Despite the many potential challenges that elite soccer throws up, and because of the brutal and demanding environment that high-performance sport brings, many players are still unsure how and where to seek the most appropriate help and support if needed (Nesti, 2010). A high percentage of intervention-based mental health literature (e.g., Kvam, Kleppe, Nordhus, & Hovland, 2016; Schuch et al., 2016) suggests that moderate to vigorous exercise can have a positive effect on psychological issues such as stress, anxiety, and depression. To be more specific, regular exercise can help raise mood, self-esteem, confidence, and lead to a higher sense of wellbeing (Rethorst, Wipfli, & Landers, 2009). Although this would be a recommended intervention for someone who is sedentary, or largely inactive, it can be argued that exercise-based interventions can be rejected within elite-level professional soccer culture, as the players already have a high level of exposure to physical fitness through their training and competition demands yet still have psychological issues? An intervention like this would simply not be appropriate and something else needs to be offered. Sport psychologists should therefore consider providing a differing type of support for elite-level soccer players as they navigate their way through the game. This can come via the means of existential sport psychology (Nesti, 2004).

In this chapter I will provide practitioners with an understanding of some of the factors that are likely to impact on the mental health of elite players. There will be also suggested strategies of identification and management of the mental health–related issue employing existential sport psychology. I will use a case-study approach to appraise a contemporary mental health challenge that an elite-level soccer player has faced within the professional game. The case study is based on a deselection experience which caused a threat to a player's identity. The aim is to present and discuss the challenge and suggest how it can be addressed by relevant sport psychology theory and practice. One of the difficulties when analysing mental health and professional soccer is the low amount of insight and academic research conducted around the mental health–related challenges which professional players regularly have to face and deal with, especially within demanding, high-performance environments. This is in part due to difficulties with distrust, confidentiality, and access to players, especially at first-team level (Nesti, 2010). Indeed, psychological-based work conducted within the game has tended to focus on samples of youth players. For example, Parker (1995) investigated the psychosocial aspects of youth trainee player journeys as they attempted to gain a professional contract, and following this there have been studies on the use of sport psychology and coaches at England youth level (Pain & Harwood, 2007), deselection (release) and the effects on identity disruption of youth players (Brown & Potrac, 2009), and athletic identity within first- and second-year scholars (Mitchell et al., 2014). Although interesting and informative research within a professional football environment is scarce, some of the main critique with these studies is that the demands and pressures within first-team-level professional soccer and the culture associated with academies and youth environments are very different indeed. Youth environments have been described as "process-oriented," "nurturing," "caring," and "empathetic," whereas first-team environments are "outcome-oriented," "ruthless," "macho," and "highly competitive" (Richardson, Relvas, & Littlewood, 2013). The environments that Richardson and colleagues (2013) described can drive, affect, and influence mental health states. The potential influence of mental health states can be seen within the current culture and climate of first-team professional soccer. Put simply, youth players tend to operate in a developmental culture and first-team players operate in a results-driven culture.

Scrutiny of performance can be high in a youth environment but is colossal in a first-team environment. As well as constant scrutiny, there are also incredible amounts of finance and rewards within the higher echelons of the game, and this means that ethics can be challenged and also decision-making processes can be faster and more abrupt. There is so little room to fail or be seen to be failing. To put this into some context, figures from a League Managers' Association Report (LMA, 2017) stated the average duration for a professional soccer manager in England is 1.66 years (The English Premier League, 2.68; The Championship, 1.07; League One, 1.37 and League Two, 1.71). Adding to these data, the Professional Footballer's Association website (PFA, 2019b) suggests the average length of a professional playing career is eight seasons, with many representing a variety of teams both from a fixed contract and loan perspective. Due to this evidence of insecurity, instability, dramatic amounts of change, and a contemporary culture for quick fixes, relationships at all levels can potentially be impacted (club, team, and individual).

Adding to the extant literature and current knowledge base of mental health and professional soccer, in this chapter I will present a semi-fictional case study using a reflective account around a critical moment at first-team level (deselection) which created a high level of anxiety. Recent work by Calvin (2017) suggested that only a few players coming through the current academy system will ever reach and accrue first-team appearances in the Premier League. To be specific, he stated that from all the players within the 9- to 18-years-old age range, only 0.012% will play in a Premier League first team. Engaging and working with this level of player can add something original to assist our understanding of the mental health challenges that first-team-level soccer players face and which type of support would be most beneficial in relation to mental health and wellbeing within an elite professional soccer culture. The information provided in this chapter will shine a light on the topic of psychological challenges and a potential mental health–related issue in elite-level professional soccer. The writing brings to the table a real, lived experience of a high-level player and provides an insight into the incredibly demanding, pressurised, and scrutinised culture of the professional game, rather than the developmental and supportive culture found within academies or at youth level.

In this section I will examine some of the academic literature wrapped around psychological challenges, mental health, and wellbeing within professional soccer. It will first focus on some of the stages and transitions that a player typically makes in their career before presenting work around more frequent experiences they encounter, which can be termed as "critical moments" (Nesti & Littlewood, 2011). The final part of the review will present an argument for why existential sport psychology in elite-level soccer may be a more effective means of support over the traditional interventions which focus on mental skills training (Nesti, 2004).

An elite soccer player who has made the grade (e.g., journeyed from youth to becoming a senior professional) will face both normative transitions and non-normative transitions along the way (Wylleman, Lavallee, & Alfermann, 1999). A normative transition is something that will usually happen within a player's career, comes in stages, and can be expected or planned for. For example, a player will typically experience the normative transitions of being a schoolboy player, to becoming an apprentice, to becoming a young professional, to becoming a senior professional, and then having to retire. A non-normative transition can be described as something that a player has not planned for or something which happens dramatically and unexpectedly. For example, this could be having a career-threatening injury to deal with or having to move to another club when being settled in an area. Non-normative transitions can bring difficult times and mental health–related challenges with them. A high percentage of the current transition literature has focused on definitive end points such as career-ending injuries or retirement (e.g., Knights, Sherry, & Ruddock-Hudson, 2016; Murphy, 1995; Wylleman & Lavallee, 2004). This body of work which focuses on career-ending injury or retirement has helped sport psychologists understand how these stages are experienced and how mental health conditions such as anxiety and depression can become a problem within these times. The mental health challenges of anxiety and depression may be in part due to leaving or having to give up a sport that players have loved and played since ages as young as five. It is natural that professional soccer has been a large part of their identity, and once this identity is lost, all manners of psychological disturbance can emerge (Nesti, 2010). Adding to this body of research, there have also been some pieces of work that have investigated the challenges of "within career transitions" (e.g., Pummell, Harwood, & Lavallee, 2008; Samuel, Tenenbaum, & Gil Bar-Mecher, 2016; Samuel et al., 2015). Although promising, this research has focused on populations such as adolescent horse riders and "competitive" athletes within sports such as judo, basketball, track and field, and gymnastics.

The research does not go into detail, or use appropriate methodology such as phenomenological interviews, to fully explore and understand the mental health challenges that professional-level athletes have experienced. Nor does this research provide definitive detail around psychological interventions or the types of support that athletes received to aid with their "within transition" experiences. The contents of this case study could go some way to help sport psychologists consider how to plug that gap.

When journeying through elite-level professional soccer, and due to the nature of a results-based culture, it can be argued that there will be a much broader range of potential mental health–related issues that players will experience, often on a more frequent basis. These issues could reside within moments such as deselection, loans, problematic coach or manager relationships, pressure to play while carrying an injury, or dealing with negative media following a poor performance. It has been suggested by researchers (e.g., Stambulova, Alfermann, Statler, & Cote, 2009) that the youth-to-senior step is the most challenging step athletes will face in their career and echo that the movement from a youth to a senior environment can challenge soccer players the most. This movement into a new environment can bring about many issues to deal with which may threaten or challenge a player's identity (Morris, Tod, & Oliver, 2015; Nesti, 2010). As the culture and highly supportive environment of youth development are markedly different to the first-team culture and environment (e.g., Richardson et al., 2013), this is an area worthy of further attention. This is because, bar Nesti (2010), there is limited insight into first-team soccer environments from both an applied and research perspective. Gaining knowledge from high-performance environments can add training value to sport psychologists wishing to operate in this domain. It is of utmost importance to understand and appreciate the array of potential mental health–related challenges that start to emerge as a player makes their way through the high pressures, expectations, and demands that the elite-level professional game brings. Further research and insight from contemporary sport psychologists working with elite-level professional soccer players would be a valuable addition.

Training and development of UK elite-level professional soccer players has shifted dramatically over the past 25 years (Kay, 2016). The move away from cleaning boots, sweeping terraces, and undertaking menial chores for little money to achieving public acclaim and high rewards quickly can potentially cause issues in player motivations. Many elite-level players post-academy (i.e., in the age window of 17–23) can become wealthy without actually playing many first-team games. This can affect desire, identity, and character development and has led Calvin (2017) to proclaim there's "no hunger in paradise." However, the window of 17–23 may be an excellent opportunity for a sport psychologist to work with a player. They are within touching distance of radically changing their lives and will seek to do anything they can ethically to progress themselves to becoming a regular elite-level first-team player.

The current base of academic mental health or psychological challenges-based research within soccer tends to cease post-academy (i.e., after 18 or 19 years old; Brown & Potrac, 2009; Mitchell et al., 2014). Other means of understanding mental health–related issues within elite-level soccer have come via self-reports within autobiographies (e.g., Carlisle, 2014; Gascoigne, 2005; Gillespie, 2013). These players have spoken openly about the challenges of elite-level soccer and dealing with the exposure, fame, and adulation associated with playing at the top levels of game. Difficulties associated with serious injury, moving clubs, and loss of identity post playing career led to severe mental health issues and poor coping mechanisms are evident, such as overuse of alcohol, poor dietary habits, drugs, and gambling. Although incredibly insightful, these accounts are not underpinned with academic theory and due to confidentiality have little indication as to what interventions and appropriate support were offered within their careers, if any? One exception to the lack of academic literature within professional soccer is the reflective work of Nesti (2010), who provided detailed accounts of the typical issues and psychological challenges occurring when working with elite-level professional soccer players for a prolonged period of time. Due to the closed culture and the general suspicion of "outsiders," the opportunity to undertake lengthy psychological work with elite-level professional soccer players at English Premier League level is extremely rare indeed. This distinct lack of academic-based research and detailed insight which could further aid our understanding can be put down to the fact that it is extraordinarily difficult to gain access due to confidentiality and trust issues (Nesti, 2010).

To further deepen and enhance our appreciation of the issues faced within an elite-level professional soccer journey, and to critique the rather smooth sounding term of "transition," the phrases "boundary situations" (Yalom, 1999) and "critical moments" have been put forward (Nesti, 2010, 2016). The regular or more frequent challenges faced by an elite soccer player can evoke anxiety and provide a threat to, or change in, a player's identity. Early work by Maslow (1968) proposed that identity is the most important component of psychological development within a human being. Very little of Maslow's work has been used in the sport psychology literature to examine the concepts such as identity and meaning, and this is a strange omission as sport, and in particular soccer, can provide a deep source of meaning in a person's life (Nesti, 2004). A high percentage of professional soccer players started playing the game when they were very young, and the construct of a strong and on occasion exclusive athletic identity can be formed (Brown & Potrac, 2009). An athletic identity can be productive in relation to high commitment and the dedication to excel and improve; however, it can be argued that other social roles can be disregarded or not engaged with, for example within important areas such as education (Mitchell et al., 2014). An overly strong, almost one-dimensional formation of an athletic identity has the potential to become a problematic issue as the player makes their way through the game, especially when having to deal with a boundary situation or a critical moment. This type of narrow identity could potentially contribute to serious mental health—related problems as players strive to funnel their way through a tiny gate and into the professional game (Brown & Potrac, 2009). Although professional soccer clubs have a responsibility to make sure young players develop a broader, richer identity and that they undertake academic and vocational qualifications, the simple view of "I'm here to become a professional football player and nothing else" remains the number one objective for a high majority (Hughes & Leavy, 2012). This can be termed as "identity foreclosure" and has the potential to diminish motivation to acquire other skills and experiences beyond the training and competition environment. To address this and other issues, Nesti (2004, 2010, 2016) suggested a radical support perspective (existential sport psychology) over the traditional, dominant uses of cognitive and behavioural psychology within sport, which primarily includes mental skills training (MST). MST is useful and has its place; however, it is technique-based and involves the use of imagery (or visualisation), self-talk, goal-setting strategies, or relaxation procedures such as breathing control. Arguably, the over-reliance by many sport psychologists to fully rely on and employ MST in high-performance environments is fundamentally flawed, as players, especially at first-team level, face a broader range of issues within their journey and therefore a broader theoretical approach is needed to support them more effectively (Nesti, 2004). This has been presented as a Socratic method (long term, developmental) as opposed to a Sophist one (short term, quick fix). The pathway of a human being must always remain open, unfinished with perspectives from both performance and care angles being considered (Anderson, 2009; Brady & Maynard, 2010). When a player faces a critical moment within their careers, it provides them with an opportunity to rigorously examine who they are and where they want to get to. This assessment of their identity can be broached from a performance perspective and a broader perspective (i.e., off the field). This can then lead to the development of self-knowledge, existential courage, and practical wisdom (Corlett, 1996b).

Developing this broader, richer identity can help with the shocks to the system which players typically face as they move through the game. These shocks can include deselection, injury, poor form, going out on loan to a lower club, media scrutiny and critique, poor relationships with managers and coaching staff and even poor relationships with teammates. Within applied sport psychology work, it has put forward that players who tend to develop and have a broader identity (within areas such as family, education, religion, or even spirituality) tend to cope with issues arising better than those players who have a narrow or exclusive athletic identity (Nesti, 2004). This is an important point as the culture of elite-level professional soccer can be a potential breeding ground for psychological challenges or mental health–related problems. It is a brutal, ruthless, and demanding world, and where there is a requirement for quick answers, minimal trust, and incredible amounts of change, players can be placed under immense mental strain (Nesti & Littlewood, 2011). Players can deal with issues in this culture much more constructively if they have a broader identity and see themselves as more than just a professional soccer player (Nesti, 2010).

In conclusion, the review of literature has considered some of the topical aspects of psychological challenges, mental health, and wellbeing within elite-level professional soccer. As a player navigates their way through the game, a broader range of issues will start to arise and have to be faced. The academic literature within this area has tended to focus on athlete end points such as retirement and terms such as "normative transitions" and "non-normative transitions" have been put forward. As there are a plethora of psychological challenges that will evoke anxiety within a player's journey (due to a threat to, or change in their identity), a more effective way of detailing these frequent issues would be through the phrase's boundary situations or critical moments. To support a player more effectively through a boundary situation, or critical moment within elite soccer, and to add something different to the traditional applications of mental skills training, an alternative approach of existential sport psychology has been suggested.

To put the review of literature into some context, a semi-fictional case-study vignette will now be presented. This is in relation to a critical moment and identity threat that was faced within an elite-level first-team professional soccer environment, including the dialogue between an existential sport psychologist and a first-team-level player. The type of psychological support provided and how the critical moment impacted on the player's mental health and wellbeing will also be discussed.

Practical Applications—Case Study

The following semi-fictional case-study vignette highlights how a critical moment can unexpectedly arise and affect an elite-level professional soccer player and their mental health. The case study is constructed using a one-to-one meeting narrative of an elite first-team-level professional soccer player and a sport psychologist within an elite-level club.

Background and Context

The player had been at the soccer club since they were 11 years old and they had transitioned through the different stages to reach the level of professional soccer. After starting their apprenticeship, they were awarded a professional contract at

17 years old and had played a number of times within the first team over the past three seasons. During this rise to play elite-level soccer, the player had gained Under-21s international recognition and the start of lengthy, successful elite career was looking promising.

Presenting Issue(s)

During the latter end of the season, the player had picked up a small injury which had sadly kept them out for the remaining fixtures. The end of the season had been reached, the player had gone on holiday for a month to recuperate and had returned to pre-season training in early July. Within the pre-season fixtures, the player had been left on the bench a lot and in his words were just "playing bit parts." These deselection experiences had hit him hard and he came to see the sport psychologist at the end of July, a week or so before the season was due to commence. The meeting held was one-to-one, fully confidential and took place in a private room at the clubs training ground.

SP: "how are you doing, you're looking fit and well, how was your break and holiday? It was well deserved"

Player: "to be honest, it's not gone as well as I'd hoped. I was really looking forwards to the rest over the pre-season as I was starting to feel mentally exhausted and needed some sunshine."

SP: "I'm sorry to hear that. Why didn't it go so well?"

Player: "I'm sure you're aware there have been incomings and outgoings over the last month, but from my perspective, I was a few days into my break, sat on my sun lounger, flicking through different soccer related sites on my phone and staring right back at me was the manager and a few players that had signed for the club. They were stood on the stadium pitch with club shirts and scarves on and the manager's arms around them, a couple of them potentially who will play in my position"

SP: "that must have come as a shock for you and difficult to comprehend. How did that make you feel?"

Player: "I've gone wow, my stomach has flipped over and I'll be honest with you the first thing that raced into my mind was I thought the manager really rated me and wanted me and now I'm going to have my hands full not only to get back into the squad, but to get back in the first eleven. I've trained hard over the last couple of weeks, got myself very fit, my diet is sound, I'm really happy off the field with my young family, but now I seem to have been pushed out and have been stuck on the bench for the last 3 pre-season matches. It's really worrying me to be honest"

SP: "so what are your options? Have you considered them? What are you going to do?"

Player: "I'm going to have to speak to my agent, and I may have to go and see the manager to basically ask him if I am in his plans for this season. If not, I'll have to try and get away. I want to play, I've been establishing myself as a

	first team player and I feel I am good enough to warrant a regular place. I'm not spending a season wasting away, sat on the bench, or hardly playing. A professional soccer career is short enough as it is. It's really disappointing because I was doing well, playing regularly in the first team, I'd managed to get under 21s international recognition. I thought I will get myself super fit over the pre-season and really push on to the next level."
SP:	"How has this made you feel?"
Player:	"It's made me feel really anxious about my long term future here" I'm not sleeping so well and it's definitely affected my self-esteem and this has really knocked my confidence for six. All of a sudden I've started questioning my ability and whether I'm good enough to play at the level and whether I'm really rated or not. I'm doubting my worth to the manager, the team and the club. I'm also starting to get friends, family and even fans asking me what's happening and why am I not playing regularly in the pre-season fixtures"
SP:	"have you had any moments like this before in your professional career and how have you reacted?"
Player:	"I have had issues like this before, but obviously not at this elite level and with this exposure. I have been sub and have even been left out in youth team games and the reserves on odd occasions, but I have responded, dug in and worked hard and managed to work my way back into the side. This has been a big reason of me reaching the first team squad and got me into the first team itself and is a substantial part of who I am as a person, to keep going, fighting and never give up."
SP:	"so what are your options from here?"
Player:	"I need to consider all angles and what is best for me. I've got one year left on my contract and I don't want to get ahead of myself, but this may affect quite a lot moving forwards. This club is all I've known, I'm happy and settled here, it's my boyhood side, I live in the area, all my family support them, so I need to get in as soon as I can and see what the manager says"
SP:	"ok, see what the next week brings and then we can sit down and can talk again."

After the conversation with his agent, the manager, and returning regularly to speak with the sport psychologist about various aspects of performance and their broader life, the player focused upon doing everything they could to get back in the side. After a few games in, the player managed to get a chance back in the starting eleven. Although not cementing a regular place after this, the player managed to play many more games than they initially expected and went on to have a decent season. Midway through the club offered him a new three-year contract which he was delighted to sign.

A key theme of existential sport psychology is to focus the person on attempting to move forwards despite the anxiety, difficulties and tough times that professional soccer will throw up. The existential sport psychology approach and dialogue employed within the player's deselection experience was to help the player become more authentic and to accept that discomfort, choice and change is a big part of gaining self-knowledge, learning, and growth (Nesti, 2004, 2010; Nesti & Littlewood, 2011).

The Intervention/Work Conducted

An existential sport psychology approach focuses on the givens of human existence such as freedom, isolation, anxiety, love, pain, suffering, sacrifice, and even death (Nesti, 2004). The work conducted by the sport psychologist within the one-to-one meeting was not about offering mental skills training (MST) on this occasion, such as using imagery or goal-setting techniques, but about using a person-centred approach, hard-hitting dialogue, and to guide the player to getting everything out and on the table. The primary focus of this and the encounters which followed, was to make the player understand that they had some control over what they can do next, as opposed to resisting the temptation to offer them something tangible. The fact that the player was returning to speak to the existential sport psychologist was an encouraging sign, as this made it clear they were getting something from the intervention. If they were not, they simply would not have returned. The whole process and work conducted by the existential sport psychologist was centred on getting the player to examine where they currently are in their journey and to clarify their sense of identity. The critical moment of deselection that the player was facing is sadly part and parcel of the ups and downs of elite-level soccer (Brown & Potrac, 2009; Nesti, 2004). This moment was creating anxiety as the player saw it as a threat to their identity as a first-team player. This was understandable as they had been at the club since they were 11 years old and had worked incredibly hard and dedicated themselves fully to get to first-team level. This was a personal issue and many elite soccer players have a strong, or even exclusive athletic identity as what they do is often a big part of who they are (Nesti, 2010). The existential approach guides the sport psychologist away from making things easy for the player, or by offering them direct solutions, and instead recognises that confronting or opening up about an issue, such as the experiences of deselection, may bring existential anxiety (anxiety brought about within our freedom as human beings to choose without being sure about future outcomes), doubt, uncertainty and make them feel uncomfortable. These feelings of anxiety and discomfort are particularly high when the player cares deeply about their sport and that playing soccer is something that they love doing. The existential sport psychology approach also recognises that despite the anxiety that the issue was creating, the player always has a choice (Frankl, 1984). Although nowhere near the horrific conditions and extremities that Frankl had to endure in the concentration camps in the Second World War, his mantra of "when you can no longer change a situation, you are challenged to change yourself" was a very strong piece of theoretical advice to draw from in this existential encounter. Choosing to ignore the critical moment (deselection), handing their fate to destiny, or not opening up about the feelings they were having can bring about a "stunted person centre" (Buber, 1999). This abandonment of freedom to choose a course of action by facing up to the uncertainty of whether the choice is right can make an elite soccer player less likely to choose for themselves in the future. This can then potentially manifest itself into a clinical mental health problem. Issues can arise when players ignore the anxiety associated with a critical moment in their career and engage with something for a quick fix, or to remove the discomfort they are feeling as quickly as possible. In the modern, fast-paced culture in which we exist, the quick fix can be a very tempting proposition and there may be occasions where a mental skills offering is useful and can help, however without asking deeper questions around how people currently see themselves and where they want to go, quick fixes will more often than not simply miss the target (Nesti & Littlewood, 2011).

Outcome Analysis

Within the ever-changing world of elite-level professional soccer, players may be faced with this situation around deselection on regular occasions, as well as a plethora of boundary situations, or critical moments. No places are guaranteed, and out of a squad of 25 players, sadly only 11 players can play at any one time, with five spaces on the substitutes bench. In a Premier League squad, this means that potentially nine players will be left out and feeling unhappy every week. Ruminating, or worrying about what is coming next can potentially impact on a player's mental health if not managed correctly. Players can become frustrated, angry, de-motivated and quickly lose confidence. Within elite-level professional soccer, it is crucial to stay visible and be involved with the first-team squad. If not, others, such as friends, family, fans and the wider media outlets, may start to question attitude, or whether players are actually doing enough to get back into the frame for first-team selection. For a player this can be anxiety ridden and uncomfortable and the only option may be to demonstrate patience and see what unfolds in the future. Facing up to the critical moment of deselection took existential courage from the player, however developing self-knowledge and facing a situation that had not been experienced at this level before was the right course of action. An important measure of the intervention and something that can quickly find a sport psychologist out, especially within the world of elite-level soccer, is that the player kept returning to see them until they got back into the starting 11. This leads to another important and pertinent point when providing sport psychology support at this level. It is absolutely crucial that the sport psychologist demonstrates certain qualities such as empathy, patience, openness, integrity, engaging in consistent critical self-reflection and should be educated and trained to develop their own self-knowledge. This can come via the means of consulting with and reading a broad range of literature. Working with a client such as an elite-level soccer player is more an art than a science and contemporary sport psychology education and training packages should acknowledge this key point. Indeed, Ravizza and Fazio (2002) have argued that the most important aspect of effective sport psychology work is not the ability and skill to construct or design a psychological intervention, but is how the sport psychologist can relate to the player/ person sat in front of them.

Case-Study Reflections

Within this case study, the sport psychologist nudged the player to reflect on whether the critical moment of facing deselection had reared its head before and how he had previously dealt with something like this. However, this was when the player was in the youth team where the culture and environment was different. Now that he had transitioned out of that environment and had gained heightened recognition as a first-team player and even represented an Under-21's international side was a different scenario. The player openly admitted in the worst-case scenario he would have to meet with the manager to discuss where he stood and even consider the option of moving on and facing his "death" at the club (Yalom, 1999). This would be particularly hard as he had been there since he was a child and had experienced a long, tough road to gaining elite-level first-team recognition. By considering differing options with the existential sport psychologist and deciding to speak with the manager and then potentially play for his life to get back in the picture, the player has demonstrated courage and their ability to cope with a critical moment. This was a constructive step forwards from a potentially destructive situation. The main potential limitation with the case study approach of existential sport psychology is that this type of work is often slow paced, and hard hitting. A contemporary fashionable way of applied sport psychology delivery, especially in the fast paced world of elite soccer, is to look for quick fixes and apply technical suggestions (such as mental skills interventions) to often non-technical problems (e.g., identity). Within Corlett's (1996a) paper this was termed a Sophist way of addressing an issue way back in Ancient Greece. The harder path to follow, which never really ends, is deemed the Socratic approach which takes time and a continuous examination of self and accrual of self-knowledge. However as elite-level soccer players recognise (including the player in the case study), the route to the top takes hard work, commitment, discipline, and does not come easy. When using an existential sport psychology approach, the key for the player is for them to decide what choices they face to get back into the starting eleven at first-team level. These choices can be narrow or broad and can impact performance directly or indirectly. It is based on anything they decide which will help them perform better, or become more competent at their work or what they do. The more experienced and higher level the players, the easier it becomes to undertake this approach as they mostly know what they need. However, the player may need to use an existential sport psychologist for the dialogue and to help make the choices become clearer in their mind. This is because when a player is in a situation of deselection, or facing a critical moment within their career, their thinking can be flawed and emotions can be poor.

Summary and Conclusions

The issue presented within this chapter is congruent to the applied experiences and reflective accounts of Nesti (2010), who wrote about his practice when working with elite-level soccer players in the English Premier League over the course of ten seasons. Although having its place and usefulness, many of the critical moments faced by players in professional soccer cannot be addressed satisfactorily by the traditional approaches and applications of mental skills training. The reasons for this can be broken into two parts. First, it can be argued that elite-level soccer players already possess excellent mental skills. This has been found by Nesti (2010) within his applied work. A second reason can be put down to mental skills training only offering a narrow, almost quick fix approach to deal with symptoms, when on many occasions deeper care, understanding, and patience are needed for the player sat in front of you. Mental skills training still tends to be popular in football-based educational packages and on university courses. This could be put down to academics and course writers needing to come away from an over-reliance on traditional, cognitive-based sport psychology offerings and consider a much broader range of literature grounded within areas such as European existential psychology or philosophy. This will enable us to present more conclusive evidence for the most effective support sport psychologists can offer players as they attempt to navigate and remain in the incredibly challenging and demanding environment of elite-level soccer. This chapter can aid sport psychology educators and course writers to consider a different angle when supporting professional players as they make their way through the professional game, specifically around the topics of critical moments, identity, and mental health challenges. Critical moments within a professional soccer player's career have the potential to affect performance and enjoyment, and by recognising these, a much-needed approach of existential sport psychology (beyond the traditional cognitive behavioural paradigms) is suggested for sport psychology practitioners to read about, train in, utilise, and apply. Future researchers should strive to keep examining how players at differing levels, differing genders, and from differing cultural backgrounds experience critical moments within professional soccer. This can further enhance our understanding of how these moments can affect a player's identity, mental health, and wellbeing and how these moments can be best supported. These moments could be within the professional development phase (18–21) and the transition into a first-team environment and beyond. There should also be a consideration of a broader range of methodological approaches employed to capture the lived experiences within the differing stages of a soccer player's career.

Key Messages and Further Reading

1. Elite-level soccer players can face a range of difficult challenges on their professional journey.
2. These challenges can be described as critical moments. Critical moments can create anxiety and can challenge, or provide a threat to, a player's identity.
3. To deal with these critical moments and the broader issues in an elite soccer player's life, a broader psychological, person-centred approach is needed.
4. This broader approach can come via the discipline of existential sport psychology.
5. Although important and having its place, mental skills training only offers techniques and deals with symptoms when much deeper care is needed for the person in front of you. To add weight to this, Nesti (2010) put forward that only 10–15% of his prolonged work with players in the English Premier League was based on mental skills training and 85–90% was based on critical moments, identity, anxiety, and broader life issues.

We have highlighted the five most pertinent further reading resources below:

Corlett, J. (1996). Sophistry, Socrates, and sport psychology. *The Sport Psychologist, 10*, 84–94.
Corlett, J. (1996). Virtue lost, courage in sport. *Journal of the Philosophy of Sport, 23*, 45–57.
Frankl, V. (1984). *Man's search for meaning: An introduction to Logotherapy.* New York, NY: Simon and Schuster.
Nesti, M. (2004). *Existential psychology and sport: Theory and application.* London: Routledge.
Nesti, M. (2010). *Psychology in football: Working with elite and professional players.* London: Taylor and Francis.

References

Anderson, M. B. (2009). Performance enhancement as a bad start and a dead end: A parenthetical comment on Mellalieu and Lane. *The Sport and Exercise Scientist, 20*, 12–14.

Brady, A., & Maynard, I. (2010). At an elite level the role of the sport psychologist is entirely about performance enhancement. *Sport and Exercise Psychology Review, 6*, 59–66.

Brown, G., & Potrac, P. (2009). "You've not made the grade, son": Deselection and identity disruption in elite level youth football. *Soccer and Society, 10*(2), 143–159.

Buber, M. (1999). *Martin Buber on psychology and psychotherapy: Essays, letters, and dialogue* (J. B. Agassi, Ed.). Syracuse; New York, NY: Syracuse University Press.

Calvin, M. (2017). *No hunger in paradise: The players: The journey: The dream*. New York, NY: Random House.

Carlisle, C. (2014). *You don't know me, but. . . . A footballer's life*. London: Simon & Schuster Ltd.

Corlett, J. (1996a). Sophistry, Socrates, and sport psychology. *The Sport Psychologist, 10*, 84–94.

Corlett, J. (1996b). Virtue lost, courage in sport. *Journal of the Philosophy of Sport, 23*, 45–57.

Gascoigne, P. (2005). *Gazza: My story*. London: Headline.

Gillespie, K. (2013). *How not to be a football millionaire*. Liverpool: Trinity Mirror Sport Media.

Hughes, L., & Leavy, G. (2012). Setting the bar: Athletes and vulnerability to mental illness. *British Journal of Psychiatry, 200*, 95–96.

Kay, O. (2016). *Forever young*. London: Quercus Editions Ltd.

Knights, S., Sherry, E., & Ruddock-Hudson, M. (2016). Investigating elite end of career transition: A systematic review. *Journal of Applied Sport Psychology, 28*, 291–308.

Kvam, S., Kleppe, C. L., Nordhus, I. H., & Hovland, A. (2016). Exercise as a treatment for depression: A meta-analysis. *Journal of Affective Disorders, 202*, 67–86.

LMA. (2017). End of season manager statistics. *Report by the League Manager's Association*, p. 1–9.

Maslow, A. H. (1968). *Toward a psychology of being*. New York, NY: Van Nostrand Reinhold Company.

Mitchell, T., Nesti, M., Richardson, D., Midgley, A. W., Eubank, M., & Littlewood, M. (2014). Exploring athletic identity in elite level English youth football: A cross sectional approach. *Journal of Sports Sciences, 32*, 1294–1299.

Morris, R., Tod, D., & Oliver, E. (2015). An analysis of organisational structure and transition outcomes in the youth-to-senior professional soccer transition. *Journal of Applied Sport Psychology, 27*, 216–234.

Murphy, S. (1995). Transitions in competitive spirit: Maximising individual potential. In S. Murphy (Ed.), *Sport psychology interventions* (pp. 334–346). Champaign, IL: Human Kinetics.

Nesti, M. (2004). *Existential psychology and sport: Implications for research and practice* (p. 114). London, UK: Routledge.

Nesti, M. (2016). Performance mind-set. In T. Strudwick (Ed.), *Soccer science*. Champaign, IL: Human Kinetics.

Nesti, M., & Littlewood, M. (2011). Making your way in the game: Boundary situations in England's professional football world. In D. Gilbourne & M. B. Anderson (Eds.), *Critical essays in applied sport psychology*. Champaign, IL: Human Kinetics.

Pain, M., & Harwood, C. (2007). The performance environment of the England youth soccer teams. *Journal of Sports Sciences, 25*, 1307–1324.

Parker, A. (1995). Great expectations: Grimness or glamour? The football apprentice in the 1990s. *The Sports Historian, 15*, 107–126.

The PFA. (2019a). *Wellbeing. Good mental health is vital for peak performance in sport*. Retrieved from www.thepfa.com/wellbeing

The PFA. (2019b). *Age. The PFA support players throughout their playing career and membership continues long after a playing career has ended*. Retrieved from www.thepfa.com/equalities/commitment-to-all/age

Pummell, B., Harwood, C., & Lavallee, D. (2008). Jumping to the next level: A qualitative examination of within career transitions in adolescent event riders. *Psychology of Sport and Exercise, 9*, 427–447.

Ravizza, K., & Fazio, J. (2002). Consulting with confidence: Using who you are to evoke excellence in others. Workshop conducted at the *Annual Conference of the American Association of Applied Sports Psychology*, Tucson, Arizona.

Rethorst, C. D., Wipfli, B. M., & Landers, D. M. (2009). The anti-depressive effects of exercise: A meta-analysis of randomised trials. *Sports Medicine, 6*, 491–511.

Rice, S. M., Purcell, R., De Silva, S., Mawren, D., McGorry, P. D., & Parker, A. G. (2016). The mental health of elite athletes: A narrative systematic review. *Sports Medicine, 46*, 1333–1353.

Richardson, D., Relvas, H., & Littlewood, M. (2013). Social and cultural influences on player development. In M. A. Williams (Ed.), *Science and soccer*. London: Routledge.

Samuel, R. D., Tenenbaum, G., & Gil Bar-Mecher, H. (2016). The Olympic games as a career change-event: Israeli athletes' and coaches' perceptions of London 2012. *Psychology of Sport and Exercise, 24*, 38–47.

Samuel, R. D., Tenenbaum, G., Mangel, E., Virshuvski, R., Chen, T., & Badir, A. (2015). Athletes' experiences of severe injuries as a career change-event. *Journal of Sport Psychology in Action, 6*, 99–120.

Schuch, F. B., Vancampfort, D., Richards, J., Rosenbaum, S., Ward, P. B., & Stubbs, B. (2016). Exercise as a treatment for depression: A meta-analysis adjusting for publication bias. *Journal of Psychiatric Research, 77*, 42–51.

Stambulova, N., Alfermann, D., Statler, T., & Côté, J. (2009). Career development and transitions of athletes: The ISSP position stand. *International Journal of Sport and Exercise Psychology, 7*(4), 395–412.

Wylleman, P., & Lavallee, D. (2004). A developmental perspective on transitions faced by athletes. In M. Weiss (Ed.), *Developmental sport and exercise psychology: A lifespan perspective* (pp. 507–527). Morgantown, WV: Fitness Information Technology.

Wylleman, P., Lavallee, D., & Alfermann, D. (Eds.). (1999). *Career transitions in competitive sports*. Biel, Switzerland: Fédération Européenne de Psychologie du Sport et des Activités Corporelles (FEPSAC).

Yalom, I. (1999). *Momma and the meaning of life: Tales of psychotherapy*. London: Piaktus.

19
SOCCER REFEREE MENTAL HEALTH

Developing a Network of Soccer Referee Mental Health Champions

Mikel Mellick

Brief Introduction and Review of Literature

The mental health of referees remains a somewhat taboo subject in soccer and across the broad spectrum of high-performance sport environments (Gouttebarge, Johnson, Rochcongar, Rosier, & Kerkhoffs, 2017). Former FIFA Referee Mark Clattenburg has admitted to using alcohol as a coping mechanism after matches: "How do you release the tension around refereeing big games? Drink lots of beer!" Stigma and the lack of understanding of mental health still permeate the elite sport community (Gulliver, Griffiths, & Christensen, 2012). Former World Cup final soccer referee Howard Webb disclosed in his 2017 autobiography his history of obsessive-compulsive disorder and how he kept the condition secret within the world of soccer fearing he would be labelled as "mentally" unsound and deemed unfit for the role of referee (Webb, 2017). Webb only felt comfortable and safe to disclose post-retirement. Soccer demands perfection from its referees, and seemingly this results in "legitimised" forms of referee role and referee personal vilification. It is hardly surprising that given this often "toxic" and unrealistic environment, referees do not feel "permitted" to experience or disclose any periods of mental health vulnerability.

It would be remiss, however, not to first acknowledge the positive impact being a referee may have on wellbeing and mental health. Beyond physical activity rewards, the sense of belonging that comes with being part of the wider football community and the value derived from making a contribution to a game one "loves" permit an altruism that promotes esteem, a sense of social connectedness, and ultimately positive wellbeing (Petracovschi, Mureşan, Voicu, & Timişoara, 2010). Referee memoirs readily acknowledge the sense of camaraderie experienced by being part of a referee society/association of like-minded individuals (e.g., Webb, 2017). Indeed, research exploring the reasons for becoming a soccer referee highlights the desire to feel part of a team, to enjoy being part of the game for which they have passion, and the sense of satisfaction that comes with a well-regarded performance (Petracovschi et al., 2010; Johansen, 2014; Bernal, Nix, & Boatwright, 2012).

Despite the potential positive impact soccer refereeing may have on an individual's mental health and wellbeing, the world of soccer is experiencing significant referee recruitment and retention challenges, with this posing a significant risk to the game itself (Dell, Gervis, & Rhind, 2016). Beyond the pragmatic constraints impacting on sport volunteering worldwide (e.g., decreased available leisure time), recent soccer refereeing exposés have shone a light on a darker side of the mental health risks associated with blowing the whistle (Webb, 2017; Mcevoy, 2018). A lack of role satisfaction as a result of "role threats and stressors" is a significant factor influencing recruitment and retention (Dell et al., 2016). Perceived and actual threats of verbal and physical violence represent the main reason for referees leaving, with the ever-present conditions of threat not surprisingly leading once-active referees to view any future participation as potentially harmful to their mental health and wellbeing (Petracovschi et al., 2010). A study by Webb, Dicks, Thelwell, van der Kamp, and Rix-Lievre (in press) demonstrated that 16% of referees in France and 14.6% of referees in the Netherlands had been subjected to physical abuse. The outcome of this "toxic" environment is unsurprisingly a referee practice community that feels disenfranchised from a game that seems to "choose" to accept referee abuse as normal.

Given these demands it is surprising that little research has examined the potential for, or existence of, common mental disorders (CMD) within the soccer referee community. A notable exception is the work of Gouttebarge et al. (2017) which investigated the symptom prevalence of CMD among professional soccer referees across Europe. Undertaking a one-season prospective study, their findings demonstrated CMD among professional football referees over a follow-up period of one season to be 10% for distress, 16% for anxiety/depression, 14% for sleep disturbance, 29% for eating disorders, and 8% for adverse alcohol use. A prevailing "stigma" inhibiting disclosure was also evidenced, with only one in five football referees reporting a willingness to seek professional/medical help for their symptoms of CMD.

There are unique referee-specific factors that result in a soccer referee's increased risk to CMDs. Samuel, Galily, and Tenenbaum (2017), for example, highlighted a number of potential psychological crisis transitions that disrupt the typical refereeing journey. The most challenging to a soccer referee's mental health was associated with coping with a very poor performance and/or a critical one-off decision error in a big match (Samuel et al., 2017). Chronic performance-related stress in referees may be reinforced by a prevailing assessment process that assumes perfection and looks for reasons to mark down a performance from the referee's first whistle. One suspects that such a process has the potential to exacerbate a mindset framed by a "fear of failure" (Voight, 2009; Corrado, Pellarin, & Agostini, 2011; Johansen & Haugen, 2013). In Zeman, Voborny, Benus, and Blahutkova's (2014) work analysing the subjective psychological experiences and mental states of soccer referees, a concept labelled "depression from failure" emerged as a frequent concern. When trapped within this mental state, soccer referees may succumb to a desire to withdraw from participation as the only viable means to avoid pressure and find emotional/psychological safety (Petracovschi et al., 2010). A referee vulnerability to a failure-based depression episode is not surprising given the unrealistic, perfectionist-driven environment current referees now operate within (Webb, 2017).

Faced with an ever-increasing psychological burden associated with a constant exposure to psychological and physical intimidation, soccer referees may be prone to periods of increased anger and frustration (Webb, Cleland, & O'Gorman, 2017). This may result in a reduction in self-confidence and increased levels of anxiety symptoms associated with clinical stress (Dell et al., 2016). Faced with this, soccer referees may choose to walk away from the game in order to preserve or indeed rescue their mental health.

Research exploring coping resources utilised by elite soccer referees acknowledges that it is refereeing colleagues who are most instrumental in providing first-line emotional and psychological support in times of mental difficulty (Slack, Maynard, Butt, & Olusoga, 2013). In contrast, research reports and published personal refereeing accounts highlight the perceived lack of psychological support initiated by Soccer Associations (Governing Body) for soccer referees in response to mental health need. Research that has explored referee intentions to quit the game indicates that a lack of support by their Soccer Association in periods of psychological crisis is a key influencing factor for referees leaving (Dell et al., 2016). Unsurprisingly, this lack of recognition, understanding, and available support upon disclosing mental health challenges exacerbates feelings of low self-worth, shame, and guilt within referees. This has the potential to disenfranchise, devalue, and isolate "at-risk" referees from the Soccer Association body and wider soccer community.

Practical Applications—Case Study

Background and Context

I was asked by a Referee Workforce Manager for a National Soccer Association (NSA) how the Referee Department could better promote and support the mental health of their match officials (referees and assistant referees) and match official developers (coaches/mentors/tutors). The Department consisted of 13 staff who were engaged in the administration and management for the development, recruitment, and education of all soccer referees involved in local (grassroots) football and the (Semi) Professional Game. The Regionally based Soccer Associations also employed at least a full-time or part-time Referee Development Officer (RDO). They were responsible for the training, education and development of registered referees and for supporting a referee performance development workforce (referee tutors, referee assessors and other referee mentors). The NSA also employed twelve part-time Regional Referee Coaches, all with substantial experience as former top-level referees and or assistant referees. Their function was both one of quality assurance, safeguarding the standard of refereeing at the higher levels of the community game, and one of talent identifying and developing referees with potential to progress to higher levels. They were expected to intervene with referees within the group if they encountered problems with fitness, health, administration and availability.

Presenting Issue(s)

What was striking from an initial review of these quite extensive workforce roles and functions was the lack of any explicit acknowledgement of referee wellbeing, welfare or mental health support. While there were clear references to the broad functions of education, development and advice, these were situated within a referee "performance" skill acquisition /enhancement framework rather than a more holistic develop/support-the-person-behind-the-referee approach.

This was surprising given the refereeing section of the National Game Strategy's primary "pragmatic" focus was about ensuring 90 per cent of youth and adult matches are officiated by a qualified referee (The FA National Game Strategy, 2015). To me, this could only be achieved however through an adequate referee retention and recruitment strategy (including support processes) that maintained an operationally viable refereeing "workforce." Yet, for a variety of mental health and wellbeing reasons previously addressed within this chapter, the game has been "haemorrhaging" referees to the point of placing the grassroots game at risk (Dell et al., 2016). Beyond pragmatics, I believed that the NSA had a moral and pastoral duty of care to better ensure the wellbeing and mental health of their soccer referee workforce. It was apparent from the publicly available information I gleaned from the NSA and from informal conversations with current referees, that there was little explicit acknowledgment of, nor any formal structured support in place, by the NSA to promote and or support the mental health and wellbeing of their soccer referee workforce.

Intervention/Work conducted

I proposed to the NSA's Referee Department a project to implement and manage a network of within-referee community, appropriately trained individuals, to provide first-line support for referees seeking help with their mental health and wellbeing difficulties. From my occupational experiences as an Academic and Practitioner Psychologist I was aware of how peer-to-peer support models have been used extensively within educational institutions and community mental health settings for at risk people of mental health difficulty. Research has suggested that peer-to-peer mental health support to be a highly successful approach leading to early intervention support and as a means to ensuring a continued sense of practice community inclusion (Sutcliffe & Matheson, 2018; O'Hagan, Cyr, McKee, & Priest, 2010). I felt adopting a similar model would have real value in referee settings where, when faced with performance obstacles and (dis)stress, previous research has demonstrated that soccer referees are most likely to turn to their refereeing peers for first-line emotional and psychological support (Slack et al., 2013). To ensure an evidence-based connection between a sport setting and mental health issue athlete support, I turned to the International Society of Sport Psychology (2019) consensus statement on improving the mental health of athletes. This provided a valuable heuristic framework that assisted in the development of the project proposal. Specifically, the following statements were used for this purpose:

> "Sport organizations should: (1) be open to discussing mental health; (2) provide the structures and resources to promote early identification and effective treatment of athletes at risk or mentally unwell and ensure that all involved persons have knowledge about these structures and resources; (3) encourage testimonials from athletes who have suffered from mental health problems to normalize and promote openness; (4) take steps to cultivate help-seeking behaviors, which includes identifying and removing barriers and reducing stigma; (5) set up educational initiatives for athletes, coaches and other stakeholders to increase mental health literacy; and (6) provide athletes with the opportunity to give back to the sport and thus experience meaning and purpose beyond their own results."

The above principles also aligned closely to the Project Committee of the Mental Health Commission of Canada's report on "Making the Case for Peer Support" (O'Hagan et al., 2010). This report emphasised that a peer-supporter must be a member of the target population and someone with considerable experience of mental health issue predisposition for that "at risk" community and who is respected by his or her peers. At a fundamental level, to ensure the credibility, usefulness and worthiness of any peer support initiative they must be tailored to the needs of the target group and have full organisational support and acceptance.

Operationalising the above principles, I provided an outline proposal to establish a national "team" of Referee Mental Health Champions using peers already embedded within the referee practice community. These "Champions" would be used to proactively support the mental wellbeing of referees, developing strong links between the NSA, the regional SA referee communities and local mental health groups and organisations. Such an approach, I believed, would help encourage and ensure referees with mental health challenges would have earlier access to an appropriate locally based support network. Building mental health awareness within refereeing communities and actively seeking opportunities to hold conversations about the typical referee mental health demands and challenges faced, would help "normalize" a within-referee community culture of disclosure and also promote timelier referee help-seeking behaviour. Referee Mental Health Champions would also provide a useful conduit to sharing guidance and information provided by the NSA with the referee community about soccer referee mental health protective factors and psychological coping skills.

The International Society of Sport Psychology (Henriksen et al., 2019) recently challenged sporting bodies to consider a number of "Expert" agreed propositions. Of particular relevance to my proposed intervention was the proposition to make mental health a core component of a culture of sporting excellence. My proposal needed to be underpinned by an approach that demonstrated to the NSA and the referee department that a high-performance referee development and support culture should pay due attention to referee mental health in their efforts to promote acceptable officiating performance, and this should be stated explicitly in training, education and protocol manuals. That is, the NSA must recognise and accept the explicit link between overall referee mental health/wellbeing and referee on-field performance success.

At an operational level, the "Experts" also argued that while mental health is everybody's business, it should, in terms of organisational accountability, be overseen by one or a few within-practice community specified members. To enable this, my proposal suggested that the National Referee Workforce Manager would be best placed to act as the proposal sponsor and activator. The already embedded RDOs were identified to serve as gatekeepers into appropriate within-region referee members with the potential (within specific inclusion criteria) to become Peer Mental Health Champions.

To help address those CMD issues highlighted earlier in this chapter, I have been working across national governing bodies of sport, embedding programmes of Mental Health Literacy Training (MHAT) within staff and athlete support teams. The aim of this has been to develop an awareness of the typical signs and symptoms of common mental health disorders experienced by those involved in high-level sport and to help facilitate a shift in sport culture to one that facilitates safe disclosure and earlier signposting to appropriate mental health issue support. Research has highlighted that providing such programmes to players, coaches and referees can enhance mental health knowledge and intentions of the sport community to offer early support (Breslin, Haughey, Donnolly, Kearney, & Prentice, 2017; Breslin & Leavey, 2019).

Soccer Referees are more likely to disclose to a refereeing colleague, that is, someone already embedded within their practice community, who has an appreciation for and experience of the unique psychological loading involved in soccer refereeing. If referees with mental health vulnerabilities can be supported to maintain a feeling of connection to, inclusiveness within and acceptance from, a soccer referee peer support network, then their access to appropriate emotional, tangible and informational support may be better guaranteed. My proposal argued that this could only be achieved with a better soccer referee community level of mental health literacy that actively acknowledges, talks about, and accepts as normal periods of referee psychological "vulnerability."

Within the proposed training syllabus, I suggested there be a specific focus on potential CMDs for referees. Given the potential sensitivities around these topics I felt that Referee Mental Health Champions would be recruited from those within referee practice community who already had a background in education or counselling and/or have or had a background in mental or occupational health. I felt also that it was important that the Referee Mental Health Champions have an awareness and understanding for how referees learn to cope and indeed flourish within the performance environment. Therefore, wellbeing training should also equip them with a knowledge of the important protective factors that soccer referees can develop in order to avoid periods of mental ill health (Breslin & Leavey, 2019; Dell et al., 2016). Mental toughness has long been emphasised by those within the referee practice community as a key psychological attribute associated with "successful" performance. Research exploring the characteristics of referee excellence has indicated a robust referee self-belief as a key defining attribute of referee mental toughness (Slack et al., 2013). Having trust in one's referee decision-making, a courage of conviction and a realistic "perfectionist" striving, has been demonstrated to cultivate a sophisticated set of protective factors against referee performance-related pressures (Slack et al., 2013). The early referee consideration of these factors through peer support and education, I proposed, would play some role in protecting soccer referees against referee environmental threats to mental health.

Beyond the above protective factors, current research has also highlighted the significant role "self-compassion" plays in maintaining one's mental health and wellbeing (Bluth, Campo, Futch, & Gaylord, 2017; Fong & Loi, 2016). While a somewhat novel research area within sport, there are however some examples of its application to athletes and coaches. The work of Ferguson, Kowalski, Mack, and Sabiston (2014), for example, found that self-compassionate athletes are actively engaged with the environment, take initiative, assume responsibility for their actions, emotions and thoughts, and act of their own volition—the outcome of which is an increase or maintenance in wellbeing. Following these actions may help soccer referees to make better sense of the environment in which they operate and permit a higher level of self-kindness and control resulting in decreased episodes of chronic self-criticism and performance failure-based depression.

My initial thoughts around how a Referee Mental Health Champion training intervention and role function would broadly look like were underpinned by the above. These are outlined below;

- *Training in the basic knowledge of the more "typical" signs and symptoms of referee distress and common mental disorders*
- *Communication "helping" skills training to promote issue/challenge disclosure*
- *Education around basic psychological self-help strategies and resource signposting*
- *Training in mental first aid and crisis intervention skills*
- *Education on referral practices and on local mental health support experts and/or services*

Within the training syllabus, I proposed a specific focus around; referee stress v distress, anxiety/depression, coping with injury and performance pathway transitions, dealing with bullying (including cyber bullying) and verbal abuse/aggressive behaviour, disordered eating and self-harm (including substance misuse and other addictions). It was proposed that an initial cohort of 15 regionally based Referee Mental Health Champions would be recruited and trained. This would allow for an adequate pilot study in which to explore any preliminary impact of the project content and delivery.

The proposed Referee Mental Health Champion attributes, tasks and role description were outlined to the NSA Referee Workforce Manager as being;

- *To work within their Regional SA to support its referees to improve their mental health*
- *To provide appropriate first-line support to referees who are experiencing mental health challenges*

The Mental Health Champions would;

- *Be appointed by the NSA Referee Department through a written EOI and interview process.*
- *Have some lived experience of a mental health problem, either personally or from a close relative or friend or through their professional—occupational experiences.*
- *Have an open and non-judgmental attitude.*
- *Adopt a positive, patient and supportive approach towards supporting referees with mental health problems.*
- *Be a positive role model*
- *Behave in a professional, confidential and non-discriminatory manner*
- *Have an appreciation for, and understanding of, the unique demands and pressures associated with Refereeing across the various game/performance pathway levels*

- *Support NSA mental health and wellbeing awareness campaigns*
- *Provide appropriate mental health first aid support*
- *Be an available point of contact for any referee experiencing mental health problems*
- *Encourage and promote conversations about mental health across their referee community*
- *Have or make links with mental health organisations in their local community*
- *Ideally have a Mental Health First Aid Training qualification (2 days or equivalent)*

Mental Health Champions would be expected to;

- *Undertake their activities in accord with ethical practice and within their own "comfort" level of competence—This includes an explicit recognition that they would not act as a psychotherapeutic practitioner providing formal therapeutic support.*
- *Provide an advisory role to the NSA Referee Department on referee mental health issue trends.*
- *Provide support to other Champions (All Champions will be supervised by a Suitably Trained and Registered Practitioner Psychologist who will provide ongoing group and individual supervision, support and guidance).*

In essence the role of the Mental Health Champion was characterised by support of referees, referee and local service engagement, referee practice community information sharing, talking openly about referee mental health vulnerability and soccer referee mental health and wellbeing advocacy.

Case-Study Outcome Analysis

While the implementation of this proposal has yet to be actioned, appreciation for how its impact may be evaluated is important to demonstrate early organisational accountability and practice community benefits. A review of best practice in this area suggested that prior to implementation the duration and frequency of the programme needed to be established with clear goals linked to specific outcomes. It was proposed that an initial pilot intervention would be conducted across one full season with a small select group of regional referee associations taking part. Initial participation would be based on an expression of interest application to the National Referee Workforce Manager.

The goals of a pilot intervention were proposed as being two-fold. First, as a means to evaluate the more operational process aspects in order to identity any constraints to its wider dissemination. Second, to explore early impact indicators evidencing improvements in referee quality of life and wellbeing, referee practice community (re) engagement, participation and performance.

A review of previous published mental wellbeing impact assessments of peer mental health support programmes highlighted that evaluations should be carried out by an external, independent evaluator in consultation with the peer support team and must include qualitative and quantitative feedback (Byrom, 2018; Campos, Sousa,

Rodrigues, Marques, Queirós, & Dores, 2016). A suitable external "Expert" with a sustained background in Mental Wellbeing Impact Assessment Methodology and Reporting was proposed to the Referee Workforce Manager to carry out an evaluation of the pilot study. In investigating initial impact, it was envisioned that consideration would be given to evaluating:

- any policy suggestions or developments aimed at helping to prevent mental health / wellbeing issues becoming problems for soccer referees
- the perceived frequency and quality of any peer referee mental health support implemented
- the availability and role demands experienced by the referee mental health champions
- the perceived and actual ease referees experienced in terms of accessing a referee wellbeing champion for help with their particular problem
- the processes, appropriateness, usefulness and frequency of referrals/signposting to mental health professionals
- the ease of availability, and perceived usefulness of education material on developing referee mental health protective factors (resiliency/coping skills/coping resources)
- the frequency and perceived benefits online training module use around referee core wellbeing/positive sport psychology in resilience, mindfulness, emotional wellbeing and mental health literacy.

Referee Mental Health Champion reflective accounts and interviews were suggested as a method to evaluate the education component of the proposed intervention. This would be actioned through exploring changes in soccer referee practice community "insight," knowledge, contextual awareness and referee practice around soccer referee mental health literacy and peer-to-peer support practice. This would be supported by a quantitative measure to explore changes in their Mental Health Literacy. A pre-training questionnaire would be used to assess prior knowledge of and attitudes towards referee mental health and wellbeing. Some within-training mental health quizzes could be used to track changes in level of mental health literacy across the training experience. Participants would be expected to complete a post-course evaluation on both content and delivery. Post their first peer-to-peer support intervention, referee mental health champions would be required to share a brief case study write-up and undertake a reflective discussion with the Supervising Practitioner Psychologist (Mental Health Professional) and Peer Support Worker colleagues.

Case-Study Reflections

My sport psychology practice philosophy for over 15 years has been about the development and support of the person beyond that of their pure athlete identity. My sport psychology consultancy, in the main, has focused on the application of psychotherapeutic counselling interventions with athletes experiencing mental health difficulties or illness. By its nature my work has tended therefore to be one-on-one and heavily influenced by my background in Nursing and Counselling Psychology. Beyond this professional/academic training context my practice has been further developed, refined and positively influenced by a personal lived experience of mental illness.

I am a sport psychologist who lives with clinical depression and anxiety and it has only been in relatively recent times that I have been prepared to appropriately disclose this within my consultancy. What changed for me as a result of this piece of work and other activities I have undertaken around mental health literacy training was a commitment for me to model the behaviour/attitude I wanted to see in the athletes (Sport Communities) I was working with. I needed to not only "talk-the-talk" of mental health issues in sport but also now felt that through my own disclosure (when appropriate) of living with mental illness and mental health difficulties/challenges, I could uniquely contribute to the development of sporting culture that accepts mental issue challenges as typical and manageable.

As sport psychologists, we predominantly define our role within a performance-focused environment working on improving athletic/team performance and perhaps do not routinely consider the significant role we can play in influencing broader governing body policies and in facilitating wider athlete mental health and wellbeing promotion activities. The challenge for me through the experience of this case study was to move beyond engaging in a one-on-one therapeutic change process and into the adoption of a more "ecological" model of cultural/organisational change. I was also conscious that it was important that I did not come across too strongly as an "activist" on a "crusade" but rather that I presented as a well informed and evidence-based sport psychologist consultant. Therefore I needed to communicate the impact evidence for what I was proposing and not just make the moral—overtly emotional argument for change.

As someone with a previous background of working as a National Referee Development Manager for a National Governing Sporting Body I should have been more aware of the organisational challenges in promoting a "new" intervention within this context. My experience of such organisations is that the various levels of professional and volunteer "oversight" administrative policy-making groups make it very difficult to smoothly progress any new initiative, and certainly within a timely manner. From my experience referee department functions are often the least recognised, understood and represented across the NGBs of Sport.

In an attempt to make sense of this and as a means by which to curtail my sense of frustration with the levels of bureaucratic decision-making bodies, I had to remind myself of the historical context of referee associations traditionally growing "outside" of the sport governing body. My experience of Referee Associations is that they exist within varying degrees of NFA independence. This may have resulted in a soccer-wide culture where referees were perceived by the game as somewhat insular and separate from those within the NGB responsible for Game Development functions. Any soccer community (NFA) changes therefore did not perhaps appropriately recognise nor consider the impact of any game-wide change on the wellbeing/performance demands placed on the refereeing role.

My experience of getting this proposal from the Referee Practice Community Endorsement phase to NSA acceptance proved problematic. While accepted and recognised as a positive and indeed much needed initiative by the Referee Practice Community representative body, its endorsement for implementation through the NSA, was stalled for two main reasons. The first was an organisational Human Resources based concern that the establishment of an NSA endorsed and managed group of referee peer-to-peer mental health and wellbeing supporters would in some way place the NSA at an unacceptable risk of reputational harm. I have been aware, through my athlete mental health advisory role to NGBs in Sport, that this concern was certainly not an isolated one. It was an argument first rehearsed when the corporate world was challenged around its Mental Wellbeing and Mental Health support practices. However as mental health literacy and mental health workforce advocacy improved there was a realignment of workplace wellbeing duty of care. As mentioned, I am heavily involved as a specialist in athlete mental health in this very same process with governing bodies of sport. I felt the intervention I proposed aligned with current corporate good practice and workforce duty of care responsibility. My response to the HR NSA concern was to highlight this and to further suggest that the greatest reputational risk to their organisation would actually come from a failure to recognise the broader mental health duty of care that all sport NGBs need to demonstrate in order to best service the needs of the game and those upon whom the game depends, including referees. Reflecting on this I should have presented this case personally and directly in front of the NFA higher-level decision-makers. To do this I should have been more prepared to engage a wider range of within organisation proposal allies and also to consider at a more strategic level how best to lobby for the actioning of the proposal. I have no doubt that I would have found this incredibly challenging, I am confident and safe working directly one-on-one, moving from this into a "corporate" strategic influencing space was a direct threat to my perceived level of expertise and sport psychologist consultancy skill set.

The second barrier and one where I have some sympathy was a legitimate desire for the NSA to consider implementing a "whole" soccer community approach to mental health awareness and support instead of an initial focus on just referees. Provided this moves beyond pure rhetoric, and or a tick-box approach, and ensures the principles of the International Society of Sport Psychology position statement on sport participant mental health are adopted, then this would be a welcome and significant move. I believe sport psychologists have a strong advocacy role to play in influencing and advising National Soccer Associations as to a "Duty of Care Charter" that ensures all in soccer including the referees receive a comprehensive mental health and wellbeing induction process, with ongoing support availability. On reflection, this perhaps would have been the best and most effective starting point for the proposed intervention within this chapter. The development of such a charter, agreed by the NSA, would have proved a valuable "psychological" contract by which to more clearly scaffold my proposed intervention.

The proposal I presented was at the very least a vehicle through which Referee Practice Community mental health vulnerability could be highlighted and discussed at a National Soccer Body level. The proposal was evidence-based and explicit in reporting current referee CMD prevalence rates. It demonstrated a clear need and articulated an intervention that was framed upon considered good practice from mental health research and support practices from both within and outside of sport.

I have presented the need for a game-wide cultural shift in the way the role of the referee should be considered. In order to better protect referee wellbeing, I believe the game requires a more realistic view of referee decision-making, with an overall referee performance assessment process that recognises decision "acceptability" rather than "accuracy" alone. Those working to support referees, including sport psychologists, can play a significant advocacy role working to create an environment which actively acknowledges that periods of mental vulnerability in referees is "typical" and "manageable" and not a defining character flaw of the individual. It will only be through the provision of adequate psychological support resources that promote a referee "collective" and individual referee resilience and efficacy, that referees will learn to "thrive" through challenging periods better ensuring on-field performance success and mental health and wellbeing (King, Newman, & Luthans, 2016).

Summary and Conclusions

There is a perceived sense within the refereeing community of a lack of organisational understanding of mental health vulnerability. This has been reinforced by the limited availability of resources targeted at improving the mental health protective factors in referees through appropriate training, education, and support. As a consequence, referees have been left to "mentally sink or swim"—those who are able to connect with a meaningful peer support network and or have the necessary coping resources (developed through a "hidden" personal experience curriculum) learn to cope and in many cases thrive. Those who do not are lost to a game they once loved. The harsh reality is that too many soccer referees are walking away from the game as they see this as the only viable means to protect or improve their mental health and wellbeing. Everyone within the soccer community has a responsibility to help close the "empathy gap" and show referees that disclosing a mental health issue is not a weakness but a sign of strength and deserving of support.

Key Messages and Further Readings

1. There remains a lack of perceived national soccer association support for referees experiencing mental health difficulties.
2. Soccer referees will only talk and seek/accept the help they deserve if all involved in soccer demonstrate an empathy and mental health literacy that permits such discussions.
3. Referees deserve to operate in a game culture that views mental health issue disclosure as a sign of strength, as something that is manageable and not a defining character flaw of the individual.
4. There needs to be a culture within soccer that accepts referee vulnerability and promotes referee help-seeking behaviour and early access to readily available support.
5. National Soccer Associations need to acknowledge and commit to a "Duty of Care Charter" that ensures referees receive a comprehensive mental health and wellbeing induction process, with ongoing peer support availability. Establishing a Duty of Care Charter, which

sets out how referees can expect to be treated and where they can go for mental health advice, support, and guidance, is a moral imperative.

Atkinson, M. (2019). Sport, mental illness and sociology. In *Research in the sociology of sport (Vol. 11)*. Bingley: Emerald Publishing.

Breslin, G., & Leavey, G. (2019). *Mental health and well-being interventions in sport: Research, theory and practice*. New York, NY: Routledge.

Gouttebarge, V., Johnson, U., Rochcongar, P., Rosier, P., & Kerkhoffs, G. (2017). Symptoms of common mental disorders among professional football referees: A one-season prospective study across Europe. *The Physician and Sports Medicine, 45*, 11–16.

Kilic, Ö., Johnson, U., Kerkhoffs, G. M. M. J., Rosier, P., & Gouttebarge, V. (2018). Exposure to physical and psychosocial stressors in relation to symptoms of common mental disorders among European professional football referees: A prospective cohort study. *BMJ Open Sport & Exercise Medicine, 4*, 1–5.

Henriksen, K., Schinke, R., Moesch, K., McCann, S., Parham, W. D., Hvid Larsen, C., & Terry, P. (2019). Consensus statement on improving the mental health of high performance athletes. *International Journal of Sport and Exercise Psychology*. Advanced online publication. Retrieved from https://doi:10.1080/1612197X.2019.1570473

References

Bernal, C., Nix, C., & Boatwright, D. (2012). Sport officials' longevity: Passion and motivation for the sport. *International Journal of Sport Management Recreation & Tourism, 10*, 28–39.

Bluth, K., Campo, R. A., Futch, W. S., & Gaylord, S. A. (2017). Age and gender differences in the associations of self-compassion and emotional well-being in a large adolescent sample. *Journal of Youth and Adolescence, 46*, 40–85.

Breslin, G., Shannon, S., Haughey, T., Donnolly, P., & Leavey, G. (2017). A systematic review of interventions to increase awareness of mental health and well-being in athletes, coaches and officials. *Systematic Reviews, 6*, 1–15.

Byrom, N. (2018). An evaluation of a peer support intervention for student mental health. *Journal of Mental Health, 27*, 240–256.

Campos, F., Sousa, A., Rodrigues, V., Marques A., Queirós, C., & Dores, A. (2016). Practical guidelines for peer support programmes for mental health problems. *Revista de Psiquiatría y Salud Mental, 9*, 97–110.

Corrado, D., Pellarin, E., & Agostini, T. (2011). The phenomenon of social influence on the football pitch: Social pressure from the crowd on referees' decisions. *Review of Psychology, 18*, 33–36.

Dell, C., Gervis, M., & Rhind, D. (2016). Factors influencing soccer referee's intentions to quit the game. *Soccer & Society, 17*, 109–119.

Ferguson, L. J., Kowalski, K. C., Mack, D. E., & Sabiston, C. M. (2014). Exploring self- compassion and eudaimonic well-being in young women athletes. *Journal of Sport & Exercise Psychology, 36*, 203–216.

Fong, M., & Loi, N. M. (2016). The mediating role of self-compassion in student psychological health. *Australian Psychologist, 51*, 431–441.

Gulliver, A., Griffiths, K., & Christensen, H. (2012). Barriers and facilitators to mental health help-seeking for young elite athletes: A qualitative study. *BMC Psychiatry, 12*, 157–171.

Johansen, B. (2014). Reasons for officiating soccer: the role of passion-based motivations among Norwegian elite and non-elite referees. *Movement and Sports Sciences – Science et Motricite. 10*, 1–8.

Johansen, B., & Haugen, T. (2013). Anxiety level and decision-making among Norwegian top-class soccer referees. International Journal of Sport and Exercise Psychology, 11, 215–226.

King, D., Newman, A., & Luthans, F. (2016). Not if, but when we need resilience in the work place. *Journal of Organizational Behavior, 37*, 782–786.

McEvoy, S. (May 14, 2018). How do you release the tension around refereeing big games? Drink lots of beer! Mark Clattenburg admits turning to alcohol after matches. *The Daily Mail*. Retrieved from www.dailymail.co.uk

O'Hagan, M., Cyr, C., McKee, H., & Priest, R. (2010). Making the case for peer support. *Peer Support, 92*, 26–56.

Petracovschi, S., Mureşan, H., & Timişoara, S. (2010). Refereeing and the perspectives of a career in football. *Physical Education and Rehabilitation Journal, 4*, 418–430.

Samuel, R. D., Galily, Y., & Tenenbaum, G. (2017). Who are you, ref? Defining the soccer referee's career using a change-based perspective. *Journal of Sport and Exercise Psychology, 15*, 118–130.

Slack, L., Maynard, I. W., Butt, J., & Olusoga, P. (2013). Factors underpinning football officiating excellence: Perceptions of English premier league referees. *Journal of Applied Sport Psychology, 25*, 298–315.

Sutcliffe, M., & Matheson, R. (2018). Developing social integration. In R. Matheson, S. Tangey & M. Sutcliffe (Eds.), *Transition in, through and out of higher education: International case studies and best practice* (pp. 139–165). Abingdon, Oxon: Routledge.

Voight, M. (2009). Sources of stress and coping strategies of US soccer officials. *Stress and Health, 25*, 91–101.

Webb, H. (2017). *The man in the middle: The autobiography of the world cup final referee*. London: Simon & Schuster.

Webb, T., Cleland, J., & O'Gorman, J. (2017). The distribution of power through a media campaign: The respect program, referees, and abuse in association football. *Journal of Global Sport Management, 2*, 162–181.

Webb, T., Dicks, M., Thelwell, R., van der Kamp, J., & Rix-Lievre, G. (In press). An analysis of soccer referee experiences in France and the Netherlands: Abuse, conflict, and level of support. *Sport Management Review*.

Zeman, T., Voborny, J., Benus, R., & Blahutkova, M. (2014). Analysis of subjective psychological experiences and states of football referees. *International Journal of Science, Culture and Sport, 2*, 69–76.

20
STRESS, BURNOUT, AND PERFECTIONISM IN SOCCER PLAYERS

Esmie P. Smith, Andrew P. Hill, Sarah H. Mallinson-Howard, and Henrik Gustafsson

Brief Introduction and Review of Literature

Pursuing and maintaining a career as a professional soccer player is stressful. The journey to become a professional soccer player starts with formal registration to a club's academy from the age of 9 years old. Thereafter, players undergo increasingly demanding training and regular reviews to secure their place at the club. The decision as to whether a player is awarded a professional contract is normally made when the player is aged 18 to 23 years old, representing in some cases 14 years of investment. With less than 1% of academy players achieving professional status, the process is fiercely competitive and most who start the journey are unsuccessful (Green, 2009). For those who make it into the professional team, they will typically have the security of only a two-year contract or less. Over a third will move club every season, often leaving their families to join clubs in different parts of the country or sometimes abroad. And, in all, their career will typically last only eight years after which most will need to seek alternative employment with minimum education or training in any area other than soccer (FIFPro, 2016; Roderick & Schumacker, 2016).

With these circumstances in mind, the aim of this chapter is to provide an overview of stress and burnout processes in soccer and explain why some soccer players are more susceptible to the development of stress and burnout than others. We first define and describe stress and burnout, and then we review research examining burnout in soccer players. Thereafter, we define and describe perfectionism, a common personality trait among athletes, and highlight how this trait may place soccer players at greater risk to burnout. This includes a review of research that has examined the relationship between perfectionism and burnout in soccer players. Finally, we provide an illustrative case study of how perfectionism fuelled burnout can manifest in soccer and how it was managed by a sport psychologist.

Stress as a Process

There are several different ways to understand stress. One of the most popular in psychology is the transactional model of stress (TMS; Lazarus & Folkman, 1984). In this model, "stress" is not a specific outcome or emotion. It is an internal psychological process that governs emotional experiences more broadly. To be "stressed" denotes the activation of this process and the experience of a range of unpleasant emotions (e.g., anxiety, fear, and frustration). A number of key concepts are important to understanding stress as a process. The term "stressor" is used to identify an event or situation that can trigger the stress process (Lazarus, 1991). "Appraisal" corresponds with a personal, typically unconscious, evaluation of the significance and consequences of the demands associated with the stressor. And, finally, "coping" refers to the specific strategies that are deployed to deal with demands. There are a wide range of different coping strategies that people can use, but coping strategies can broadly be categorised as emotion-focused (how we attempt to manage our emotions), problem-focused (how we attempt to remove a stressor), or avoidant (how we attempt to avoid or escape a stressor) (Lazarus & Folkman, 1984).

In terms of the sequence of events in the stress process, when a stressor occurs the appraisal process begins. There are two types of appraisal that take place. First, primary appraisal takes place to ascertain if a stressor is irrelevant, positive, negative, or harmful (e.g., "Is losing this match important to my goals?"). Next, if the stressor has personally meaningful consequences, secondary appraisal takes place so to ascertain available coping resources to deal with the stressor (e.g., "Do I have the ability to perform how I want to or how I am expected to?") (Lazarus, 1991). What kind of coping strategies are deployed depends on the appraisal of resources, with problem-focused coping normally used when resources are high and avoidant coping normally used when resources are low. Although what determines if individuals are successful in their attempts to cope is complex, problem-focused coping is typically regarded to be a better way of coping than avoidant coping and emotion-focused coping when utilised regularly (Biggs, Brough, & Drummond, 2017).

It is important to note that experiencing stress is part of everyday life and is not problematic for most people. In accord, many soccer players will successfully cope with the stressors they encounter, whereas others will not. The stress process takes into account this individuality in the way in which appraisal is influenced by an individual's values, goals, and beliefs. As these can be different for everyone, the personal meaning and significance of any event will also differ from person to person, as will perceptions of personal resources. This means that two individuals can respond quite differently to the same event. That said, there are events and personality characteristics that are more likely to make most people prone to stress. For instance, research has found that certain stressors are common among soccer players and include performance demands (e.g., making mistakes), team issues (e.g., relationships with teammates), coach issues (e.g., coaches personality), and practical issues (e.g., travel management) (Holt & Hogg, 2002; Kristiansen, Murphy, & Roberts, 2012; Reeves, Nicholls, & McKenna, 2011). It is consideration of these environmental factors and the different characteristics of the soccer players themselves that helps us identify who is more susceptible to stress and its consequences.

Athlete Burnout and Burnout in Soccer Players

One consequence of long-term stress is athlete burnout. Burnout was first studied in organisational psychology (e.g., Maslach, 1993). The relevance of burnout to sport was first recognised by Raedeke (1997; Raedeke & Smith, 2001), and it has since become a popular area of research for sport psychologists (see Gustafsson, DeFreese, & Madigan, 2017). Raedeke (1997) proposed that athlete burnout is characterised by three core symptoms: physical and emotional exhaustion, a reduced sense of accomplishment, and sport devaluation. In regard to these symptoms, physical and emotional exhaustion is fatigue that is experienced beyond that which would arise because of the typical demands of sport participation. When this symptom is high, athletes feel sapped of energy and have difficulty recovering a sense of vigour. A reduced sense of accomplishment, by contrast, is the perception of feeling inadequate and ineffective. Athletes perceive that they are consistently performing below their capabilities or unable to reach their goals, regardless of their actual success. Finally, sport devaluation is a decreased interest in sport participation. This is when athletes develop cynical attitude and resentment towards their sport and may choose to drop out.

In terms of understanding how these symptoms develop, Smith (1986) has produced one of the best supported models of athlete burnout. In this model, athlete burnout is the result of chronic "overload" in the stress process. Mirroring the stress process, burnout includes the long-standing experience of high environmental stressors (high competitive demands, low social support, low autonomy, and low rewards) and low resources (perceived or actual insufficient skills/ability to cope with demands). The appraisals involved in burnout reflect a sense of being overwhelmed by demands with little means to manage them effectively or gain any respite. The three core symptoms of burnout themselves are actually part of a broader psychological response in the stress process that includes a range of negative emotions (e.g., anxiety and anger), physiological reactions (e.g., fatigue, insomnia, and illness susceptibility), and behavioural signs (e.g., decreased performance and avoidant coping strategies).

The prevalence of burnout in sport and soccer is currently unknown. This is because there has been no systematic attempt to estimate the number of athletes or soccer players exhibiting burnout and its symptoms in existing studies. However, for this chapter we collated all studies that have examined burnout in soccer. To do so we conducted a computerised search of published research using the databases PsycINFO, PsycARTICLES, MEDLINE, and SPORT-Discus. The search terms were burnout *and* soccer. The search date was between January 1990 and December 2018. The search was limited to peer-review journals published in English. The search produced 54 studies. The abstract of each study was reviewed, and studies were removed that did not provide an empirical examination of burnout exclusively in soccer players or were duplicates. The number of studies was reduced to $k = 17$. There was one further published peer-review article that we were aware of but that was not retrieved through the review (Smith, Hill, & Hall, 2018); with the addition of this article, the total number of studies included in the review was $k = 18$. Information provided in Table 20.1 is from these published articles.

Most studies we identified used the Athlete Burnout Questionnaire (ABQ; Raedeke & Smith, 2001) to measure burnout. This is a self-report questionnaire that has five questions for each of the three symptoms. Each question is measured on a five-point scale that indicates how often an athlete experiences a symptom: 1 = "almost never," 2 = "rarely," 3 = "sometimes," 4 = "frequently," and 5 = "almost always." To interpret the questionnaire, an average total burnout score and an average score for each symptom are calculated. There is no cut-off or threshold for the questionnaire that signals when an athlete has burned out. Therefore, in Table 20.1 we have reported the percentage of athletes that report an average of 3 out of 5 and 4 out of 5 (i.e., soccer players who reported experiencing symptoms "sometimes" and "frequently"). We adopted this approach for all other instruments too.

When examining the prevalence of total burnout across studies, it was found that the percentage of athletes who typically reported experiencing total burnout *sometimes* was 7.1% (range <1% to 18.4%) and *frequently* was <1% (range 0% to 1.4%). When observing the individual burnout symptoms, it was found that the percentage of athletes who typically report experiencing exhaustion *sometimes* was 18.4% (range <1% to 38.6%) and *frequently* was 2.2% (range 0% to 6.3%). The percentage of athletes who typically report experiencing reduced accomplishment *sometimes* was 14.8% (<1% to 44.0%) and *frequently* was <1% (0% and 4.9%). Finally, the percentage of athletes who typically report experiencing sport devaluation *sometimes* was 7.9% (<1% and 32.6%) and *frequently* was <1% (0% to 1.8%). These figures reveal that burnout is not especially common but, nonetheless, can be observed to some degree in most groups of soccer players.

TABLE 20.1 A summary of research examining burnout in soccer players ($k = 18$)

Study	Sample	Burnout prevalence					Instru.	Criterion variable	BO r	RA r	EE r	DEV R
			M	SD	Sometimes (%)	Frequently (%)						
Adie, Duda, and Ntoumanis (2012)	91 male junior soccer academy players ($M = 13.82$; $SD = 1.99$)	Exhaustion (T1)	1.91	0.76	7.64	0.30	ABQ	Autonomy support (T1)	—	—	−.25	—
								Autonomy (T1)	—	—	−.03	—
								Competence (T1)	—	—	−.05	—
								Relatedness (T1)	—	—	−.11	—
								Subjective vitality (T1)	—	—	−**.31**	—
		Exhaustion (T2)	2.03	0.85	12.71	1.02		Autonomy support (T2)	—	—	−.21	—
								Autonomy (T2)	—	—	−.04	—
								Competence (T2)	—	—	−.18	—
								Relatedness (T2)	—	—	−.10	—
								Subjective vitality (T2)	—	—	−**.32**	—
		Exhaustion (T3)	2.31	1.01	24.83	4.75		Autonomy support (T3)	—	—	−**.30**	—
								Autonomy (T3)	—	—	−.07	—
								Competence (T3)	—	—	−**.32**	—
								Relatedness (T3)	—	—	−.17	—
								Subjective vitality (T3)	—	—	−**.25**	—
		Exhaustion (T4)	2.31	1.01	24.83	4.75		Autonomy support (T4)	—	—	−.06	—
								Autonomy (T4)	—	—	.01	—
								Competence (T4)	—	—	.03	—
								Relatedness (T4)	—	—	−.09	—
								Subjective vitality (T4)	—	—	−.07	—
		Exhaustion (T5)	2.36	0.98	25.78	4.75		Autonomy support (T5)	—	—	−.22	—
								Autonomy (T5)	—	—	−.07	—
								Competence (T5)	—	—	−.14	—

(*Continued*)

TABLE 20.1 (Continued)

Study	Sample	Burnout prevalence					Instru.	Criterion variable	BO r	RA r	EE r	DEV R
			M	SD	Sometimes (%)	Frequently (%)						
		Exhaustion (T6)	2.24	0.89	19.77	2.39		Relatedness (T5)	—	—	−.39	—
								Subjective vitality (T5)	—	—	−.18	—
								Autonomy support (T6)	—	—	−.34	—
								Autonomy (T6)	—	—	−.12	—
								Competence (T6)	—	—	−.14	—
								Relatedness (T6)	—	—	−.18	—
								Subjective vitality (T6)	—	—	−.38	—
Balaguer et al. (2012)	725 male junior soccer academy players (M =12.57; SD =0.54)	Burnout (T1)	1.89	0.70	5.59	0.13	Spanish-ABQ	Autonomy support (T1)	−.24	—	—	—
								Controlling style (T1)	.38	—	—	—
								Need satisfaction (T1)	−.34	—	—	—
								Need thwarting (T1)	.53	—	—	—
								Subjective vitality (T1)	−.16	—	—	—
		Burnout (T2)	1.98	0.75	8.69	0.36		Autonomy support (T2)	−.33	—	—	—
								Controlling style (T2)	.40	—	—	—
								Need satisfaction (T2)	−.38	—	—	—
								Need thwarting (T2)	.59	—	—	—
								Subjective vitality (T2)	−.19	—	—	—
Cheval, Chalabaev, Quested, Courvoisier, and Sarrazin (2017)	110 male junior soccer academy players (M =16.54; SD = 1.99)	Burnout (T1)	2.27	0.47	6.06	0.01	French-ABQ	No bivariate correlations reported	—	—	—	—

Study	Sample	Variable	M	SD			Measure	Correlate			
Curran, Appleton, Hill, and Hall (2011)	149 male junior soccer academy players (M =16.20; SD = 2.00)	Burnout (T2) Burnout (T3) Reduced Accomplishment	2.16 2.18 2.15	0.46 0.50 0.67	3.36 5.05 10.20	0.00 0.01 0.29	ABQ	Harmonious passion	—	−.31	−.08	−.27
Curran, Appleton, Hill, and Hall (2013)	173 male junior soccer academy players (M =15.46; SD = 1.47)	Exhaustion Devaluation Burnout	2.46 1.63 2.00	0.86 0.73 0.55	26.43 3.01 3.44	3.67 0.06 0.01	ABQ	Obsessive passion Self-determination index Harmonious passion	— — −.17	−.25 −.54 −.21	−.02 −.39 −.12	−.29 −.54 −.09
		Reduced Accomplishment Exhaustion Devaluation	2.10 2.37 1.59	0.62 0.70 0.72	7.35 18.41 2.10	0.11 0.99 0.04		Obsessive passion Need satisfaction	−.07 −.42	−.13 −.57	−.00 −.21	−.04 −.31
Gonzalez, Garcia-Merita, Castillo, and Balaguer (2016)	360 male junior soccer academy players (M =12.60; SD =0.53)	Burnout (T1)	1.88	0.70	5.48	0.12	Spanish-ABQ	No bivariate correlations reported	—	—	—	—
Gonzalez, Tomas, Castillo, Duda, and Balaguer (2017)	725 male junior soccer academy players (M =12.57; SD =0.54)†	Burnout (T2) Burnout (T3) Burnout (T4) Burnout (T2)	1.89 1.85 2.01 1.98	0.70 0.68 0.80 0.75	5.59 4.55 10.75 8.69	0.13 0.08 0.64 0.36	Spanish-ABQ	Autonomy support (T1) [a]	−.20	—	—	—

(Continued)

TABLE 20.1 (Continued)

Study	Sample		Burnout prevalence				Instru.	Criterion variable	BO r	RA r	EE r	DEV R
			M	SD	Sometimes (%)	Frequently (%)						
Gustafsson, Skoog, Podlog, Lundqvist, and Wagnsson (2013)	238 junior soccer academy players (30% females; $M = 17.0$; $SD = 0.90$)	Reduced Accomplishment	2.36	0.71	18.41	1.04	Swedish-ABQ	Controlling style (T1) [a]	.37	—	—	—
								Autonomy satisfaction (T2)	-.29	—	—	—
								Competence satisfaction (T2)	-.28	—	—	—
								Relatedness satisfaction (T2)	-.34	—	—	—
								Autonomy thwarting (T2)	.47	—	—	—
								Competence thwarting (T2)	.58	—	—	—
								Relatedness thwarting (T2)	.52	—	—	—
								Subjective vitality (T2)	-.19	—	—	—
								Hope	—	-.48	-.27	-.40
		Exhaustion	2.33	0.83	20.90	2.22		Perceived stress	—	.57	.58	.55
		Devaluation	2.10	0.85	14.46	1.25		Positive affect	—	-.45	-.42	-.47
								Negative affect	—	.33	.36	.31
Hill (2013)	171 male junior soccer academy players ($M= 16.17$; $SD= 1.57$)	Burnout	2.16	0.55	6.30	0.04	ABQ	Personal standards perfectionism	-.23	-.33	-.03	-.22

		Reduced Accomplishment	2.28	0.60	11.51		Evaluative concerns perfectionism	.29	.22	.27	.23
		Exhaustion	2.45	0.69	21.19	1.22					
		Devaluation	1.74	0.70	3.59	0.06					
Hill, Hall, Appleton, and Kozub (2008)	151 male junior soccer academy players ($M = 14.40$; $SD = 2.40$)	Reduced Accomplishment	2.35	0.69	17.36	0.84	ABQ	Self-oriented perfectionism	—	−.39	−.25	−.42
		Exhaustion	2.28	0.81	18.67	1.70		Socially prescribed perfectionism	—	.46	.41	.40
		Devaluation	1.86	0.92	10.75	0.99		Unconditional self-acceptance	—	−.19	−.31	−.15
								Satisfaction with goal progress	—	−.47	−.29	−.43
Lai and Wiggins (2003) ††	73 adult amateur soccer players (53% females; $M = 19.38$; $SD = 1.45$)	Burnout (T1)	2.09	0.52	4.09	0.01	BIA	Age (T1)	.12	—	—	—
								Years playing soccer (T1)	.22	—	—	—
								Years of competitive soccer (T1)	.20	—	—	—
		Burnout (T2)	2.05	0.47	2.12	0.00		Years of club soccer (T1)	.20	—	—	—
								Age (T2)	−.08	—	—	—
								Years playing soccer (T2)	.20	—	—	—
								Years of competitive soccer (T2)	.14	—	—	—
		Burnout (T3)	2.15	0.58	7.08	0.07		Years of club soccer (T2)	.08	—	—	—
								Age (T3)	.12	—	—	—
								Years playing soccer (T3)	**.33**	—	—	—
								Years of competitive soccer (T3)	.08	—	—	—

(*Continued*)

TABLE 20.1 (Continued)

Study	Sample		Burnout prevalence				Instru.	Criterion variable	BO r	RA r	EE r	DEV R
			M	SD	Sometimes (%)	Frequently (%)						
		Burnout (T4)	2.21	0.70	12.92	0.52		Years of club soccer (T3)	**.28**	—	—	—
								Age (T4)	.08	—	—	—
								Years playing soccer (T4)	.22	—	—	—
								Years of competitive soccer (T4)	.07	—	—	—
								Years of club soccer (T4)	.17	—	—	—
		Burnout (T5)	2.31	0.76	18.41	1.36		Age (T5)	.09	—	—	—
								Years playing soccer (T5)	**.28**	—	—	—
								Years of competitive soccer (T5)	.14	—	—	—
								Years of club soccer (T5)	**.24**	—	—	—
Li, Ivarsson, Stenling, and Wu (2018)	10 male adult blind Paralympic soccer players ($M = 24.80$; $SD = 2.53$)	Burnout[Av]	1.51	0.46	0.06	0.00	ABQ	No bivariate correlations reported	—	—	—	—
Lopes Verardi et al. (2014, 2015)	71 male adult professional soccer players ($M = 22.77$; $SD = 3.98$)	Reduced Accomplishment	2.08	0.50	3.29	0.01	Portuguese-ABQ	No outcome variables reported	—	—	—	
		Exhaustion	1.91	0.52	1.79	0.00						
		Devaluation	1.77	0.64	2.74	0.03						

	63 male junior amateur soccer players (M=17.18; SD=0.84)	Reduced Accomplishment	2.07	0.39	0.87	0.00		
	193 female junior amateur soccer players (M=16.10; SD=1.10)	Exhaustion	1.87	0.44	0.51	0.00		
		Devaluation	1.70	0.53	0.71	0.00		
		Reduced Accomplishment	2.56	0.87	30.50	4.85	MBI	Perceived competence	—	−.51	−.22	−.33
Price and Weiss (2000) ††		Exhaustion	2.59	0.92	32.64	6.30		Anxiety	—	.67	.39	.36
		Devaluation	2.11	0.90	16.11	1.79		Enjoyment	—	−.48	−.31	−.64
								Training and instruction	—	−.20	−.05	−.12
								Democratic	—	−.32	−.32	−.24
								Autocratic	—	.20	.19	.22
								Social support	—	−.11	−.14	−.09
								Positive feedback	—	−.27	−.13	−.24
	162 male junior soccer academy players (M=16.15; SD=1.84)	Reduced Accomplishment (T1)	2.16	0.64	9.51	0.20	ABQ	Self-oriented perfectionism (T1)	—	−.25	−.32	−.40
Smith, Hill, and Hall, (2018)		Exhaustion (T1)	2.05	0.70	8.69	0.26		Socially prescribed perfectionism (T1)	—	.27	.24	.16
		Devaluation (T1)	1.55	0.51	0.23	0.00		Depressive symptoms (T1)	—	.51	.44	.44
		Reduced Accomplishment (T2)	2.18	0.64	10.03	0.23		Self-oriented perfectionism (T2)	—	−.17	−.16	−.19
		Exhaustion (T2)	2.02	0.75	9.51	0.41		Socially prescribed perfectionism (T2)	—	.09	.26	.27
		Devaluation (T2)	1.52	0.61	0.75	0.00		Depressive symptoms (T2)	—	.65	.40	.53

(*Continued*)

TABLE 20.1 (Continued)

Study	Sample	Criterion variable	Burnout prevalence M	SD	Sometimes (%)	Frequently (%)	Instru.	Criterion variable	BO r	RA r	EE r	DEV R
Tabei, Fletcher, and Goodger (2012)	98 male adult semi-professional soccer players (50 = English; 48 = Japanese; M =20.25; SD =1.20)	Reduced Accomplishment[Av]	2.92	0.52	44.04	1.88	ABQ and Japanese-ABQ	No outcome variables reported	—	—	—	—
		Exhaustion[Av]	2.84	0.56	38.59	1.92						
		Devaluation[Av]	2.73	0.60	32.64	1.70						
Yildiz (2011)	107 male adult professional soccer players (M =25.70; no SD reported)	Burnout	2.47	0.57	17.62	0.36	Abbreviated BM	Marital status	−.12	—	—	—
								Age	.55	—	—	—
								Educational status	.03	—	—	—
								Professional playing experience	.53	—	—	—
								Leader-member exchange	−.44	—	—	—

Note. Instru. = instrument; BO = Burnout; RA = Reduced Accomplishment; EE = Emotional Exhaustion; DEV = Devaluation; † = same sample as Balaguer et al. (2012); †† = Statistical significance of correlations not provided in the original study. In Table 20.1 they are calculated based on sample size; [Av] = Average burnout score across time points or across samples; ABQ = Athlete Burnout Questionnaire measured on a five-point Likert scale (Raedeke & Smith, 2001); Spanish-ABQ = Spanish version of the Athlete Burnout Questionnaire measured on a five-point Likert scale (Balaguer et al., 2012); French-ABQ = French version of the Athlete Burnout Questionnaire measured on a five-point Likert scale (Isoard-Gautheur, Oger, Guillet, & Martin-Krumm, 2010); Swedish-ABQ = Swedish version of the Athlete Burnout Questionnaire measured on a five-point Likert scale (Smith, Gustafsson, & Hassmen, 2010); BIA = The Burnout Inventory for Athletes measured on a five-point Likert scale (Van Yperen, 1997); Portuguese-ABQ = Portuguese version of the Athlete Burnout Questionnaire measured on a five-point Likert scale (Pires, Brandao, & Silva, 2006); MBI = Maslach Burnout Inventory measured on a five-point Likert scale (Maslach & Jackson, 1981a, 1981b); Japanese-ABQ = Japanese version of the Athlete Burnout Questionnaire measured on a five-point Likert scale (Tabei, Fletcher, & Goodger, 2012); Abbreviated BM = ten-item Burnout Measure originally measured on a seven-point Likert scale but converted here to a five-point Likert scale with a .71 correction factor (Malach-Pines, 2005); all correlations with burnout for longitudinal studies are within time points unless otherwise indicated; [a] = correlations between burnout at time two and outcome variables measured at time one.

The studies providing evidence of prevalence also examined burnout alongside a range of other factors and in various groups. Of the 18 studies reviewed, five of the samples were adult soccer players and the rest were adolescent soccer players. Two of the five adult samples were identified as being professionals and one as being semi-professionals. Eleven of the 18 adolescent samples were from soccer academies of professional clubs. In all, 15 of the samples were all male, one was all female, and two were a mix of males and females. Regarding the factors examined, the studies typically focused on how burnout was related to (1) features of the training and performance environment created by others, particularly the coach, and (2) individual features such as personal motives for participating in soccer and other personality characteristics. We have provided the correlation coefficient between the different features and burnout symptoms in each study in Table 20.1. Correlation coefficients range from −1.00 to +1.00. A positive correlation coefficient signals that as the feature increases burnout increases, and a negative correlation coefficient signals that as the feature increases burnout decreases. Larger correlation coefficients signal stronger relationships.

Regarding features of the training and performance environment, burnout among soccer players has typically been found to be higher when they report that coaches are more controlling and autocratic. That is, when the soccer player has little or no input into decision-making. Similarly, burnout has also been found to be higher when soccer players report that coaches, teammates, and parents thwart their needs for competence (belief in personal abilities), relatedness (feeling connected to others), and autonomy (being in control of one's actions/life). By contrast, burnout has typically been found to be lower among soccer players when they report higher social support, autonomy support, and a democratic coach style. This means that when soccer players report support from others (social support), are given choice without coercion or pressure (autonomy support), and their opinions are taken into account (democratic style), burnout is less likely. Similarly, research has found that burnout is lower among soccer players when they report others are satisfying their needs of competence, relatedness, and autonomy. Finally, burnout has also been found to be lower when soccer players report receiving positive feedback and believe the coach is satisfied with their goal progress.

Regarding individual features, burnout among soccer players has been found to be lower when soccer players report higher harmonious passion (i.e., that they are choosing to take part of their own volition and due to a sense of value in the sport) and when participation is accompanied by other positive features such as enjoyment, hope, and subjective vitality (i.e., positive feelings of energy). By contrast, burnout has typically been found to be higher among soccer players when they report obsessive passion (i.e., their motives include a sense of being compelled to participate because they "have to") and when participation is accompanied by other negative features, such as stress, anxiety, and depressive symptoms. The personality characteristic that has received the most attention is perfectionism. Burnout has been found to be higher when soccer players report some aspects of perfectionism and lower when they report other aspects of perfectionism (Hill, 2014; Hill et al., 2008; Smith et al., 2018). Because of the potential importance of perfectionism, we now focus on this characteristic and the mechanisms underpinning its relationship with burnout.

Multidimensional Perfectionism

Perfectionism is a trait that is broadly defined as the pursuit of exceedingly high standards accompanied by overly critical evaluations (Frost, Marten, Lahart, & Rosenblate, 1990). In Hewitt and Flett's (1991) popular model, perfectionism comprises three dimensions: self-oriented perfectionism (SOP), socially prescribed perfectionism (SPP), and other-oriented perfectionism

(OOP). SOP is self-directed and is a requirement of perfection from the self ("I expect myself to be perfect"). Those high in SOP set their own high personal standards and adopt a harsh critical style when evaluating themselves. SPP is the perception that other people have unrealistically high standards ("Others expect me to be perfect"). Those high in SPP believe that perfectionistic standards are imposed on them, and if standards are not met, they will be subjected to harsh criticism from others. Finally, OOP is externally directed ("Others should be perfect"). Those high in OOP have unrealistic expectations for others, and when standards are not met, it leads to harsh criticism of others.

Hewitt and Flett (2002) argued that perfectionism is associated with four stress-related mechanisms. The first mechanism pertains to how perfectionism creates more stressful events by encouraging individuals to pursue unrealistic rather than appropriate goals (stress generation). The second mechanism pertains to how perfectionism contributes to a greater preoccupation with possible stressors and their personal significance (stress anticipation). The third mechanism pertains to how perfectionism can maintain and prolong stress because of a tendency to overthink and obsess during stressful episodes (stress perpetuation). The fourth and final mechanism pertains to how irrational beliefs can subvert appraisal processes so that even minor events are considered monumentally important, mistakes are considered indicative of profound personal flaws, and coping becomes avoidant and ineffective (stress enhancement). Given the close association of stress and burnout, these same mechanisms also explain why perfectionism may contribute to the development of burnout in athletes.

Perfectionism and Burnout in Soccer Players

At present, there are three studies that have examined the relationship between perfectionism and athlete burnout in soccer. In the first study, Hill et al. (2008) examined the relationship between perfectionism and burnout and whether unconditional self-acceptance (accepting oneself regardless of approval from others) mediated or explained this relationship. One hundred and fifty-one adolescent male soccer academy players took part in the study (M age = 14.53 years, SD = 2.29 years). All players completed questionnaires that measured perfectionism, burnout, and unconditional self-acceptance on one occasion. It was found that SPP had a positive relationship with all burnout symptoms whereas SOP had a negative relationship with all burnout symptoms. In addition, unconditional self-acceptance partially mediated the relationship between both dimensions of perfectionism and burnout. That is, the view that one needs to constantly win approval from others linked both SOP and SPP to higher burnout in soccer players.

In the second study, Hill (2013) examined the relationships between combinations of dimensions of perfectionism and burnout. This included high levels of SOP and high levels of SPP, low levels of both, and a mix of low and high SOP and SPP. One hundred and sixty-seven adolescent male soccer academy players took part in the study (M age = 16.17 years, SD = 1.57 years). All players completed measures of perfectionism and burnout. Findings revealed that (i) low SOP/high SPP was related to higher levels of total burnout and all symptoms of burnout in comparison to individuals exhibiting low levels of perfectionism, (ii) high SOP/low SPP was related to lower levels of total burnout and reduced accomplishment in comparison to those individual exhibiting low levels of perfectionism, (iii) a mix of high SOP/high SPP was related to lower levels of total burnout, reduced accomplishment, and sport devaluation in comparison to those exhibiting low SOP/high SPP, and (iv) a mix of high SOP/high SPP was related to higher total burnout, reduced accomplishment, and exhaustion than those exhibiting high SOP/low SPP. Based on these findings, low SOP/high SPP and high SOP/high SPP are the worst combinations of perfectionism for soccer players in terms of burnout.

In the most recent study, Smith et al. (2018) examined the relationships between perfectionism, burnout, and depressive symptoms over time. One hundred and eight adolescent male soccer academy players (M age $=16.15$ years, $SD= 1.84$) completed measures of perfectionism, burnout, and depressive symptoms twice three months apart during the competitive season. The findings showed that the relationships between perfectionism and burnout are more complex when observed over time. SOP did not predict any burnout symptoms over time, nor was it predicted by any burnout symptoms. However, the relationships between SPP and burnout were reciprocal with SPP related to increases in sport devaluation over three months, and sport devaluation also related to increases in SPP over the same time period. In other words, while perceptions that others expect you to be perfect can increase burnout in soccer players, the experience of burnout may itself lead to a greater reliance on others' expectations to maintain participation. The implications being young soccer players may become entrapped, participating because they believe they "have to" rather than because they "want to."

In summary, so far, research examining perfectionism and burnout in soccer players demonstrates that SPP is problematic for soccer players, particularly as the relationship between SPP and burnout has been found over time. As such, early indication is that SPP is a risk factor for burnout among soccer players. In comparison to SPP, SOP has a more complex relationship with burnout. SOP has a negative relationship with burnout when measured on one occasion, a positive indirect relationship via conditional self-acceptance, and no relationship when examined over time. The role of SOP in the development of burnout among soccer players is therefore currently unclear. In keeping with these findings, when examining combinations of perfectionism, it is the presence of high SPP either in combination with high or low SOP that is important and what makes soccer players most at risk of burnout.

Practical Applications—Case Study

Next, we present a case study of perfectionism-fuelled burnout in soccer. The case study is based on the experience of one of the authors from their applied work. We have altered some of the details and circumstances, so the individual remains anonymous. However, overall, the case study documents similar issues to those presented by athletes in his actual work and the steps that were taken to help address these issues.

Background and Context

Jen is a 22-year-old elite-level soccer player. She had been part of the national squad for two years and was in her first season at one of the major professional clubs in Europe. She combined her soccer career with university studies and planned to be a lawyer after her soccer career was over. She had recently moved towns and clubs so to allow her to continue her studies. This move was also partly motivated by the belief that playing for the new club would give her a better chance of becoming a starting player in the national team. As a consequence of her move, her life changed significantly, with new teammates, new coaches, and new surroundings. The sport psychologist was introduced to Jen at the new club where he worked part-time. A few weeks into the competitive season, Jen sought him out to discuss what she described as "motivation issues."

Presenting Issue(s)

Jen reported in informal conversations with the sport psychologist that she was struggling with the workload of combining studying with soccer and always felt tired. The coach had also made comments about her apparent lethargy to both the player and the sport psychologist. From what Jen described, it appeared that she was displaying signs of mental and physical exhaustion. She was not currently in the first team at the club, and she reported that she was performing poorly, well below the perfectionistic standards she had for herself and the levels that she believed helped her secure the move to the club. She said that she found her new teammates to be friendly but, overall, the environment at the club was far more competitive than her previous club, so she wanted to be professional about her interactions with her teammates. Jen said that because she has little time to do other things and meet new people she felt isolated and lonely. Sometimes she cried at night when she was on her own due to the pressure of her new life and feelings of stress.

The Intervention/Work Conducted

Intervention work with Jen included eight formal sessions. Reflecting the experience and expertise of the sport psychologist, the sessions were guided by cognitive behaviour therapy (CBT). CBT is a short-term, problem-focused, goal-directed therapy with roots in both behavioural and cognitive therapy (Craske, 2017). It is based on two basic premises: first, that our cognitions influence our emotions and behaviours and, second, that our behaviours influence our emotions and cognitions (Wright, Basco, & Thase, 2006). It is thought to be an effective intervention for perfectionism because individuals displaying perfectionistic tendencies typically have negative thoughts and irrational beliefs associated with the need to be perfect. The sport psychologist had also used CBT when working with other athletes reporting similar issues. In formulating the approach, the intervention work was guided by Egan, Wade, Shafran, and Antony (2014).

Session 1: Initial Analysis

The aim of the first session was to provide some initial analysis of the issues being presented and Jen's reasons for wanting to change. The principles of CBT were also explained, and the typical sequence of the work outlined.

The session started by asking why Jen was seeking support and what she thought she needed help with. Jen said she was here because she was feeling stressed and had started to feel low in motivation. She described having no energy for training and feeling tired. She was asked to describe an ordinary day in detail. Jen indicated that she had two training sessions per day with the soccer club, one in the morning (10.00–11.30 am) and one in the evening (17.00–18.30 pm). She attended university classes in between. She had decided that this was not enough training and so had also added an extra session in the morning before breakfast (7.00–8.00 am). She also tended to complete a "light" training session on her rest days (days when players were instructed by the club not to train). The extra training was being both positively reinforced ("I feel good about myself as I was doing something the other players were not") and negatively reinforced ("If I don't do it, I get anxious and worry that I am not doing enough"). She estimated that with her additional training sessions and sessions on rest days, she had trained more than anyone at the club. This was something she was proud of.

Jen mentioned that she considered herself to be a perfectionist. When discussing her goals and expectations, it was clear that Jen was extremely demanding of herself. These demands seem to be tied to proving to others that she is both an exceptional student and soccer player. Her father was a professional soccer player and had been instrumental in her career so far. She referred to his achievements and advice often. Her only sibling, an older brother, was also an elite-level athlete and had competed internationally with some notable successes. The need to "prove herself" equal to her brother and win the approval of her father was a reoccurring theme when she described her motivation and why soccer was important to her.

Her perfectionism was also evident in how she prepared for matches and training. Jen prepared meticulously for training as to when and what she ate and always arrived at training and matches early, well before her teammates and sometimes before her coaches. She also kept detailed notes on her own performances in the form of a performance diary (something her father recommended). She did not like to rest and always liked to be doing something, even on rest days when she completed her own separate training sessions. Generally, she considered being a perfectionist to be a good thing. However, she also acknowledged that when things didn't go well in games or training, she had difficulty focusing. She got angry with herself and others often but hid her anger from others. The worst moments were when the team lost and she had performed badly. When this happened, she felt ashamed and guilty and contemplated leaving soccer completely.

Session 2: Case Formulation, Behavioural and Functional Analyses

The aim of the second session was to develop a case formulation of the issues Jen presented and then conduct an analysis of her behaviour. In doing so, a conceptual framework and set of working hypotheses for the problem and its consequences were created.

Through discussion, an initial picture of Jen's problem was constructed, including how it developed and what was maintaining it. This focused on her mental and physical fatigue and approaches to training and competition. A "problem list" was created that made explicit what the key issues were (e.g., "Tired all the time" and "Feel like I am letting people down"). This included discussing the short-term and long-term consequences of these problems if they were not addressed (e.g., "I won't perform to my ability" and "I will probably have to leave the club") and the benefits of addressing these problems (e.g., "I will feel better about myself"). This was an important step for building an alliance with Jen and fostering a commitment in her for the work ahead. It was decided that the problem list and a list of the consequences would be copied into the start of her performance diary.

After outlining the problems that Jen was experiencing in behavioural terms, functional analysis was conducted so to understand the relationships between the antecedents, behaviours, and the consequences. A functional analysis can help clarify the role of perfectionism and the influence it has on the wellbeing of the individual and can also help determine whether you should focus on the treatment of perfectionism first, the treatment of the symptoms first (here, mental and physical exhaustion), or on both together. As part of Jen's functional analysis, we focused on the origins and consequences of her perfectionistic and rigid way of thinking which had inadvertently become tied to the belief that she "needed to always be professional." This is illustrated in Figure 20.1. This allowed us to identify specific distorted ways of thinking/cognitive biases and how her extra training and over-preparation were safety behaviours (i.e., being used to prevent or minimise negative things happening). In concert with Jen, the extra training, over-preparation, and lack of physical "down time" were identified as the major source of Jen's feelings of exhaustion. In addition, her perfectionistic tendencies, self-criticism, and the unrealistic demands that she placed on herself were identified as major sources of the psychological stress she was experiencing.

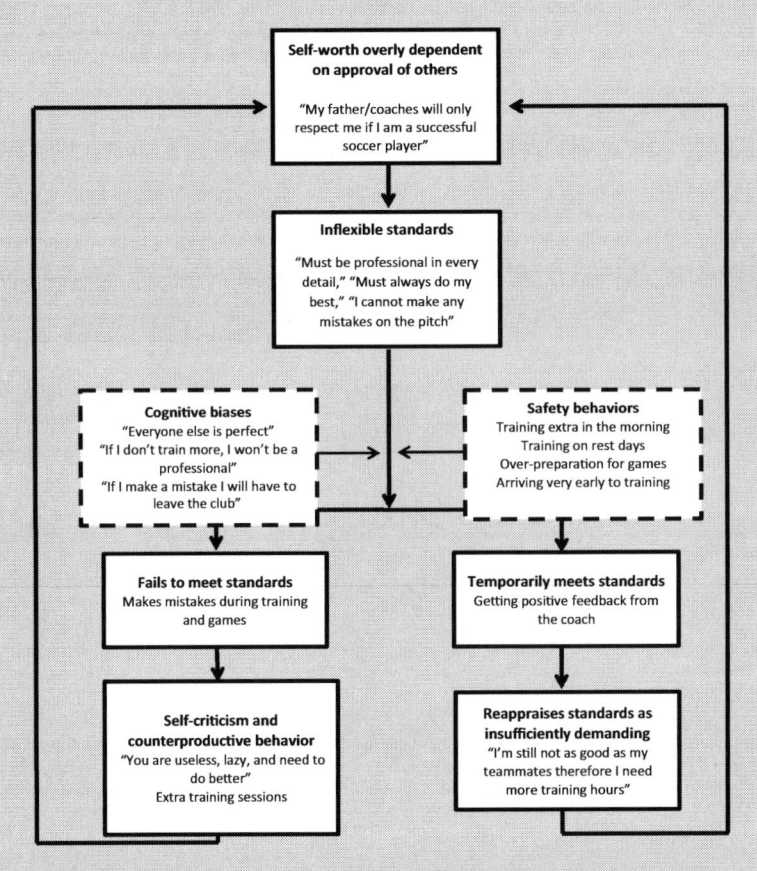

FIGURE 20.1 A cognitive behavioural model of Jen's perfectionism. Based on the cognitive-behavioural model of perfectionism presented by Shafran, Copper, and Fairburn (2002, p.780)

Session 3: Psychoeducation and Self-Monitoring

The aim of the third session was to discuss some of the myths regarding perfectionism. In addition, perfectionistic thoughts and associated emotions and dysfunctional behaviours that Jen was engaging in, as well as their perceived function, were also focused upon.

In this session the psychologist described and discussed the problems associated with perfectionism, such as myths like "practice makes perfect." It was important to show Jen that being less perfectionistic didn't mean lowering her standards and help her take a broader view of her participation in soccer. Also, importantly, addressing perfectionism meant she would need to focus more on how she felt about herself when things were not perfect and why she felt that way. By presenting how her thoughts, emotions, and behaviours were linked, this provided a rationale for the interventions that were designed later. Via structured questioning ("Socratic dialogue"), Jen's thoughts about possible disadvantages of her current behaviours were explored. One important insight was that the extra morning training sessions may be undermining her ability to rest, recover, and perform well the following day. A further insight was how her meticulousness and over-preparedness made it difficult for her to get mental respite from soccer and her studies.

Jen was introduced to the notion of monitoring her perfectionistic way of thinking. She was asked to provide examples of some of the thoughts she had ("my preparation needs to be perfect"), how strongly she believed the thought ("95%"), what behaviours followed ("turning up an hour early to training"), and how this made her feel ("anxious"). Using a small number of examples, the discussion focused on how productive or counterproductive the subsequent behaviours and feelings were. Jen was asked to spend some time doing this alone for other thoughts and behaviours and to bring her attempts to the next session where they could be discussed. She was provided with a worksheet to record this exercise.

Session 4: Behavioural Experiments and Inflexible Standards

The aim of the fourth session was to introduce the use of behavioural experiments and to co-create behavioural experiments that could be used to test the problematic behaviours identified as part of the problems.

Undertaking behavioural experiments with clients is a way for them to gather information themselves first-hand and to test unhelpful thoughts and beliefs. Jen had identified several counterproductive behaviours related to both sport and university work. These included staying up all night studying and comparing her performances with her teammates despite differences in age, experience, and playing positions ("I always need to be better than the others"). Different behavioural experiments were considered in context of the practicalities (what behavioural experiments were feasible) and her own apprehension (what behavioural experiments felt challenging but manageable). She did not want to include other players or coaches in the experiments. It was agreed that Jen should skip three of the extra morning training session until the next meeting (two days with extra training and then three days without it) and then evaluate the consequences. This behavioural experiment was designed to test the validity of the beliefs she held that "more training was better than less," "the extra training is helping my performance," and "the extra training makes me feel better." As part of the behavioural experiment, she was asked to monitor how tired she felt each day (0–100%), how well she performed in the other training sessions (0–100%), and how positive she felt (0–100%).

Session 5: Evaluating Behavioural Experiments and New Insights

The aim of the fifth session was to review Jen's experience of the behavioural experiment and for her to reflect on the experience.

Jen described how the assignment had been tough and had provoked a lot of anxiety. However, she also reported that after a few days she felt like she had more energy and was more alert during training sessions. She reported that this helped her confidence. Reflecting upon the behavioural experiment, she compared how she used to feel during training camps with the junior national team ("full of energy") and how she had been feeling ("exhausted") and identified the additional training and lack of fun as major sources of her lethargy. Her new insights and further discussion about what it means to be "professional" formed the basis of the session. Her initial beliefs were revisited and she had the opportunity to rephrase them. In each case, the beliefs were revised based on her experience ("the right amount of training is important" and "I feel best when I am rested and can perform well"). It was decided that Jen would skip the additional morning training sessions and training sessions on rest days and see how she felt. It was also agreed that she should continue to challenge her thinking errors and explore the consequences of changing other behaviours such as turning up on time (not too early) and planning fun events such as socialising with friends on her rest days (as opposed to training).

Session 6: Challenging Cognitive Biases

The aim of session six was to challenge the excessive concerns Jen expressed regarding mistakes and explore how this was linked to some of her beliefs.

Jen was first asked if she was a player who always needed to be in control and feel comfortable (rating 0–100%). She replied, 100%. The second question was whether she was a player who wanted to learn new things and to develop (rating 0–100%). She replied, 100%. The sport psychologist then proceeded to discuss the compatibility of these two answers with Jen. In addition, it was discussed how she viewed other members of her team, the standards she had for herself and others, and her selective attention to the errors she makes while discounting positive aspects of her performances. This latter issue was evident in her performance diary that focused almost exclusively on the mistakes she had made and technical weaknesses. It was agreed that she would record at least the same amount of positive aspects of her performance as negative aspects in her performance diary (e.g., "ability to pass with backspin from left foot has got better").

Building on the monitoring exercise in an earlier session, Jen was introduced to the idea of using a thought diary and consciously challenging and amending her negative thoughts (cognitive restructuring) and behaviours. This process was modelled in the session with the help of the sport psychologist. Jen was asked to "think aloud" as the sport psychologist described various scenarios she might encounter. This included turning up late to training, making a mistake in training, and not being selected to be a starter in the team for an important match. Afterwards, her thoughts were recorded and reviewed with a focus on identifying which thoughts were "helpful" or "harmful" towards her performances. The reasoning behind the decision was discussed and, for thoughts identified as "harmful," alternative thoughts were created. For example, "I need to prove myself to the coaches" was replaced with "the coaches believe in me and want me to be successful" and "if I am late, people will think I am not professional" was replaced with "even the best players at the club are late sometimes." It was also agreed that this exercise would be a regular part of her own performance diary.

Session 7: Scheduling Time for Recovery and Pleasant Events

The aim of session seven was to help Jen understand that she could balance her participation in soccer with time for rest and relaxation.

Individuals demonstrating perfectionism often feel that they must always be doing something productive. One important aspect of Jen's problems was related to insufficient mental recovery. Insufficient recovery is a critical aspect of burnout. Jen thought that "doing more was better," and she made little time for activities other than soccer or university study. Social events were the last things on her "to-do list" even though she would have benefited from the social support and distraction that can be provided by time with friends and family. The focus of the session was on the different ways she might spend her "rest day" (the one day of the week the club did not ask her to come). After considering various options Jen decided she would like to join a recreational canoeing club. This was one of her hobbies she enjoyed with friends before moving towns. She felt it would allow her to meet new people, people who were not involved in soccer, and still be active (but not too active). It was also decided that Jen should talk with her coach about whether he had ideas about how her recovery could be improved. Finally, it was decided that Jen should talk to her father about the pressure she feels. Jen and her father had a brief conversation when she moved to the new club, and she thought it was a good idea to follow this up and be more open about the experiences she had been having.

Session 8: Maintenance and Relapse Prevention

The aim of the final session was to focus on ensuring that Jen was ready to bring the sessions to a close and could maintain the work we had done together.

Jen had good news. Her talk with her father had been a relief. He was very understanding and had shared some of his own experiences. He also told her that he provided advice and was eager to help because he wanted her to feel supported. He didn't want her to feel pressure from him. With the coach, she also planned several changes that would help her recovery. The coach stressed the importance of balancing "light days" and "heavy days" so her body could recover. Hearing the coach encourage her to rest more was important to Jen. One of the main goals of CBT is that the athlete becomes conscious of their own thoughts and able to manage them, in effect becoming self-sufficient. In this respect, the athlete should be able to better handle future challenges without the sport psychologist. This session helped prepare Jen for this by creating an action plan. This plan was developed based on questions from Butler, Fennell, and Hackman (2008): How did the problem(s) develop? What kept them going (maintenance)? What have you learned (insights, methods, etc.)? What were your most unhelpful thoughts, and do you have alternatives? How can you build on what you have learned to continue working in the right direction? What will help me do this? Jen copied this into the back of her performance diary.

Outcome Analysis and Case-Study Reflections

Working with Jen was challenging. She found it difficult to discuss the issues that she thought underpinned her behaviours and was particularly sensitive to discussing scenarios in which she wasn't successful at the club. The idea that she would become a lesser player, or even mediocre, if she accepted anything less than perfection from herself meant that she was also initially reluctant to considering that she might need to address her perfectionism. Some key turning points in this regard were the notion that being less perfectionistic did not mean lowering her standards. The behavioural experiments, too, were useful as it gave Jen something "to do" and provided tangible outcomes. Her physical recovery improved almost immediately once she stopped the extra training sessions and, in turn, so did her performances and, in turn, confidence. She recognised this and so did her coaches. As such, the intervention was considered successful. Jen found it more difficult to "switch off" psychologically, but some of the related over-preparation was reduced (e.g., turning up extremely early), and she was able to find more opportunities for other activities as she better integrated into the new town. The advice from the coach regarding the importance of rest appeared to legitimise her attempts to "recover better" as did the coach's idea that "being good at rest also takes practice." The importance of Jen's father was evident at various junctures. Jen benefited from being more open with him, and he responded by adopting a more overtly supportive role. This was reassuring to Jen and helped dispel her fears that how he felt about her depended on her success as a soccer player.

Summary and Conclusions

In this chapter we provided an overview of stress and burnout processes in soccer. In doing so, we explained how risk of burnout is influenced by both the soccer environment and the characteristics of the soccer players. In this regard, research has found that soccer players report higher burnout when their coaches, teammates, and parents are perceived to be less supportive and when their participation was accompanied by less enjoyment and less internal motives for taking part (i.e., participating because they want to). We also identified perfectionism as an especially important personality characteristic in terms of risk of burnout in soccer players. In particular, perceptions that others expect you to perform perfectly, when accompanied by internal pressures to be perfect or on its own, have consistently been found to be related to higher burnout in soccer players. With this in mind, our case study of an elite female soccer player illustrated how sport psychologists can work effectively with players by using a CBT approach to help manage burnout when it is underpinned by perfectionistic thoughts and behaviours.

Key Messages and Further Reading

Below we provide five key messages from the chapter and related directions for future research.

1. Soccer is an environment in which stressors are common. Common stressors include performance pressures, managing relationships with others, and day-to-day practicalities of being in a sport environment. Research is increasingly looking at how sport is organised and what features might lead to more stress or less stress for athletes (see Fletcher, Hanton, & Mellalieu, 2008). An increased focus on the structure of soccer in this regard is likely to offer further insight into burnout.
2. There are currently no accepted cut-off points to identify when soccer players (or athletes generally) are burned out or not. Our review revealed that the percentage of soccer players who typically reported experiencing burnout symptoms *sometimes* ranged between 7.1% and 18.4% and *frequently* ranged between <1% and 2.2%. Other reviews are required like ours to compare these figures to other sports.
3. Several environmental and personal factors have been identified in research that are related to burnout in soccer players. However, the last review of research examining athlete burnout in all sports was over ten years ago (Goodger, Gorely, Lavallee, & Harwood, 2007). As there has been a considerable amount of research since publication of the review, an updated review is sorely needed. This should include a focus on comparing different sports.
4. Perfectionism is emerging as a key characteristic when seeking to identify soccer players who are at risk to burnout. However, so far, only a small number of studies exist, all are in male adolescent academy players, and there has been only one examination of this relationship over time (three months). To better establish perfectionism as a risk factor, research is required that examines the perfectionism–burnout relationship in a wider range of soccer settings, including in adults, females, more elite groups (e.g., professional soccer players), and over prolonged periods of time (e.g., an entire season).
5. Very few studies have been published that have documented or formally evaluated interventions aimed at reducing athlete burnout. Research that does so is a priority. In the meantime, and so to better inform future work of this kind, researchers and practitioners should consult work outside of sport (e.g., Awa, Plaumann, & Walter, 2010).

Below are five key further readings for those interested in learning more about the topic;

DeFreese, J. D., Raedeke, T., & Smith, A. L. (2014). Athlete burnout: An individual organizational phenomenon. In J. M. Williams & V. Krane, *Applied sport psychology: Personal growth to peak performance* (7th ed., pp. 444–461). New York, NY: McGraw-Hill.

Gustafsson, H., DeFreese, J. D., & Madigan, D. J. (2017). Athlete burnout: Review and recommendations. *Current Opinion in Psychology, 16,* 109–113.

Hill, A. P. (2016). Conceptualizing perfectionism: An overview and unresolved issues. In A. P. Hill (Ed.), *The psychology of perfectionism in sport, dance, and exercise* (pp. 3–30). London: Routledge. ISBN 9781138958692

Jowett, G. E., Mallinson, S. H., & Hill, A. P. (2016). An independent effects approach to perfectionism in sport, dance, and exercise. In A. P. Hill (Ed.), *The psychology of perfectionism in sport, dance, and exercise* (pp. 85–149). London: Routledge. ISBN 9781138958692

Smith, A. L., Pacewicz, C. E., & Raedeke, T. D. (2019). Athlete burnout in competitive sport. In T. S. Horn & A. L. Smith (Eds.), *Advances in sport and exercise psychology* (4th ed., pp. 409–424). Champaign, IL: Human Kinetics.

References

Adie, J. W., Duda, J. L., & Ntoumanis, N. (2012). Perceived coach autonomy support, basic needs satisfaction and the well- and ill-being of elite youth soccer players: A longitudinal investigation. *Psychology of Sport and Exercise, 13*, 51–59.

Awa, W. L., Plaumann, M., & Walter, U. (2010). Burnout prevention: A review of intervention programs. *Patient Education and Counseling, 78*, 184–190.

Balaguer, I., Gonzalez, L., Fabra, P., Castillo, I., Merce, J., & Duda, J. L. (2012). Coaches' interpersonal style, basic psychological needs, and the well- and ill-being of young soccer players: A longitudinal analysis. *Journal of Sports Sciences, 30*, 1619–1629.

Biggs, A., Brough, P., & Drummond, S. (2017). Lazarus and Folkman's psychological stress and coping theory. In C. L. Cooper & J. Campbell Quick (Eds.), *The handbook of stress and health: A guide to research and practice* (pp. 351–364). West Sussex: Wiley-Blackwell.

Butler, G., Fennell, M., & Hackman, A. (2008). *Cognitive-behavioral therapy for anxiety disorders: Mastering clinical challenges*. New York, NY: Guilford Press.

Cheval, B., Chalabaev, A., Quested, E., Courvoisier, D. S., & Sarrazin, P. (2017). How perceived autonomy support and controlling coach behaviors are related to well- and ill-being in elite soccer players: A within-person changes and between-person differences analysis. *Psychology of Sport and Exercise, 28*, 68–77.

Craske, M. G. (2017). *Cognitive-behavioral therapy*. Washington, DC: American Psychological Society.

Curran, T., Appleton, P. R., Hill, A. P., & Hall, H. K. (2011). Passion and burnout in elite junior soccer players: The mediating role of self-determined motivation. *Psychology of Sport and Exercise, 12*, 655–661.

Curran, T., Appleton, P. R., Hill, A. P., & Hall, H. K. (2013). The mediating role of psychological need satisfaction in relationships between types of passion for sport and athlete burnout. *Journal of Sports Sciences, 31*, 597–606.

Egan, S. J., Wade, T. D., Shafran, R., & Antony, M. M. (2014). *Cognitive-behavioral treatment of perfectionism*. New York, NY: Guilford Press.

FIFPro. (2016). 2016 FIFPro global employment report: Working conditions in professional football. Retrieved from www.fifpro.org/attachments/article/6706/2016%20FIFPro%20Global%20Survey%20-%20TopFindings_1128.pdf

Fletcher, D., Hanton, S., & Mellalieu, S. D. (2008). *An organizational stress review: Conceptual and theoretical issues in competitive sport*. New York, NY: Nova Science.

Frost, R. O., Marten, P. A., Lahart, C., & Rosenblate, R. (1990). The dimensions of perfectionism. *Cognitive Therapy and Research, 14*, 449–468.

Gonzalez, L., Garcia-Merita, M., Castillo, I., & Balaguer, I. (2016). Young athletes perceptions of coach behaviors and their implications on their well- and ill-being over time. *Journal of Strength and Conditioning Research, 30*, 1147–54.

Gonzalez, L., Tomas, I., Castillo, I., Duda, J. L., & Balaguer, I. (2017). A test of basic psychological needs theory in young soccer players: Time-lagged design at the individual and team levels. *Scandinavian Journal of Medicine & Science in Sports, 27*, 1511–1522.

Goodger, K., Gorely, T., Lavallee, D., & Harwood, C. (2007). Burnout in sport: A systematic review. *The Sport Psychologist, 21*, 127–151.

Green, C. (2009). *Every boy's dream*. London: A & C Black Publishers.

Gustafsson, H., DeFreese, J. D., & Madigan, D. J. (2017). Athlete burnout: Review and recommendations. *Current Opinion in Psychology, 16,* 109–113.

Gustafsson, H., Skoog, T., Podlog, L., Lundqvist, C., & Wagnsson, S. (2013). Hope and athlete burnout: Stress and affect as mediators. *Psychology of Sport and Exercise, 14,* 640–649.

Hewitt, P. L., & Flett, G. L. (1991). Perfectionism in the self and social contexts: Conceptualization, assessment, and association with psychopathology. *Journal of Personality and Social Psychology, 60,* 456–470.

Hewitt, P. L., & Flett, G. L. (2002). Perfectionism and stress processes in psychopathology. In G. L. Flett & P. L. Hewitt (Eds.), *Perfectionism: Theory, research and treatment* (pp. 255–284). Washington, DC: American Psychological Association.

Hill, A. P. (2013). Perfectionism and burnout in junior elite soccer players: A test of the 2 x 2 model of dispositional perfectionism. *Journal of Sport & Exercise Psychology, 35,* 18–29.

Hill, A. P. (2014). Perfectionistic strivings and the perils of partialling. *International Journal of Sport and Exercise Psychology, 12,* 302–315.

Hill, A. P., Hall, H. K., Appleton, P. R., & Kozub, S. A. (2008). Perfectionism and burnout in junior elite soccer players: The mediating influence of self-acceptance. *Psychology of Sport and Exercise, 9,* 630–644.

Holt, N. L., & Hogg, J. M. (2002). Perceptions of stress and coping during preparations for the 1999 women's soccer world cup finals. *The Sport Psychologist, 16,* 251–271.

Isoard-Gautheur, S., Oger, M., Guillet, E., & Martin-Krumm, C. (2010). Validation of a French version of the athlete burnout questionnaire (ABQ). *European Journal of Psychological Assessment, 26,* 203–211.

Kristiansen, E., Murphy, D., & Roberts, G. (2012). Organizational stress and coping in U.S. professional soccer. *Journal of Applied Sport Psychology, 24,* 207–223.

Lai, C., & Wiggins, M. S. (2003). Burnout perceptions over time in division I soccer players. *International Sports Journal, 7,* 120–127.

Lazarus, R. S. (1991). Progress on a cognitive-motivational-relational theory of emotion. *American Psychologist, 46,* 819–834.

Lazarus, R. S., & Folkman, S. (1984). *Stress, appraisal and coping.* New York, NY: Springer Publishing Company.

Li, C., Ivarsson, A., Stenling, A., & Wu, Y. (2018). The dynamic interplay between burnout and sleep among elite blind soccer players. *Psychology of Sport and Exercise, 37,* 164–169.

Lopes Verardi, C. E., Nagamine, K. K., Micelli Domingos, N. A., De Marco, A., & Santos Miyazaki, M. C. D. (2015). Burnout and pre-competition: A study of its occurrence in Brazilian soccer players. *Revista de Psicologia del Deporte, 24*(2), 259–264.

Lopes Verardi, C. E., Nagamine, K. K., Neiva, C. M., Pessona Filho, D. M., Micelli Domingos, N. A., Ciolac, E. G., & Santos Miyazaki, M. C. D. (2014). Burnout and playing position: A study of Brazilian soccer players. *Journal of Physical Education and Sport, 14,* 324–330.

Malach-Pines, A. (2005). The burnout measure short version. *International Journal of Stress Management, 12,* 78–88.

Maslach, C. (1993). Burnout: A multidimensional perspective. In W. B. Schaufeli, C. Maslach & T. Marek (Eds.), *Series in applied psychology: Social issues and questions. Professional burnout: Recent developments in theory and research* (pp. 19–32). Philadelphia, PA: Taylor & Francis.

Maslach, C., & Jackson, S. E. (1981a). The measurement of experienced burnout. *Journal of Organisational Behaviour, 2,* 99–113.

Maslach, C., & Jackson, S. E. (1981b). *The maslach burnout inventory: Research Edition.* Palo Alto, CA: Consulting Psychologists Press.

Pires, D. A., Brandao, M. R. F., & Silva, C. B. (2006). Validação do questionário de burnout para atletas. *Revista da Educação Física, 17,* 27–36.

Price, M., & Weiss, M. (2000). Relationships among coach burnout, coach behaviors, and athletes' psychological responses. *The Sport Psychologist, 14,* 391–409.

Raedeke, T. D. (1997). Is an athlete burnout more than just stress? A sport commitment perspective. *Journal of Sport and Exercise Psychology, 19,* 396–417.

Raedeke, T. D., & Smith, A. L. (2001). Development and preliminary validation of an athlete burnout measure. *Journal of Sport and Exercise Psychology, 23,* 281–305.

Reeves, C. W., Nicholls, A. R., & McKenna, J. (2011). The effects of a coping intervention on coping self-efficacy, coping effectiveness, and subjective performance among adolescent soccer players. *International Journal of Sport and Exercise Psychology, 9,* 126–142.

Roderick, M., & Schumacker, J. (2016). The whole week comes down to the team sheet: A footballer's view of insecure work. *Work, Employment, and Society, 31*, 166–174.

Shafran, R., Cooper, Z., & Fairburn, C. G. (2002). Clinical perfectionism: A cognitive-behavioural analysis. *Behaviour Research and Therapy, 40*, 773–791.

Smith, A. L., Gustafsson, H., & Hassmen, P. (2010). Peer motivational climate and burnout perceptions in adolescent athletes. *Psychology of Sport & Exercise, 11*, 453–460.

Smith, E. P., Hill, A. P., & Hall, H. K. (2018). Perfectionism, burnout and depression in youth soccer players: A longitudinal study. *Journal of Clinical Sport Psychology, 12*, 179–200.

Smith, R. E. (1986). Toward a cognitive-affective model of athletic burnout. *Journal of Sport Psychology, 8*, 36–50.

Tabei, Y., Fletcher, D., & Goodger, K. (2012). The relationship between organizational stressors and athlete burnout in soccer players. *Journal of Clinical Sport Psychology, 6*, 146–165.

Van Yperen, W. (1997). Inequality and vulnerability to dropout symptoms: An exploratory causal analysis among highly skilled young soccer players. *The Sport Psychologist, 11*, 318–325.

Wright, J. H., Basco, M. R., & Thase, M. E. (2006). *Learning cognitive-behavior therapy: An illustrated guide*. Washington, DC: American Psychiatric Press.

Yildiz, S. M. (2011). Relationship between leader-member exchange and burnout in professional footballers. *Journal of Sports Sciences, 29*, 1493–1502.

INDEX

Note: **Bold** page references indicate tables. *Italic* references indicate figures and boxed text.

3Rs 63–64
5Cs model 137, *139*, *144*, *146–147*, 174, *192*, *238–241*, 243
5R Shared Leadership Program (5R⁵) 64, *66–69*, **68**

ABC (Antecedence-Behaviour-Consequence) model *164*
ABC(DE) model 45, *45*, *48–49*, 56
acceptance, unconditional other *51–57*
Achievement Goal Theory (AGT) *138*
Alfermann, D. 222
Allied Health teams (Australia) 64
Andersen, M. 235
anterior cruciate ligament (ACL) rupture management: background/context of case study *252*; beliefs and, challenging *255–256*; case study *252–260*; cognitive restructuring and *255–256*; emotions related to *255*; fear of re-injury and 250; imagery and *256–257*; intervention/work conducted in case study *254–258*; issues of case study *252–254*; literature review 249–252; messages, key 260; outcome analysis of case study *258–259*; overview 260; pre-game fitness test and *258*; pre-injury performance and 250; psychological intervention strategies in 251–252; Q angle and 249; reflections on case study *259–260*; return-to-participation rates and 249–252, *257–258*; sport injury-related growth and 250, *253*; of Sullivan (Andi) 249; "whole-person" approach and *254*
anti-awfulising *49–51*
anticipation/uncertainty stage in organisational change 208, *211*

Antony, M. M. *306*
anxiety 6, 30–33; *see also* penalty kick psychology
applied psychology in academy soccer settings: background information 172–173; literature review 172–175; models/frameworks to optimise youth development and 174–175; organisational structures of 173–174; systems-led approach to 176–178, 180–183; *see also* systems-led approach
appreciation of parents, showing small tokens of 130
approach focus *195–196*
athlete burnout *see* burnout
Athlete Burnout Questionnaire (ABQ) 294
athlete rational resilience credo (ARRC) *54–55*
athletic leadership goals task *68–69*
Athletic Talent Development Environment (ATDE) model *157*, *160*, 221; *see also* talent development environment (TDE)
attentional control theory (ACT) 31
Audas, R. 206
awfulising *49–50*
Azar, O. H. 33–34

Bacca, C. 29
"badness scale" *50*
Bakker, F. C. 32
Bar-Eli, M. 33–34
Barker, J. B. 63–64, *66*, 107, *109*
barriers/solution action plan task 69
Barros, C. P. 207
Baumeister, R. F. 32
Benus, R. 279
"big calls" 75, 77
"Big I little i technique" *55–56*
Blahutkova, M. 279

Blinde, E. M. 92
Boardley, I. D. 135
Bowley, C. 92
Bridges, W. *214–215*
Brown, B. *226*
Brown, M. C. 207
Buffalo Bills (American football team) 105
burnout: analyses, behavioural/functional *307–308*; Athlete Burnout Questionnaire and 294; background/context of case study *305*; behavioural experiments and *309–310*; case formulation *307–308*; case study *305–312*; cognitive behaviour therapy and *306*, *308*; cognitive biases, challenging *310–311*; evaluating behavioural experiments and *310*; Hill's studies of 304; inflexible standards and *309–310*; initial analysis of *306–307*; intervention/work conducted in case study *306–312*; issues of case study *306*; maintenance of good mental health and *311–312*; new insights and *310*; outcome analysis of case study *312*; overview 312–313; perfectionism fuelling *305*; performance and 294, 303, *307*, *309–312*; prevalence of 294, **295–302**, 303–305; psychoeducation *309*; recovery time and *311*; reflections on case study *312*; relapses and *311–312*; research summary on 294, **295–302**, 303–305; self-monitoring of *309*; Smith's (E. P.) study of 305; stress and, long-term 293–294; stressors and 294; time for pleasant events and, scheduling *311*

Calvin, M. 266–267
case studies: anterior cruciate ligament rupture management *252–260*; burnout *305–312*; challenge culture *191–200*; culture/environment in women's international soccer *223–231*; efficacy of coaching youth *138–147*; leadership, on- and off-field *65–71*; mental health/wellbeing of elite soccer players *269–274*; organisational change in professional soccer *210–216*; parents' role in developing young players *126–129*; penalty kick psychology *35–39*; personal-disclosure mutual sharing *108–117*; positive psychology *20–26*; positive youth development *93–101*; rational emotive behaviour therapy *47–57*; referee mental health *280–289*; referee psychology *75–84*; social identity approach *65–71*; sport psychology provision in elite youth soccer *235–243*; systems-led approach *175–186*; talent development environment *156–168*; transition from elite youth to elite adult soccer *7–14*
challenge culture: approach focus and *195–196*; background/context of case study *191*; case study *191–200*; challenge concept and 190; confidence and *194*; consequences of to player, meaningful 189–190; control and, emotional *195*; intervention/work conducted in case study *192–196*; issues of case study *191–192*; literature review 189–191; messages, key 201; motivated performance and 189; outcome analysis of case study *196–197*; overview 200–201; performance and 189–190, *192*, *195–197*, 200; self-efficacy and *194*; social support and *196*; Theory of Challenge and Threat States in Athletics and 190–191, *192–193*, *195*, *197*, *199–200*, 200–201; threat-state cardiovascular reactivity pattern and 190

change, stages of 208
Chase, M. A. 134
Christensen, M. 222
chronic performance-related stress 279
Chung, Y. 92, *95*
City PASS framework *178*
Clarke, N. J. 122, 125
Clattenburg, Mark 278
coach-athlete relationship 92
coaches: 5Cs-related education of 136–137, *138–145*; appreciation to parents and, showing small tokens of 130; communication with parents and 130; confidence of *101*, 133–134, 136–138, *138–147*, 148–149; frustrations of, managing 128; influences of 133–134; learning and, role in 92–93, *96–98*, *100–101*, 102, *159*; organisational change in professional soccer and, perspective of *211–212*; parents' role in developing young players and, perspective of *127*; performance and *211–212*; positive youth development and 92–93, 102; reflections of case study of transition of *13–14*; self-reflection of *145*; sport psychology provision in academy youth soccer and *240*; *see also* efficacy of coaching youth
coaching *96*; *see also* coaches; efficacy of coaching youth
coaching efficacy scale (CES) 134–135
coaching practice *98–99*, 102
coach-parent relationship, facilitating conflict resolution in 128
cognitive behaviour therapy (CBT) *306*, *308*
cognitive biases, challenging *310–311*
cognitive restructuring *255–256*
Collins, K. 92, *95*
commitment in 5Cs model 137, *139*, 144, 146–147, 174, *238–241*
common mental disorders (CMD) 279, *282*
communication in 5Cs model 137, *139*, 144, 146–147, 174, *238–241*
communication with parents 130; *see also* language
concentration in 5Cs model 137, *139*, 144, 146–147, 174, *238–241*
confidence: of coaches *101*, 133–134, 136–138, *138–147*, 148–149; describing *178–179*; in 5Cs model 137, *139*, 144, 146–147, 174, *239–241*; injury-related 250, 252, *252*, *256–257*; in penalty shootout *36–38*; of players 8–9, 24–25, 27; self-efficacy and *194*; in supporting others with mental health 78, *82*; in team 63–64; Theory of Challenge and Threat States in Athletics and *192–193*
conflict resolution between coaches and parents *128*

Connor-Davidson Resilience Scale (CD-RISC) *81*
constructivism 97
control: in 5Cs model 137, *139*, 144, *146–147*, 174, *238–241*; emotional *124–125*, 136, 137, *139*, *192–193*, *195*; injury and *253*, *256*, *258–259*; perceived *81*, 190, *193*, *195*; Theory of Challenge and Threat States in Athletics and *192–193*, *195*
Coping Function Questionnaire for Adolescents in Sport (CFQ) *113*
coping-oriented PDMS 107–108, *109–110*, *112–114*
Corlett, J. *274*
Coyle, D. 222, *226*
Crace, R. K. 105
"critical moments" 266, 268, 275
Cruwys, T. 64
Culley, G. 121–122
Culture Code, The (Coyle) 222
culture/environment in women's international soccer: background/context of case study *223–224*; case study *223–231*; Coyle's publication and 222; factors necessary when conducting ecological interventions and 222; female role models and 221–222; in German soccer 220; Henriksen's studies of 221–222; holistic approaches and 220–221; intervention/work conducted in case study *225–230*; issues of case study *224–225*; Larsen's studies of 221–222; messages, key 231; methods of improving psychosocial development and 222; overview *230–231*; performance and *224–226*, *229–231*; purpose and, establishing 223; reflections on case study *230–231*; safety and, building 222; storytelling and *227–229*; team identity and, developing *227*; team vision, values, and goals and, developing *226–227*; theoretical background 220–223; US Navy's SEAL Team and 222; vulnerability and, sharing 222–223, *225–226*
Cushion, C. *163*

Damarjian, N. 136
Danish Football Association (Danish FA) 155
Darwin, C. 30
Davis, H. S. 107
De Paola, M. 207
depreciation *55–56*
depression from failure 279
descriptive models of transition *4–5*
Developmental Model of Sport Participation (DMSP) 174–175
development pathways *see* transition from elite youth to elite adult soccer
Dier, E. 29
disputation of irrational belief *53–55*, **54**
Doosje, B. 70
Dryden, W. 106
Dunn, J. G. H. 106–107, 124, 136
Dutch Eredivisie clubs 207
Dutch football 207

efficacy of coaching youth: background/context of case study *138–139*; background information 133–134; case study *138–147*; 5Cs and *139*, *144*, *146*; 5Cs-related education and 136–137, *138–145*; improving 136–137, *145*; in-service sessions *138–145*; intervention/work conducted in case study *139–145*; learning and 134, 137; literature review 134–135; longitudinal adaptive training and 136–137; messages, key 148–149; model of, conceptual 134–135, *134*; overview 134, 138, 148; performance and 134–135, 137, *138*, 148; Program for Athletic Coach Education and 135; P.R.O.G.R.E.S.S. and *141–142*, *144–145*; from psychological perspective 135–138; psychosocial factors and 135–138; reflections on case study *145–147*; scale 134–135; from social perspective 135–138; supportive environments and 136–137
efficacy of positive psychology 20
Egan, S. J. *306*
eight-step model for leading change *183*, **184–185**
Ekman, P. 30–31
Elite Player Performance Plan (EPPP) 172–173, *235–236*
Ellemers, N. 70
emotions: of anterior cruciate ligament rupture *255*; anxiety 6, 30–33; control of *124–125*, 136, 137, *139*, *192–193*; Darwin and 30; evolutionary-inspired theories of 30; fear *8*, *12*, 33, *49*, 250; healthy negative 45; injury-related 250, *255*; interpersonal effects of 33–35; laboratory-based manipulations of 29, 32; parents' role in managing own *124–125*; in penalty kick psychology 31–35; penalty shootout and 29–30; physiological process and 31; of stress 30; themes of 31; *see also* rational emotive behaviour therapy (REBT)
emotions as social information (EASI) model 34
emotion theory 30–31
English Football League (EFL) 205, 206, 209
English Premier League (EPL) 206, 209, 266
environment *see* culture/environment in women's international soccer
environmental success factors (ESF) 221
Environment Success Factor (ESF) model *157*, *161–162*
Evans, A. L. 106–107, *115*
exclusive identity 5
exit, voice, loyalty, and neglect (EVLN) model *214*
explanation models of transition 5–6
Eysenck, H. J. 20

failure: depression from 279; fear of *8*, *12*, *49*
fairness, preference for *47–49*
fear: of failure *8*, *12*, *49*; performance pressure and 33; of re-injury 250
Feltz, D. L. 134–136, *142*
female role models 221–222
Ferguson, L. J. *283*
Fletcher, D. *228*

Flett, G. L. 303–304
Football Association (FA) four-corner model 172
foreclosed athletic identity 5
Foundation Phase teams *192*
four-corner model 92
four-step intervention: analysing club's TDE/culture (Step 1) *159–160*; implementation of behaviours/ongoing evaluation (Step 4) *165–166*; organisational awareness (Step 2) *160–164*; organisational behaviors, coherent (Step 3) *164–165*; overview *158–159*, **158**
Frankl, V. 272
Fransen, K. *66, 71*
Fraser-Thomas, J. 148
Frick, B. 207
Fridlund, A. 29
frustration intolerance (FI) *52–53*
frustration tolerance *51–57*
Furley, P. 33

Galily, Y. 279
German soccer culture 220
Gilmore, S. 208–210
Give and Take (Grant) 222–223
goal-setting *9–10*
González-Gómez, F. 207
"good," concept of *101, 237–238*
Gould, D. 92, *95*, 136
Gouttebarge, V. 279
Grant, A. 222
guided imagery *256–257*

Hägglund, K. *226*
Hancock, G. R. 134
Hanton, S. *228*
Hardy, C. J. 105
Hartman, E. 33
Harwood, C. G. 122–125, 133, 136–137, *138*, 173–174
Haslam, S. A. 64
healthy negative emotions (HNEs) 45
Henderson, J. 29
Henriksen, K. 221
Hewitt, P. L. 303–304
Hill, A. P. 304
holistic approach: to culture/environment of women's international soccer 220–221; to developing life skills *94*, 102
holistic athletic career transition model 5
holistic ecological approach (HEA) *156–157*; *see also* four-step intervention
Holt, N. L. 106–107, 124, 136, 221
humanistic counselling/psychology *11*

identity: development 4–5, *227*, 268–269; embedders 62; entrepreneurs 62; mapping *68*; multidimensional 5; social theory of 61; team *227*; *see also* social identity approach
Identity Leadership Inventory (ILI) 62, *70*
"illness scripts" *26*
imagery *256–257*

individualism in soccer, myth of *176*
inference chaining *48*
in-group champions 62
in-group prototypes 62
injury *see* anterior cruciate ligament (ACL) rupture management
integration/experimentation stage of organisational change 208, *211*
International Society of Sport Psychology *281–282*
irrationality of player 44–46, **46**, *47–48*, 57
irrational Performance Beliefs Inventory (iPBI) *49*

Jones, R. L. 97, *163*
Jordet, G. 33–34

Kane, H. 29, *37*
Karg, A. 206, 209
Karius, L. 46
Kavussanu, M. 135
Keidar-Levin, Y. 33–34
King, T. 136
Knight, C. J. 123–124
Knight, P. T. *96*
knowledge-in-action *99–100*
Koning, R. H. 207
Kotter, J. P. *183*, **184–185**
Kowalski, K. C. 283

language *101*, 129–130, *178–179*
Larsen, C. H. 221–222
Lauer, L. 92, *95*
Lazarus, R. 30
leadership, on- and off-field: case study *65–71*; identity embedders and 62; identity entrepreneurs and 62; Identity Leadership Inventory and 62, *70*; in-group champions and 62; in-group prototypes and 62; literature review 61–64; messages, key 71; overview 71; Pogba 60, 63; shared sense of "us" and, cultivating 61–64; *see also* social identity approach
leadership succession: organisational functioning and 208–210; performance and 207–210, *215*; prevalence in professional soccer 206–207; in professional soccer 205–206; *see also* organizational change in professional soccer
League Managers' Association (LMA) 205, 265
League Managers' Association Report (2017) 265
learning: coaches' role in 92–93, *96–98, 100–101*, 102, *159*; constructivism and *97*; culture and 97; efficacy of coaching youth and 134, 137; environments and *97*; goal-setting and *9*; Larsen's studies and 221–222; message-reinforce-transfer and *98*; mutual 178; orchestration and *97–98*; outcomes *95–96*; positive youth development and opportunities for 91–93; P.R.O.G.R.E.S.S. and *141*; stage in organisational change 208, *211–212*; teaching and *96*; Theory of Challenge and Threat States in Athletics and *193*, 201

life skills, developing young people's *see* positive youth development (PYD)

literature reviews: anterior cruciate ligament rupture management 249–252; applied psychology to soccer settings 172–175; challenge culture 189–191; efficacy of coaching youth 134–135; leadership, on- and off-field 61–64; mental health/wellbeing of elite soccer players 264–269; organisational change in professional soccer 205–210; parents' role in developing young players 121–126; penalty kick psychology 29–35; personal-disclosure mutual sharing 105–108; positive psychology 19–20; positive youth development 91–93, 137; rational emotive behaviour therapy 44–47; referee mental health 278–280; referee psychology 74–75; sport psychology provision in elite youth soccer 234–235; stress 292; talent development environment 155–156; transition from elite youth to elite adult soccer 3–7

Mack, D. E. *283*
MacNamara, A. 174
Major League Baseball (MLB) 206
"Making the Case for Peer Support" (2010 Canadian report) *281–282*
Malete, L. 134–136, *142*
managerial change *see* organisational change in professional soccer
Marback, T. L. 135
Maslow, A. H. 268
mastery-oriented PDMS (MOPDMS) 107–108, *109*
McCallister, S. G. 92
McTeer, W. 207
Medbery, R. 136
mental health literacy (MHL) of referees 75, 78–79, 82–83, 286; *see also* referee mental health
Mental Health Literacy Training (MHAT) *282–283*
mental health/wellbeing of elite soccer players: background/context of case study *269–270*; case study *269–274*; challenges to 269; "critical moments" and 266, 268; help and, seeking 264–265; identity development and 268–269; intervention/work conducted in case study *272–273*; issues of case study *270–272*; literature review 264–269; mental skills training and 268, 272; messages, key 275; outcome analysis of case study *273*; overview 266, 274–275; range of issues and 267; reflections on case study *273–274*; Rose (Danny) and 264; scrutiny of performance and 265–266; transition from elite youth to elite adult soccer and 268–269; understanding 267
mental skills training (MST) 268, *272*
Mesquita, I. *143*
message-reinforce-transfer *98*
messages, key: anterior cruciate ligament rupture management 260; challenge culture 201; culture/environment in women's international soccer 231; efficacy of coaching youth 148–149; leadership, on- and off-field 71; mental health/wellbeing of elite soccer players 275; organisational change in professional soccer 216–217; parents' role in developing young players 129–131; penalty kick psychology 40; personal-disclosure mutual sharing 118; positive psychology 27; positive youth development 102; rational emotive behaviour therapy 57; referee mental health 289; referee psychology 85; sport psychology provision in elite youth soccer 245; systems-led approach *186*; talent development environment 168; transition from elite youth to elite adult soccer 15

Model for Life Skill Development Through Coaching: changes as a result of *101*; coaching practice element of *98–99*, 102; environmental development element of *97–98*, 102; overview *93–94*; philosophy element of *94–95*, 102; plan element of *95–96*, 102; reflections on *101*; reflective practice element of *99–100*, 102

Moll, T. 34
Morley, D. 221
Morris, R. *10*
motivated performance 189–190; *see also* challenge culture
multidimensional identity 5
multidimensional perfectionism 303–305
Myers, N. D. 134–135

National Basketball Association (NBA) 206
National Football League (NFL) 206
National Game Strategy *280*
national governing bodies (NGBs) 92
National Hockey League (NHL) 206
National Soccer Association (NSA) *280*
Nesti, M. 267–268, 274
Neymar 37
non-normative transition 269
normalisation/learning stage of organisational change 208, *211–212*
normative transition 269

observable behaviours *95*
"optimal" challenge mindset 77–78
optimal player development 156; *see also* talent development environment (TDE)
orchestration of learning *97–98*
organisational awareness *159–164*, **167**
organisational behaviours *164–165*
organisational change in professional soccer: anticipation/uncertainty 208, *211*; background/context of case study *210–211*; case study *210–216*; coaches' perspective *211–212*; exit, voice, loyalty, and neglect model of *214*; integration/experimentation 208, *211*; intervention/work conducted in case study *213–215*; issues of *211–213*; leadership succession events and 205–206; leadership succession and organisational functioning 208–210; leadership succession and performance 207–208; leadership succession

prevalence an, d 206–207; literature review 205–210; messages, key 216–217; normalisation/learning 208, *211–212*; outcome analysis of case study *215–216*; overview 210, *215–216*; performance and 205; players' perspective *213*; practitioner's perspective *213–215*; recurrent 209; reflections on case study *215–216*; season ticket holder study and 209; "shock effect" and 208; staged-based model of 208, *214*; upheaval/realisation 208, *211*

organisational culture 156, *157–160*; *see also* challenge culture

organisational functioning and leadership succession 208–210

Ospina, D. 29

other-oriented perfectionism (OOP) 303–304

our shared behaviours task 68–69

our shared values 68

over-identification with own athlete's role 5

parents: coaches' communication with 130; expectations of child's performance and *13*; peer-to-peer support among 130–131; relationship with coaches and *128*; sport psychology provision in academy youth soccer and *240–241*; stressors and 122, 124

parents' role in developing young players: alignment with child's needs, changing to meet 125–126; appreciation and, coaches' showing small tokens of 130; background/context of case study *126*; case study *126–129*; coach perspective of *127*; communication and, encouraging continual 130; culture of clubs/academies and *126*; demands of youth soccer, coping with 125; early engagement and, importance of 130; emotional support, providing 123; emotions at competitions, managing 124–125; experiences within soccer and 122–123; intervention/work conducted in case study *128–129*; issues of case study *126–128*; language and, importance of 129–130; literature review 121–126; messages, key 129–131; optimizing 123–126; overview 130; parent perspective of *127*; peer-to-peer support among parens and 130–131; player perspective of *127–128*; relationships with others in soccer environment, developing 125; soccer opportunities, selecting 122, 124; soccer sessions, registering/paying for 122; stress and 122; style of parenting and, adopting 124; *Sun* newspaper article on 121; tangible support 122–123

Parker, A. *198*, 265

peer-to-peer support among parents 130–131

penalty kick psychology: attentional control theory and 31; background/context of case study *35*; background information 29; case study *35–39*; confidence and, building *36–38*; emotions in 31–35; emotion theory and 30–31; goalkeepers and 31–34, *38*; individual effects of emotions and 31–33; intervention/work conducted in case study *36–39*; issues in case study *35*; literature review 29–35; messages, key 40; outcome analysis of case study *39*; overview 30, 39; performance pressure and 32–33; player selection and *36–37*; reflections of case study *39*; social effects of emotions and 33–35; team and *38–39*; training for kicks and *37*; World Cup quarter-final match (2018) and 29, *36–38*

penalty shootout 29; *see also* penalty kick psychology

Pepping, G.-J. 34

perfectionism 292, 303–305, 313; *see also* burnout

performance: anxiety about 6; assessing *236–242*; burnout and 294, 303, *307*, *309–312*; challenge culture and 189–190, *192*, *195–197*, 200; chronic stress due to 279; coaches and *211–212*; "critical moments" and 275; culture/environment in women's international soccer and *224–226*, *229–231*; diary *307*, *310–311*; efficacy of coaching youth and 134–135, 137, *138*, 148; Elite Player Performance Plan and 172–173, *235–236*; fear of failure and *12*, *49*; goal-setting and *9–10*; imagery for reducing injury-related concerns and *256–257*; irrationality of player and 44; leadership succession and 207–210, *215*; mental skills training and 268; motivated 189–190; organisational change in soccer and 205–206; parental emotional support and 123; parental expectations and *13*; personal-disclosure mutual-sharing and 105, 107–109, *116*; players and *213*; positive psychology and 19; practitioners and *213–216*; pre-injury 250, 260; pressure 6, *8*, 32–33, **78**; psychological characteristics of developing excellence and 174; psychosocial factors and 136; rational emotive behaviour therapy and 46, *54*; referee 74–75, *76–84*, **78**, 84–85, 279, *280–285*, *287*, *289*; safe environment and *224*; scrutiny of player 265–266; scrutiny of referee 74; social identity approach and 61–64, 70; sport psychology and 155; systems-led approach and 174–175, *179*, *182–183*, 186; Theory of Challenge and Threat States in Athletics and 190, *192*, *197*, 201; *see also* penalty kick psychology

personal-disclosure mutual-sharing (PDMS): background/context of case study *108–109*; benefits of 106; case study *108–117*; changes resulting from, positive 106; contract *111–112*; Coping Function Questionnaire for Adolescents in Sport and *113*; coping-oriented 107–108, *109–110*, *112–114*; describing 105; instructions *111*, *113*; intervention/work conducted in case study *109–112*; issues of case study *109*; literature review 105–108; mastery-oriented 107–108, *109*; messages, key 118; outcome analysis of case study *112–114*, **115**; overview 105, *110*, 117–118; performance and 105, 107–109, *116*; rational emotive 107; reflections on case study *115–117*, **116**; relationship-oriented 106–107, *109–110*, 112, 114–115;

social validation and *114–116*, **116**; suitability of using, appraising 117
person-centred theory/therapy 20, *22–25*, 26–27, 106, *272*, 275
Pickford, J. 29
players' perspective of organisational change in professional soccer *213*
Pogba, P. 60, 63
positive psychological interventions (PPIs) 19–20
positive psychology: background/context of case study *20–21*; background information 19; case study *20–26*; describing 19; efficacy of 20; interventions 19–20; intervention/work conducted in case study *22–24*; issues in case study *21–22*; literature review 19–20, 137; messages, key 27; outcome analysis of case study *24–25*; overview 26; performance and 19; person-centred theory and 20, *22–25*, 26–27; reflections of case study *25–26*; self-concept and 27; Seligman and 19
positive youth development (PYD): background/context of case study *93–94*; case study *93–101*; coaches and 92–93, 102; coaching and *96*; coaching practice and *98–99*; environmental development and *97–98*; four-corner model and 92; holistic approach to developing life skills and *94*, 102; intervention strategies *99*; intervention/work conducted in case study *94–100*; issues of case study *94*; learning and 91–93, *96–97*; literature review 91–93, 137; message-reinforcement-transfer and *98*; messages, key 102; outcome analysis of case study *100–101*; overview 102; philosophy and *94–95*; planning and *95–96*; reflections on case study *101*; reflective practice and *99–100*; skills as being taught rather than caught and 92–93; social validation and *100–101*; teaching and *96*; zone of proximal development and 93; *see also* Model for Life Skill Development through Coaching
practitioner effectiveness 234
pre-game fitness test *258*
Prinz, J. 207
Professional Development Phase teams 175, *192–193*, *239*
Professional Footballer's Association (FPA) 264–265
Program for Athletic Coach Education (PACE) 135
P.R.O.G.R.E.S.S. *141–142*, *144–145*
Project Committee of the Mental Health Commission of Canada *281–282*
psychoeducation *309*
psychological characteristics of developing excellence (PCDEs) 174
"Psychology for Football" course 172
purpose in women's international soccer, establishing 223

Raedeke, T. D. 293
Ranieri, C. *65*

Rashford, M. 29
rational emotive behaviour therapy (REBT): ABC(DE) model and 45, *45*, *48–49*, *56*; anti-awfulising and *49–51*; athlete rational resilience credo and *54–55*; awfulising and *49–50*; "badness scale" and *50*; "Big I little i technique" and *55–56*; case studies *47–57*; depreciation and *55–56*; disputation of irrational belief and *53–55*, **54**; fairness and, preference for *47–49*; frustration intolerance and *52–53*; frustration tolerance and *51–57*; healthy negative emotions and 45; irrationality of player and 45–46, **46**, *47–48*, 57; irrational Performance Beliefs Inventory and *49*; literature review 44–47; messages, key 57; overview 57; performance and 46, *54*; preference for fairness case study *47–49*; rationality of player and 45–46, **46**, 57; unconditional other acceptance case study *51–57*
rational-emotive PDMS (REPDMS) 107
rationality of player 45–46, **46**, 57
readying in 3Rs model and 5R^5 program 64, *67–68*
realising in 3Rs model and 5R^5 program 63–64, *67*, *69*
rebound resilience 77
Reckase, M. D. 134
reductionist approach *181*
referee mental health: background/context of case study *280*; case study *280–289*; chronic performance-related stress and 279; Clattenburg (Mark) and 278; common mental disorders and 279, *282*; depression from failure and 279; depression and, future-based 279; intervention/work conducted in case study *281–285*; issues of case study *280–281*; literature review 278–280; memoirs of referees and 278; Mental Health Literacy Training and *282–283*; messages, key 289; outcome analysis of case study *285–286*; overview 289; proposed training syllabus *284–285*, *287–288*; Referee Mental Health Champions and *282*, *284–286*; reflections on case study *286–289*; self-compassion and *283*; stigma of mental illness and 278–279
Referee Mental Health Champions *282*, *284–286*
referee psychology: abuse of referee and 76; background information 85; "big calls" and 75, 77; case study *75–84*; characteristics of performance under pressure and *78*; Connor-Davidson Resilience Scale and *81*; intervention/work conducted of case study *76–81*, **78**, *79*, **80**; literature review 74–75; mental health literacy and *75*, *78–79*, *82–83*; messages, key 85; "optimal" challenge mindset and *77–78*; organisational culture and *78–84*, **80**, 85; outcome analysis of case study *81–83*; overview 84–85; overview of case study 75, *75–76*; performance 74–75, *76–84*, **78**, 84–85; reflections of case study *83–84*; resilience training and 77, *79*, *82*; scrutiny of performance of referee and 74; short-term approach to

soccer and 74, *82*; stress and 77, **78**, 84–85; technological changes and 75–76, 84–85; video assistant referees and 75–76
reflecting in 3Rs model and 5R⁵ program 63–64, 67–68
reflective practice *99–100, 145*
re-injury, fear of 250
relationship-oriented PDMS (ROPDMS) 106–107, *109–110, 112, 114–115*
reporting in 3Rs model and 5R⁵ program 64, *67, 69*
representing in 3Rs model and 5R⁵ program 63–64, *67–69*
resilience training 77, *79, 82*
retirement from soccer 5
return-to-participation (RTP) rates 249–252, *257–258*
Richardson, D. 265
Ring, C. 135
Ritov, I. 33–34
robust psychological resilience 77
Rogers, C. R. *11, 24–25*
role models, female 221–222
Ronaldo, C. 37
Rooney, W. 105
Rose, D. 264
Rowe, W. G. 207

Sabiston, C. M. *283*
safety in women's international soccer, building 222
Samuel, R. D. 279
Sapieja, K. M. 124
Schein, E. H. *157, 162*
Schein, G. 33–34
Scoppa, V. 207
season ticket holder (STH) study 209
self-categorisation theory 61
self-compassion *283*
self-concept 27
Self Determination Theory (SDT) *138*
self-efficacy 135, *138–139*, 190, *193–194, 241, 244*, 250
self-monitoring *309*
self-oriented perfectionism (SOP) 303–305
self-reflection *145*
Seligman, M. 19
Senior Leadership Team (SLT) 63–64, *66*, 68–71
Shafran, R. *306*
Shankly, B. 44
shared language *179*
shared model of practice *179*
shared sense of "us," cultivating: benefits of 61; by leaders 62–63; programmes for 63–64
"shock effect" 208
Short, S. E. 135
short-term approach in soccer 74, *82*
Sillince, J. 208
Slater, M. J. 61–64, *66*
Smith, E. P. 305
Smith, J. 209–210

Smith, R. E. 294
Soccer Associations 279–280, *280*, 288
social identity approach: background/context of case study *65*; basis of 61; benefits of 61; case study *65–71*; consequences of 61; describing 60; 5R⁵ intervention and 64, *66*, **67**, *68–69*; identity entrepreneurs and 62; importance of 61; issues in case study *65–66*; leadership and 62–63; outcome analysis of case study *69–70*; performance and 61–64, 70; reflections on case study *70–71*; team performance and 61; 3Rs and 63–64
social identity theory 61
socially prescribed perfectionism (SPP) 303–305
social network analysis (SNA) *66*
social validation *100–101, 114–116*, **116**, 137
sociocultural constructivism 97
Spears, R. *70*
"spontaneous remission" 20
sport injury-related growth (SIRG) 250, *253*
sport psychology 26, 155; *see also specific method*; sport psychology provision in academy youth soccer
sport psychology provision in academy youth soccer: background/context of case study *235–236*; case study *235–243*; coaches and *240*; doing "right thing" and *242–243*; effectiveness of practitioner and *243*; Elite Player Performance Plan and *235–236*; fit/priorities of work and *236–238*; 5Cs and *239–241*; "good" and, concept of *237–238*; integrity and, maintaining *242*; intervention/work conduct in case study *238–241*; issues of case study *236–238*; literature review 234–235; messages, key 245; outcome analysis of case study *241*; overview 235, 243–245; parents and *240–241*; practitioner effectiveness and 234; promoting psychology rather than psychologist *239*; reflections on case study *241–242*
sport-specific model of transition 6
staged-based model 208, *214*
stages within life of sports performer 4
Stambulova, N. B. 6
Steffens, N. K. 63
Steptoe, K. 136
stigma of mental illness 278–279
storytelling *227–229*
stress: appraisal of stressor and 293; chronic performance-related 279; coping with 293; emotions of 30; literature review 292; overview 312–313; of parents 122; as process 292–293; referee psychology and 77, **78**, 84–85; stressors causing 74–75, *75–77*, **78**, *80, 83*, 84, 122, 124, 177, 190, 279, 293–294, 304, 313; transactional model of 292–293; transition from elite youth to elite adult soccer and 4; *see also* burnout
Sullivan, A. 249
Sullivan, P. J. 135
systems-led approach: to applied psychology *176–178, 180–183*; applied psychology in academy soccer settings and 172–175; background/

context of case study *175–179*; case study *175–186*; describing *176–177*; eight-step model for leading change and *183*, **184–185**; integration of applied psychology through *175–176*; intervention/work conducted in case study *183–185*; language and *178–179*; messages, key 186; overview 172, 186; paradox of language and *178–179*; parenting issues and *180–183*; performance and 174–175, *179*, *182–183*, 186; reflections on case study *185–186*

talent development environment (TDE): ABC model and *164*; analysing club's *159–160*; Athletic Talent Development Environment (ATDE) model and *157*, *160*; background/context of case study *156–158*; case study *156–168*; characteristics of 221; defining 155; developmental characteristics and 155; Environment Success Factor (ESF) model and *157*, *161–162*; evaluation and, ongoing *165–166*; factors influencing 155–156; holistic ecological approach and *156–157*; implementation of behaviours and *165–166*, **167**; intervention/work conducted in case study *158–166*, **158**; issues of case study *158*; literature review 155–156; messages, key 168; organisational awareness and *159–164*, **167**; organisational behaviours and *164–165*; organisational culture and 156, *157–160*; outcome analysis of case study *166*, **168**; overview 156, 168; reflections on case study *166–168*; Team Denmark case and 155; *see also* four-step intervention

teaching 96
team: confidence in 63–64; 5R[5] intervention and 64, *66–69*, **68**; identity development 227; vision, values, and goals of *68*, *226–227*
team-based intervention *see* personal-disclosure mutual-sharing (PDMS)
Team Denmark case 155
Tenenbaum, G. 279
ter Weel, B. 207–208
Theory of Challenge and Threat States in Athletics (TCTSA) 190–191, *192–193*, *195*, *197*, *199–200*, 200–201
threat-state cardiovascular (CV) reactivity pattern 190
Tod, D. 235
transactional model of stress (TMS) 292–293
transition from elite youth to elite adult soccer: background/context of case study 7; case study *7–14*; challenges 6; client reflections of case study *13*; coach reflections of case study *13–14*; descriptive models 4–5; empirical research 6–7; explanation models 5–6; goal-setting and *9–10*; help in overcoming challenges 6–7; holistic career transition model 5; human adaptation 5; humanistic counseling and *11*; identity development and 4–5; intervention/work conducted in case study *9–11*; issues of case study *7–8*; literature review 3–7; mental health/wellbeing of elite soccer player and 268–269; messages, key 15; non-normative 269; normative 269; outcome analysis of case study *11–13*; overview 3, 15; psychological 4–5; reflections on case study *13–14*; sport-specific model 6; stages within life of sports performer and 4; stress and 4; theories/models 4–7; workshops and *10–13*
Trowler, P. R. 96
Turner, M. J. 107

UEFA European Championships (2016) 61
unconditional other acceptance *51–57*
Under-17 soccer team 221
upheaval/realisation stage of organisational change 208, *211*
US Navy SEAL Team Six 222

value statements 95
video assistant referees (VAR) *75–76*
Voborny, J. 279
vulnerability in women's international soccer, sharing 222–223, *225–226*
Vygotsky, L. S. 93

Wade, T. D. *306*
Wagstaff, C. R. D. 208–210, *211*, *214*, *228*
Walcott, T. 105
Wallace, M. 97
Walters, I. 121–122
Weiss, W. M. 92
"whole-person" approach 254
Wilson, M. R. 31–32
Windsor, P. M. 107
women's soccer *see* culture/environment in women's international soccer
workshops for transition from elite youth to elite adult soccer *10–13*
World Cup Final (2018) 60, *71*
World Cup quarter-final match (2018) 29, *36–38*
Wylleman, P. 4

Young Lions (English national youth soccer club) 3
Youth Development Phase teams *94*, 175, *193*
youth-to-senior transition in soccer *see* transition from elite youth to elite adult soccer
Yukleson, D. 105

Zeman, T. 279
zone of proximal development 93

Printed in Great Britain
by Amazon